PEDESTRIAN
MODERN

PEDESTRIAN MODERN

Shopping and American Architecture,
1925–1956

David Smiley

University of Minnesota Press
MINNEAPOLIS · LONDON

This book is supported by a grant from the Graham Foundation for Advanced Studies in the Fine Arts.

The University of Minnesota Press gratefully acknowledges the work of Edward Dimendberg, editorial consultant, on this project.

Portions of chapter 6 were published in "History of the Victor: Varieties of Shopping, 1955," *Lotus* 118, Entrance/Sidewalk/Room (September 2003): 4–25.

Published by the University of Minnesota Press
111 Third Avenue South, Suite 290
Minneapolis, MN 55401-2520
http://www.upress.umn.edu

Library of Congress Cataloging-in-Publication Data

Smiley, David J., 1958–
Pedestrian modern : shopping and American architecture,
1925–1956 / David Smiley.
Includes bibliographical references and index.
ISBN 978-0-8166-7929-4 (hc)
ISBN 978-0-8166-7930-0 (pb)
1. Commercial buildings—United States—History—20th century.
2. Architecture and society—United States—History—20th century.
3. Consumer behavior—United States—History—20th century. I. Title.
NA6212.S65 2013
725'.2109730904—dc23

2013003504

Printed in the United States of America on acid-free paper

The University of Minnesota is an equal-opportunity educator and employer.

20 19 18 17 16 15 14 13   10 9 8 7 6 5 4 3 2 1

This book is dedicated to
the life and memory of my sweet mother,
Barbara

CONTENTS

Preface and Acknowledgments / ix

Introduction: Centers and Peripheries / 1

ONE   The Store Problem / 17

TWO   Machines for Selling / 51

THREE   Park and Shop / 93

FOUR   Pedestrianization Takes Command / 133

FIVE   The Cold War Pedestrian / 175

SIX   The Language of Modern Shopping / 207

Conclusion: Pedestrian Modern Futures / 243

Notes / 255

Bibliography / 293

Index / 337

PREFACE AND ACKNOWLEDGMENTS

I spent very little time in shopping malls during the first half of my life; they simply did not interest me. This did not stem from any nascent politics I can recall, but I found the places both boring and distracting. It was not until my first teaching job in the American Midwest that I rediscovered the mall. Most of my students had grown up in the suburbs, and the mall was second nature to them. My position about the mall was a matter of getting to see what they saw, viewing the mall as a legitimate place on anyone's social map, but also as a place that was, like everything else, designed. As a conceived and constructed place, it was the site of conflicting motives, pasts, futures, and sensibilities. Writing this book has not pushed me to love or hate malls or other sites organized for consumption, but I continue to be fascinated by their spatial experience, by what Fredric Jameson in 1984 called (for the Bonaventure Hotel) a "constant busyness" matched with "packed . . . emptiness." Perhaps it is unique to my generation, my ideological blinkers, or a particular thread in my profile, but I still find malls and the proliferation of quasi-public places like them to be slightly worrisome, more than a little strained, and all the more exciting for it. I am interested in malls not only as places of shopping but also as architecture, as places and representations drawn up by architects and circulated as part of architectural knowledge.

This book has been in the works for more time than I would like to admit, and I owe thanks to many. Friends and colleagues who gave me things to think about include, first and foremost, Gabrielle Esperdy, whose insight, support, and humor have been vital. Ed Dimendberg has been a guiding spirit and an acute reader. Andy Shanken, Liz Hutchinson, Owen Gutfreund, Eric Mumford, Debra Fausch, and Nancy Levinson all shared ideas and methods. Early conversations with Jeff Hardwick helped spur my interest in Victor Gruen, and Robert Fishman has always been as fascinated with the mall as I. A special thanks to Mark Robbins for roping me into looking at "dead malls." Leonard Groopman always lends a sympathetic ear.

During my studies at Princeton University, I was fortunate to work with and learn from Alessandra Ponte, Georges Teyssot, Christine Boyer, Mark Wigley, Beatriz Colomina, Antoine Picon, Stani von Moos, and especially Dan Rodgers. Each, in his or her own inimitable way, impressed on me particular modes of thinking, seeing, and scrutinizing, all of which I still ponder. At Columbia University's Graduate School of Architecture, Planning, and Preservation, I had the benefit of learning from and then working with Richard Plunz, Robert Beauregard, and Gwendolyn Wright, who offer their time and knowledge on a regular basis.

At Barnard College, Karen Fairbanks, the chair of my department, and Raleigh-Elizabeth Smith were both supportive and good-humored about my progress through this book as I also struggled with the demands of full-time teaching. Many students assisted me in small and large ways; thanks much to Emily "Red" Samaniego, Stephen Davan, Stefie Gan, and Najim Kim.

I had the pleasure of speaking with Norval White about his experiences as a young architect at Lathrop Douglass's office. He laughed when recalling that shopping centers and supermarkets were done in a separate area from the "real" work. Alvin Ubell, now of Accurate Building Inspections (that is a plug), worked with Morris Ketchum and helped me get a sense of the man; Erik Furno also shared his thoughts about Ketchum's office. Donna Ochenryder of Niles, Michigan, was uniquely helpful in gathering material about Morris Ketchum's modernization of the town's main street, as well as later information about redesign and restoration. Niles has seen it all.

Many people gave me their time, knowledge, and e-mail addresses, some for just a few minutes and others for days and weeks. They constitute this book's infrastructure, on which I heavily depended. Many thanks to K. C. McCrory, PPG Industries, Inc.; Marjorie McNinch, Hagley Museum and Library; Nancy Dean, Division of Rare and Manuscript Collections, Cornell University; Karen M. Widi, library and records manager, Skidmore, Owings & Merrill; Carolyn Davis, Peter D. Verheyen, and Jonathan Jackson, Syracuse University Library; Mary Daniels, Frances Loeb Library, Graduate School of Design, Harvard University; Malgosia Myc, Bentley Historical Library, University of Michigan; Michelle Klose, Local History–Genealogy Department, Niles Library, Niles, Michigan; Nancy Thorne, Architectural Archives of the University of Pennsylvania; Gerd Zillner and Tatjana Okresek-Oshima, Austrian Frederick and Lillian Kiesler Private Foundation, Vienna; Christian Larsen and Michelle Harvey, Museum Archives, Museum of Modern Art; Janet Parks, curator of drawings and archives, and Kitie Chipnick, associate director, Avery Library, Columbia University; Nancy Hadley, Library and Archives, American Institute of Architects; Carol Bowers, American Heritage Center, University of Wyoming; Kristina Bicher, Rye Historical Society; Andreas Nutz, Vitra Design Stiftung, Weil am Rhein, Germany; Dan Naylor, Elkhart Library, Indiana; Chris Hanington, Princeton Shopping Center, Princeton, New Jersey; Patrick Kerwin, Manuscript

Division, and Erica Kelly, Library of Congress; Christina Bollinger, Pei Cobb Freed and Partners; Lisa Crotea, program manager, Niles Main Street, Downtown Niles, Michigan; and the always helpful people at Harvard University Archives, Pusey Library; the Research Center, Chicago History Museum; and the Archives of American Art. A very special thanks to the Graham Foundation.

My children, Leah and Elliot, regularly make sure I understand the pleasures of shopping. My wife, Lauren Kogod, my secret weapon, my better half, my sounding board, and my logic consultant, has never failed to inspire and fuel my work. This book would not exist had it not been for her ever-creative RISD eye and her critical and pragmatic view of everything in her orbit, and then some.

INTRODUCTION

CENTERS AND PERIPHERIES

IN OCTOBER 1956, between farms and single-family home subdivisions outside Minneapolis, a fully enclosed shopping center opened its glass doors (Figure I.1). For its architect, Victor Gruen, the project represented a triumph, and not only because it made the pages of *Life* magazine. Southdale was the most ambitiously realized of Gruen's continuing ventures into retailing.[1] Two years earlier, his Northland Shopping Center (Figure I.2) opened outside Detroit; its landscaped malls, fountains, and sculptures received positive acclaim in both popular and professional media. These were not the first shopping centers in the country, but Southdale was the first realized large-scale, fully enclosed, and air-conditioned center—later known as a "shopping mall."[2] At the time the success of this new building type was far from assured for suburban shoppers. Although obviously convenient, various merchandising publications, planning magazines, and architectural journals alike expressed caution and some skepticism regarding the lack of precedent and market analysis, not to mention the inability to predict the results of an untested formula of site design, store mix, and financing. The economic risk of this experimental organization of material, earth, infrastructure, jobs, and merchandise was patent. After fits and starts beginning around 1950, highly sympathetic changes to the federal tax code in 1954, and evidence of the new type's profitability, the pace of suburban shopping center construction quickened considerably.[3] By 1960, hundreds of large shopping centers had been built or were in construction or planning stages throughout the United States.[4]

As a landscaped island amid a sea of cars and asphalt surrounded, in turn, by empty fields or a carpet of new homes, the 1950s shopping center was something of a conceptual paradox. The tidy, planted serenity of its pedestrian areas was at odds with the sociotechnical systems required to operate a development of such complexity.[5] Neither the scale nor the extent of design control was easily registered in images of the new shopping center. As a model for reading representations, take Leo Marx's 1964 description of pastoralism in images such as George Inness's painting *The Lackawanna Valley* (1855), which suggested that new technologies of factory and railroad coexisted peacefully, as if "naturally," alongside wooded and agricultural landscapes. Compare the rendered view of Gruen's Bayfair Shopping Center proposal through a car windshield as a similarly pastoral view of the landscape (Figure I.3). We are moving through what could be a park, with trees and low plantings, where we see a bridge crossing over a river on which a boat drifts along without the aid of its apparently napping passenger. In the distance is the barely discernible silhouette of

Figure I.1. Victor Gruen Associates, Southdale Shopping Center, Edina, Minnesota, 1956. Interior view, 1964.

the buildings, hidden behind a slight rise of the land that will dramatize our arrival and reveal the scale of the complex. Like Inness's painting, Gruen's rendering normalized the new conditions, taking in the roads and infrastructure, the architectural and planning techniques, and, implicitly, the social modernization in which they were to fuse and operate smoothly. Seamless visual harmony is vital: no gaps or incongruities give us pause in our appreciation of the new designed environment nestled in the suburbs. Gruen's perspective also includes the driver, who is a woman. Because we see her and see more or less from her point of view, she becomes both a subject, the eager participant, and an object and framing device, an aestheticized part of the picture. Gruen's Bayfair image offers the shopping environment as pastoral, in which a massive construction appears as if it were a quasi-natural phenomenon, a legitimate and "proper part of the landscape," as Marx wrote.[6] Once we are inside the shopping center, the completeness of the designed realm erases all reference to other places, old or new.

While Gruen was planning his first large shopping centers around 1950, José Luis Sert, president of the Congrés Internationaux d'Architecture Moderne (CIAM), was writing about the need to create new community centers and civic cores, where

Figure I.2. Victor Gruen Associates, Northland Shopping Center, Southfield, Michigan, 1958. Fountain court with sculpture by Joe Smith. Walter P. Reuther Library, Wayne State University.

gathering among friends and strangers could take place and where a public life, presumably lost to modernization and media, could be found.[7] Central to Sert's thesis was the pivotal role of an emerging, modern "architect-planner" in bringing such meaningful new places into being. Architects have historically participated in making cities, however, in the discourse generated by CIAM, it was precisely the modernity of the Modern Architect—his new professional and curricular training in analytic, technological, programmatic, land-use, and sociological areas—that made him uniquely able to create and transform the "heart of the city." This was exactly the role Gruen envisioned himself as fulfilling with his large-scale commercial work. In the many shopping center and urban proposals that followed, Gruen and many lesser-known peers, in concert with magazine editors and critics, articulated a specifically modern architectural project, albeit one using the medium of a merchandising operation for its social—indeed civic—ends. The project of this book is to replace the "lesser" and "suburban" association of shopping centers with one of "the modern."

Since modernism's earliest representations in the United States, attempts to define it had been rife with claims, counterclaims, speculation, and polemics. What did shopping have to do with the modern? From the 1920s forward, some observers claimed that the design of stores offered an unmediated demonstration of modernism's utility, its hopes for the machine age and, by extension, its promise of a better life. The uses of formal modernist techniques, such as visual transparency and overlapping interior and exterior spaces, satisfied an architectural avant-garde as well as the forward-thinking store owner. Over the next three decades, as modernism matured, narrowed, and became the normative model of architectural practice, store architects and, later, shopping center architects understood their work as part of the modernist trajectory. Extensive plate glass, extruded aluminum mullions, and air-conditioning were the material correlates of new scales of site planning, construction

Figure I.3. Victor Gruen Associates, Bayfair Shopping Center, San Leandro, California, 1956. From "View from the Windshield," *Shopping Centers of Tomorrow*. Courtesy of Gruen Associates.

management, commercial coordination, and social organization. At any scale and in any site, modernist methods and materials could address merchandising problems no less well than any other architectural undertaking. Southdale and its cousins may well have been integral to America's modernizing and suburbanizing landscape, but within the evolving discourse of architecture they were framed as modernist research into the transformation of the midcentury metropolis. Any history of American architecture across the middle decades of the century must therefore examine how the store and shopping center were unique vehicles for experimentation as Modern Architecture. Yet, even as stores and shopping centers earned significant attention in the literature and design theories of the profession, they never quite escaped a second-class architectural citizenship, qualified, as they were, by the dilemmas of consumption.

Pedestrian Consumption

During the early part of the twentieth century, as the organization and reach of capital expanded, so too did the merchandising trades. Specialization of many retail-related occupations turned the store into an intricate territory populated by interior designers, display managers, window trimmers, buyers, stylists, set designers, and manufacturers' representatives, all of whom claimed expertise in ensuring the swift movement of goods off the shelves and out the door.[8] In large cities, schools of applied design supplied store owners with new professionals trained in store layout, cabinetry, display techniques, and advertising.[9] In the 1920s and 1930s, industrial designers such as Raymond Loewy, Norman Bel Geddes, and Walter Dorwin Teague happily worked alongside retailers, advertisers, and mass-production-based firms— later they were called "consumer engineers."[10] The increasingly consumable work of these industrial designers, although published in the architectural media, also confirmed and reinforced the historical character of the profession as disinterested, non-commercial, untouched by the culture of consumption, and socially invested in its own "objective" status. The lures of mass merchandising conflicted with the aesthetic and educational standards by which the profession typically distinguished itself.[11]

The representation of stores in the journals of the American architectural profession was ambiguous. The small store, even for the "carriage trade," was in general not designed but simply built according to the whims of owners, managers, and, starting in the 1920s, many new technical specialists. Most shop and store owners treated their establishments as overstuffed showcases, earning the censure of planners, architects, and retail reformers for their "unrefined" attitudes toward signage and their lack of any systematic approach to display and arrangement. High-end, elite stores were shown in architectural magazines as one-off "artistic" tours de force, as though they were upper-class residential interiors and salons. The emergence of chain stores in the 1920s radically changed the dynamics and scale of merchandising as their architects began experimenting with design methods for multistore recognition, regional marketing, and unified operations.[12] No matter how progressively designed or organized these stores were, however, the connotations of selling on this new, mass scale further undermined the traditional professional aspirations of architects toward art, much less status or cultural autonomy.

Most architects treated large stores and department stores as businesslike, bill-paying commissions. While the famed "palaces of consumption" offered desirable opportunities for distinctive massing, lobbies, or facade design, the requirements of merchandising, promotion, and other commercial enticements were treated gingerly and separately. A monument on the outside and a machine on the inside, the store relied on ever-shifting needs to which traditionally defined architectural talent added little.[13] After World War II, many department stores were built as opaque boxes with new skins and elevations—windows were considered distractions from selling and a hindrance to storage—and interior layouts became temporary and "informal" arrangements of racks and shelving units that department managers could reposition as needed, released from the orthogonal structural grid.[14] Calculation and spectacle remained primary programmatic requirements even as commercial commissions expanded among a growing niche of specialized store design architects. More broadly, stores posed a professional conundrum: they were essential urban institutions and stable commissions, but they were precariously tainted by what the architecture critic Talbot Hamlin referred to in a 1939 essay as the "art of the barker."[15] In sum, as an architectural commission no less than as a daily activity, shopping remained *pedestrian*: prosaic, a bit lowbrow, compromised by banality and afflicted with doubt about its cultural merit.

Dismay over consumption has historically stressed the corrupting effects of goods and the desires they create.[16] Department stores in the nineteenth century had helped to "domesticate" urban space and create a public life acceptable for "respectable" women, yet they were simultaneously "cathedrals of consumption" or "theaters of goods" that clouded the demarcation between necessary and luxury items, inducing impulse purchases. Émile Zola and Theodore Dreiser had explored with empathy how the tantalizing presence of the seemingly infinite supply of just-affordable merchandise created a social-psychological dreamworld that encouraged the incremental relaxation of willpower and self-restraint. For many social critics, this synchrony with the less seemly aspects of money—the cycles of fashion, the rise of ersatz, mass-produced, and perhaps second-rate merchandise—threatened the dignity and autonomy of individuals.[17] And, as Gruen's Bayfair Shopping Center rendering so beautifully illustrates, the subject of shopping, the protagonist of mass consumption, especially of this larger-scaled retailing, was feminized. Even as a vast system of production and distribution grew up around these precise interactions, women's self-control was assumed to be weak. And the sites of shopping's necessary activities—the display windows, interior halls, and atriums, as well as all the services and operations—became synonymous with the exhilarating but untrustworthy spectacle of commodities through which the modern city attained its identity, its allure, and its risks.[18]

Civic Pedestrianism

If one meaning of *pedestrian* is weighed down with the dubious baggage of the commercial, the word has another meaning that is unambiguously wholesome. This pedestrian is a self-directed and rational protagonist, who, like Kant and Rousseau, meditates as he walks. Unencumbered by doubt and confidently open to the new, the walker thoughtfully—and publicly—navigates his world. Across the "great divide" of cultural value, this ideologically male pedestrian embodies a constructive (if also historically selective) civic role—quite literally, for example, when Clarence Perry measured out the physical dimensions of a cohesive "neighborhood unit" according to the comfortable reach of a seemingly universal pedestrian.[19] Distinct from the bemused, aleatory wanderings of the Parisian *flâneur,* and almost the inverse of the "pedestrian speech acts" of de Certeau, this American pedestrian was a community maker and political participant.[20]

The self-empowered pedestrian-as-citizen offered remediation for the choking crowds and traffic of the industrialized city, against which, Theodor Adorno wrote, "human dignity insisted on the right to walk." The trope of the walker found wide expression among observers of urban life.[21] The cover image of the May 1925 *Survey Graphic,* for example, a visual set piece provided by the Regional Plan Association of America, contrasted two worlds: in one, the smog-induced darkness of the anonymous gray urban intersection; in the other, a father and his children walking across a rolling greensward toward their cozy bungalow (where the mother is, no doubt, cooking), a distant hydroelectric dam stabilizing the image. Similarly, the 1939 American Planning Association film *The City* represented the obstacles of the industrial city with muddy, unpaved streets and used neatly paved country lanes to signify the improved social milieu promised by the association's reformist proposals.[22] The verdant ground plane available to the healthy citizens of Le Corbusier's urban proposals of the 1920s was opposed to the dark, tubercular streets of the old European cities.[23] And to Sigfried Giedion, whose seminal 1941 *Space, Time and Architecture* had gone into eleven printings by 1956, the conceptually open meaning of modern architecture was available only through the perceptions of the person in motion, revealed through the interval of his meander (or, in dialectical contrast, on the open road).[24]

The walking figure offered a remedy for a lost connectedness among anonymous urban crowds and automotive-based environments. Perhaps most succinctly demonstrated in a simple 1943 sketch by Willo von Moltke for an article by Joseph Hudnut (Figure I.4), the realm of the pedestrian was associated with well-manicured greenways, controlled land use, family-friendly spaces, and a (somehow) safe urban realm.[25]

In 1947, Talbot Hamlin argued that "true democratic planning" would necessarily treat the pedestrian as the primary lens for large-scale work.[26] In sum, asserting, as did Le Corbusier, the *"royauté du piéton"*—the right of the pedestrian—(and the right to "kill" the street) addressed what many perceived as the compounded social and physical shortcomings of aging metropolitan downtowns and Main Streets as well as new suburban subdivisions. Architects and urban theorists believed the "citizen afoot" could constitute the conceptual and literal core of an organic, civic, and modern culture.

Figure I.4. Willo von Moltke, shopping sketch, 1943, *Architectural Record* 93 (January 1943): 62.

The two typal constructions of *pedestrian* serving as themes in this book cannot remain unalloyed or unexplored. Each figure—the seduced shopper and the rational citizen—necessarily contains its inverse: in the former, shopping has a respectable place on life's ordinary stage, and in the latter, the agency of the solitary walker might be a simulation masking the absence of true alternatives within a regulated, mass-culture industry. Thus I reach here for a Geertzian "thick" representation of the tensions through which architectural design and practice and the discourse of modernism were brought into the ever-changing realm of commerce across the middle decades of the twentieth century.

Sites of Modern Merchandising

Catching the eye of the pedestrian has always been crucial to store owners and primary among their requirements from architects. In 1939, the editors of the magazine *Architectural Forum* noticed that retailers were beginning to employ the "dramatic, attention-getting qualities of modern architecture as an extra salesman."[27] This adoption of the modernist style, the editors implied, was the latest "thing" in the continuous cycles of fashion, to be followed by whatever stylish looks the future would bring. In other words, modernist architecture in retail design in 1939 was considered superficial, the newest lure in the perpetual quest to ring up sales.

Over time, however, many advocates of modern architecture came to counter that suspicious attitude toward retailers and champion the relationship between stores and modernism as one of substantive affinity. Ten years later, the same magazine, now under the energetic leadership of Howard Myers, George Nelson, and Henry Wright Jr., described the modern store as "the result of a demand for an environment which only the *modern techniques* can furnish," techniques the magazine's editors understood to be more legitimately modern than the mere "recognition of the esthetic merits of modern architecture by business men."[28]

Modernist design, in this holistic conception, was not a choice of surfaces but an organizational necessity—the inevitable result of bringing rational thought to the program of selling. Partaking of contemporary management systems, industrial processes, production efficiencies, and "scientific" planning, merchandising was already modern. Store design based on explicit needs, a clear mandate, and common sense would yield a "100 percent modern" result. In fact, the *Forum* editors argued, modern architectural principles were not especially well investigated in projects for institutions or residences, the latter "mired in 1776." Modern architecture was best established in the design of stores and, through their synergy, a new, modern building type would emerge.[29]

Another significant transformation in attitude took place in the same ten-year period. The same 1939 article in *Forum* reinforced the traditional location of retailing as urban, arguing that "customers are thickest" in small-town Main Streets and big-city downtown centers. The busy sidewalk, the famed "100 percent location" so coveted by merchandisers and integral to economic success, made any other site unthinkable. The recognition of urban problems—increasing traffic congestion, aging building stock, and obsolete infrastructure—required serious study and active remediation, but the healthy and profitable operation of American downtowns remained central.[30]

Ten years later and in the same journal, Main Street was "wasteful" and downtown "a trap." After countless generations, the traditional centralized diagram of urban and commercial concentration was reconsidered. Myers, Nelson, and Wright described the emergence of new uses and scales that portended a "complete . . . reversal" of retailing patterns such that a substantial proportion of shopping dollars soon would be spent in branch stores and new "store groups" well outside the city core.[31] New sites for shopping required experiments with the fabric and elements of the city and suggested new forms for planning and organization while also offering an expanded role for the architect.

By the mid-1950s, leading proponents of modern architecture such as Sert and Giedion predicted a happy outcome for this suburban relocation of retail. Properly designed, the shopping center could "recentralize" social life in the "incomplete" suburbs by providing sites with urban complexity and density for genuine social contact.[32] The 1955 opening of the Roosevelt Field Shopping Center in Queens, New York, designed by I. M. Pei (Figure I.5), was hailed in this context: a review in *Progressive Architecture* described the ensemble as a place "for assembly and community recreation in a spirited and coordinated architectural setting."[33] And, while admiring Pei's Miesian architectural refinement in the pages of *Architectural Record,* Giedion emphasized the center's potential to support social and civic life.[34] As a modernist enterprise, the shopping center was invested with social meaning as a new community space: the aggregation of retail was the physical means to a greater, public, end.

Discourse and Setting

Historical narratives of modern architecture in the United States generally focus on its midcentury acceptance by institutions and corporations. The museum, the city hall, and the corporate headquarters were invested with the symbolic gravitas of worthy commissions. And the embrace of modern architecture by corporate America, which created the ubiquitous curtain-wall office building, was a central means by which modernism became normative in the United States.[35] To frame the store as an integral protagonist in the creation of modern American architecture challenges the assumptions and borders of the discipline and questions the historiography of modernism. Embracing merchandising might be construed as an ideological blindness—a picture of willing accommodation on the part of American architectural

Figure I.5. I. M. Pei Associates, Roosevelt Field, Queens, New York, 1956, *Architectural Record* 122 (September 1957): 208.

practice to the structures of capital. Indeed, this is often the trajectory by which the "true" content of European modern architecture has been traced: the inexorable desiccation of the modern social program as fruit of the original sin in Henry-Russell Hitchcock and Phillip Johnson's 1932 *Modern Architecture: An International Exhibition.* This received view does not explain or give historical texture to the ways in which architects shaped the terms of modernism through their multifaceted work, writing, and other professional activities. In this book, I examine how architects interpreted what modernism could be and what it could accomplish under unprecedented conditions.

I will argue that the store and the shopping center expanded upon and effectively disseminated modernist architectural tenets and practices across the profession no less than across the American built landscape. The pejorative associations of shopping and of the suburbs pushed shopping to the fringes of an architectural profession whose identification with "high cultural" practice could be maintained.[36] I will show that the architects of stores and shopping centers normalized modernism and shaped it in different ways: architects, writers, and critics wove together the aesthetic, technological, and planning threads of modern architecture with the programmatic necessities of merchandising and shopping between the 1930s and the mid-1950s.

This book examines the overlooked thread joining the architectural representation of the store to architectural representations of modernism. With the exceptions of Richard Longstreth, Dell Upton, and Gwendolyn Wright, historians of American architecture have not, for the most part, treated stores as legitimately architectural. Other than the earliest, monumental stores, such as H. H. Richardson's 1887 Marshall Field Wholesale Store or Louis Sullivan's 1899 Carson, Pirie, Scott, architectural history has given retail and commerce a wide berth and a narrow reading. Histories of architecture that engage sites of merchandising tend to produce revealing economic, real estate, and land-use information in which architects play a secondary role. This is not to say that architects are absent: Longstreth's powerfully encyclopedic work examines in rich detail the architecture of shops, department stores, and shopping centers as well as the roles of their developers and builders.[37] But the discursive machinery of architecture remains obscure, suggesting that those editors, architects, and architectural writers working with retail design operated outside the dominant discourse, as if in some other, parallel, realm. This was not the case, and the design of stores and shopping centers was a key part of modernism's institutionalization. In this book I treat the trajectory and transformation of this contribution, hoping thereby to fill in the intellectual history of the American landscape.

Charting the intersections of architecture, modernism, and modernization is fraught with the tensions of *habitus,* cultural politics, and unevenly operating capital, but others have recently pushed scholarship forward. Gabrielle Esperdy and

Andrew Shanken have illuminated the complicated social and discursive map in which architecture has taken place.[38] Alison Isenberg and Robert Fogelson have substantially added to the literature on the real and imaginary constructions of urban place, and their histories intersect with the discipline of architecture. I hope to complement their contributions by examining how the terms, methods, and imagery of what was called "modern" gave shape to social and technical shifts that were part of the merchandiser's expanding world. M. Jeff Hardwick has written an insightful biography of Victor Gruen, the best-known architect of the commercial landscape, and Alex Wall has added considerable architectural context to Gruen's work and thinking; this book extends their projects and places Gruen among his professional peers.

This book is neither a history of built form nor a social history, in the sense of offering a map of the relations among builders, users, and bankers; rather, it is a history of the architectural culture and discourse. In charting the conversations among architects of stores and shopping centers, I hope to show how they integrated that work into the formation of modernist practice. By *discourse* I mean not (only) face-to-face dialogues or presentations but the disciplinary conversation created by architectural texts, debates, ideas, images, and unbuilt projects in addition to constructed buildings. The ways these architects contributed to modernism were not as effective as they hoped—the tenets often honored in the breach, as Colin Rowe later wrote—but the modernist imaginary retained its considerable power as a wellspring of ideas and methods, even as social tensions and limits loomed.[39] In varied and distinct ways, my interrogations of disciplinary identity draw from the work of Mark Wigley, Beatriz Colomina, Robert Fishman, Margaret Crawford, Robert Beauregard, and Christine Boyer.[40] Disciplines exist and shape thought and action, but never in a social vacuum.

The story of *Pedestrian Modern* travels both chronologically and in loosely concentric scales from the store to the city to the region, charting architectural practices and propositions for these specific sites. Chapter 1, "The Store Problem," traces how the individual shop was represented in architectural literature through the 1920s. One thread described store design in terms of visual openness, another in terms of new spatial relations with the street; another, influenced by functionalism, rendered the store as a site of the utilitarian circulation of provisions; finally, yet another thread staged the fantasy of goods. Touching on the work of Morris Lapidus, Knud Lönberg-Holm, and Frederick Kiesler, the modernism of the store was apparent but yet to be pinned down.

Chapter 2, "Machines for Selling," explores how retail work shaped and abetted the normalization of particular modernist tenets in the 1930s and 1940s. The formal language of the "steel and glass" modernism that emerged in the United States in the 1930s was variously characterized by transparency, replicability, and function;

store design was described in architectural literature as uniquely appropriate to the new, modern methods of practice in these terms. Kenneth Welch, Morris Lapidus, Victor Gruen, and Morris Ketchum considered store work a demonstration of the modernist design outlook, and this also entailed participation in the phantasmagoric realm of mass media: magazines, manufacturers' catalogs, and publicity campaigns.

Chapter 3, "Park and Shop," examines the effect of urban congestion on the design of stores and shopping districts. Starting in the 1920s, the efficacy of the "curbside paradigm" (the sidewalk-facing store) began to break down. The need to accommodate drivers—and manage their metamorphosis into pedestrians—fueled attempts to transform the conventional urban diagram and rethink the relations among street, car, pedestrian, and store entrance. Retail design began to incorporate parking—above, below, and behind stores—as well as pedestrian access from newly proposed lots and garages. Examples of this reapportioning of streets and inner blocks by Kenneth Welch and many others—some architects and others not—illustrate a reconfiguration of urban space and the architectural scope of work.

Chapter 4, "Pedestrianization Takes Command," examines how the "right of the pedestrian" became integral to modernist planning and the emerging form of the shopping center. In the 1940s, Welch, Lapidus, Gruen, Ketchum, and George Nelson at *Architectural Forum* experimented with the creation of shopping precincts separated from automobiles. Building on interpretations of Clarence Perry's neighborhood unit, pedestrian-centered proposals for retail districts and shopping centers endowed commercial design with legitimating civic substance as well as a design method.

Chapter 5, "The Cold War Pedestrian," focuses on the activities of Gruen and Ketchum around 1950, when Cold War anxiety added new incentives to shift building patterns away from the centralized metropolis. Against the wide circulation of incendiary images, real and imagined, of bombed-out cities, architects amplified the importance of protected precincts. Ketchum took part in the Project East River atomic bomb survival study, and Gruen presented one shopping center as an "emergency shelter." Most telling was Gruen's creation of a trendsetting arts program to sublate fears of the bomb as well as worries about consumption; art could signify the culture and complexity of an imagined city.

Chapter 6, "The Language of Modern Shopping," continues the investigation of urban symbolism by looking at the site plan types used, types whose associations provided meaning and reference for the new constructions. Examples from this period—before any formula cohered—show that architects experimented with linear "Main Streets," gathering piazzas, picturesque sequences of views, monumental civic plazas, and American town greens. As retail architects began to specialize, becoming increasingly expert in technical-consumer metrics and claiming positions of leadership on development "teams," a discursive emphasis on this symbolic aspect of planning minimized their entanglement with profit-driven goals and shielded their professional status. The pastoral contradiction—the need for artifice to create the dream of the natural—guides my reading of the "total" design of Gruen's Fort Worth Plan and Southdale Shopping Center, which together explicate a modern paradox.

Urban proposals that close off streets to cars, presenting shopping as a pedestrian activity, have been derided as "suburban" since the 1960s. The pedestrianization of Times Square, for example, has been described as an attempt to turn this congested network of intersections into a bland shopping mall. In expanding my historical investigation beyond the *pedestrian* commercial culture barrier, I hope to show, instead, that its pedigree as an architectural intervention is Modern.

Pedestrian Modern confirms that modernist architecture was normalized and brought into mainstream usage among architects in part by its application to store and shopping center work inside and outside cities. This expansion of architectural history breaks down the culture barrier that brackets off commerce and consumption from the consideration of architectural practice. It also shows that the shopping center was as connected to modernist design tenets as it was to the processes of suburbanization to which it is usually wedded. Moreover, if the shopping center is displaced as a creature of suburbanization, then the application of shopping center principles to city centers after the 1950s might be reconsidered as part of the modernist enterprise of reshaping cities. Thus Gruen's Fort Worth Plan (1955) and the subsequent flood of pedestrianization plans for American cities can be understood as the historical expansion of modernism. While *suburbanization* and *urban renewal* are often the terms, usually pejorative, applied to this work, pedestrianization in civic and commercial forms offers another framework through which to view the spaces and uses of the "modernist city," warts and all. The quixotic role of shopping is central to a more robust conception of modern architecture.

ONE

THE STORE PROBLEM

The modern movement in architectural and decorative design may be
applied with peculiar success to the design of shops and stores.
—RANDOLPH W. SEXTON
American Commercial Buildings of Today, 1928

THE REPRESENTATION OF STORE DESIGN in American architectural
magazines through the 1920s was only partly about selling goods. Editors
deemed it necessary to ensure that such work first and foremost be considered a high-minded architectural enterprise—that is, respectable, professional, artistic, and anything but commercial. For the most part, small
stores and storefronts were described in terms ranging from facade composition and eclectic associations to framed mise-en-scènes and historical
precedents. The mechanics of sales and display were treated in terms of
elite furnishings or cabinetry, and the entire operation was treated as a
tasteful expression of an urbane culture. Elite shops carried value because
of the class they catered to as well as for their "proper" representation of
architectural quality. Overall, storefronts were considered subsidiary parts
of the larger building masses in which they were housed. This system of
conventions began to shift in the 1920s when heated debates about modernism emerged across the profession and in the magazines.

The varied terms through which modernism was given architectural
meaning were laden with crisscrossing associations, affiliations, and refrac-
tions. American architectural periodicals of the time joined the modern
to, inter alia, pragmatics, organicism, coherence, straightforwardness, the

machine, objectivity, logic, simplicity, and progress, all of which indicated that the modern was as much wish image as truth claim—especially since many of the terms were claimed equally by the "traditionalists" or others seeking a so-called middle ground so as not to jettison the forms or methods of what Lewis Mumford called the "genteel reaction." Fiske Kimball, for instance, defended the work of McKim, Mead & White as modern in its simplicity and abstraction, an improvement, he said, upon an earlier eclecticism or mere structural expression.[1] Like an echo of the eighteenth-century battle between "the ancients and the moderns," early twentieth-century architects were caught up in interpretations of authority, order, and rule making as much as they were in the specifics of any one building, image, or space.[2] Defining modern design and modern architecture was tendentious.

In 1929, Ralph T. Walker (of the New York firm Voorhees, Gmelin & Walker) was highly critical of the "fetish" made of utility and the machine, but the same year *Architectural Forum* praised these qualities in Duiker and de Klerk, among others; in 1930, John Harbeson (partner of Paul Cret) was highly dismissive of Le Corbusier's machinic metaphors, but the same year Henry-Russell Hitchcock demanded "conversion" to machinelike logic over stylistic "syncretism"; also in 1930, George Howe decried the limits of American "stylistic tradition" and, aided by illustrations of Le Corbusier, Oud, and others, called for a return to "sound tradition" in which "a sane and logical formula" might "solve new problems."[3] While many praised the Museum of Modern Art's 1932 framing of a newly found architectural coherence based on what Hitchcock described as "the aesthetic crystallization of the engineering solution to the building problem," others, such as Fuller and other writers for *Shelter* magazine, saw in the International Style a brute exercise in disciplinary, aesthetic, and political cleansing.[4] The 1933 Century of Progress exhibition in Chicago was also seen by some critics as a testing ground for various forms of modernism, European and otherwise, and not always with praise.[5]

More catholic in his tastes, Lewis Mumford (not unlike Giedion) went so far as to praise as incipiently modern the well-executed utilitarianism of the subway station and the "cheap popular lunchroom"; in similar terms he lauded the seventeenth-century farmhouse, the nineteenth-century factory, and the work of the engineer and the shipbuilder, all of which connected use and form.[6] In these terms, Mumford also held in high esteem the modernist rationalism he saw in German "objectivity" *(Sachlich)*, not because of a formal preference (he said) but because the entire range of production—from cities to buildings to household goods—was socially and organically integrated.[7]

So why did the eclectic editor and chronicler of architecture Randolph Sexton write that modern architecture could be applied with "peculiar success" to store work? Sexton was no purist, and perhaps he worked with a looser or inchoate interpretation of the modern as representing "the new" rather than taking any organicist, aesthetic, or functionalist position. Yet this was also the problem of the store: because the store was by definition a temporary or fleeting type, an offshoot of an ever-modernizing system of goods distribution, it was presumed to have less at stake, architecturally, than other types of buildings. Even if the store was viewed, as it was in some quarters, as a harbinger of architecture to come, its ephemeral status lowered it in the eyes of other professional observers. On the other hand, the store's low investment of time, money, and even cultural capital enabled it to serve as a site of experimentation and architectural or even urban polemic. From this point of view, a store design could be modern and could therefore rise to the level of capital-*A* Architecture.

The Conventional Store

The architecture magazines of the early twentieth century were genteel portfolios of design work in which treatment of stores typically entailed the legitimations of history and convention and a discreet distance from the less seemly associations with commerce or fashion. "Modern" often meant up-to-date, and although the technical needs of display were noted, they were always qualified. New books on the business and "science" of merchandising flooded the market in the 1920s, but the literature on the planning of stores remained general and rote. In some cases, articles and images focused on fine woodworking, custom interior furnishings, or the stately and "correct" treatment of the decorative program or the facade—all of which appeared to have little to do with merchandising. Dispassionate discussions of small and usually elite shops as well as new department stores were concerned with propriety, where elements of novelty were held within the bounds of convention. "Taste" was balanced by "showmanship" to the degree best suited to the presumed upper-class clientele.[8] Design discussion wavered between allegiance to "tradition" based in a wooly version of "the past" and, in a hint of the future, responsiveness to new technological developments. In a 1924 article on "store designing," Ely Jacques Kahn called for a "practical" and pragmatic approach and suggested—sounding much like an earlier advocate of the Deutscher Werkbund (or even the Bauhaus)—that the type and quantity of the merchandise should determine the design.[9] At the same time, the projects illustrating his article were various iterations of historical, classically derived composition. Continuing this bifurcated position, joining the modern to history, Kahn wrote that the best store work would evidence simplicity and the "plain surface" because, "after all, there is no new principle involved, for through all time the same theory has dominated those works that remain to us as masterpieces."[10] Modern did not have to be wholly new or ephemeral.

In praising a store design by architect Eugene Schoen in 1922, the *American Architect* editors felt compelled to transfer its value onto other, more respectable types of work: "While it cannot be said that the shop looks like anything but a store, yet it is treated with a dignity and repose, quite as a library or office of a cultured gentleman might be treated."[11] The store attained its dignity by association, not on its own terms; it was acceptable if the design was elevated and tasteful, if it looked away, so to speak, from its main function. The store was thus by implication a problematic or at least handicapped undertaking, and it was classified, according to an *Architectural Forum* editor in 1921, as a "minor architecture."[12] More often than not, articles about store design paid far more attention to the shop fronts than to interior planning. Noteworthy as well, the term *shop front* was typically used, not *storefront,* as if the latter carried a slightly lesser social weight, but in either case, the proper display was central.

The size, scale, and articulation of the shop front—the representation of the goods—was the key moment in any store consideration. The "advertising value" of the shop front was undisputed but needed to remain within the bounds of taste, with "character, with distinction and, above all, with unique quality."[13] Thus, even as the wide commercial availability of large sheets of glass in the early twentieth century was considered a triumph of engineering and science and "the natural outcome of modern methods of trade," the architectural result was not necessarily consonant with the goals or taste cultures of the profession.[14] Fully accessible display was considered "vulgar [and] tawdry" in some of the architectural literature, and seeing all the goods was not necessarily salutary. The typical store owner's "insistence in blank plate glass, gilt lettering, crude forms and gaudy colors," some argued, was uncomfortably close to the wiles of Barnumesque lower-class stores.[15] Freighted with the fear of a loss of control and the overwhelming of propriety, one writer inveighed against "all-glass display cages" that promoted a "promiscuous assemblage" of goods. Instead, "architectural distinction" with goods "half displayed" was said to be more alluring and proper than "getting the whole story at a glance."[16] This language of restraint and disinterestedness was a means by which mass consumption could be differentiated from "higher" pursuits, untainted by desire. The disorganized and overstuffed windows of putatively lower-class stores and their overt associations with seduction and the feminine did not mesh with the empyreal realms of Architecture, or its elite proponents. And integral to the call for sobriety and for the properly Architectural—in any expressive language—were claims for the composition of the building as a whole, not any single one of its parts.

Contrary to the time-honored architectural conventions of wholeness and completeness, the tendency of many shop owners, claimed the architects, was to put up large sheets of glass without sufficient consideration for the visual effect on the building elevation as a whole. This was compounded with the advent of iron and steel construction, which, complained one architect in 1901, made the entire building front "appear to be supported upon a wall of glass" (Figure 1.1). In this intolerable

The Problem of the Store Front.

By J. Randolph Coolidge, Jr.

A CLIENT intending to build stores or offices in a building of many stories where it will be impossible to provide top light for any part of the ground floor, wishes the front of his stores or offices to be as nearly as possible an unbroken surface of plate glass, and demands of his architect a design in which the lower story or two shall be a void, — a mere blank, an opening or series of openings bounded by no more than the absolutely indispensable supporting members of the structure.

What is the architect to do? If he attempts to design for masonry, its limitations will speedily appear and embarrass the practical solution of his problem. Lintels, even of granite, can be used for short spaces only, and piers or columns ten or twelve feet on centres must be ruled out. Masonry arches are scarcely more available, for although such arches may readily span twenty feet instead of twelve, a round arch of this span will be very high at the crown unless its springing is very low, which is unsightly, and a segmental arch, though not so high for an equal span, must be much more solidly abutted. Moreover, any arch, whether circular or segmental, cuts off a deal of light that would pass under a straight window-head of equal width and height, and the loss of light is greatest where the light rays might penetrate the furthest: near the top. Until the advent of steel, however, the only method of opening wide the lower stories of a brick or stone building was to construct a colonnade or arcade, as in the Palazzo Pietro Massimi or the Place des Vosges.

Richardson himself seems to have designed the Ames Building in Bedford street, Boston, following the suggestion of the Pont du Gard. It required not less than his genius to attain the effect of massiveness in which he so delighted, while using as

Fig. 1.

situation, he asked, "What is the architect to do?"[17] The result of this seemingly inorganic approach to the design was a compositional or "structural" disruption. This was especially problematic since most store work entailed renovations of extant buildings, adding to the need for sensitive handling of new materials and elements. Instead of the increasingly popular large plate-glass window, several journals showed elevations with smaller panes of glass (Figure 1.2), which, the authors claimed, could be appropriate to some stores and, more important, would maintain the visual integrity of the facade, allowing the building to be treated as an architectural whole. This tapped into the long-standing architectural demand for "honesty" of built expression—of the Albertian or Ruskinian sort—for which the larger aesthetic whole entailed the subservience of the parts.[18] The small pane, in these terms, could achieve the necessary openness for display and, by remaining part of the composition of the building, still retain the broader values of composition. Architects made the case for smaller panes and openings that could, with more "smartness" and "distinction," show off the sellers' wares.[19]

Visual unity and stability may have been the hallmarks of a properly architectural discourse, but the transience of commerce could not be ignored. Propriety aside, one architect reminded his readers, "primarily a store front is there to catch the eye. It must brazenly herald forth the fact that something is for sale."[20] An *American Architect* writer described as necessary the "architectural untruth" of "inconsistency" and visually unsupported elevations to achieve the "spectacular presentation" of goods. After all, he wrote, the store and shop front are, in the end, "created to serve a certain well defined purpose."[21] Architect Edwin Trowbridge added that the problem of designing stores and store buildings was "the manifest incapacity of glass to carry weight." He went so far as to admit the impossibility of reconciling these incompatible values, and he argued for the separation of the "decorative" elements of the store design from the "fundamental" parts of the building.[22] The store sat uncomfortably at the intersection of architectural and commercial values.

Yet opportunity called for architects interested in commercial work as chains, independents, and department stores expanded during the years following World War I.[23] One observer in the architectural press wrote that the new small shop was "gaining a place for itself in American Architecture."[24] Another predicted that store growth presaged a "new branch of architecture."[25] This was an opportunity for the modern. One writer in *Architectural Record* claimed in 1921 that new store work was "alive with the modern spirit" but, mindful of the bounds of taste and the professional mores involved, noted that instead of "overzealous modern" designs, the better architects "have not discarded tradition."[26] Sexton, too, called for modernism in the design of stores, but his view that stores should be "striking, unusual and yet up-to-date" was bounded by the caveat that such work remain "within the bounds

The Architectural Review

| Volume XIV | June, 1907 | Number 6 |

Modern Store Fronts

By Henry L. Walters

MEN still living, and not so very old, remember the era of 1850–1880, when architecture suffered from the reign of terror, followed by anarchy. Even to those of us who did not witness the perpetration of those deeds, their memory still lives. The doubter has only to gaze abroad from the nearest windows to be fully convinced.

Perhaps the saddest sights of those days were the business parts of the towns, where brick Gothic and dingy sandstone Jacobean store fronts exhibited the wares of the retail district. When heights increased cast-iron pillars came in, unshrinkingly copying leafy capitals, bosses, and rosettes. The cast-iron rosette, covered with thick black paint, is the final word of that era.

To-day, in almost every city in the country, or almost every street in the retail districts, one may see new store fronts being built into old buildings. The masses of masonry and cast iron are taken out, light steel columns are being put in, and the intervening spaces filled with great sheets of plate glass. Deep girders of steel carry the weight of the façade above, which formerly was carried on piers so close together that only an indifferent display of goods could be made.

The problem varies, considering on the one hand the utilization of every available inch of space for display, and on the other hand the obtaining of an attractive store façade, one which will draw the attention from a distance on account of its good — or noticeable — design. An example of the first sort, where the window is merely a frame for displaying the greatest amount of goods, is shown on page 154, a drug-store window in New York City. Little depends on the architect here; it is a prob-

Music Store, West Street, Boston.

lem for the window-dresser. An example of the second sort of façade, where a quite attractiveness is necessary, is shown on this page. Since this store deals in music, and its customers are persons of education, to whom brilliant window-display would fail to appeal, it is not obliged to sacrifice architecture to window-space.

A third example is shown on page 154, the jewelry-store of A. Stowell and Co. in Boston. This is done in galvanized iron made to imitate oxidized copper in the following manner. The iron is painted black or dark brown. When this paint is dry a coat of green paint is put over it and partially rubbed off with a cloth, leaving streaks of the black showing unevenly through the green, and producing a very fair imitation of oxidized copper. In the Sowell store a frieze of veined marble has been inserted, and the base course along the sidewalk is also of marble. The effect of this store is distinctly brilliant and sparkling, lending a much-needed cheerfulness to a dingy street. Though its rococo quality — of the style of Louis XIII.— has called forth considerable criticism, it seems to the author to be one of the best things which have been done in store fronts. The streets in our retail districts are generally narrow and rather dark, and the effect of dirt and dust are to reduce everything to dinginess; therefore, we should introduce color and brilliancy. A street in the retail district is really a bazaar; why not make it frankly look like one?

The illustrations of the entrance to the Berkeley Building, Boston, and of Huyler's store, in that building, show great originality in design. The material is cream-colored terra-cotta, glazed. Deep red curtains in the store give a striking contrast to the white

Figure 1.2. "Modern Store Fronts," *Architectural Review* 14 (June 1907): 155.

of good architecture"; his interpretation of the modern was, like that of many before him, circumscribed. The store required "individualism" and could be "striking," but it should never be "radical" or "outside basic architectural principles."[27] Thus the store was programmatically appropriate to convey "the modern"—no matter how vague—but it was also caught between the professional and aesthetic traditions of the field and the vagaries of change and fashion.

The tensions between the familiar and the new generated a host of caveats for store design seeking an affiliation with modernism. In the portfolio section of a 1929 "Shops and Stores" issue of *Architectural Record,* whatever is represented as "modern" or "*nouveau*" in each store is also checked by "restraint" and "taste." There is nothing "extreme" or "startling" in any of the designs, say the editors, yet none uses merely "conventional" strategies; there are "new forms" as well as associations with past types. In all cases, materials are used "frankly" and with "simplicity," and the design strategies come from a "purely objective handling of the problem" of merchandising. Each project in the magazine paid homage to the tradition of craftsmanship while also recognizing, as if restating Frank Lloyd Wright's call to embrace the "web of the machine," that there might be a "modernist craftsman" comfortable with "modern technology."[28] Yet these views were nothing if not elastic, and praise for the store and storefront elevations by McKim, Mead & White or Carrère and Hastings, for instance, could well assert that they fell within the "spirit" of modern while still retaining the "classic tradition of perfect form."[29] Other store treatments showed the suitability of art deco and the moderne, especially after the 1925 Paris Exposition Internationale des Arts Décoratifs et Industriels Modernes, but this work too could be, according to some, "extreme," so the best design accommodated a classical restraint as well.[30] So even while new forms, new needs, and being "up-to-date" were integral to a conception of modernism, limits were set by the social conventions of the profession as well as by the taste cultures of the clientele. In effect, the store suffered interwoven limitations: the program of the store to sell goods conflicted with its potential role as Architecture—the former requiring novelty and seduction, the latter requiring stability and restraint. The tensions of mass culture were becoming apparent. The paradoxical pulls on the modern store, as in modernity itself, created a constant problem in store work: between convention and experiment, the store needed to be new but could not really be new.

Yet one area of store work appeared to offer a new and serious role for its design, to wit, that the store was part of the city. An *American Architect* editor expressed the tensions of the city as a site when he wrote that one store was "advertisingly good" but not "harmonious with its surroundings."[31] Recourse to larger scales of planning, to the city beyond, implied a new reach of engagement and change as well as a sense of permanence and stability, a new scale that might lend legitimacy to professional work on store design.

The Expanding Modern Store: Arcades

Architectural debates about stores evidenced the tensions between commerce and culture, and there soon emerged a formal device that satisfied both, in part, and expanded the relevance of the store as part of the ebb and flow of the city. Architect and writer John Taylor Boyd noted in 1921 that the tension between the use of the all-glass front and small panes could be resolved through a new "method of planning" in which the ground-floor street wall would be recessed. This ground-plane shift would create "a small corridor or vestibule" that could be used "for show window space" and allow for fuller treatment of the building as a whole. If not at the scale of the arcades of Bologna or the famously enclosed arcades of Paris, the vestibule between street and storefront was considered an important rearrangement of store elements, balancing the concerns of professional and architectural standards with display needs and the problem of the distracting "sidewalk throng."[32] To compensate for the small store and the typical narrow urban lot's minimal display frontage, and to provide additional weather-protected display space off the bustling sidewalk, the arcade would turn the sidewalk display into part of the showroom and enable architects to treat the street elevation in new terms.

The "recessed shop front" where a customer could "quietly admire" goods for sale was usually given humble beginnings, but its importance was widely noted. The single outdoor vestibule containing the door swing was originally small scale—and largely without authorship—and it slowly made its way into professional design vocabularies on both sides of the Atlantic. In the United States, the vestibule, later called the "recessing system," was noted just after the turn of the century, and its use increased dramatically during the 1920s. The potential for experimentation was evident. Mixing architectural and commercial logic, one architect praised "advancing and retreating with planes, with bays, and recesses which give great play of light and shade and opportunity for ingenious arrangement of decorative surfaces."[33] Although references to Parisian arcades were typical, the simpler recessing system became a standard architectural tool for commerce; it appeared to be a pragmatic method for store owners to advance their businesses and architects to invent new store-to-street relations.

The 1921 Avedon shop arcade in New York City by Harry Allen Jacobs was considered an "original" and "perfectly adapted" example of the arcade, demonstrating how merchandising needs could foster a change in the architectural understanding of the street-store relationship.[34] Jacobs inserted an open vestibule or "rotunda" into the street-facing mass of an extant building and lined it with large, glazed display cases. Ely Jacques Kahn (becoming Jacobs's partner a few years later) praised the rotunda for its commercial potential because it offered "protection" from the "annoyance from street crowds or solicitous clerks or inclement weather."[35] Advertisements portrayed the new space as a sheltered extension of the sidewalk, as if the city were somehow a threat, a perennial theme in urban representation (Figure 1.3). Another store in New York City designed in the "English Gothic" style was entered through an outdoor vestibule complete with groin-vaulted ceiling.[36] Indicative of the possibilities of the arcade, Jacobs proposed in 1922 the addition of a continuous arcade to the fronts of buildings on New York City's Fifth Avenue to address congestion of pedestrians and vehicles and to improve the accessibility of shop fronts. Such large-scale

Figure 1.3. Avedon store advertisement, *New York Times* (June 1924).

retooling of the urban fabric—proposed perennially for midtown—was not feasible, however, and smaller-scale versions would continue to be proposed.[37]

The single-building or single-store arcade became a catalyst to rework the relation between building and sidewalk, and "arcading" became both a planning technique and a verb. In 1924, noted planner Russell Van Nest Black wrote: "Architecturally, the arcaded sidewalk frequently gives opportunity for interesting effect and often enables attractive show window display with minimum damage from sunlight exposure."[38] The "arcade style" could also be undertaken by individual store or building owners under their own initiative and thus entailed little in the way of policy or planning work. In the June 1924 *Architectural Forum* "Shop Reference Number," the arcade emerged as the strongest thread among the articles (Figures 1.4 and 1.5). In its typical form, the new entry zone acted as a thickened spatial layer between store and street and was often populated with "island displays" or vitrines projecting into the expanded pedestrian realm.[39] One writer saw that the new "vestibule" could accommodate "kiosk-like showcases" that could further make the display a draw from the street.[40] John Taylor Boyd praised the three-dimensional possibilities of the arcade as well as its utility. The new design idea, he said, was tied to both "salesmanship, quantity production, selling, psychology and window display" and "new architectural

Figure 1.4. "The Development of the Arcaded Shop Front," *Architectural Forum* 40 (June 1924): 270.

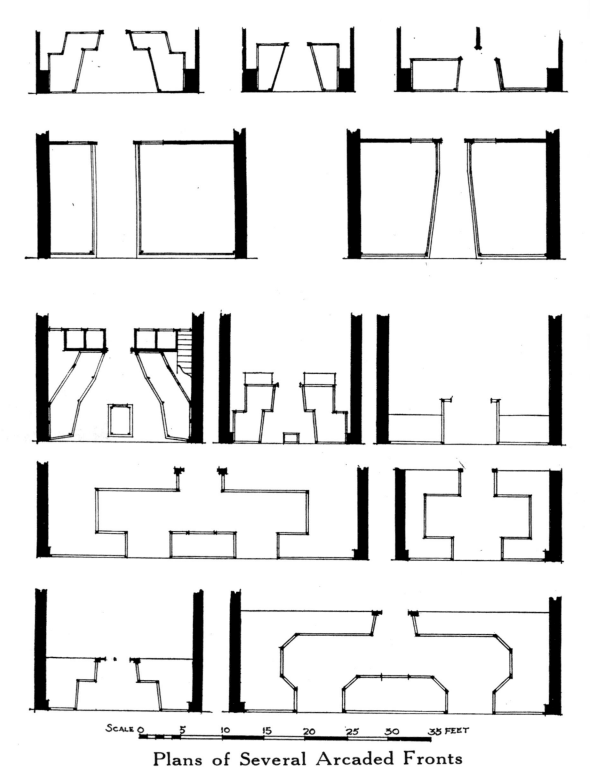

Plans of Several Arcaded Fronts

Figure 1.5. "Plans of Several Arcaded Fronts," in "The Development of the Arcaded Shop Front," 271.

and social needs." Another writer described how "our shopkeepers have brought out a new idea" of "recessing the display front" and connecting the sidewalk to the store. An extended *Forum* treatment of stores in 1925 deemed the "recessed or arcaded treatment" suitable for "period" or "modern" styles but noted that the latter styles allowed for greater experimentation with the new recessing system, for which it offered diagrams.[41] Joseph Urban's 1929 Bedell Store in New York City utilized a large arcade (Figure 1.6)—called both a rotunda and a promenade in the press—and the project was framed in *Architectural Forum* as a modern design *and* a business innovation. The distinctive "moderne" design was praised for making the architecture its "own advertisement"—for being straightforward, ahistoric, and "functional"— instead of a substructure for garish signage or unnecessary detail. In business terms, the author praised the "display vestibule" for addressing sidewalk congestion and the weather so that goods and store would be visible.[42] The arcade pleased various audiences, professional, popular, and commercial. The new relation of store to street, the new scale of the work, the reduction of "obstacles" preventing a customer from entering, and the additional display space created a unique urban experience, a *new* semipublic, if slightly commodified, social realm.

On the West Coast, as Richard Longstreth has documented, architectural experimentation with the store-to-street relationship in the form of arcades, setbacks, and courtyards depended less on sidewalk commercial needs than on new locations accessed by car. The Pasadena Arcade by Marston, Van Pelt and Mayberry (1929) utilized a pedestrian-friendly courtyard (also used by cars) as well as an arcade in the

Above. New Front of the Bedell Store, New York
Designed by Joseph Urban, Architect
George A. Schonewald, Architect of the Building Alteration

Right. Plan of the shop front, showing unusual arrangement and extent of show windows. The Bedell Store, New York

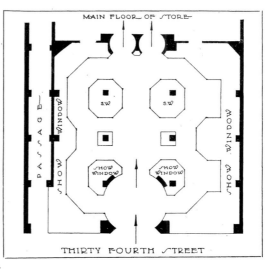

957

Figure 1.6. Joseph Urban, Bedell Store, New York, in "A Modern Store Alteration," *Architectural Forum* 50 (June 1929): 957.

"Spanish Style," and other projects included the Palm Drive-In by J. B. Severance (1929)—later photographed by Albert Frey—the Plaza Market by Morgan, Walls & Clements (1929), and Richard Neutra's Los Angeles Drive-In (1929) (Figure 1.7), all of which expanded the vocabulary of access for the motorist.[43] These projects stressed spatial flow for the car and driver as a functional pair needing bathrooms, gas pumps, and groceries but *not* places to walk. In other cities, arcaded stores could

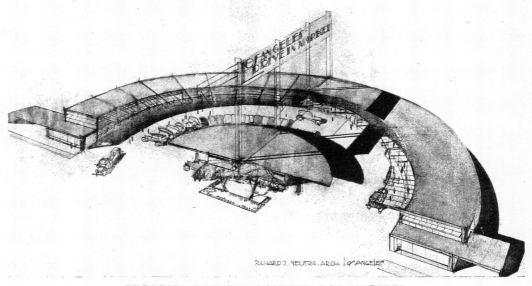

PROPOSED DRIVE-IN MARKET, LOS ANGELES
RICHARD J. NEUTRA, ARCHITECT
Stores in outer semicircle; awnings are of glass; the central unit contains
filling station and rest rooms

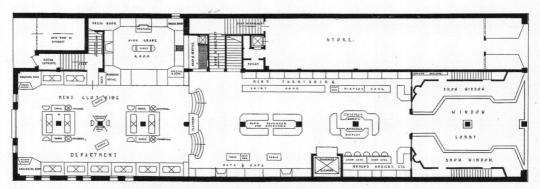

PLAN OF ROOS BROTHERS' STORE, HOLLYWOOD, CAL.
Auto entrance at rear with car storage in basement
DESIGNED BY GRAND RAPIDS STORE EQUIPMENT CORPORATION

Figure 1.7. Richard Neutra, "Proposed Drive-In Market, Los Angeles," and Grand Rapids Store Equipment Corporation, "Plan of Roos Brothers' Store, Hollywood, California," in "Store Buildings," *Architectural Record* 65 (June 1929): 591.

be found, but they were exceptions—recessed entryways became the only popular adjustment of the connection of the street to the individual store. Yet, among architectural observers, the arcade, with "double the display space," smoothed the tasks of the merchandiser *and* the architect, and "arcading" appeared to offer a unique spatial solution for both fields.[44] Most important, by meshing the space of the street with the space of the store, the arcade could raise questions of planning, of city-scale thinking, and a new sense of architectural possibility.

The Rational Store

In January 1928, *Architectural Forum*'s editors split the magazine into two sections, "Architectural Design" and "Architectural Engineering and Business." This dramatic move indicated that the older model of a genteel portfolio presentation would now coexist with the expanding technological and economic realms of practice. The January 1929 issue of the *Architectural Record* shifted as well and featured a new cover design consisting of a silhouette of the Parthenon and the steel frame of a skyscraper, positing a continuity between accepted monuments and the new "facts" of the modern age. The new approach was most evident in the "Technical News and Research" section, introduced, wrote editor Michael Mikkelsen, as a way to address the architectural implications of mass production and specialization.[45] The increased use of standardized materials and assembly processes would have a profound effect on design and building, Mikkelsen wrote, and, with a heady mix of modernist ideals and Taylorist pragmatism, he asserted that the profession would need highly specialized and quantitative information.[46] Mikkelsen embraced the broad social and architectural changes under way, yet he still framed the situation as a question: the new technical section, he wrote, would determine *if* scientific method could benefit the fine arts. These changes were made real in the new editorial voices Mikkelsen brought to the journal's masthead—architects, technical specialists, and historians, all just beginning to demonstrate their architectural mettle. They included Henry-Russell Hitchcock, Douglas Haskell, Fiske Kimball, Robert Davison, and Theodore Larson, and to lead them, Mikkelsen hired architect and educator Lawrence Kocher.[47]

Kocher was a canny choice to run the *Record*. Hired in 1926 and becoming managing editor in 1929, he was well positioned to navigate the unstable ground of architectural debates, given that he had a foot in the "traditional" world and one in the "modern" world.[48] He was a spokesman for "an American style" of architecture while simultaneously addressing the putatively radical voices emanating from Europe. His Americanist credentials were extensive. He had taught American architectural history at the University of Virginia, conducted studies of American colonial building practices, and served on the Architectural Advisory Board for the polemical Williamsburg Restoration.[49] At the same time, he published the highly rationalist and abstract, technically derived Sunlight Towers project in 1929 and collaborated with Albert Frey on the 1931 Aluminaire House, a demonstration of new construction and technological methods. Both projects were couched in a matter-of-fact language of technical possibilities, siting, climate, and health research. Kocher also examined real estate and subdivision methods.[50] Like Lewis Mumford and Sigfried Giedion, among others, Kocher saw a demonstrable affinity between the rationalism and objectivity already claimed by would-be modernist architects and the frankness of American eighteenth-century architecture. In fact, Kocher was an early advocate for Richard Neutra, and he sought to bring Walter Gropius to the United States as early as 1934; Kocher and Gropius discussed a curriculum linking products, manufacturers, and design distinctly parallel to Bauhaus ideas of art and industry.[51] Kocher was uniquely suited to demonstrate that the modernism of *Sachlich* and the *Neues Bauen* might be "at home" in the United States.

The June 1929 "Shops and Stores" issue of the *Architectural Record* demonstrated the balancing of so-called traditional and modern approaches. The articles and plates in the design portfolio in the first half of the magazine balanced convention and novelty, craft and technology, and gentility and simplicity. One store was praised for its "restraint" even as it experimented with "new forms" and for its exploration of "modern craft" without "fantastic" design.[52] In this telling, tradition was integral to the architect's ability to integrate new circumstances or technologies. Most of the work was deco and moderne in image, with flourishes of detailing and a hint of cubism, and photographs of Parisian stores gave the articles a certain cultural legitimacy. Even Vahan Hagopian's expressionistic shoe store (Figure 1.8) was described in terms of objectivity and "harmony." The "Technical News and Research" section that followed, however, used utterly different language.

The *Record*'s 1929 "Store Buildings" feature was first and foremost an exercise in utility and sobriety (Figure 1.9).[53] The lead image of the piece showed the entry to the "rear parking area" of the Mullen & Bluett store building (Morgan, Walls & Clements) in Pasadena, California, not a tasteful street facade or garden court. With a utilitarian attitude—buildings, not designs *(Baukunst* over *Stilarchitektur)*—the special section was a manual and a set of standards; the introductory line could not have been more manifesto-like: "The store building should be considered by the architect as primarily a problem of merchandising." The store, the editors added, is no more and no less than a "device for selling goods."[54] The article started with "Economic Factors in Planning" for the store building, stressing location, types of goods, and types of customers. The following sections on "design factors" and "structural and operation factors" focused on technical and best practices for goods handling and customer circulation and suggested methods and dimensions for furnishings. Illustrations included fixture diagrams, typical plan layouts, lighting details, and built examples. There was little mention of facade or building elevations. Several projects—including Neutra's Los Angeles Drive-In proposal—entailed new

Photo. Amemya

OUTER VESTIBULE
A. S. BECK SHOE STORE
V. HAGOPIAN, ARCHITECT

Figure 1.8. V. Hagopian, "A. S. Beck Shoe Store," *Architectural Record* 65 (June 1929): 543.

TECHNICAL NEWS
AND
RESEARCH

· REAR PARKING AREA
STORE OF MULLEN & BLUETT, PASADENA, CALIFORNIA
MORGAN, WALLS & CLEMENTS, ARCHITECTS

Featuring

STORE BUILDINGS

Previous studies of Building Types include: Swimming Pools, Storage Garages, Apartment Houses, Airports.

Future issues will include analyses of the following: Kitchen Planning (Hotel, Club and Restaurant) and Soundproofing the Hospital.

Figure 1.9. Title page of "Store Buildings," featuring rear parking area of Mullen & Bluett, Pasadena, California, in "Technical News and Research," *Architectural Record* 65 (June 1929): 583.

site-planning ideas derived from the use of the car. Overall, the technical section was a complement to the portfolio, although from another point of view, the two forms of representation were irreconcilable. The split view of the store, in other words, demonstrated the tensions between an emerging understanding of modernism as machinic and utilitarian and a view of modernism as another convention with valued historic associations.[55]

The pragmatic concerns of the *Record* "Store Buildings" article were also evident in the list of industry specialists consulted by the editors: alongside two architects from Starrett & Van Vleck—well known for commercial and store buildings—were Kenneth C. Welch, an architect and vice president of the Grand Rapids Store Equipment Company, and two engineers, one from Curtis Lighting and one from Erikson Electric Company. Consultation with industry experts for editorial assistance was not new to architectural publishing, but notable in this case was that all of the consultants also showed their own work—several plans by Starrett & Van Vleck, cabinet layouts by Welch (Figure 1.10), and details by the lighting companies. As an overt integration of the design, production, and editorial communities, the "Store Buildings" article went beyond advertisements or endorsements and represented the overlaps in practices wrought by an embrace of industrial production, in effect restating the goals of the Bauhaus. A moderne store by Ely Jacques Kahn somehow found its way into the section, but it bore little relation to the terse attitude of the article or the editorial position of the "Technical News and Research" section as a whole.

For the *Record* editors, the new approach to the design of stores had wide implications for the professional claims and responsibilities of the architect. While many store owners might have scoffed, the editors wrote that "it is the architect more than the owner who should determine the financial success of a new store building."[56] Based on a rational evaluation of needs and possibilities, which the architect was best equipped to carry out, the architect would shape the success of the store. Architects had long claimed such control for their work, but the modern store seemed to offer a newly transparent relation between program and form—if, that is, the field adapted. The editors wrote that the typical architectural school curriculum needed to include the study of buying habits, purchasing power, and principles of showcase and window display—exactly those pedestrian forms of knowledge the leaders of the field had so assiduously pushed beyond its borders. Architectural practice needed to incorporate the necessities of the store as a viable and legitimate commission, even if these new skills ran counter to the historical image of the architect.[57]

The relation of the pragmatics of merchandising to the expertise of the architect was soon taken up as an explicitly modernist project. In a 1931 *Record* piece titled "Planning the Retail Store," which featured J. J. P. Oud's Hook of Holland project (1929) at its opening (Figure 1.11), Danish architect Knud Lönberg-Holm described the store as a technical project for which objectivity was the determining feature. Lönberg-Holm had immigrated to the United States in 1923 and was appointed to the magazine in late 1929 to head the "Technical" section. He embraced the integration of industrial production with architectural design and strongly advocated a productivist interpretation of modernist tenets. He became director of research for *Sweet's Catalog* in 1932 and was writer and organizer of *Time-Saver Standards* of 1935—both remarkable documents of standardization at the heart of any project of rationalization. In 1932, he joined Buckminster Fuller (among others) to take over the Beaux-Arts–leaning *T-Square* magazine, renaming it *Shelter* and taking polemical positions about, inter alia, the necessity of industrialization of

THE ARCHITECTURAL RECORD

¶ 591

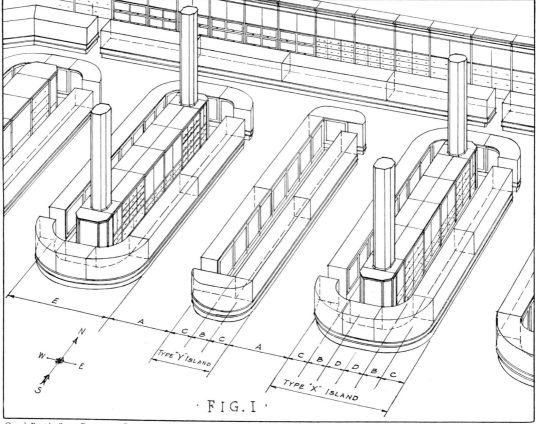

Grand Rapids Store Equipment Corp.

TYPICAL SCHEME OF FIRST FLOOR FIXTURES FOR A DEPARTMENT STORE

Figure 1.10. "Typical Scheme of First Floor Fixtures for a Department Store, Grand Rapids Store Equipment Corporation," *Architectural Record* 65 (June 1929): 591.

PLANNING THE RETAIL STORE

By K. LÖNBERG-HOLM

NEIGHBORHOOD STORE, HOEK VAN HOLLAND, J. J. P. OUD, ARCHITECT

Figure 1.11. Title page of "Planning the Retail Store," featuring "Neighborhood Store, Hoek Van Holland, J. J. P. Oud, Architect," in "Technical News and Research," *Architectural Record* 69 (June 1931): 495.

architectural production.[58] And a modern store was a unique site of a progressive view of modernization.

The tight fit of the store to the rationalist thread of modernist tenets was demonstrated in Lönberg-Holm's utilitarian treatment:

> The retail store is an outlet unit for distribution of commodities. It should provide accommodations for receiving, storing and selling merchandise, and for administration and human comfort. The goods should move through the store with a minimum of friction in a minimum amount of time.[59]

Stores, in other words, were mechanisms for service, display, and distribution, and Lönberg-Holm found support for such pragmatics in the technical materials from the U.S. Chamber of Commerce, among other industry sources such as *Progressive Grocer* magazine.[60] Rhetorics of friction and the reduction of waste, of unnecessary exertion of energy, were central to the rationalist thread of modernism, especially in its roots among the architectural avant-garde in interwar Europe, and the store smoothly and uniquely fit into this representation. If the "streamlining" that would soon become popular also utilized an aesthetics of friction, the rationalist view of the store was polemically opposed; a store had nothing to do with surface, style, or fashion.[61]

Alongside rationalized layouts and organization, the necessity to quite literally see all the goods was pivotal, and the storefront—not shop front—was an essential part of the store project. No longer "promiscuous," architectural transparency and knowledge fused with the fundamental laws of merchandising. Lönberg-Holm's primary example was a small store at Oud's Hook of Holland housing complex, an early and unabashedly modern project that was widely published. The widely circulated store photographs (included in the Museum of Modern Art's 1932 *International Exhibition of Modern Architecture*) foregrounded how extensive glazing provided a continuous sight line into and through the store—that is, the store was utterly open, unencumbered by signage, trumped-up or exaggerated displays, and other impediments to the information provided by the goods themselves. With a circular plan and a fully glazed storefront, Lönberg-Holm wrote, the "whole selling space is made display space." In fact, he added, with unsubtle aplomb, "the best store front is no store front. The store itself is the best display window."[62]

Lönberg-Holm's understanding of visibility had deep roots in the European avant-garde. For him, design was a product of transparency, rationality, and efficiency and directly represented the necessities of merchandising—seeing equaled selling. This was as good a modernist manifesto as any—the object was its own best representation, or presentation was better than representations—and his framing of the store matched the discourses on objects and expression offered by Hannes Meyer, Walter

Gropius, and (to a lesser extent) Erich Mendelsohn, the latter well known for his department store work in Germany. Hannes Meyer's Co-op Vitrine project of 1924 demonstrated the limits and the potential of production, and Mendelsohn most dramatically wrote that the merchandise is central: "all commercial and architectural measures serve the necessity of its highest praise." This was the architectural milieu from which Lönberg-Holm emerged and that he pursued.[63]

The European rationalism and productivism at the heart of Lönberg-Holm's thinking was supported by the other projects illustrating his *Record* article, including Gropius's store in Dessau, a store in London by Welles Coates, and a cooperative store in Stockholm. This work was said to exemplify a much-needed clarity of programming, materials, and interior planning that could, without the deceptions of consumption, provide for social need and that found expression as severe, geometrically simple forms. Quite simply, the modernism articulated by Lönberg-Holm was defined by and fused with the functional necessities of store design.[64] The store was, to use a phrase that was later a marketing slogan, a machine for selling. Objective analysis and flowchart logics could define a new architectural approach and, at the same time, confirm and epitomize the role of social and economic modernization. This tension was at the root of store work, defining its possibilities as well as its limits as architecture, but there yet remained other ways of exploring the design of selling.

The "Tensionist" Store

Frederick Kiesler's 1930 book *Contemporary Art Applied to the Store and Its Display* yoked together two utterly different genres. Part art manifesto and part design manual, it employed a defamiliarizing juxtaposition of literary forms and presentation methods, nothing like an instructional manual, that demonstrated the avant-gardist principle in which Art and the Machine could be unified and a "new spirit" produced. For Kiesler, as for his peers in various European art and architecture movements of the time, a properly modern approach lay in the embrace of Art and the Machine. Kiesler, like Lönberg-Holm, saw in the store "a new spirit in art" derived from mass production that could further establish and spread a renewed social life. This was a uniquely American situation, he wrote, since the "expression of America is the mass, the expression of the masses, the machine." Echoing the fascination with America's industrial complex that had beguiled Le Corbusier, Gropius, and Mendelsohn, Kiesler, too, framed the country's vigorous productive apparatus as liberative. He added a not insignificant detail to this framework by suggesting that the distributive apparatus—that is, the store—would be a key means of circulating new ideas to the public. "Unprecedented though it may be in the annals of art," he wrote, "a main channel through which the new style will approach popularization is the store."[65] As a site for the fusing of human want, social process, and technology, the store was, for Kiesler, not destructive or wasteful in a Veblenian or Adornian sense or déclassé or pedestrian in the bourgeois sense, but redemptive. He was not naive about this and later wrote that an art-for-art's-sake approach would be just as socially destructive as "industry for industry's sake."[66] In any case, the store's specific role as a purveyor of consumer goods and dreams was integral to a possible modern world.

Artist, designer, and architect, Frederick Kiesler was an unlikely candidate to reveal a deep connection between a modernist aesthetic position and a merchandiser's on-the-ground logic. In the 1920s Kiesler trained in Vienna and moved widely in European avant-garde art, theater, and architecture circles; he joined the De Stijl group in 1923.[67] His work was experimental and varied. His swirling "Endless Theater" and constructivist "Space Stage" for a theater exhibition in Vienna in 1924 and his "City in Space," exhibited in the Austrian pavilion at the 1925 Paris Exposition, all drew wide acclaim and made clear his commitment to a merged social and aesthetic program.[68] His projects demonstrated a strong sense of the possibilities of constructivist and neoplastic programs, using what he called "tensionism" to surrealistically blur or merge environments—we shall have "NO MORE WALLS," he wrote.[69] In later years, Reyner Banham praised the open aesthetic of "City in Space" as comparable to the Russian *proun* in its formal as well as social potential.[70] Based on the success of Paris Exposition installation, Jane Heap of the radical magazine the *Little Review* asked Kiesler to organize an "International Theater Exposition" to be held in New York in 1926, and Kiesler relocated to New York City. The show opened in February, and reviewers deemed the show and the new theater work revolutionary: an introduction to an American audience of surrealist, futurist, constructivist, and De Stijl examples of art, architecture, and theater design.[71]

While setting his sights on larger projects, Kiesler directed his design thinking toward smaller-scale (paying) work: the commercial storefront. Kiesler found temporary work as a window designer for Saks Fifth Avenue department store in 1927 and 1928, which provided him with an income and publicity (Figure 1.12).[72] A *New York Times* architecture critic commented that Kiesler's windows were the most dramatic among those tending toward the modern—such as contemporary windows by Donald Deskey—since in his windows "well-known geometrical symbols have been distorted and deformed to make a foil" for the consumer goods on display. Other designers had used shapes and materials suggestive of "engineering, architecture and machinery," but Kiesler's were "the most abstract" yet the most effective, drawing the passerby into the scene.[73] Even as he was working for Saks and developing new theater projects, Kiesler was cultivating peer and patronage relationships that brought him the commission for the Film Arts Guild Theater, which opened in early 1929. The theater's "immersive" space, much praised by the *New York Times,* was made by walls built as screens that could become part of the performance, thus joining staging and audience.[74] Kiesler's avant-gardist attempt to fuse art and experience and to remove the social distinctions of performance and action were central tenets in his

Sigurd Fischer

Window display contributes to selling of merchandise. Goods and the architectural setting are coordinated, illustrating the close tie-up between selling and display.

SHOP WINDOW DISPLAYS
SAKS AND COMPANY
NEW YORK CITY
F. J. KIESLER
DESIGNER

Figure 1.12. Frederick J. Kiesler, Saks Fifth Avenue storefront, New York, *Architectural Record* 20 (September 1930).

work, as they were for many of his peers, and he sought in modernism more broadly to break down social and psychological barriers.

Kiesler's design work, from De Stijl–affiliated projects to the theatrical and quasi-surrealist Saks windows to the remaking of spaces for theater and film as experiential and haptic, formed part of a larger project he later called "correalism" or "design correlation." This program sought to break down the artificial walls erected by the restrictive social conditions and institutions shaping daily life and to enable creative and alternative visions.[75] Instead of framing political, natural, and technological realms as autonomous experiences or fields of inquiry—the world constructed by and for the bourgeoisie—radical artists such as Kiesler from 1910 through the 1920s sought collapse, overlap, and continuity, where social flow would replace life-sapping perceptual-psychological containers. In this restatement of the *Gesamtkunstwerk*, "correlation" of once separated social fields, the bringing together of experience and technology would, in Kiesler's modernist terms, emancipate humankind. His endeavors in all this included a variety of employment, organizational, and art and architecture projects.

Kiesler was among the founding members of the American Union of Decorative Artists and Craftsmen (AUDAC) in 1928; this organization sought to reform the design, production, and distribution of goods in ways "appropriate" to the times. Clearly modeled on the Deutscher Werkbund as well as the Bauhaus, the members of the organization were not, unlike some architectural critics, ambivalent about advances in technology, industry, and merchandising. AUDAC advocated for cooperation among designers, "industrial organizations," manufacturing processes, and "heads of stores" and other professionals. The group's members were critical of what they considered the overly ornamental works of the 1925 Paris Exposition as well as the inferior mass-produced goods flooding the American marketplace, and they advocated for a simultaneous embrace of the market and a disciplined approach to design, seeking to "direct the so-called modern art movement . . . along more intelligent lines."[76] Earlier in the 1920s, the Metropolitan Museum of Art organized annual decorative and industrial art exhibits, and while AUDAC members praised the efforts of curator Richard Bach, they saw the museum's work as "one of a kind" and insufficiently integrated with mass production. That the membership included as diverse a group as William Lescaze, Paul Frankl, Norman Bel Geddes, William Muschenheim, John W. Root, Eliel Saarinen, Walter Dorwin Teague, Joseph Urban, Lucien Bernard (a Werkbund designer), Witold Gordon (painter), and Robert Leonard and Kem Webber (designers) indicated that "modern" and "intelligent lines" were not particularly restrictive with respect to claims to simplicity and industrial process—a very different vision that the Museum of Modern Art would soon support. And while the members' individual works varied considerably—the group's 1930 exhibits in Brooklyn and Manhattan were nothing if not liberal with respect to a particularly "modern" form or approach—AUDAC stressed the integration of design, produc-tion, and merchandising; for Kiesler, this entailed a direct engagement with goods.[77]

Kiesler's 1930 *Contemporary Art Applied to the Store and Its Display* was a mani-festo that aimed, like many of the European avant-garde, to collapse the differenti-ated and straitjacketed spaces of social life that resulted from industrialization and its mass-produced goods. The book's simple dedication to "a sound cooperation between public, artist and industry" did not sound particularly new at the time, but Kiesler's melding of aesthetic and social theory with the needs and techniques of storefront design was specific and experimental.[78]

Contemporary Art was a synoptic if selective account of the ways in which modern painting, sculpture, and architecture would enable an unmediated unity and experi-ence of daily life, including commerce. The first third of the book explores the work of Picasso, Matisse, Sheeler, Brancusi, Vantongerloo, and Gabo, among others, and shows how their simplicity, dynamism, and abstraction enabled an empathetic con-nection to users and viewers. The same qualities were to be found, Kiesler argued, in the work of Mies, Oud, and Chareau, which had a simplicity and openness that would "break down insularity." He also described a new "horizontalism" as the result of openness, where walls would disappear, although he was critical of Mendelsohn's work, in which the horizontal was, he wrote, "decoration without functional rea-son."[79] In any case, the unified movement of the new art—and here Kiesler sounds much like Sigfried Giedion in his broad strokes and polemical syntheses—would revitalize social life and give to architecture a renewed relevance. For Kiesler, the store was a unique communicative mechanism in which modern art would shape a new age of commerce and fast-paced urban life.

The overlapping principles of art and merchandising take up the latter two-thirds of *Contemporary Art*. "Unprecedented though it may be in the annals of art, a main channel through which the new style will approach popularization is the store. Here is where a new art can come into closest contact with the stream of the mass, by employing the quickest working faculty: the eye."[80] Beyond theater and set design but making use of their techniques, the modern store would expand access, visually and literally, to modern art and goods and enhance their centrality and agency in the social life of the city. The store could physically enable the joining of art with social life.[81] The task of the storefront, therefore, was to engage the passerby with the goods on display through particular design techniques, or what Kiesler later called "biotechniques."[82]

If visually joining the pedestrian with goods for sale was typically accomplished via ever-larger panes of glass, Kiesler saw this as too passive—the eye was not auton-omous—and here he differed from many retailers as well as Lönberg-Holm and other rationalist-leaning designers. Instead he sought to heighten, focus, and acti-vate the relationship between goods and pedestrian (Figures 1.13–1.15). "Tension and relaxation," he later wrote, were necessary to engage the passerby.[83] This included formal experiments with the building line—"scalloping" the plan, creating projections and recessions, creating a "funnel type" of arcaded entryway, and treating doors like windows and windows like doors.[84] In a detailed exposition of window, ceiling, sidewall, and floor strategies for creating displays, he showed how the architect could bring the shopper into closer contact with the items for sale, creating an enlightening tension between access and visibility. Framing methods, slightly off backgrounds, asymmetry, and proportion were all aimed to disturb "normal" perception

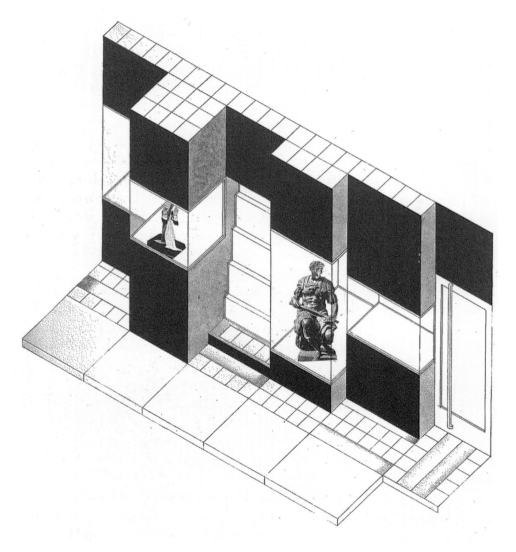

Figure 1.13. Frederick J. Kiesler, "Experiment in Rhythmic Storefront," in *Contemporary Art Applied to the Store and Its Display*, 83.

and expectation, which matched merchandising interests as well as avant-garde tenets. Regarding this approach, Kiesler praised the store windows of designers from the Berlin-based Reimann School (which shared students and teachers with the Bauhaus) and the London-based Arundell Display School, the work of both being similar to Kiesler's in their simplicity and dissonant compositions.[85] At the extreme end of this vision, Kiesler proposed "kinetic" window displays with push buttons and built-in radio and television giving the pedestrian access to information and ever-more-engaging images—an extension of the mediated relationship he advocated (as

Figure 1.14. Frederick J. Kiesler, "Storefront," in *Contemporary Art Applied to the Store and Its Display,* 95.

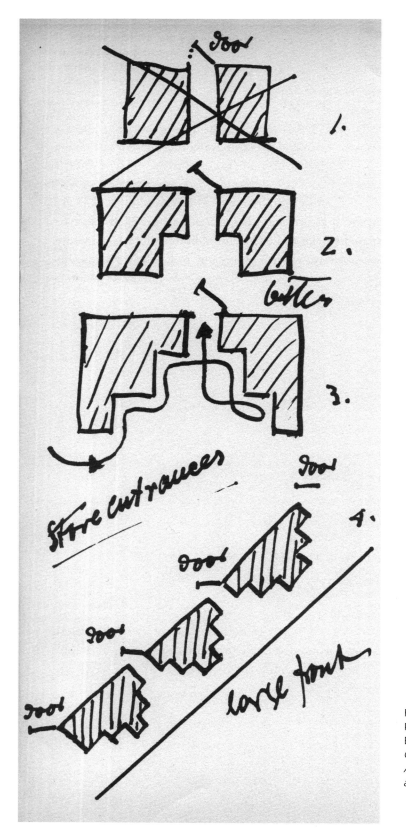

Figure 1.15. Frederick J. Kiesler, "Zigzag Funnel Entranceway," in *Contemporary Art Applied to the Store and Its Display,* 81.

opposed to pure transparency) and one that would provide the consumer/citizen with a new interpretation of the potential of the goods. For Kiesler, the storefront offered a technical, material, aesthetic, even psychic mechanism through which modernist techniques and ideals could be inserted into and transform American mass culture.

Kiesler's work was not easily interpreted, but his insistence on breaking down social and spatial boundaries was more than evident. Critics Douglas Haskell and Walter Rendell Storey praised Kiesler's *Contemporary Art* less for its detailed formal proposals than for its attempt to bring art and design to prosaic problems of retailing. Haskell favorably compared Kiesler to Le Corbusier; both architects, he wrote, brought the arts into the "constructive world." Storey saw in Kiesler's book an important attempt to use the broad reach of commerce and merchandising to circulate principles of "new art."[86] Kiesler continued to develop the tensions between art and commerce and the fusing of perception, space, and experience—his 1933 "Space House" for the Modernage Furniture Company, his design for the "Art of This Century" gallery in 1942, and his writings on "correalism" all indicated his unique position on the transformative power of modernism, especially as it might exist at the interstices of art, culture, production, and consumption.[87] In sum, Kiesler's store book and his practice were indicative of an optimistic and fluid traffic among the arts, architecture, and merchandising.

Kiesler's position on modernism was nondogmatic; he praised Mies van der Rohe's exhibit work of the 1920s, but his embrace of commerce also matched the thinking of American industrial designers such as Norman Bel Geddes. He was sometimes skeptical of what he referred to as decorativeness in some industrial design—criticizing the lack of "practicality" in some of Bel Geddes's work—but he praised any attempts to overcome the autonomy of disciplines and practices.[88] Kiesler was as technically focused as Knud Lönberg-Holm, always noting specifications and "mathematical ratios" and precisely researching construction techniques, but at the same time he was unafraid of and embraced the images and the spectacle he saw as central to stores *and* modern architectural practice.[89] Although he was later described in *Architectural Forum* as an "avant-garde European astray in the American commercial woods," it would be more accurate to say that Kiesler's book and his work in the 1920s and 1930s promoted a modernism in which commerce and consumption did not preclude serious architectural research.[90]

Merchandising and/or Modernism

The curators of the infamous 1932 Museum of Modern Art *International Exhibition of Modern Architecture*—Henry-Russell Hitchcock and Philip Johnson—concretized what they deemed properly modern architecture and created a uniform and conventionalized modernist practice. Their shaping of the new style and an embrace of the concept of style minimized the rationalizing tendencies exemplified in the work of Lönberg-Holm and elided the bio-emotive frisson in the work of Kiesler even as the new style easily assimilated key parts of their formal vocabularies. The three qualifications for the new style—volume over mass, regularity over symmetry, and material over ornament—heralded a simplicity and clarity of form appropriate, according to the museum, to practice in a new age. It was an aesthetic that was reproducible, easily circulated, and professionally adoptable. Rejecting nineteenth-century eclecticism and the art deco and moderne "styled" work of the 1920s, Hitchcock and Johnson saw themselves as protecting and enabling the discipline of architecture by controlling what they saw as its basic visual tenets and its claims to a grand history.

Most important, the museum framed modern architecture as distant from overt associations with merchandising and commerce. The exhibit and catalog subsumed store work, including Oud's Hook of Holland project, among others, into the visual survey of the new architecture, but the specific role or social life of stores was not evident. In other words, as in the discussions of stores up until the early 1920s, para-mount questions included appropriate formal techniques, deployment of materials, and conventionalized practice. Under what became known as the International Style, store design would be incorporated into a standardized aesthetic framework within which it could be considered Architecture, not commerce. This separation of architecture from commerce placed the International Style into direct conflict with the liberal tendencies of industrial design and many of the members of AUDAC. The integration of commerce, modernization, and design that so fueled the indus-trial designers, especially given the blossoming of consumption after World War I, became a problem for those trying to limit, define, and reestablish a "purer," inde-pendent, and notably more elite sense of the field of architecture. In the subsequent 1934 *Machine Art* exhibit at the Museum of Modern Art (and in the 1938–39 Bauhaus exhibit), the curators further isolated aesthetic principles from what they saw as social, technical, or programmatic externalities, and they policed the terms of architecture and design in order to create a clear and secure discipline.

Through the 1930s, there remained considerable latitude about the modern. Ken Stowell, in his 1935 book on modernization, saw the modern as the newest and simplest route for new work,[91] and in 1936, historian-critics Sheldon and Martha Cheney wrote that the new architecture was an "indissoluble part of Modern Indus-trial Design" and would come from those who practiced "consumer engineering."[92] They praised industrial designers such as Raymond Loewy, Norman Bel Geddes, and Walter Dorwin Teague, who reconciled the traffic between design and mass production far better than did many architects.[93] Most dramatically, the compet-ing "machine age" buildings of the 1939 New York World's Fair, designed mostly by industrial designers, famously exemplified the interpretive latitude with which "the modern" could be described. In comparison with the strict principles of MoMA's

1932 project, a tug-of-war was clearly under way across the 1930s, and one of the key elements of that struggle was the architectural profession's relation to commerce, advertising, and consumption.[94]

In the tensions between a modernism understood as a broad set of practices engaged with the machinery of modernization and a contrasting view for which an interpretation of the machine would enable disciplinary autonomy and unity, the store held a fraught position. The store sat atop a disciplinary fault line. In the 1920s and 1930s, the store gave shape to ideas of what modernist architecture could do, but, more than almost any other building type, it could never be detached from the operations of capital and investment that were its ever-present monitors. The development of merchandising in the early twentieth century and the development of concepts of modern architecture were not merely synchronous but intertwined.

Propriety and an aesthetic anchor were the key elements of store work with which this chapter began; stores large and small were, essentially, conservative. A rationalist or functionalist approach was anathema, but the late 1920s and early 1930s saw experimentation with these and other forms of architectural thinking, where program, organization, and technique were said to be the drivers of store design work. The 1930s also saw a new aesthetic integration of form and program under various interpretations of modernism—especially the International Style, which reintroduced convention and offered visual and professional stability. However, the tensions between commerce and architecture did not abate.

TWO

MACHINES FOR SELLING

Functionalism is an overworked word. Nevertheless the remarkable progress in design for shops and stores is based largely on a new understanding of the meaning of functional design. The shop exists for trade: it can only serve to attract customers and to please them once they are inside. . . . In no field has the triumph of the modern architect been more complete. Reasons: the comparative lack of prejudice against change in the commercial field, and the necessity for every shopkeeper to meet the highest standards set by his competitors.

—"Design Decade," *Architectural Forum,* October 1940

THAT THE EDITORS OF *Architectural Forum* could claim in 1940 that modernism was uniquely suited to the design of stores no doubt raised some eyebrows. Other critics were more circumspect, wondering if the adoption of the modern was "sometimes for efficiency, sometimes for publicity, sometimes to be 'smart.'"[1] In 1939, *Forum* editors noted that "the dramatic attention getting qualities of modern architecture" could serve as an "extra salesman," and while this was certainly not the highest compliment in aesthetic or professional terms, they went on to praise the store in the already normative language of modernism. More than in other types of commissions, in store work, "form must follow practically in function's footprints." The modern store was said to emerge from co-ordination of programming, planning, and new technologies. Progress in American architecture, they wrote, was most evident in the design of shops.[2]

By 1940, form following function might already have been a cliché, but its rhetorical power was more than evident, and in design terms, modernism and the architecture of merchandising maintained a useful partnership. Architects and critics praised the arcade and the "open front" all-glazed store design techniques for making the "transition from pavement to interior painless." Standing just outside one store, *Architectural Record* editors wrote, "produces a sensation . . . of being already within the store."[3] Bringing together modernist methods and formal techniques with the desideratum of selling goods was firmly established in the 1940s; no longer radical, it became conventional and normative.

This chapter explains how particular modernist tenets in the 1940s were infused and entwined with store design, each lending credibility and legitimacy to the other. The first part of the chapter describes four architects whose practices were deeply embedded in the commercial world, in store design, and in the professional debates about retailing. The work of the four—Victor Gruen, Morris Ketchum, Morris Lapidus, and Kenneth Welch—was also unevenly woven into modernist discourse. All of these architects maintained different relations to debates, institutions, and outlets for the framing of modern architecture, and all were aware of the questions raised by retailing work in the status-conscious professional world. They were deeply interested in the logic and trajectory of modernism and, in the 1940s, played a role in making those principles part of the architectural landscape and of architectural discourse. This included the reach of architectural media, including magazines, catalogs, monographs, and conferences, treated in the latter half of this chapter. Considering the breadth of discussion about modernism and merchandising, it is more than notable that store work later came to stand outside the historiographic picture of modernism, hidden in plain sight.

Victor Gruen, Showman

Victor Gruen claimed to be a "contemporary" architect, not a modern architect. Modern architects, he often said, were too concerned with style, status, and an image of restraint and abstraction, whereas the "contemporary" label enabled the architect to act as both a researcher and a "client advocate."[4] The contemporary architect is pragmatic and takes the time to create form through understanding client needs and program functions; only in this manner, said Gruen, could a true modernism be sustained. He asserted that professional elites supported overly aesthetic standards that had little basis in the lived experience of most people. In his opinion, modernism had already become primarily a form-giving enterprise, cut off from needs and quotidian concerns, and he was happy to challenge the situation. Gruen was quite comfortable mixing art and commerce, and for him, merchandising was just another program. Staking out a professional position as an ardent spokesman for the pragmatic needs of his clients, including store owners, he was both keenly aware and unafraid of cultural questions about consumption, and he later became a lightning rod for criticism in debates about the status of merchandising work and consumption.[5]

Between the 1927 founding of his own firm in Vienna and his immigration to New York in 1938, Victor Grünbaum (hereafter Gruen) completed small residential renovations and several stores.[6] The American trade magazine *Display* published a review of Gruen's 1935 Bristol Parfumerie, and his store work also appeared in European journals; one British discussion of Austrian architecture lauded Gruen's stores as particularly forward-looking. Perhaps the ultimate architectural compliment was offered in 1938 by a French critic who praised one of Gruen's wide and open storefronts "*à la manière de Le Corbusier.*"[7] In 1937, Gruen completed a small interior residential project for retailer Fritz Lederer, important because a few years later their chance meeting in New York (according to Gruen) would result in one of his first stores in the United States. Gruen also wrote reviews and commentaries for several Viennese newspapers, including a review of Le Corbusier's large-scale urban ideas, for which he offered qualified support. Gruen felt Le Corbusier was handicapped by his "visionary" approach, and while Gruen too sought discipline-challenging work, he was equally passionate about the hurdles of what he saw as the gritty pragmatics of building.[8]

Gruen moved to New York in 1938, just ahead of the *Anschluss,* and, considering the difficult times, he landed on his feet professionally by getting swept up in the wave of work generated by the upcoming New York World's Fair. He worked as a draftsman for the Ivel Corporation, designers and installers of exposition exhibits, and for George Wittbold, a designer known for "settings" and showrooms for General Motors in the 1930s.[9] For Wittbold, Gruen worked on Norman Bel Geddes's famed automotive extravaganza, the Futurama Pavilion.[10] Aside from the fruitful tensions between Le Corbusier's and Bel Geddes's conceptions of a regulated landscape dominated by the car, Gruen witnessed firsthand the fluid relations among business, technology, and design, especially the new field of industrial design. Industrial designers were, to varying degrees, less constrained by the traditions of hierarchy, status, and gentility that characterized (and encumbered, according to some) the architectural profession. For better or worse, the World's Fair epitomized for many observers the confluence of consumption and design that had taken shape across the previous decade. The fusion of highly corporatized management methods and theatrical, streamlined design appeared to confirm for some that the world of goods would become total, or totally compromising. The World's Fair, according to designer Raymond Loewy, was a "big department store" in which goods were part of a new merchandised way of life.[11]

Gruen's first recognition by the American architectural press focused on the clear relation in his work between merchandising needs and modernist tenets, even as the work raised an equally clear tension between them. *Pencil Points* critic Talbot Hamlin praised Gruen's Vienna stores Deutsch Herren Moden and Bristol Parfumerie and wrote that Gruen's contrasting Lederer and Ciro stores (the latter done with architect Morris Ketchum; see below) were excellent demonstrations of modern materials and methods of work (Figures 2.1 and 2.2). Ciro offered a smooth, solid, slightly concave street wall with a relatively narrow punched opening leading into a twelve-foot-diameter arcade with domed ceiling—very similar to Harry Allan Jacobs's Avalon store of 1924. The crisp corners and subtle curve of the Ciro facade were, perhaps, an attempt to demonstrate the ascendant International Style. In a 1939 issue of *Architectural Forum,* the Lederer store was praised as a "highly original interpretation" of the arcaded storefront in which the shop "merges" into the window. The elegant "recessed" entryway framed a door set twenty feet back from the street wall and was lined with Pittsburgh Plate Glass's pigmented glass. The store's projecting and freestanding glass display cases more than fulfilled the functions of merchandising and were praised by John McAndrew of the Museum of Modern Art for their "semi-invisibility."[12]

Talbot Hamlin specifically cited the deeply recessed entries of both the Ciro and the Lederer stores because they offered an "intermediate zone between outside and inside, which not only serves to give additional space for display but also acts as a true architectural vestibule—that is, an aesthetic connection between outdoors and in." A "quiet" arcade space separated the stores from the ebb and flow of the street, although the displays were flush with the wall and created a continuous visual line from the street into the vestibule.[13] Gruen's 1939-40 Strasser Studio, Barton's Bonbonniere, Canterbury Shop, and Altman-Kuhne Candy were described by a *Forum* writer in similar terms, the last for "eliminating the entire window display."[14] Editors praised Gruen for working within the idiom of modernism, using new materials and blurring the interior and exterior while simultaneously working with the efficiencies and economies of modernized retailing. This was a thin line to tread, and even Hamlin cautioned that stores more than other commissions were necessarily theatrical and "creatures of fashion." Lewis Mumford expressed the tension between modern and modernized merchandising when he described Lederer, Ciro, and other work as elegant but better "mousetraps."[15]

Hamlin's and Mumford's description of the shop as a pedestrian form of architecture was tied up with the not uncommon perception that a salesman's work lay just shy of manipulation and deception. Gruen was not above flirting with this role. His pragmatic and rationalist understanding of architecture did not prevent him from interpreting the store as a site for drama, "arousal," and visual interest, and, as many observers have noted, his favorite referent for store design was the stage. Gruen was active in alternative theater groups in 1930s "Red Vienna," and he helped start a Viennese theater group when he came to the United States; showmanship and

Figure 2.1. Morris Ketchum and Victor Gruen, "Lederer de Paris," New York, 1939.
Photograph by Ezra Stoller. Copyright ESTO. All rights reserved.

Figure 2.2. Morris Ketchum and Victor Gruen, "Retail Fronts: Ciro" (New York), *Pencil Points* 20 (August 1939): 505. Photograph by Ezra Stoller of Underwood & Underwood.

staging were never far from his interests, day and night.[16] He routinely used theater references, such as the storefront as a "display stage" and the vitrines as "performance techniques." More literally, the entryway of his Canterbury Shop (Figure 2.3) was shaped by four proscenium arches, each articulating a glass display case, and stepped down across the twenty feet from street wall to front door. One published photograph—joining advertising with Bauhaus techniques—was dynamic and almost kinetic. The entry arcade, too, was enlivened with a theater technique, which could, Gruen wrote, offer "a tour of the little theater displays."[17] Unlike other modernist thinkers, such as Kiesler and Lönberg-Holm, Gruen approached merchandising not by reducing or defamiliarizing the presentation of goods but by increasing it to the level of spectacle.

Figure 2.3. Gruenbaum, Krummeck, and Auer, Canterbury store, White Plains, New York, 1940, in "Women's Shop," *Architectural Forum* 75 (September 1941): 194. Photograph by Robert M. Damora.

Theatrical and scenographic references enabled Gruen to craft an elastic connection between merchandising and modernism. In a 1941 *Forum* article, Gruen's first full feature treatment in the American architectural press, he explained that the exterior of the store should be treated as an "exhibit" enticing the shopper to enter the interior "sales factory." This factory was designed for efficient selling but not, as rationalist tenets might dictate, as the exposure of "the machinery," since, in Gruen's terms, the commercial "levers must be hidden" and the "cogs and wheels" *not* revealed.[18] This hidden component of theatricality would eventually collide with other modernist tenets. Transparency and the easy "step from outside to the inside" did not translate into any larger social ideals but instead meant visual access to goods and a smoothed consumption. More frankly than other architects, Gruen demonstrated that the invisible storefront or a plastically conceived vestibule greatly facilitated the merchandiser's first requirement: turning the passerby, the passive pedestrian, into an active purchaser. This later became known as the "Gruen effect" or "transfer."[19]

In his dramatic 1940 Grayson's Ready-to-Wear, in Seattle (Figure 2.4), Gruen reshaped and rescaled the street-store relation and thereby also rescaled his practice.[20] He later described that he had merely been asked to make small drafting changes for an existing design and, no doubt fueled by his bravado, ended up with a grand redesign of the entire storefront, entry and section, as well as an introduction to the Grayson's vice president. Grayson's was a national low-priced retailing chain that expanded massively before and during World War II, especially with the increased demand for working women's clothing.[21] For Gruen this was an entrée to a new type of client, the chain store.

Taking his knowledge of "exhibit techniques" to a new level, Gruen reshaped the Seattle Grayson's storefront with a massive, and visually simple, arc that was thirty-five feet tall and reached a depth of thirty feet from the street wall. It was broken only by two dramatically lit structural columns, capped off with a six-foot-tall neon sign. At the street, the "arcade" was filled with two "island" show windows and flanked by two more show windows. Inside the store, the display space just inside the glazed front was set several feet below street level (Figure 2.5), approaching something like the relation of an orchestra pit to a stage. In addition, there was a continuous view from the street to the three-story interior, and the proscenium composition attained a monumental drama; the arrangement had the visual effect of drawing the store forward into the street. Gruen also placed two weight scales in the columns flanking the show window; this "subtle form of suggestive advertising" was supposed to relate each observer "personally to the display" and lure the (presumably female) customer into the merchandising process before she even entered the store.[22] In sum, the Seattle Grayson's was a modernist spectacle.

Grayson's chain stores were an integral part of the American postwar consumerist landscape, and Gruen's work appeared in cities all over the country, from the East

Figure 2.4. Gruenbaum, Krummeck, and Auer, Grayson, Seattle, Washington, in "Women's Ready-to-Wear Store," *Architectural Forum* 75 (September 1941): 196. Photograph by Baskerville.

Figure 2.5. Gruenbaum, Krummeck, and Auer, Grayson, Seattle, Washington (detail), in "Women's Ready-to-Wear Store," *Architectural Forum* 75 (September 1941): 197. Photograph by Baskerville.

Coast to the Deep South to California. He completed thirty-five new and renovated locations by 1951, some distinctive, other less so. These stores had to be perceived as unique—grandly, if simply scaled, and often using an enlarged store signature as their signs—and many were built within strict wartime materials restrictions. The standardization and cost efficiencies axiomatic for chain store operations were thus multiplied. With or without the wartime limits, chain store economics enmeshed Gruen in the complexities of mass merchandising, yet he always maintained that good design was a profitable and necessary part of any retailing operation. For the 1944 San Francisco Grayson's, Gruen designed an eye-catching undulating wooden screen, twenty-five by sixty feet in size, across the facades of three smaller stores.[23] Designs like this could be built quickly, were distinctive, and dominated their Main Street or downtown locations.

Gruen was aggressive in ensuring that his work entered the nonprofessional media and was placed in manufacturers' literature—such practices were not at all unheard of for an architect, but certainly few reached the level Gruen perfected. His work was featured in *National Painters Magazine, Women's Wear Daily, Display World,* and *Chain Store Age,* as well as in newspapers in the various cities where new stores opened.[24] He was an active agent in cultivating and broadening the audience for his work, sending out clippings and often initiating correspondence with potential corporate clients, even if such marketing behavior tested the proprieties of a profession that only a few decades earlier had scorned explicit advertising and self-promotion.[25] America's postwar socioeconomic landscape was clearly changing, and Gruen was unafraid to grab his piece of it.

Despite his self-promotional efforts in a profession where traditional mores of gentlemanly publicity still lingered, Gruen was not entirely shunned by the architectural establishment. His efforts to interpret the modern were recognized and supported, with certain qualifications—an asterisk. His Altman-Kuhne Candy shop was accepted for the Architectural League's 1940 annual show, and his Seattle Grayson's, Canterbury, and Barton's stores were all shown in the League's 1941 *40 under 40* exhibit.[26] And perhaps most telling, his work was included in the Museum of Modern Art's 1940 *Guide to Modern Architecture: Northeast States,* in which the editor, John McAndrew, offered mixed praise for store work. Shop owners and their architects "welcomed" modernism into their projects, he wrote, but their reasons for doing so were subject to the "less-than-pure motives of merchandising." Despite this limit, McAndrew wrote that stores were good demonstrations of modern design principles of logic, clarity, simplicity, and openness. Half of the twenty stores shown in the *Guide* were designed by Victor Gruen (and Morris Ketchum), and the Lederer store was deemed worthy of illustration in axonometric (Figure 2.6), only one of a half dozen in the entire book.[27]

Gruen's simple yet "daring" use of materials and fusing of store with street in these projects showed that the terms of modern design and modern merchandising could be interwoven, and although others were conducting similar experiments, he appeared to reshape convention more overtly.[28] Stores, "which exist for trade," could be seamlessly modern.

Morris Ketchum, Favored Son

Victor Gruen and Morris Ketchum designed several projects together, and although Gruen asserted that he was the design force in their informal partnership, Ketchum also garnered early publicity. The editorial handling of their work at the time often deferred to Ketchum, perhaps following the letter of the law and referring to him as "architect" and the unlicensed Gruen as "associate." And despite their joint work, the 1939 *Forum* "Stores" survey was filled with praise for Ketchum, not Gruen:

Galleries for Associated American Artists, Inc, 711 Fifth Ave (55 St). Victorine & Samuel Homsey, architects. 1939. Open 10-6 daily except Sun; closed Sat in July and Aug.

Lederer de Paris, Inc, 711 Fifth Ave (55 St). Victor Gruenbaum in association with Morris Ketchum, Jr, architect. 1939.

A fresh and trim new version of the XIX century shopping arcade gives this store an unusual amount of exterior display space despite the narrow (22') frontage on Fifth Ave. Separate showcases are used in order to display different specialties of the firm. These cases are technically neat and apparently very light, without support below and without metal frames around the glass, achieving a handsome semi-invisibility, never in competition with the wares displayed. At night they are individually lit by

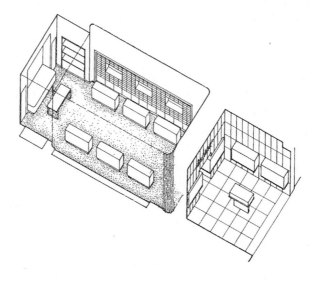

spotlights concealed near the edge of the suspended ceiling of stock corrugated factory skylight glass. Walls are of suède finish Carrara glass. The unframed doors of Herculite glass permit an uninterrupted view of the more conventional salesroom (chairs by Aalto).

Ciro of Bond St, Inc, 711 Fifth Ave (55 St). Morris Ketchum, Jr, architect. 1939.

Another restudying of the shop arcade. Exterior floor of Monocork, a pleasantly resilient mixture of cork and cement.

Figure 2.6. "Lederer de Paris," New York, in Victor Gruen with Morris Ketchum, *Guide to Modern Architecture: Northeast States* (New York: Museum of Modern Art, 1940), 78.

If this optimistic conclusion [of new work] seems to be based on a portfolio, many of whose pages are devoted to the work of one architect, it is still all to the good, for the suddenness with which Morris Ketchum has emerged from comparative obscurity to a position as one of the most brilliantly imaginative designers in this field is in itself evidence of the willingness of the merchandiser to take the best the architects have to offer.[29]

This was quite an endorsement for someone with little built work to his name.

It is unclear who introduced Gruen and Ketchum, but it was a fortuitous meeting. Gruen deprecatingly recalled that he refused a job offer from Ketchum—indicating that Ketchum already had an office up and running—and that he only needed to "associate pro forma" with a licensed architect.[30] That Gruen knew retailer Fritz Lederer from Vienna lends credibility to his view of the relationship, but it is almost impossible to separate Gruen's and Ketchum's roles. More important, however, is how their joint work produced significant technical and formal advances at the intersection of modernism and merchandising. A rendering of Ciro and Lederer (Figure 2.7) further muddies attribution (it was done by neither architect)—indicating that the two architects were, in effect, an author, describing the breadth of modernism to include merchandising.[31]

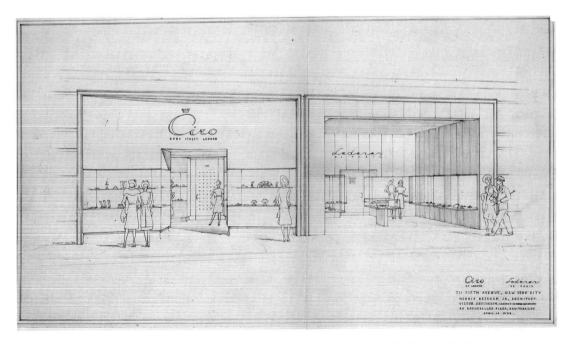

Figure 2.7. Morris Ketchum and Victor Gruen, perspective sketch of Ciro and Lederer stores, New York, April 1939. Box 11, Victor Gruen Collection, American Heritage Center, University of Wyoming.

Morris Ketchum Jr. was born into an establishment New York family, and much of his career reflected his privileged roots. Ketchum studied at Columbia University from 1924 to 1928 and received his architectural license in 1934, the same year he married a wealthy socialite he had met at one of the many charity balls he attended.[32] Ketchum's early employment put him at the heart of the architectural establishment.[33] From 1928 to 1930, he worked for the busy Beaux-Arts firm York and Sawyer (an offshoot of McKim, Mead & White). He next worked for his former Columbia professor, Francis Keally, who had a small practice, published regularly in the architectural magazines, and was involved in professional architectural culture, including the Architectural League, the AIA, and the Municipal Art Society.[34] In 1931, under Keally's guidance, Ketchum published European travel sketches in *Pencil Points*.[35] In 1933, Ketchum worked at Mayers, Murray & Phillip (successor to Bertram G. Goodhue's firm). In 1935 and 1936, he shared office space (and perhaps some work) with Edward Durell Stone at Rockefeller Center.[36] In 1937 and 1938, Ketchum was drawn into the design frenzy of the coming World's Fair—through which he may have met Gruen.[37] With Stone and Phillip Goodwin, Eric Kebbon, and Richard B. Snow, Ketchum worked on the fair's large and unremarkable (except for its mural by Witold Gordon) "Food Building South."[38] More important than the building at the fair were the circles this work enabled Ketchum to enter.

Ketchum's relationship with Stone and Goodwin put him at the heart of New York design culture when the new building for the Museum of Modern Art was under way. In fact, a biographical note on Ketchum in a 1944 kitchen proposal in *Better Homes and Gardens* cited him as "co-designer of New York's Museum of Modern Art." Although there is no evidence to support this description of Ketchum's work on the museum, Ketchum and Stone did in fact work together on a 1938 competition for a post office building, for which they received an honorable mention.[39] And even as he embarked on his own practice in 1938, Ketchum was also a part-time associate at Harrison, Fouilhoux & Abramovitz, downstairs from Stone's office in Rockefeller Center. Stone was friends with Wallace Harrison and *Architectural Forum* editor and publisher Howard Myers, a peripatetic promoter of modernism in America.[40] That Ketchum dedicated his 1948 book on stores to Myers further indicates the social glue of New York's architectural "club" of the time and, moreover, that he was part of the milieu in which modernist ideas, projects, and politicking were central.[41]

Ketchum's practice expanded slowly, and his experiments with a modern vocabulary coexisted with a variety of other period styles, as perhaps befitting a pragmatic, aspiring, socially connected architect. In 1938, Stone introduced him to designer Paul Frankl, for whom Ketchum became the associated architect for the much-praised moderne design of the Mosse Linen Shop on Fifth Avenue.[42] Through his and his wife's social connections, Ketchum was commissioned for a variety of small new and renovation projects, including a riding academy for the Myrtle Beach Club and several residences in Westchester and Long Island, one of which was the home of his wife's aunt. The latter was a Greek Revival restoration, yet a *House & Garden* article stressed the design's "clean lines" and "simplified" language, which many observers considered to be modern "in spirit."[43] Ketchum's 1939 *Architectural Forum* "Productive Home" competition entry was a more explicit experimentation with the technologies and aesthetics of modernism and, displayed at Macy's and Wanamaker's, also indicated that the engines of distribution and publicity were a central part of modern architectural culture.[44]

Ketchum's early store work experimented with modern tenets of transparency and the fusion of interior and exterior space, especially through the invisible line of glass. His 1939 Steckler shop (Figures 2.8 and 2.9) was one of the earliest stores to use a full glass wall that dramatically emphasized the continuous space and surfaces from the exterior lobby into the store. One magazine wrote that the "entire shop function[s] . . . as a show window." A popular magazine praised its "fishbowl" design, noting that the "entire interior" could be seen from the sidewalk. Ketchum and other architects such as Morris Lapidus quickly capitalized on the capacity of the fully glazed shop front to give a full view of the interior and, echoing Lönberg-Holm a decade earlier, to treat the entire shop as the display.[45] In a 1942 *Interiors* article, Ketchum named the growing design phenomenon the "Open Faced Shop" and went so far as to criticize the deep entry and the arcade. Calling the vestibule designs of the Steckler and Lederer shops an "intermediate step" on the way from the "old arcade front" to the open-faced shop, Ketchum concluded that his Trade Winds Shop and America House reached the pinnacle of intelligent retail principles in which "the whole interior has become part of the show window."[46] The primacy of transparency and the fusing of space was confirmed in Ketchum's design for the Artek furniture showroom, a highly regarded project for a highly regarded client (Figure 2.10). *Architectural Forum* dramatically photographed the showroom outward from the interior mezzanine to show the two-story glazed (although not single-paneled) street wall, illustrating how the store, its products, and its patrons would "join" with the street.[47] Ketchum was interpreting a modernist vocabulary with roots in Bauhaus notions of volume and transparency, but for the program of merchandising.

Ketchum's role in the spreading of a particular modernist formal vocabulary was matched by his equally vigorous circulation within the institutions of architectural culture. In 1939, he began to participate in the juries and affairs of the Beaux-Arts Institute of Design (BAID), the home of the old-line proponents of the French atelier system. The members of the BAID were a who's who of New York and national architectural elite—the institute was "a place for rich men's architects," according to member Wallace Harrison.[48] The BAID was not only a social club but also a key

Figure 2.8. Morris Ketchum, "Steckler Shop," New York, storefront, 1945. Photograph by Ezra Stoller. Copyright ESTO. All rights reserved.

Figure 2.9. Morris Ketchum, "Steckler Shop," New York, interior, 1945. Photograph by Ezra Stoller. Copyright ESTO. All rights reserved.

conduit for shaping architectural and, eventually, specifically modernist ideas and images. Its circulating programs and competitions reached as many as 75 percent of American architectural students during the 1930s and early 1940s, and these were juried by well-known architects, critics, and educators.[49] Moreover, the stylistic classicism of the institute's origins mellowed across the 1930s, making way for a variety of modernist-leaning approaches. After 1940, a glass-and-steel (or aluminum) modernism became the norm of the work coming through the institute. By 1944, the BAID director was proud, if also perhaps preemptively defensive, of the organization's evolution from monumental projects echoing its Beaux-Arts heritage to more "up to date and progressive" projects, many entailing commerce or merchandising.[50] The BAID was a key social node in shaping the discourse of modernism in the United States. Through its New York City activities as a meeting place for local and national players in architectural culture and through its widely circulated

Figure 2.10. Morris Ketchum and Francis Gina, Artek showroom, 1941–42. Photograph by Ezra Stoller. Copyright ESTO. All rights reserved.

monthly *Bulletin,* the methods and practices of American modernism were debated, codified, and circulated. In Ketchum's case, this normalization took the form of the store.

Making a quick ascent through the gentlemanly realm of the BAID, Ketchum joined the Architecture Committee in 1942 and the board of trustees in 1944, participating in many of the institute's affairs and programming. He joined an elite group of younger and already established architects and magazine editors, including Ken Stowell (then at *Architectural Record*), Howard Myers (publisher of *Architectural Forum*), and Kenneth Reid (at *Pencil Points*). Gruen did not participate in BAID affairs until almost 1950.[51] Ketchum's store expertise was immediately put to use, and he wrote the briefs for many of the BAID's nationally circulated commercial and store competitions. In 1941 he wrote "A Mural for a Handicraft Shop," and in 1942, "A Merchandise Display Window," in which the winning designs were selected on the basis of their use of large, glazed fronts.[52] In 1943, Ketchum wrote the program for "A Decorators Accessory Shop," for which Jedd Reisner, a Harrison, Fouilhoux & Abramovitz contact and occasional Ketchum collaborator, wrote the jury report praising the projects for their use of glass and concern with transparency.[53] Ketchum also worked at the BAID with his future partners: Stanley Sharp, then in the employ of Stone, served on juries starting in 1941, and Francis X. Gina wrote the 1944 program for "A Costume Jewelry Shop," for which Ketchum wrote the jury report.[54] From the BAID there emerged a body of work for which store and commercial work could be undertaken by advocates of modernism.

In 1942, Ketchum served on the jury for a "small stores development" with André Fouilhoux, George Nelson, Reid, and Stowell, and the entries were praised for the plasticity with which they handled storefronts and display spaces. The projects were later published in *Architectural Record* along with a note that cash prizes were awarded by the glass and storefront manufacturer Kawneer.[55] In late 1943, Ketchum wrote the BAID program for "A Shopping Group and Motion Picture Theater Entrance," with jurors including Kenneth Reid and Ely Jacques Kahn. This competition was now called the Kawneer Prize, demonstrating the continued weaving together of interests of designers and manufacturers, with Ketchum as star.[56]

Pencil Points editor Kenneth Reid wrote a glowing piece about Ketchum in 1942 that located his work in the ongoing debates about modern architecture. Reid portrayed Ketchum as a rational practitioner who saw no conflict with merchandising but instead saw it as an exemplary commission with which to apply modernist ideas. Ketchum's stores were "smart, business-like, and thoroughly rational," and in them "good planning" was "unobtrusively" joined to "attractive appearance." The stores had "no fakery," only solid "analytical planning" enhanced by "superior taste." Taking his praise to an utterly personal level, Reid called Ketchum a "handsome," "mild-mannered and serious" architect whose "six foot stature, black hair, dark eyes and well tanned skin" might remind one of an "exceptionally fine looking Indian" except for the fact that he was "of English extraction."[57] Ketchum's pragmatic, home-grown, authentic modernism was being capped off with the ultimate in achievements: the architect was renovating an *old* farmhouse in the establishment Long Island town of Wainscott, New York (in the Hamptons). Reid thus succeeded in connecting up several threads of American modernist self-representation: Ketchum was the level-headed, objective, masculine thinker of the sort that modern architecture appeared to require; modern architecture in Ketchum's practice entailed a traditional pragmatism rather than a pretentious styling; and finally, Ketchum's rationalism was well suited to the challenges to modernism posed by the limitations and requirements of nationally scaled merchandising operations. The store and the modern architect, in other words, were made for each other.

And the praise kept on coming. Reid lauded Ketchum as representative of the new generation embracing "architectural rationalism." In particular, Ketchum was among the new breed of architects who could find clients in the pragmatic field of design for merchandising and services, where "no arbitrary preconceptions" hampered the work. Ketchum was widely represented as the stellar example of the new architect able to fuse the strict visual logic on which the increasingly normative version of modernism was based with the no less strict program of merchandising.[58]

Kenneth Welch, Calculator

The Grand Rapids Store Equipment Company (GRSEC) holds but a small place in the annals of retailing and manufacturing history. Grand Rapids, Michigan, was a major producer of factory-made furniture—sometimes considered popular and second-rate, yielding the pejorative term *Grand Rapidism*, but equally indicative of a strong connection between design and mass production.[59] GRSEC vice president and architect Kenneth Welch played a key role in shaping the connection between art and commerce. Welch wore several professional hats, providing retail architectural services, writing for architecture magazines, offering "expert" advice and layout information, documenting the work of other architecture and fixture firms, and making sure the GRSEC name appeared in the mass media. In the 1930s, Welch emerged in the professional architecture magazines as an expert on store operations and design. For several decades, he was a sought-after consultant, retail architect, and materials and fixtures supplier, and this multifaceted role demonstrated the pragmatic elasticity of his professional practice.

The GRSEC was started by Welch's father before the turn of the century, and about 1920 it merged with the Wilmarth Show Case Company. In the early 1920s, the Welch-Wilmarth Corporation produced respected reports on store equipment and design.[60] Welch became the corporation's vice president in charge of design in 1928, supervising design, fixture coordination, and business expansion.[61] During the

1920s and 1930s, the national rise of chain stores and the expansion of distribution networks required standardized and mass-produced store fixtures; the GRSEC was very much part of this growth of production and selling. For stores in Pittsburgh, Indianapolis, Detroit, and other cities, Welch was sometimes listed as architect or associated architect even as correspondence and magazine credits referred to him as vice president of the Grand Rapids Store Equipment Company.[62] Welch worked both sides of the street.

Welch participated in many design, planning, and retailing forums. In 1929 he was an editorial consultant for *Architectural Record*'s "Store Buildings" feature, and work by the GRSEC illustrated the article (see Figure 1.10).[63] In 1933, Welch, now a member of the AIA, acted again as editorial adviser, this time for an *Architectural Forum* special issue on stores, serving alongside current and would-be GRSEC customers, including the presidents of Hahn, Macy's, and Kaufmann's department stores. Reaching beyond "fixturing," Welch's own article "The Logic of Layout" focused on the principles and the details of smooth customer and product movement.[64] Welch used language that was prosaic and replete with Tayloristic, efficiency-based considerations and prescriptions, sounding very much like Lönberg-Holm. The store design was a "problem to be solved," with service areas designed to eliminate extra space and unnecessary motion. Welch also kept a keen eye on business and referenced his firm's name and work throughout the article. In addition to GRSEC-designed furnishings, other featured stores were designed by another architect with the "Grand Rapids Designing Service" as "consultants"; still other stores shown had no relation to Welch, but the photos were "courtesy of Grand Rapids Store Equipment Corporation." Welch was nothing if not ambitious, and he designed stores, laid out store fixtures, sold store furnishings, and was an avid photographer of everything to do with stores.[65]

For much of his career, Welch was listed as both associate architect and design head of the GRSEC. *Architectural Record* published an article on a men's shop by Welch in 1934 that was largely concerned with typical fixtures, display types, storage, and lighting. The article provided a "store modernization checklist."[66] The GRSEC figured prominently in a 1935 *Record* feature titled "Retail Store Planning." The lead article was not a glamorous presentation of new shops but a dry bibliographic survey of store literature. The GRSEC was well represented: one article by Welch and another by a GRSEC associate, both consisting of specification lists for counters, storage, circulation, and other detailed merchandising issues.[67] The treatments were thoroughly pragmatic, and the authors made it quite clear that store design consisted primarily of merchandising principles and site requirements, the proper attention to which would yield good design. The language of the merchandising needs more than paralleled the emerging modernist doctrine of transparency and continuity: the designer should "provide a view of the store interior, thus making the window display doubly effective."[68] In the design and technical programming of stores, it appeared, the tenets of modernism could be demonstrated.

Indicative of his growing professional reach, Welch also participated in a national project to boost the commercial construction business. Welch was a jury member for the 1935 "Modernize Main Street" competition sponsored by *Architectural Record* (then under Kenneth Stowell) and Libby-Owens-Ford Company, a leading glass and storefront supplier. The competition was conceived in tandem with the shift in policy of the U.S. Federal Housing Administration (FHA) to open up its lending guarantee criteria to include larger funding levels for commercial work. Faced with the drastic belt-tightening effects of the Great Depression, bankers and other lenders, as well as many manufacturers, owners, and designers, sought not to build new, expensive stores but to make modest improvements to the appearance of existing stores as a means of increasing business.[69] Welch served on the jury with marketing specialists and architects, including Albert Kahn, John W. Root, William Lescaze, and André Fouilhoux. Occupying a unique niche as both an architect and a manufacturing representative, Welch worked among professionals for whom discussions of program, space, dimension, and efficiency were second nature.[70] In addition, Welch was developing national contacts that broadened his customer base as well as brought him into large debates about architecture.

Welch rose to national prominence and continued to combine design services and "fixturing." For the *Record,* he wrote an article on the interior of Wanamaker's in New York City in 1936, for which his firm also manufactured the cabinets; in 1937, he wrote and illustrated with GRSEC work a feature article on the department store; in 1938, the GRSEC was represented in half the stores shown in the *Record*'s "Retail Stores" special issue. In an *Architectural Forum* feature in 1938, the GRSEC was the furnishing supplier for one project and the furnishing designer on another.[71]

Aside from working all the angles in the store business, Welch demonstrated an interest in the architectural representation of modernism. He was adamant that the architect needed to determine selling areas, efficient layouts, and furnishing requirements, and he noted that modern design "lends itself" to store work because its "simplicity" provides for the store's technical requirements as well as the display and accessibility requirements of the merchandise.[72] Although trimmed of Lönberg-Holm's overt social goals, Welch's view of the modern store was equally pragmatic: the movement of goods was primary.

Welch was an avid publicist for his firm, a leader in market analysis, and a spokesman for good design techniques. An address he gave to an Indianapolis retailers group in 1938 was entirely about the details of fixtures and lighting; in 1942 and 1943 he wrote articles with prosaic titles such as "Self-Selection Is Sensible," and he conducted a market analysis of the new stores at the Parkchester housing project (Shreve, Lamb and Harmon, 1939–41) in New York. From the late 1930s into the mid-1940s, he was a widely cited source on lighting, fixtures, and store layout, and, of course, the GRSEC was regularly the source of store furnishings.[73] Market analysis and regional income studies became almost his hobby as well as his professional identity, and he was soon traveling from coast to coast, working for developers, lenders, and other architects. Complementing his business acumen, Welch advocated the simplicity of modern architecture—"letting the merchandise play the part that ornament has played in many dated styles"—for both good design and good sales. Clearing the shelves was the desideratum of the modern and the modernized store.[74]

Morris Lapidus, "Design-Builder"

In 1935, a one-page set of storefront plan diagrams and sash details by "Morris Lapidus, Architect for Ross-Frankel, Inc.," accompanied an *Architectural Forum* article on the just-announced FHA loan liberalization program for store modernization. The drawing showed a mundane fluency with the details of construction and especially with the functioning of the store and storefront plans with respect to goods, display, and pedestrian flow (Figure 2.11). One sketch for a women's hat store had "long lights to attract pedestrians"; another design had a "slightly bowed front offering maximum display and a natural guide into the store." An entry plan for a bookstore was broken up into smaller display areas, and the overall plan was "designed to encourage entry into the store itself." A bakery and a jewelry store were designed with the scale and visual access of the specific goods in mind—the former with a wide and long storefront, the latter with a smaller and shallower one. Although Lapidus would later be infamous in the professional world, at this point in his career he was learning the architectural nitty-gritty as the in-house designer at Ross-Frankel, a well-known store and display contracting firm.[75] Pragmatics, construction, and economy shaped his position on the relation of the street to the goods for sale.

From his graduation from Columbia University's architecture school in 1927—where he later claimed that the 1925 Paris Exposition catalog was circulated under the desks—until 1943, Lapidus worked for Ross-Frankel.[76] At the firm, Lapidus became adept at working with new materials, new and old construction methods, construction management, and new merchandising formulas. In 1929, he began storefront and furnishings work for Mangel's chain store, which had grown from five stores in 1916 to eighty-nine stores by 1935, with locations from New York to Dallas. At Ross-Frankel, Lapidus also executed dozens of commercial projects for well-known chains, including Lerner, Bond's, Wallach's, and Florsheim, as well as corporate interiors for firms such as Bulova Watch Company.[77] Designing and supervising the construction of dozens of stores at Ross-Frankel during the 1930s placed Lapidus at the intersection of one of retailing's most important modernizing engines—the chain store—and the emerging stylistic and aesthetic debates on

BASIC PLANS AND PROFILES
OF STORE FRONT CONSTRUCTION

MORRIS LAPIDUS, ARCHITECT FOR ROSS-FRANKEL, INC.

At right: Types of store front sash with cheapest at top.

Kalamein

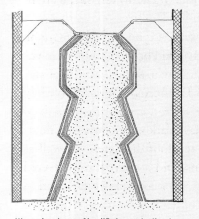

Women's shoes: Simplified saw-tooth plan for different display groupings, with long lights to attract pedestrians

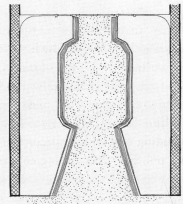

Women's apparel: Long lights at proper angle to be seen from both directions with rear rotunda for organized display

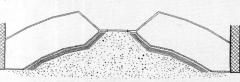

Men's shoes: Acknowledges man's distaste for window shopping by slightly bowed front offering maximum display and natural guide into the store.

0   5   10   15   20 FEET

Drawn front
Face screw

Drawn front and back.
Face screw

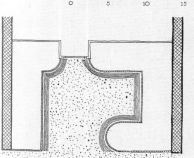

Men's apparel: Divided for suitings on left, haberdashery on right, with long lights on both sides.

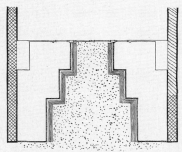

Books: Permits grouping of books into recognized classifications, with minimum street window areas, and plan designed to encourage entry into the store itself.

Drawn sash
Patent lock

Extruded sash
Patent lock

Bakery: Recognizes that bakery products are sold from windows, and thus provides maximum display space on the street.

Jewelry: Small display space because unit of merchandise is small and stock is frequently limited. Shallow windows permit easy access to wanted items. Divisions for jewelry proper and usual accessories.

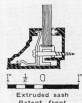

1" ½ 0   1"

Extruded sash
Patent front
snap-on

Figure 2.11. Morris Lapidus, "Basic Plans and Profiles of Store Front Construction," *Architectural Forum* 63 (July 1935): 53.

modernism. As his 1935 sketches show, retailing needs could definitely shape architectural results.

Lapidus enthusiastically adopted the arcading system—expanding and merging display and outdoor space within the building line—that had become popular in the 1920s. Among the projects he did with Ross-Frankel, many included arcades of various sizes and scales: the entryway of Lapidus's 1936 Doubleday Doran Bookshop in Chicago stepped in plan to a depth of fifteen feet from the street; the vestibule of his 1936 Sachs Furniture Store (Figure 2.12) in New York City contained floating display cases—including one with a spectacular ten-foot diameter—as well as curved entry windows, polished freestanding columns, and a curved, cantilevered entry canopy. The display cases in the vestibule of his 1939 Postman's retail shop in New York City were floating glass boxes. The editors of *Architectural Record* praised Lapidus for making the vestibule "as spacious as possible—both apparently and actually."[78] In 1941, Lapidus added his voice to the discussions about store design in a *Record* feature in which he combined the pragmatic and rationalistic threads of

Figure 2.12. Morris Lapidus, architect, Sachs Quality Furniture Store, New York, 1936. Photograph from Library of Congress, Prints and Photographs Division, Gottscho-Schleisner Collection, LC-G612-38863 (photograph taken November 5, 1940).

modernism with a remarkable showmanship and humor. The design of stores and storefronts, he wrote, was a simple question of merchandising techniques—to display goods, to identify the store, and to provide a clear and enticing entry to the store. The key means of completing these tasks, he declared, was through the use of the arcade, examples of which (by him as well as by Gruen and others) dominated his article. Alongside this pragmatic advice, however, was a graphic representation that was anything but dry, with arrows, sketches, cartoons, and catchy captions. An image of his 1941 Postman's shop (Figure 2.13)—with a display device that might be called a ribbon vitrine, suspended in a cube of light—is supplemented with a sketch indicating that a good display will draw in a continuous line of customers. Elsewhere in the article, Lapidus dramatically asks (in a parody of a modernist manifesto), "Where is the Building Line?" demonstrating that merchandising and the modernist use of space and glass could comfortably work together.[79] The floating glass line and the arcade could be both transformative architectural devices and subtle merchandising techniques.

In a coda to the 1941 *Record* stores article "Is Store Design Vital?," Lapidus called for architects to take store work more seriously, since consumer goods were becoming

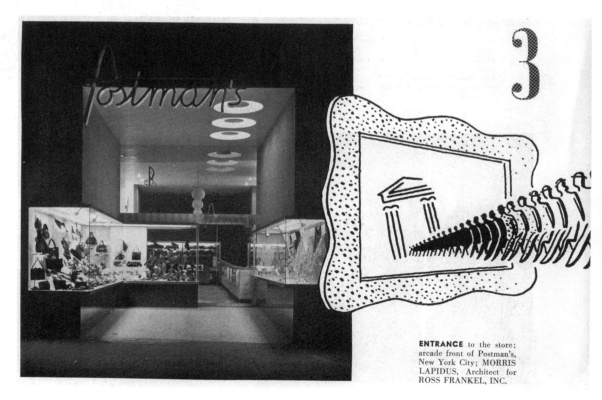

ENTRANCE to the store; arcade front of Postman's, New York City; MORRIS LAPIDUS, Architect for ROSS FRANKEL, INC.

Figure 2.13. Morris Lapidus, architect for Ross-Frankel, Inc., Postman's store, New York, 1941, *Architectural Record* 89 (February 1941): 119.

more widely available. He lamented that retail design had not been fully "recognized" by architects, so merchandisers with stores to build took their business to other professionals or, worse, designed the stores themselves. Yet design for merchandising was, he wrote, as simple as measuring a drawer and asking a few questions, after which the design would be "dictated by form and function." The *Record's* editors concurred when they wrote that the "broader planning" of stores and groups of stores was an architectural "opportunity" and that the "architect's skill" could be added to the landlord's self-interest.[80] Lapidus had cut his teeth on the design and construction of stores, and he saw little tension between the needs of retailing and what he saw as the premises of modern architecture.[81] The simplicity and rationalism of the "steel-and-glass" language of emerging modernist practice was equally suited to stores and, with a considerable immersion in modern media, would become the new norm.

Expanding Representations of Modernism

During 1942, the Kawneer Company, like many manufacturers at the time, embarked on a new advertising and production program for anticipated postwar work. Typical of much advertising during the war, Kawneer's advertising reflected how vital it was to keep a company name in circulation, since many industries had retooled for arms manufacturing or were severely hobbled by materials limits. Companies were looking to the future; a typical Kawneer advertisement included the copy "War work today . . . Store fronts, Aluminum Doors and Windows Tomorrow."[82] In October, the company announced "Store Fronts of Tomorrow: *New Pencil Points*–Kawneer Competition," with William Lescaze as professional adviser and editor Kenneth Reid as assistant adviser.[83] Signaling his ascent in the professional hierarchy, Morris Ketchum was the chairman of the jury and served with Mies van der Rohe, among others. Instead of the high-end stores typical of architectural work, the competition brief called for designs for the "shopping area of an American city or part of a shopping center in an outlying residential district."[84] In other words, submitted designs should seek replicability, which was key to the project of modernism, if not also modernization, and signaled as well the role of circulated architectural representations as integral to the modern project.

The designs submitted to the *New Pencil Points*–Kawneer competition helped to standardize an image of a pared-down, glass-and-steel modernism. The design techniques receiving jury praise typically included the combination of full-height glazing (or no visible glazing at all) and an exterior "deep lobby" carved from behind the building line. These two strategies created continuity from interior to exterior, using a portion of the lot width to create a semipublic zone between entry door and sidewalk. The perspective submitted by the competition winner (Figure 2.14) shows how fully the design ideas and representation techniques of leading modernist architects (such as the leading juror) had permeated architectural culture. Floor and ceiling are gridded with no visible means of enclosure or support, the two walls are rendered as repetitive panels of color rather than material, and the empty "space" of the rendering itself hints that any context will do.

One typical refinement of the inset entry, also dramatically used by the winner, was the seemingly continuous display case, which, running from the entry "through" the glass and into the store, emphasized the overlap of interior and exterior and highlighted the use of the pedestrian realm of the street for merchandising. The shifting glass line carried dual positive meanings—it was a better display technique, and it evidenced a modernist sensibility.[85]

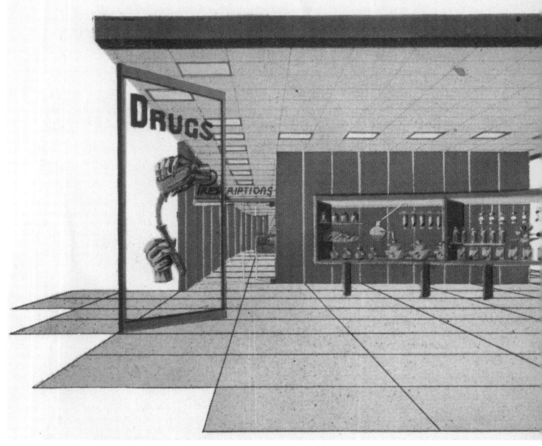

Figure 2.14. Seymour R. Joseph, first-prize winner of Kawneer Pencil Points Competition, *Pencil Points* 24 (February 1943): 32. Copyright 2012 Penton Media, Inc., 90488:612SH.

Store improvement discussions reached a higher pitch in 1944. With the general sense that retailers had to prepare (and hope) for postwar prosperity, the magazines, the manufacturers, and the architects actively engaged in calls for improvement, modernization, and new architectural visions. In August, *New Pencil Points* published "Stores of the Future," an excerpt of the soon-to-be-released Pittsburgh Plate Glass company catalog. Editor Kenneth Reid introduced PPG's catalog with an emphatic framing of store design as the sine qua non of modernist practice. Unlike the house, he noted, the store is one of those "rare architectural instances where we are all in essential agreement, and logic rules the design!" He continued: "It is . . . instructive to observe that when design honestly sets out to serve the broader concept of public

need—as in stores—the architecture is almost automatically progressive." In addition to its important linkage of merchandising with modernism, this logic was a pitch for the architectural profession: the potential of research and design found its greatest expression in the "talent for organization" that was the architect's specialty.[86] And in Reid's glowing portrait of the easy logic of the store, only one image appears, a shop interior by Morris Ketchum—highly noticeable since Ketchum's work was *not* included in the very PPG catalog promoted by the article.

In fact, Ketchum was already in the employ of Pittsburgh Plate Glass competitor Kawneer—the company he had worked with at the Beaux-Arts Institute of Design and then in the *Pencil Points* competition—doing studies for a new line of storefront products. In early 1944, Ketchum's firm began an extensive study of the retail redevelopment on the Main Street of Kawneer's hometown of Niles, Michigan, and in October of that year, the results were published in *Architectural Forum.* The Niles project was a leap in scale, moving from the building to the district. Niles was a "typical American community," the editors wrote, in that it suffered from the increasingly common ailment of obsolete stores, street patterns, and services.[87] Making improvements required working at the scale of an entire "downtown shopping center" and gaining the collective cooperation of business owners—the individual actions of whom, the editors argued, had created the problem in the first place. Thus the project was conceived at a district scale, and the remodeling proposals combined pragmatism, programming and use, and aesthetic unity. And all this without tearing down buildings and instead working mostly at the sidewalk level.

Ketchum's Niles study was an extensive catalog of storefront and store ideas based on full glazing, minimum structure, and use of the deep and open front (Figure 2.15). The traditional street wall was maintained, so the most dramatic feature of the design language was the plasticity of the design along the street—although upper-story recladding was introduced as well. Entry walls, partitions, display cases, vestibules, planters, and lobbies advanced and receded from the building line, and the interiors of the stores were, to varying degrees, visible from the street. Each store type was accompanied by a description of program and needs, and this complemented the reshaping of the plan at grade. Modernist transparency and spatial continuity were achieved, and an integration with industrial and merchandising practices had provided the means.[88] And the street looked and performed in a new, uniform, and modern way.

With the end of the war in sight, Kawneer embarked on a more ambitious campaign to boost its image and products. In mid-1944, the company started using the slogan "Machines for Selling" in its ads, and in July 1945 the company announced its "Machines for Selling" campaign, with storefront designs by Ketchum. In early 1946, the company issued a hefty eighteen-by-twenty-four-inch hardcover, full-color, indexed catalog titled *Machines for Selling.*[89] The catalog introduction made it

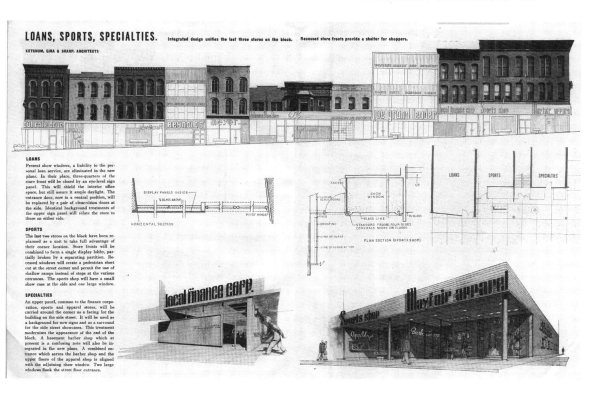

Figure 2.15. Ketchum, Gina, and Sharp, "Remodeling Main Street: Niles, Michigan," *Architectural Forum* 81 (October 1944): 110, 111.

clear: commercial success depended on "machine-like coordination of every working part of a store," and the parts, like "hidden gears and levers," had to "work together."[90] Offering just such a coordinated representation of parts, *Machines for Selling* presented a dramatic fusion of the visual imagery of modernist forms and techniques with continuing industrialization and economic modernization. It is unclear if the title of the catalog was a reference to Le Corbusier's oft-cited dictum "A house is a machine for living in," but such metaphors were not uncommon. Just as important in Kawneer's case (as in Gruen's) were the "hidden gears" of the store, indicating that the tenets of modernism changed as they entered normative practice.

Machines for Selling was organized by store type—from "women's furnishings" to hardware and furniture—each type flagged with special labels for easy navigation. Programmatic and physical needs for different kinds of stores were demonstrated through renderings of typical storefronts, interior spaces, and large details. The catalog was a blend of technical manual and design portfolio—all designed by Ketchum and his firm (Figure 2.16). The store designs were highly consistent and evidenced experimentation with continuous glass; planes of wood, stone, and metal; deep and clear sightlines from exterior to interior; and variously shaped and sized glass display

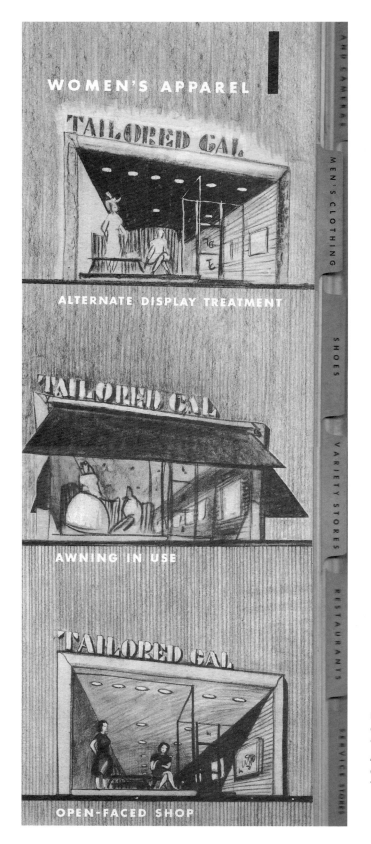

Figure 2.16. Ketchum, Gina, and Sharp, "Tailored Gal," in *Machines for Selling* (Niles, Mich.: Kawneer, 1946).

cases that floated, projected, hovered, or stood alone in the arcade or vestibule areas. For the pedestrian, this created a veritable modernist exhibit celebrating window shopping and strolling. A formal inventiveness at the street wall bridged the modernism of transparency and the modernization of rationalized selling—the visual connection of interior and exterior spaces established a dream of unfettered access to goods. In effect, the catalog was a definitive modernist primer, albeit without an explicit social program other than increased and efficient sales; it was a complete guide for other architects to learn from and emulate.[91]

The circulation of *Machines for Selling* was more important than any particular storefront or building that may have emerged from its pages. The catalog's scope and unity were at the core of midcentury modernization, where the constellation of mass production included the professional magazines, advertisers and publicists, distributors, and other commercial buyers and middlemen. In 1947, *Progressive Architecture* (then edited by Thomas Creighton) praised Kawneer for "so distinctively" aiding the profession by allowing Ketchum to redesign the company's entire product line. The book demonstrated the deep interconnections between the visual and aesthetic unity of modernism and the utility and standardization of modernization.[92]

Parallel attempts were made by other companies. Libby-Owens-Ford, the Toledo glassmaker that had sponsored the 1935 "Modernize Main Street" competition, published its *Visual Fronts* pamphlet in 1945. With the term *visual* distinctly in the title, the emphasis was clear. Although smaller than the Kawneer volume, the pamphlet was unified by a street-facing design program. It extolled the emerging "open-faced" architecture for stores and featured color renderings by Sumner Gruzen, Morris Sanders, Morris Lapidus, and José Fernandez as well as the company's in-house designers. The projects shown in the pamphlet were eclectic—from hints of the traditional to deco and moderne—and the renderings were cartoonish, but all demonstrated the plastic conception of the street front with exterior lobbies and vestibules of great variety.[93]

The promotional catalog released by Pittsburgh Plate Glass in 1945 took an approach different from that of the Kawneer catalog. *There Is a New Trend in Store Design* did not focus on a single designer but instead used an array of designs by well-known architects such as Holabird and Root as well as by emerging commercial architects such as Gruen, Morris Sanders, José Fernandez, and Morris Lapidus. The roster also included architects from the elite and emerging elite realms of modernist practice, including William Lescaze; Eero Saarinen; Skidmore, Owings & Merrill; Stonorov and Kahn; and Pietro Belluschi. Topping off the list of participants with modernist credentials was Walter Gropius.[94]

Gropius contributed two store designs to the PPG catalog, a jewelry shop and a drugstore, both of which demonstrated a clear modernist spatial and material palette (Figure 2.17). In both cases, the storefront was essentially invisible and served as a

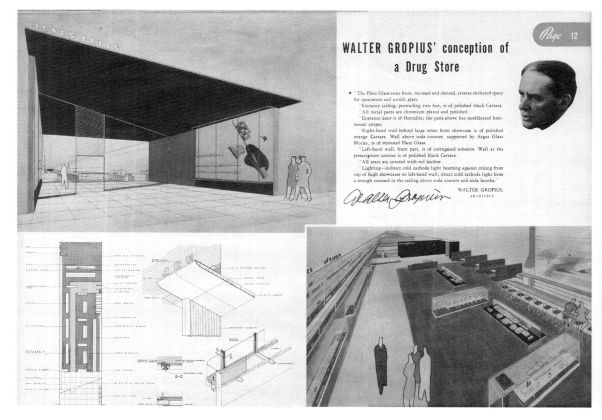

Figure 2.17. "Walter Gropius' Conception of a Drug Store," in *There Is a New Trend in Store Design* (Pittsburgh: Pittsburgh Plate Glass Company, 1945).

mere weather line between inside and outside; the space of the street and the volume of the store were continuous. Each project used a floor pattern and simple furniture to subdivide the space. In the jewelry store, a planter continued from the outside space "through" the glazing and into the interior. Each project showed a reduction of elements and a planning simplicity; each store was designed with the details of its program—special cases for the jewelry shop and counters for the drugstore. The designs were resolutely modern in image and treated the program with the precision and efficiency that was the hallmark of modernism. In addition, the catalog's page for each of the projects included the signature of the architect as well as a tight head shot. In sum, the catalog communicated to readers that they were in the presence of very esteemed authors undertaking a uniform project, and the idea of the design of a store thereby gained considerable status and legitimacy.

PPG's *There Is a New Trend* did not overstate its case. The differences among the projects were slight, and the work was a checklist of modernist visual and construction techniques: work by Gruen, SOM, Lapidus, Belluschi, and Stonorov and Kahn showed extensive glazing, overlapping planes, sculpted fronts and volumes pulling away from the lot line, arcades, and, perhaps most touted, interior and exterior spatial overlaps.[95] Most striking in the collection was the uniformity and the consistency of the design of the stores. The standardization and wide acceptance of these design strategies was confirmed in the PPG catalog, and, in fact, Gropius was just one of the crowd. There was now an established modernist set of techniques.

Consisting of a display of names, the PPG catalog's cover indicated that the work derived not from the hand of a single designer but from the sheer number of "names" who contributed to the catalog (Figure 2.18). The architect's signature, the hand of the designer, was paramount, and the collected names were more important than any single design. Like the Rockettes, the signatures march across the page in lockstep, their power, grace, and effect stemming from their unity, not their uniqueness. This was the paradox of the modernist collective—the ideal famously claimed by Gropius—where individual action was but a step in the progress of the group; the work was uniform and standardized even though executed by many designers.

Figure 2.18. Cover of *There Is a New Trend in Store Design*.

Even as PPG sought out the collected expertise of modern architects in this enterprise, the company hedged its bets and engaged in a very different model of publicity between 1938 and 1960. During these years PPG produced the *Design of the Month* brochure series, which was largely the work of in-house architect Elmer A. Lundberg (Figure 2.19). Lundberg joined PPG in 1934 and eventually became head of architectural development and architectural sales promotion. PPG's monthly brochures included renderings of storefronts and store entrances that, like those depicted in *There Is a New Trend,* experimented with the spatial and material relations of store and street. Designs were eclectic and ranged from deco to modern, from monumental to casual, and included floating cases, projecting walls and planes, and, of course, extensive use of glass. Some were signed by Lundberg. The two projects, *Design of the Month* and *There Is a New Trend,* were complementary—the latter based on status and uniqueness, the former based on anonymity and repetition—and together they exemplified the intersection, in the hands of one company, of modernism and modernization.[96]

OPEN FRONT

Here the idea has been to bring into the window display the liveliness of color and form of the flowers shown inside, and to show the flowers along with natural materials. Hence, behind the completely open front, the stone pylon with structural glass shelves, and the planting beds running from the show window into the store. The recessed, flagged entry offers a transition from the street's artificiality to the naturalistic interior and affords the entering buyer some protection from foot traffic on the sidewalk. Inside, the refrigerator is made the dominating feature of the active selling space, which is to be more brilliantly lighted than the carpeted lounge space. The store is planned for a louverall ceiling; louverall's egg-crate lighting shield provides a reasonable approximation of natural lighting, and spotlights can be incorporated into it to highlight special displays.

Figure 2.19. E. A. Lundberg, "Store Modernizations," *Progressive Architecture* (October 1948): 82.

By different routes, Ketchum and Gruen became widely cited experts on store design by the mid-1940s, with Gruen responsible for dozens of new and renovated stores across the country.[97] Both were praised for their advocacy for and use of a modernist vocabulary. Just as important, they and their many peers expanded the discourse of stores and the modern architect.

Complementing the ways in which architects worked with and through the manufacturers of storefronts and furnishings was a growing literature on "modern stores." Among the best spokespersons for the modernity of the store in American architectural literature was architect Emrich Nicholson, whose 1945 book *Contemporary Shops in the United States,* with an introduction by Nelson, offered a wide-ranging visual survey. The book was a compendium of store work, all of which Nicholson described as based on "logic, rather than style," and a "progressive" understanding of the development of new technologies and materials.[98] Showing the work of architects including Ketchum, Gruen, and Lapidus as well as José Fernandez, Raphael Soriano, Raymond Loewy, Edward Durrell Stone, SOM, Walter Dorwin Teague, and Russell Wright, the book did not so much stress "logic" but showed that the plastic and three-dimensional possibilities of modernism were quite rich. George Nelson joined the two threads and stressed the "organic" relation of stores to their program and thus their appropriateness for modernism. For him, the store was an opportunity and a catalyst for architectural research: "In no section of the building field has there been the amount of fruitful experimentation, the depth of understanding of the problem, or the variety of expression that has gone into shops."[99]

Los Angeles architects Eugene Burke and Edgar Kober published *Modern Store Design* in 1946, offering a contrasting yet equally important technical view of the store. Having designed a considerable number of store interiors and worked as associated architects for other firms, Burke and Kober were also regular speakers at retailing conferences and later specialized in shopping centers. The subtitle of their book— *A Practical Study of the Influence of Store Style on Modern Merchandising*—indicates that theirs was a pragmatic approach. In the very first chapter, the authors stress that modern style is simple, functional, and practical and produces "things primarily for use rather than essentially for effect or ornament." In other words, the merchandising program was fundamentally similar to the aims of modernism as method and strategy, not an image or form. Adding to the sense that the rigors of merchandising matched those of modernism was the book section on typical details, in the manner of "graphic standards" for store interiors and furnishings. Standardized construction, efficiency, and ease of product display and movement of goods were framed in quasi-Taylorist terms and showed the easy overlap of modern and merchandising programs, not unlike the positions of Lönberg-Holm and Ken Welch in previous years.[100] Yet the "Typical Show Window Dimensions" page (Figure 2.20) could be mistaken for a functionalist parody: the specificity of display for shoes, hats, and

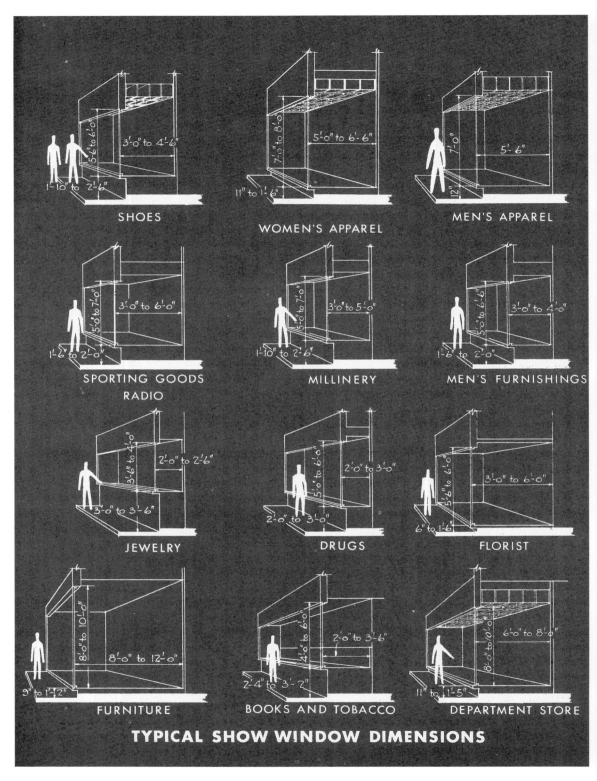

TYPICAL SHOW WINDOW DIMENSIONS

Figure 2.20. Eugene Burke and Edgar Kober, "Typical Show Window Dimensions," in *Modern Store Design: A Practical Study of the Influence of Store Style on Modern Merchandising* (Los Angeles: Institute for Product Research, 1946), 99.

tobacco, each requiring unique, precisely calculated measurements, conflicted with modernist notions of standardization. In this and the growing literature on stores, one could see that modernism and merchandising were comfortable bedfellows, yet the books also evidenced the distance between standardization and individualization—a struggle deep within modernism that would continue to underlie discussions about the design of stores.

In 1947, the New York University School of Retailing sponsored the first "Store Modernization Show," with "clinics" devoted to an array of technical and design issues. These sessions featured a who's who of retail architects, interior designers, industrial designers, lighting manufacturers, showroom builders, engineers, air-conditioning specialists, and business professionals.[101] Kenneth Welch, Morris Ketchum, Victor Gruen, Morris Lapidus, and many other noted retail architects contributed to the shows and the discussion panels. Presentations were, in part, highly technical, show-casing discussions of lighting, heating and air-conditioning, storage, and even accounting—but few of the architects took such a bracketed view of their work. Most framed their discussions as part of the growth and maturing of modernist techniques even as they were well aware that the rule of sales and profit was part of the Faustian bargain.

Modernist tropes of continuity were central to the design discussions. On the design of the storefront, José Fernandez said that there is "no dividing line or barrier between front or exterior" and the interior must be "visible to the passerby." Gruen made good on his reputation for overstatement: "I was asked to speak today about modernizing store fronts. To begin with let me say I am against it." In other words, in good modernist terms, he said that the "exterior of a building is only the reflection of the interior." He continued, sounding a modernist clarion: "The only trend in modern store design, as in modern architecture generally, is a trend toward serious and honest analyses of existing conditions and a thorough study of the needs." Ketchum too weighed in, more reasonably, to say the store, like any other modern building, is "best designed from inside out."[102] In all cases, they asserted that the street wall was no longer static or literally flat, and instead a "three-dimensional" treatment would answer the needs of merchandiser and customer and fit properly into the urban context.[103] Through the logic of planning, the role of the eye and the status of merchandise could be construed as modern.

The architectural representation of store work as a modern and professional undertaking culminated in the publication in 1948 of Morris Ketchum's *Shops and Stores*.[104] The book was a step-by-step, "practical" discussion of the store design process, from planning and concepts to store examples, layouts, and typical details. Several chapters were taken from earlier publications of Ketchum's work, including Kawneer's *Machines for Selling* and the Niles Main Street projects, and some were drawn from his firm's many commissions for stores and store interiors (work shown by other firms is minimal). The book took a dry, authoritative tone, in contrast to the breathless prose of Gruen, and was well reviewed for its reasonable approach and its presentation of the unique capacity of the architect to understand the "essential reasoning of the merchant."[105] More specifically, Ketchum joined merchandising needs and store design to specifically modernist architectural thinking. "The store is fundamentally a simple thing," he began, but in the early years of the twentieth century store design was a "costume ball" in which the architect had little to offer beyond imagery. Since the 1920s, however, research into the needs of merchants, contractors, and manufacturers had enabled store work, he wrote, to join "architectural integrity" and the "logical answers to the requirements of modern merchandising." "Uniting the exterior with the interior sales space" was not merely a technical guideline but a modern spatial means of demonstrating the organic connection of form and content, image and program.[106] The culmination of years of writing, publicity, conferences, catalogs, and widely circulating images and information, Ketchum's book was the coda to the professional fusing of modern architecture and merchandising.[107]

Merchandising Modern

In a 1950 article, the editors of *Architectural Forum* described how the design of the typical store had come to exhibit fully the best features of modern architecture:

> The building line has vanished into the recessed store front, the sales counters shrunk to hook strips in the wall, island fixtures were reduced to skeleton forms clothed in merchandise and the light fixtures were recessed into the ceiling, the ceiling and walls themselves began to be replaced by easily removable drybuilt panels.[108]

Modern architecture as a rational and frictionless process and as a visual expression of such fluidity was by the late 1940s clearly established. That the programmatic necessity of the store to move goods could be equated with a modernist position seemed now self-evident. *Forum* editors had earlier pointed out that the program of merchandising, like the best modernist practices, entailed an embrace of change and experimentation as well as "systematic study." Thus "the many improvements which are found later in residential and institutional buildings are proved first in the retailing section of town."[109] This was certainly an exaggeration (witness the early 1940s Case Study Houses, among other experiments), but the narrative pairing of retailing and modernism helped to legitimate retailing commissions that otherwise might not have been acknowledged in the profession. Gruen, Welch, Lapidus, and Ketchum embraced store work as part of their ambition as modern American architects. In addition, the store, through professional activity, educational research, conferences, publicity, writing, and design—through the culture and social life of the discipline—demonstrated that the rationalities of merchandising could be coupled with modernist tenets of transparency and spatial and three-dimensional possibility. There was a lingering, ever-present tension that the processes of modernization—economic rationality—would limit the architectural role of store work, but at the same time, such work helped to concretize and normalize modernism as both method and image. Modern architecture was nearly axiomatic, if too easily slipping into a style, but its increasingly successful rationalist tenets and the emergence of new sites outside the city pointed toward a new scope of work for the modern architect.

THREE

PARK AND SHOP

The parking problem will never be solved at the curb.

   —Eno Foundation, *The Parking Problem,* 1942

To GREAT FANFARE, Milton Bradley proclaimed in 1954 in an advertisement for its new game Park & Shop that "every child will enjoy the hustle and bustle of parking and a trip to the stores." The game mimicked a day's errands in town, including library and post office visits, medical appointments, and bill paying, but mostly the game was organized around shopping (Figure 3.1). The game board was a diagrammatic map of a small gridded town or urban district: a four-block by five-block grid, with a main intersection plus a perimeter road dotted with ten identical single-family home icons and one chamfered corner making room for parking ticket cards and the game logo. Ten Park & Shop parking lots were sprinkled along or near the perimeter road, near such auto-centered if less glamorous programs as Auto Dealer, Hay Grain Feed, and Car Wash.

Each player began with an automobile marker on a house and then moved the marker according to the rolls of a single die until he or she reached a Park & Shop parking lot. There the car was parked and the player switched to a pedestrian marker of the same color; the player then rolled two dice to "walk" to all the places on his or her shopping list and pay for purchases before returning to the car to drive home again. The player to arrive home first won. Moves were dictated by a combination of

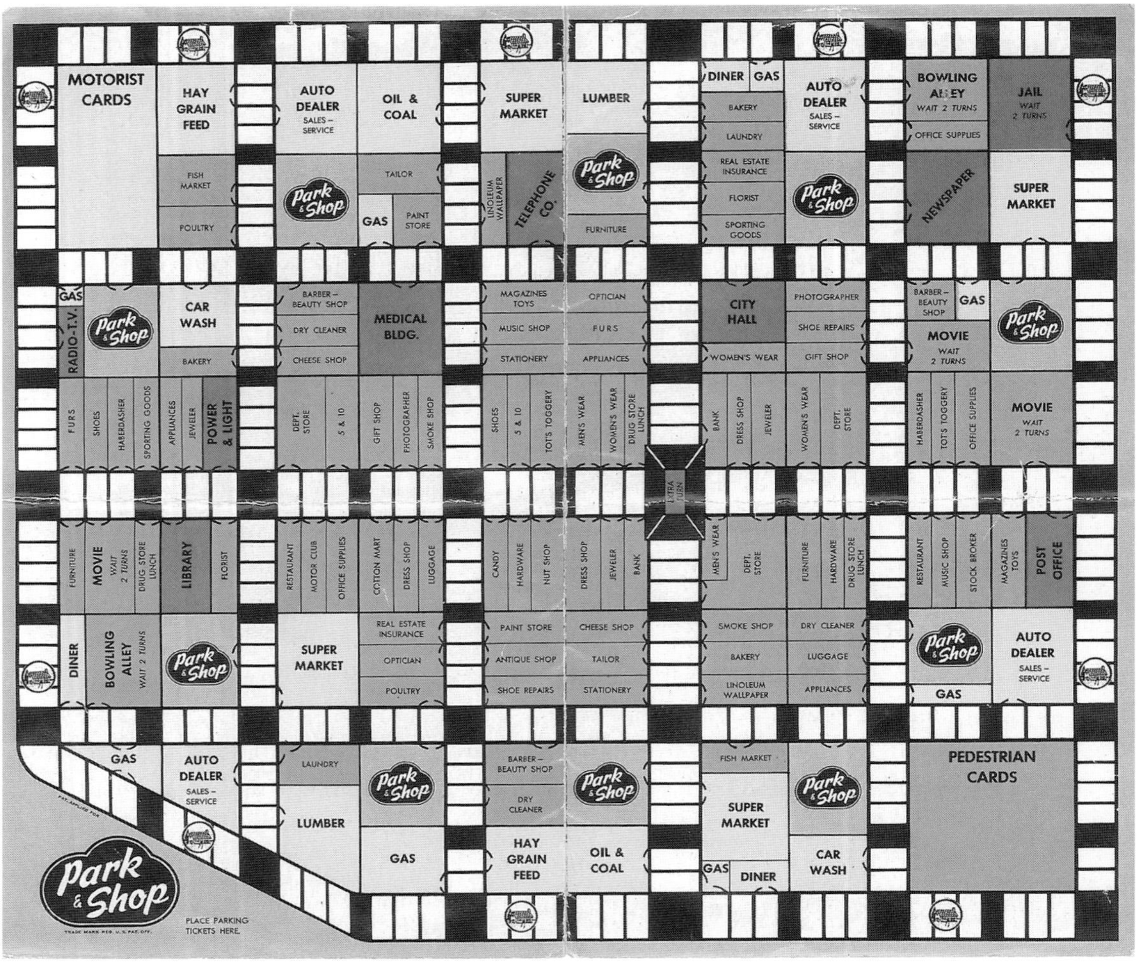

Figure 3.1. Game board for "Park & Shop," Traffic Game, Inc., Allentown, Pennsylvania, 1951.

dice rolls and chance cards drawn; the cards gave players extra errands ("Pick up a sack of chicken feed while you have the car."), bonuses ("Traffic thinned out. Take an extra free turn!"), or penalties ("There's a woman driver in front of you. Lose one turn."). A player might move his or her car from one lot to another or try to do the assigned errands with the car left in the same lot; strategic car parking was key, and, more broadly, the very premise of the game was a demonstration of a shifting attitudes about the planning of cities and towns.[1]

Park & Shop was certainly not the first board game to utilize an urban map—Monopoly, the famed game of real estate, mortgages, and rent, goes back to the start of the twentieth century—but it was unique in representing the city core as a quasi-real map and, more specifically, a core that was more than slightly dysfunctional.

Park & Shop also confirmed planners' concerns about the "terminal problem" in many cities, that there were too many cars, too little street space, and too few places to put cars when not in use. The fun of Park & Shop revealed a major conflict in the use and perception of American cities across the middle decades of the twentieth century. However, Park & Shop did not come from the minds of Milton Bradley's famous marketers or inventors; Milton Bradley bought the game from Traffic Game, Inc., which was formed by the Merchants Association of Allentown, Pennsylvania, in 1951 and headed by the game's inventor, Campe Euwer, artist and member of the photography and printing department at Allentown's *Call-Chronicle* newspaper.[2]

Typical of planning efforts of the time, business and political leaders of the small city of Allentown, as described by John Jakle and Keith Sculle in *Lots of Parking,* saw traffic congestion and a lack of parking as a threat to the viability of the local shopping district, and they organized to address the problem.[3] In 1947, store and landowners formed Park and Shop, Inc., to improve the perception and reality of parking downtown. By 1949, interested merchants and owners pooled their money, leased or bought vacant property within walking distance of the shopping district, advertised heavily, and gave free parking stamps to subscribing stores, which then distributed them to customers. This inventive program was praised among planners nationwide—and was profiled in *Collier's* magazine—for improving the troubled "Main Street situation" in Allentown.[4]

This unique collective approach, one observer wrote, would show that urban stores were as accessible as suburban stores, and the district was "pleasing to the eye."[5] Together, Allentown officials, planners, and store owners had taken steps to address stores beyond their individual functioning or design. The city's Park and Shop, Inc., focused on the design and operation of the shopping district as a whole, and thereby expanded the retailers' perception of, and participation in, district planning. The instructions for the Park & Shop game pointed to this conjunction, and the original 1951 instruction insert (Figure 3.2) included an aerial view of Allentown with parking lots noted in white and, in bold letters, announced, "More than a Game—It's the Story of a Great U.S. City!" The game, the text continued, was a "fairly accurate reproduction of Allentown's now famous Park & Shop set-up." The "coordinated Parking Program" ensured the retailers' necessity: "300 steps from Car to Counter."[6] Repeated across the country among planners and architects as well as engineers and merchandisers, this was a clear statement that the city needed to be redesigned, or at least tinkered with, to ensure the success of its shopping (and real estate) in light of automobile use and the increasing competition from the suburbs.

Urban interventions for shopping had long been considered. As discussed in chapter 2, Morris Ketchum rethought the Main Street of Niles, Michigan, as a distinct shopping district in 1945, and the "park and shop" concept—as a game and as a tactical urban intervention—enabled a coherently planned shopping destination

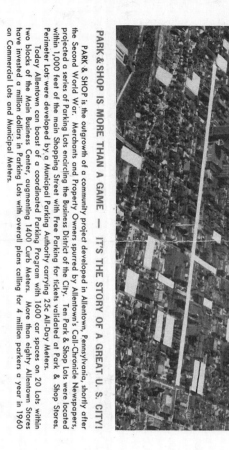

PARK & SHOP IS MORE THAN A GAME — IT'S THE STORY OF A GREAT U. S. CITY!

PARK & SHOP is the outgrowth of a community project developed in Allentown, Pennsylvania, shortly after the Second World War. Merchants and Property Owners spurred by Allentown's Call-Chronicle Newspapers, projected a series of Parking Lots encircling the Business District of the City. Ten Park & Shop Lots were located within 1,000 feet of the main Shopping Street with Free Parking for tickets validated at Park & Shop Stores. Perimeter Lots were developed by a Municipal Parking Authority carrying 25¢ All-Day Meters.

Today Allentown can boast of a coordinated Parking Program with 1600 car spaces on 20 Lots within two blocks of the Main Business Center, augmenting 1400 Curb Meters. More than eighty Allentown Stores have invested a million dollars in Parking Lots with overall plans calling for 4 million parkers a year in 1960 on Commercial Lots and Municipal Meters.

Park & Shop

Trade Mark Reg. U. S. Pat. Off

The Nation's

Traffic Game

Sensation

INSIDE THIS FOLDER YOU WILL SEE REPRODUCED IN MINIATURE THE PLAYING SURFACE OF PARK & SHOP, AMERICA'S NEWEST GAME. HOWEVER WHAT YOU SEE IS MUCH MORE THAN THAT. IT IS A FAIRLY ACCURATE REPRODUCTION OF ALLENTOWN'S NOW FAMOUS PARK & SHOP SET-UP, WHICH IS SERVING THE MERCHANTS OF THIS BUSY PENNSYLVANIA CITY AND THEIR CUSTOMERS WITH A MILLION CAR SPACES A YEAR "300 STEPS FROM CAR TO COUNTER".

TRAFFIC GAME, INC.
Allentown, Penna.

Figure 3.2. Instructions for "Park & Shop."

by focusing on smoothly functioning parking. Since the mid-1920s, planners, architects, and engineers had sought to reconcile the car with the city, and the customer with the store, and new efforts in the 1940s and 1950s created a new set of methods. At small and large scales, the professionals tinkered with the city and its constituent parts. Parking options, street layout experiments, driving policies, open-space uses, and building redesigns became central in urban discourse. The city's spaces and buildings, all agreed, needed to be altered in some way to accommodate the moving and especially the parked car. And architects hoped to play a leading role. "In this wider sphere," wrote Cornell dean and landscape architect Gilmore Clarke, "the architect's training and abilities are both particularly apt and sorely needed."[7] Traffic engineers typically had more leverage in these matters, but architects claimed a voice in the design of the city and its working parts. With each proposal or intervention, even concerning only a small piece of the larger puzzle, there took shape a new sense of how the city could be organized and reassembled as modern through the rethinking of parking, stores, circulation, and mobility.

The Limits of the Curbside Paradigm

During the Roaring Twenties, traffic congestion was a major concern for retailers, store owners, property owners, and their planning and political associates. Traffic and parking problems began to "interfere" with business. The "100 percent corner" of high foot traffic was in trouble, and business suffered from "strangulation," or, as the planner Wilbur Smith put it years later, the street had "backfired." Police departments were throwing up their hands at the impossibility of enforcing parking rules and restricting movement, and they begged policy makers for more precise regulation.[8] And while the Depression saw a dip in registered vehicles, most cities did not see a decrease in reports of congestion at their cores. The curb simply could not accommodate the numbers of cars and trucks that sought space, and, as cities pulled out of the Depression, they had reached a parking "saturation point."[9] The streets were so overrun, and the problem of getting about so straining, that merchants and planners feared that "downtown shopping fatigue" and the "parking blues" would become a serious threat to profits. Yet, for most observers, the street was still guided by the historical notion of the unimpeded "king's highway"—where movement was privileged over parking.[10] In a situation where a shopper still expected to simply walk into a store from the sidewalk, the system was more than stretched.[11]

Throughout the 1920s, professionals and magazines weighed in on the parking problem, including the magazine *American City,* the Institute of Traffic Engineers, and, of course, the American Automobile Association. All published studies of traffic regulations and infrastructure, from signage to the new road systems.[12] The simplest means to address the parking problem and clear the streets, according to many, was merely to enforce existing parking, loading, and traffic regulations and, more important, to coordinate all modes of movement. The next step was to expand and refine the regulations on the use of the street. While the planning and implementation details were often contentious—with acrimony about oversight, proceeds, and costs—cities from coast to coast tested and initiated changes to rules of flow and parking.[13] Municipal regulation of street use and design became the norm and included partial and whole parking bans, loading bans, through streets and designated turn lanes, left-turn bans, one-way streets, new forms of signaling, restricted lanes, and "platform safety" islands. To cure the "parking evil" the traffic engineer became a contributor to debates about the street as a multifaceted object of design.[14]

Managing and reorganizing the street was a key element of discourse about urban change. "The Traffic Problem" was one of several sessions at the 1925 International

City and Regional Planning Conference in New York City, attended by luminaries such as Ebenezer Howard as well as planners and architects from around the world, including Eliel Saarinen from Finland, Parker and Unwin from Great Britain, and Josef Stübben from Germany.[15] Planners, engineers, and architects agreed, first, that a reconsideration of the design, use, and policing of the street was required, and second, parking needed to be taken off the streets and relocated in garages, warehouses, and existing or new service courts in store buildings. In 1926, *American City* published "To Park or Not to Park," the crux of which was a call to planners and professionals to think about urban organization based on the off-street storage of cars.[16] In the *Highway Traffic* volume (1927) of the *Regional Plan of New York and Its Environs* (RPNYE), planner Harold Lewis called for an array of congestion management techniques to "provide more space" for cars and trucks and to unclog the sidewalks, and he too argued for more parking spaces. He wrote that improvement required several scales, including new garages within building envelopes and "terminal" garages at the core and at the edges of congested areas tied to transit systems.[17] The 1931 RPNYE volume, *The Building of the City,* called for an "elastic" street design that could accommodate more and varied users, arguing that with a more robust system, walking would become a "pastime . . . and shopping would be a joy."[18]

Although the RPNYE planners worried that store owners would be too faithful to their older "100 percent location" model of American cities—where crowded streets and sidewalks were the goal—many owners seized upon plans to alter the road and parking system.[19] In the mid-1920s, Macy's initiated a nighttime warehouse delivery system to keep its trucks off the streets during shopping hours.[20] As early as 1922, one St. Louis department store opened its own four-story garage with "inclines" (ramps) at the heart of the city, and more were planned. During the 1920s, one survey reported that dozens of stores in different cities had built their own garages by purchasing adjacent or nearby buildings or lots, and many more were leasing space in public garages. The department store garages were entirely subsidized by their owners, and they were expected to generate little if any direct profit.[21]

The city parking garage appeared in architectural literature and was quickly recognized as a key element in a new urban landscape. The "commercial garage," wrote *Architecture and Building* editors in 1922, "is a necessity in the modern city." Yet building such a garage was not a simple task, because the "modern garage" raised unique technical and design questions and there was neither precedent nor a unified position about "how a building to house automobiles should appear." Most garages were published in the technical or engineering sections of various magazines, which focused on improvements in garage operations such as ramp systems, "turntable" elevators, and access dimensions.[22] A 1923 garage by Albert Kahn featured in *American Architect* and the Kent Automatic Parking Garage system (starting in 1927) were praised as technical solutions to the parking problem of the city.[23] In many instances, the style of the garage had little to do with its function; while garages were praised for their operations, eclecticism was typical, from Gothic to Federal to vaguely spartan and "industrial."

A modernist treatment of design and construction standards for garages was the focus of a 1929 special section, written by Robert Davison, in *Architectural Record*'s then new "Technical News and Information." The piece was a powerful exercise in modernist methods and rhetorics, stating that the "appropriate and characteristic expression for garage design . . . will be attained by architects without conscious effort. . . . [Concrete and steel construction] will endow the garage with frankness and modernity."[24] Even as the examples shown ranged from deco to neoclassical, the magazine focused on construction and rental costs, car dimensions (providing a chart with thirty-five car models), ramp system types, circulation layouts, vertical circulation methods, typical plans, construction details, and subsidiary services.[25] More generally, the editors envisioned the auto as essential to the urban future and called for garages "attached to or within" all new construction, showing stores and office buildings, such as Albert Kahn's 1928 Fisher Building garage.[26] The *Record*'s handling of the garage, like its "Stores" feature a few months later, showed an editorial commitment to a modernist—that is, a frank, stark, and seemingly objective— view of architectural production. Focusing on the "practical function" of the garage and its need in the heart of the city demonstrated the *Record*'s editorial experimentation with the modernist project.[27]

The parking garage was not simply a matter of building, since the location of an appropriate site was considered a serious hurdle by most experts. During the 1920s and at a Depression-fueled fever pitch in the 1930s, tearing down large, financially "obsolete" buildings became commonplace, and the replacement of buildings by parking lots was typical. What became known as taxpayer lots—land held in abeyance for a better-yielding investment climate—were excellent candidates for parking, although planners and city officials usually saw these as compounding the congestion problem. Although such lots offered an immediate fix to local parking problems, critics pointed out that they were ad hoc and unplanned in relation to road capacity and proximity to stores or offices, and use of them for parking could just as easily worsen congestion. And since, by definition, the owners of taxpayer lots were merely waiting for a better investment climate, such parking facilities could not be factored into any long-term solutions. Other urban surveys showed available parking sites located far from shopping destinations, so they too offered little to solve the parking problem.[28] That some change was required was not contested, but exactly how to provide more terminal space in the city was vexing.

After the Depression, a wider array of architects came to recognize that the garage had become part of architectural discourse and expression. Henry R. Shepley wrote in *Federal Architect* that the Park Square Garage in Boston was a suitable mix of classical and modern design elements, and that it could be a model for the "rule of necessity" that determines good design.[29] This was not an unusual position for an architect to take in the 1920s or 1930s, with "modern versus traditional" debates raging across the profession, but others were both polemical and pragmatic about the rise of the new building type. Hunley Abbott, of Abbott, Merkt, wrote that his and other firms were designing garages in simple, straightforward, and minimal forms for various department stores, including Kaufmann's (Pittsburgh), Marshall Field's (Chicago), and Hecht's (Washington, D.C.), and that the work was a new and modern element of the urban landscape.[30]

During the 1940s, with the broad transition from a wartime economy, the professional literature and newspapers in many large cities spilled considerable ink on the question of parking and traffic. By the early 1950s there was a boom in urban garage construction: driving into the city and finding a place to park became a central urban question, as if the parking garage were the linchpin in the ever-expanding metropolitan system, the modernity of which was no less important than its mere technical functioning.[31] Architects considered parking part of a modernist approach to the city, largely fueled by retail and commercial work.

Tinkering with Buildings

In a 1936 report by the Regional Plan Association (RPA), one image in particular stands out for its clarity in the remaking of the city and its shopping areas (Figure 3.3). Through five different site plans, the ground plane is opened up for parking areas among the buildings, and arcades lead from parking to adjacent commercial streets; off-street parking, in other words, had transformed even as it had preserved the gridded fabric of the city. This almost typological reworking of the city plan did not resemble the normative view of modernist cleared sites (or the political economic machinery that supported such clearance), and this attitude toward remaking of buildings and neighborhoods to accommodate cars produced a considerable array of projects at different scales.

New York architect and planner Robert Weinberg wrote in 1937 that cities could address congestion by locating parking spaces in, under, behind, and on top of new buildings. Weinberg hoped to reallocate and rethink the spaces of the city to "find" or create space for the car. He called on architects to use the new possibilities of modern construction to design department stores, office buildings, and housing that included substantial parking within their lot lines. Echoing (if also reversing) Le Corbusier's argument for *pilotis,* Weinberg wrote that "eliminating the ground floor" would resolve the conflicts of the movement and storage needs of cities in the automobile age. At the broader scale, Weinberg also proposed that blocks and open spaces could be reprogrammed for parking, and he praised the layouts and siting of parking facilities at Jesse Clyde Nichols's Country Club Plaza (Edward Buehler Delk,

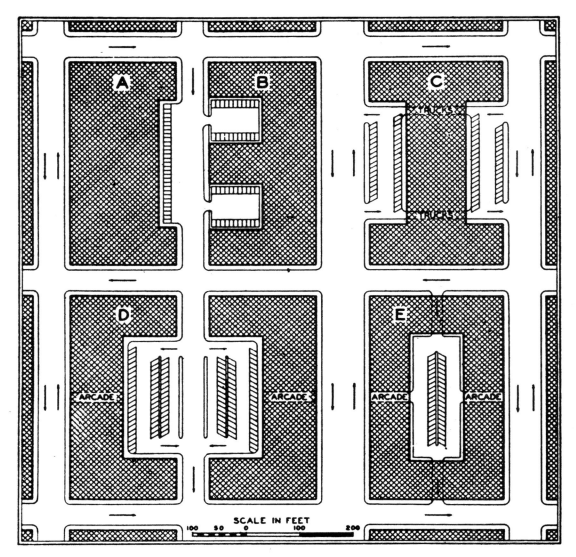

Figure 3.3. "Block Study," in Regional Plan Association, "Parking Facilities Found Inadequate in Communities of the Region," *Information Bulletin* 30 (May 18, 1936): 7.

1923) outside Kansas City and at the Gloucester Street shopping area at Colonial Williamsburg (Arthur A. Shurcliff, landscape architect, 1930).[32] A few years later, Weinberg proposed pedestrian arcades inserted into new and existing buildings to increase traffic flow on New York City's Eighth Street (Figure 3.4). For Weinberg, the parking question had both practical and social effects, and he saw the siting of the car as central to any discussion of a modern city.

New York architects Albert Mayer and Julian Whittlesey proposed in several articles in 1943 that planners and architects with a good "horse sense" about the city

1952   COVERED SIDEWALKS FOR DOWNTOWN SHOPPING AREAS   165

SKETCH PREPARED BY HOWARD T. FISHER ASSOCIATES, CHICAGO, ILLINOIS
Sketch of proposed arcades for E. 8th St., N. Y. C.

Figure 3.4. Bruno Funaro, "Arcades for Eighth Street" (New York), from Robert C. Weinberg and Alvin E. Gershen, "Covered Sidewalks for Existing Downtown Shopping Areas," *Journal of the American Institute of Planners* 18 (Fall 1952): 165. Reprinted by permission of the publisher, Taylor and Francis, Ltd. (www.tandfonline.com).

could tinker with the elements of the fabric to better accommodate the car.[33] Both were committed to a rationalist approach to urban questions, and their firm was active in housing research; Mayer was a designer, planner, and writer with a long association with the Regional Plan Association of America. From a pragmatic point of view, Mayer and Whittlesey wrote, reconfigured buildings and blocks where parking was conceived as an "integral part of the building design" would improve general urban movement and improve shopping. Key to any improvement in the city's capacity to handle cars was simply finding space, and they offered a variety of ways in which parking decks could be inserted over service areas, on top of single-story "taxpayer" buildings, and underneath, between, and on top of new buildings (the last of these accomplished, they noted, at the 1939 Pico Boulevard Sears store in Los Angeles).[34] Mayer and Whittlesey also sought to change the typical block and lot patterning in a series of diagrams (Figure 3.5) for ground-floor insets, widened sidewalks, arcades and store setbacks, reoriented ground floors facing onto shared (and quiet) open courtyards, and midblock arcades. A city planner from New Haven, Connecticut, also an architect, proposed in 1945 a similar reconfiguration of a "hollow-core" block interior (Figure 3.6) into a parking and shopping amenity.[35] Remade lots and building organizations were widespread in the literature shared by architects, planners, and engineers; they brought not merely a pragmatic sense to the problem but also a vision of their work as a modern architectural route toward seeing the city anew.

Victor Gruen and Morris Ketchum also participated in the reconfiguring of the urban building to accommodate the automobile. In 1940, Ketchum published in *Architectural Forum* a "store block" (Figure 3.7) that consisted of a low-rise block housing a department store, facing a typical Main Street, and topped by a high-rise office building set back to the rear of the lot—a massing diagram that could be mistaken for Lever House a decade later.[36] The addition of an office building above,

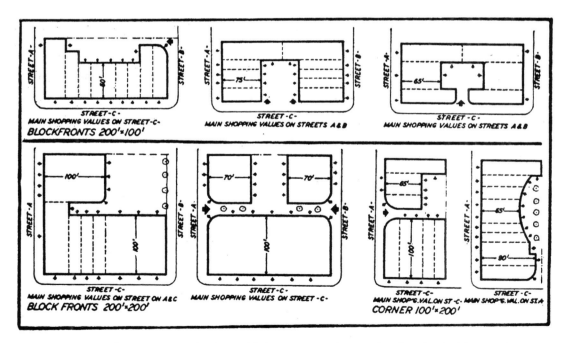

Figure 3.5. Albert Mayer and Julian Whittlesey, "Horse Sense Planning, 2," *Architectural Forum* 79 (December 1943): 77–82.

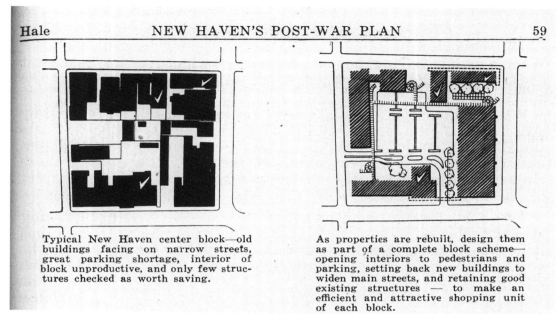

Typical New Haven center block—old buildings facing on narrow streets, great parking shortage, interior of block unproductive, and only few structures checked as worth saving.

As properties are rebuilt, design them as part of a complete block scheme—opening interiors to pedestrians and parking, setting back new buildings to widen main streets, and retaining good existing structures — to make an efficient and attractive shopping unit of each block.

Figure 3.6. Peter Hale, "New Haven's Post-war Plan" (New Haven, Connecticut), in *1945 Proceedings of the Institute of Traffic Engineers* (New Haven, Conn., 1946), 57. Copyright 2012 Institute of Transportation Engineers, 1627 Eye Street NW, Suite 600, Washington, D.C. 20006, www.ite.org. Reprinted by permission.

however, opened new territory: the "store block" project vertically replicated the business, retail, and parking features of downtown and worked within its gridded fabric.

In 1944, *Architectural Record* published a Ketchum store project with rear yard, on-site parking as well as a sidewalk-facing elevation. Since existing grade of the proposed store's back lot was five feet higher than the store floor, Ketchum further raised the parking grade to one full story above the store floor; customers would walk beneath the new rear entryway uninterrupted by cars (Figure 3.8). The store was faced entirely in glass and thereby performed a sectional demonstration of the resolution of pedestrian movement in an automotive context. This was an urban store that accounted for and even displayed its parking. In 1947, for his Milliron's store outside the core of Los Angeles, Gruen took advantage of the horizontal expanse of an open lot and used grandly scaled exposed ramps to get cars to the rooftop parking, from which store access was also provided (Figure 3.9). The building also had a traditional sidewalk-facing front entry, with projecting windows and displays. Here dual loyalties were at work—to the emerging programming for the car and to an older notion of the street.[37]

By 1950, Gruen and Ketchum both experimented with grand reorganizations of the store and parking: Gruen's proposal for the Olympic Shopping Circle in Los

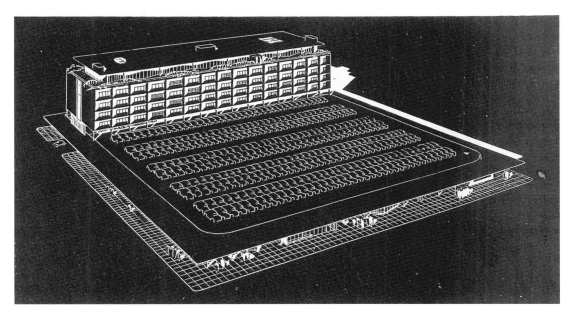

Figure 3.7. Morris Ketchum, "Store Block," *Architectural Forum* 73 (October 1940): 294.

Figure 3.8. Ketchum, Gina, and Sharp, "A Variety Store," *Architectural Record* 95 (April 1944): 97.

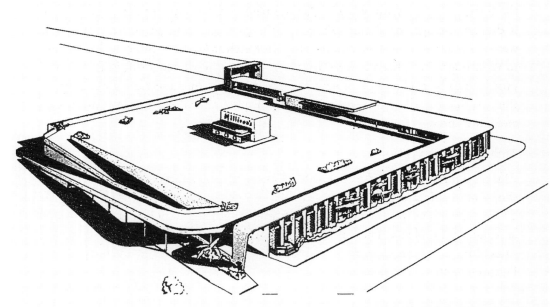

From any parking space on the roof, it is only a few steps to the entrance at the center of the roof or to the entrances of the restaurant, auditorium, children's playroom and beauty shop.

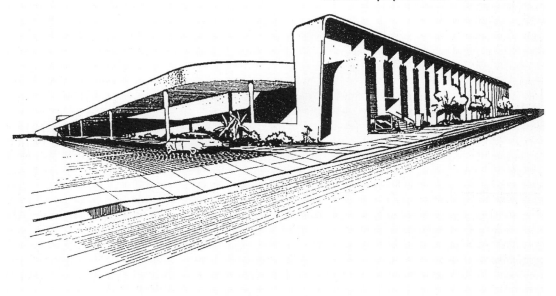

Figure 3.9. "A New Suburban Department Store," by Gruen and Krummeck, Architects, from *Arts & Architecture* (June 1949): 39. Copyright David Travers. Reprinted with permission.

Angeles (Figure 3.10) and Ketchum's "Store-on-Stilts" proposal (Figure 3.11). In the former, a quasi-symbolic, circular site plan and massing appeared radical, but it did not change the simple relation of the parking lot to the store entry—cars were parking inside and outside the ring. In Ketchum's "stilts" project, the distance to walk might have been covered over, but the plan remained autocentric.[38] These projects can be read as tests of new relations between store and car—a challenge to the curbside paradigm—even if they did not quite alter the conditions of parking and store entry.

Tinkering with Sites

Efforts to find, create, and rescale space for cars in small subcenters and Main Street shopping districts were widely watched among design and planning professionals. There were many proposals to reprogram extant space to solve automotive and accessibility problems. These prosaic projects offered new directions in any reconsideration of the street, store, and car. In many locations, the back lot, the block interior, or the space behind the stores was "discovered" as viable parking space,

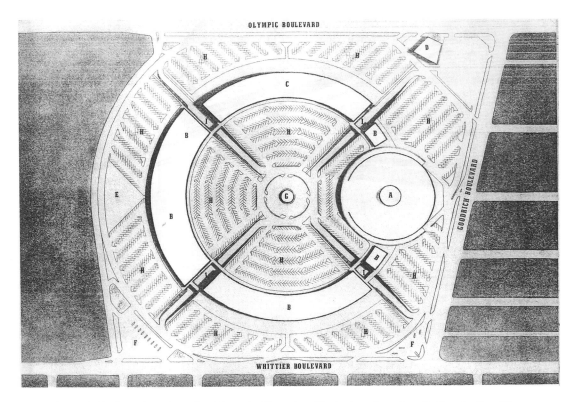

Figure 3.10. From brochure for Olympic Shopping Circle, Los Angeles, California. Box 12, Victor Gruen Collection, American Heritage Center, University of Wyoming.

STORE-ON-STILTS turns a design concept upside down.

Figure 3.11. Ketchum, Gina, and Sharp, "Store-on-Stilts," *Architectural Forum* 92 (February 1950): 102.

as was demonstrated so simply in the 1936 RPA plan study. The RPA went further and noted that several communities in the New York area were using back lots or open spaces as parking space; towns such as Hackensack, New Jersey, and Hempstead, New York, provided parking areas near their central and shopping districts. The RPA's advocacy of this new use was widely circulated—from the Automobile Association of America to many technical journals—and the report became a key reference in discussions of methods to reorganize cities for parking.[39]

During the early 1930s, smaller towns and cities addressed their parking problems in ways that made planning news. In Montclair, New Jersey, and Quincy, Massachusetts, town authorities and local businesses sought to condemn and clear land behind their main street shops for parking. Over the course of a decade Montclair slowly acquired back lots, and in 1931 Quincy started acquiring land behind its main street. Over the next two decades Quincy's plan was expanded to include more back lots, and images of the town's parking solution were widely circulated.[40] The Downtown Property Owners Association in Oakland, California, started planning in 1929 to run a large parking lot system behind the city's main street blocks, and, after partial implementation, revenue deficits were covered by association members. Even small shopping centers provided small "garden courts" for access to rear parking areas.[41] The reprogramming of shared back lots and nearby parking areas initiated a professional rethinking about the patterning of the built-up urban fabric.

Among the widely cited examples of redesigning for back-lot parking was the project undertaken by the town of Garden City on Long Island, New York, begun in 1932 and partially opened in 1937 (Figure 3.12).[42] In this parking plan, the organization of parking lots behind main street stores indicated that the design was woven into a larger-scale conception of the district. Paving, landscaping, pedestrian routes, and auto access from adjacent roads were all considered part of the design. One study noted that the plan gave store owners the idea of not merely placing doorways from the new parking area but also providing new display windows facing the cars. In addition, the "walkways" from the parking area to the main street set a new "pattern" of movement. Another observer noted that retailers in "suburban communities and small cities will have their principal entrances and most elaborate window displays facing interior parking fields."[43] This was a tremendous understatement, since the challenge to the street facade and the curb would eventually have considerable effects on store and shopping district work.

The back-lot parking system was widely adopted. Garden City's program was widely replicated over the next two decades, for example, in 1941 in Greenwich, Connecticut, and Los Angeles and Beverly Hills, California; in 1942 in Hempstead, New York (expanded), and in 1945 in Kalamazoo, Michigan; Pasadena, California; and Plainfield, New Jersey.[44] Typical publicity materials such as Hempstead's brochure told motorists they could "Park and Shop with Ease" and showed the locations of back-lot and inner-block parking fields. With the use of rear lots, one writer observed, the "old front on the main street becomes less important."[45] This simple statement and the scale of design revisions signaled a profound shift in the conception not only of the shopping district but also of typical urban form, scale, and organization.

The reorganization and reshuffling of the architectural elements of the building and the block were not taken lightly or accomplished easily. While the 1929 Los Angeles Bullocks Wilshire store (John and Donald Parkinson, architects) was designed according to the dual, if paradoxical, mandate of pedestrian street frontage and rear automotive access, the situations of most existing cities were not so easily addressed. The shift from front to back, from street to lot, was not simple. In some cases, architects and planners had to convince merchants that curb parking was no longer significant, that the curbside paradigm no longer held, and that off-street and inner-block parking would increase foot traffic and sales. A 1947 joint study by the Bureau of Highway Traffic at Yale University and the Eno Foundation (the results

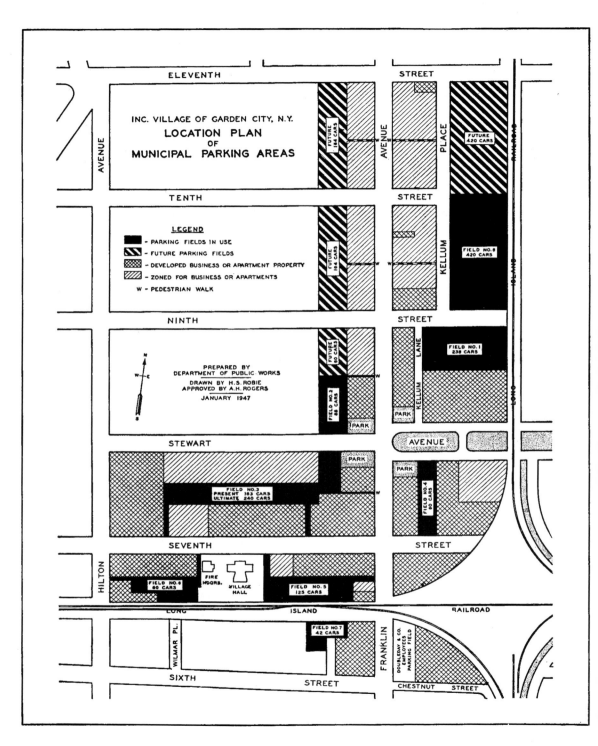

Figure 3.12. "Garden City Parking Plan" (Garden City, New York), 1938, in Harold M. Lewis, *Planning the Modern City,* vol. 2 (New York: John Wiley and Sons, 1949), 86.

of which were published in the inaugural edition of *Traffic Quarterly*) measured the costs and gains to cities of interior-block acquisition programs; not surprisingly, the conclusion was that the local tax base ultimately benefited from the extensive rethinking and redesign of the urban block.[46]

In 1940, modernist architect and advocate Walter Curt Behrendt, then the technical director of planning in Buffalo, New York, argued for a larger-scale, systemic approach to the off-street parking needs of most cities. As shown in a diagram for Buffalo (Figure 3.13), he reprogrammed back streets as "service streets," widened to

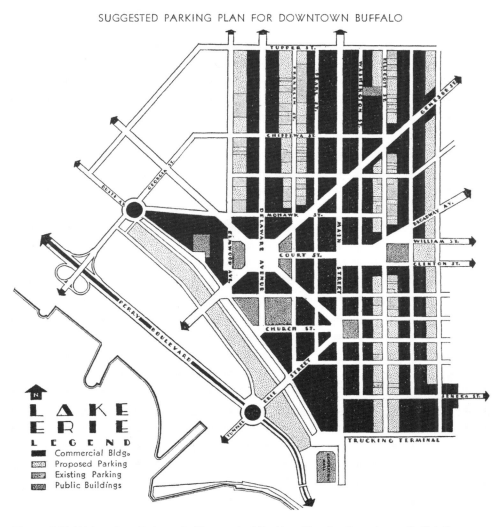

Figure 3.13. Walter Curt Behrendt, "Suggested Parking Plan for Downtown Buffalo" (Buffalo, New York), originally published in *Journal of Land and Public Utility Economics* 14 (November 1940): 467. Copyright 1940 by the Board of Regents of the University of Wisconsin System. Reproduced by permission of the University of Wisconsin Press.

include parking areas just behind the main shopping streets, and proposed stores facing in both directions. This would create the "permanent institution" of a solution to parking needs and not the "makeshift," ad hoc system that was, he wrote, typical of the time.[47]

While smaller cities were more able to implement change, larger cities did not lack for experiments and changes to street, lot, and block configurations. Planners in Milwaukee, Wisconsin, proposed a "quadrangle" of four blocks with stores facing a parking area—a superblock for cars—tied into the street grid.[48] Kansas City, Missouri, planners sited new parking lots behind the main street of stores, and store owners planned new entries, windows, and even new stores facing the back lots.[49] Hollywood, California, planners considered a large-scale remapping of blocks behind their main commercial street, and a corresponding study by architecture students from the University of Southern California was published in *Architectural Record*. Newly paved and landscaped lots behind buildings and reconfigured rear entries and windows would ensure the shopping district would remain viable.[50]

Other challenges to the distinctions between front and rear were scattered across the country. Small- and large-scale parking studies for the Los Angeles area showed the application of the rear-lot parking principle at a level that effectively challenged any traditional urban conception of entry.[51] Planners in Anaheim, California, planned in 1945 to create thirty lots (Figure 3.14) behind the city's two intersecting shopping streets, and in Miami, Florida, planners proposed in 1950 to install parking lots behind the Lincoln Road shopping district (almost a decade before Morris Lapidus proposed to close the street entirely).[52] Architects and planners in Detroit, Michigan, offered a variety of proposals. A 1945 underground parking facility sited under Washington Boulevard would, planners insisted, create a good merchandising "zone of influence," and another proposal placed garages in the middle of the city's wide avenues and connected to the proposed regional highways.[53] At various scales, new forms of parking altered the space and functioning of the city.

Among the most detailed plans using a combination of planning and design techniques for restructuring the city was offered in 1947 by planner Harland Bartholomew for Beverly Hills (Figure 3.15). The plan maintained the city's through-traffic and grid system but was overlaid with a network of closed streets, block interior lots, and underground and additional perimeter parking, all of which would ensure that parked cars and local business would be well accommodated. As an example of how to treat parking and building masses, Bartholomew specifically cited and illustrated a suburban shopping center proposal by Morris Ketchum that had just been published in *Architectural Forum* (Beverly; see chapter 4).[54] By the mid-1940s, variously scaled and sited parking solutions were part of many architectural and planning efforts to dramatically rethink existing urban and shopping fabrics.

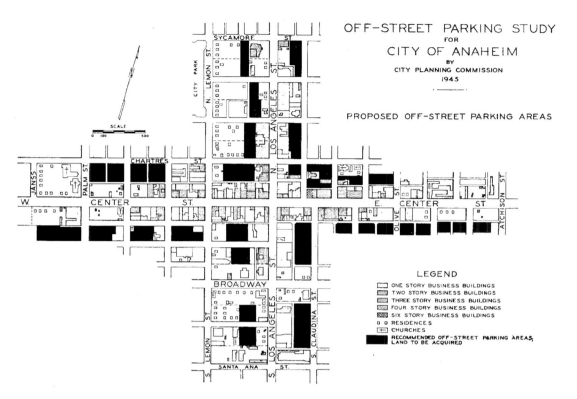

Figure 3.14. "Off-Street Parking Study for City of Anaheim" (Anaheim, California), from Wilbur Smith and Charles LeCraw, *Parking* (Saugatuck, Conn.: Eno Foundation, 1946), 85. Reprinted with permission of the Eno Transportation Foundation, Washington, D.C. Copyright 1946 Eno Center for Transportation.

The rhetorical keys to larger proposals were "comprehensiveness" and an ideal of smooth automobility that might span the metropolis. Shopping areas of the city needed to connect to parking terminals, which, in turn, would connect to new or proposed expressways.[55] This was one of the central threads in a key document that confirmed and fueled highway logic in the United States: the 1944 *Interregional Highways* report. In addition to outlining a national network of limited-access highways—for which it is widely cited—the report made the equally important observation that any proposed system would require garage and terminal connections for smooth and successful operation. The head of parking in Washington, D.C., wrote that a functioning urban region depended on the connection of the highway system to the city's "terminal parking." More emphatically, another traffic expert noted that roads and vehicular movement were of "no great consequence if terminal facilities are not provided." The provision of terminal facilities should be considered an "extension of the roadway system." By the mid-1940s, the call for overall planning was typical

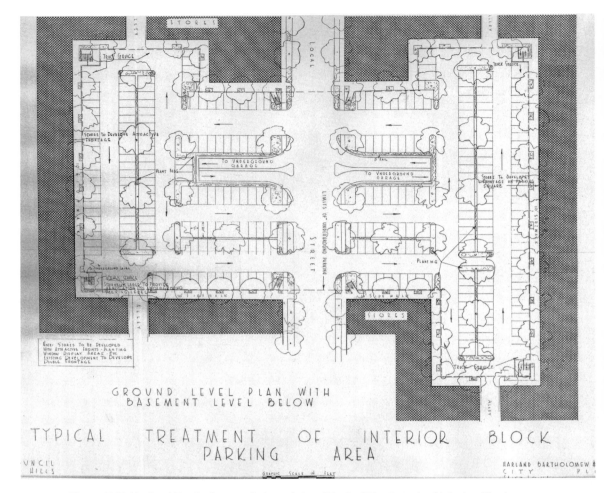

Figure 3.15. Harland Bartholomew & Associates, "Typical Treatment of Interior Block Parking Area," in *Report upon Streets, Parking, Zoning, City of Beverly Hills, California* (St. Louis, Missouri, January 1948).

and shared across the architectural and planning professions: ad hoc parking lots and connector systems were insufficient; large-scale, "modern" automobile systems were necessary to connect regions to garages.[56]

Larger patterns of the remade metropolis emerged. Architects and planners in Flint, Michigan, proposed in 1937 a "block-wide belt" of parking areas—taken from delinquent properties or "obsolete blocks"—that paralleled the main street of the shopping district. New alleys or service streets inserted into the system would help create a hierarchy of movement systems. One 1944 project for Detroit placed a dozen garages in and around the core of the city, near an inner loop expressway (Figure 3.16). A 1945 proposal for Pittsburgh, Pennsylvania, remapped the city core into walkable zones centered on at least one garage each near stores and businesses

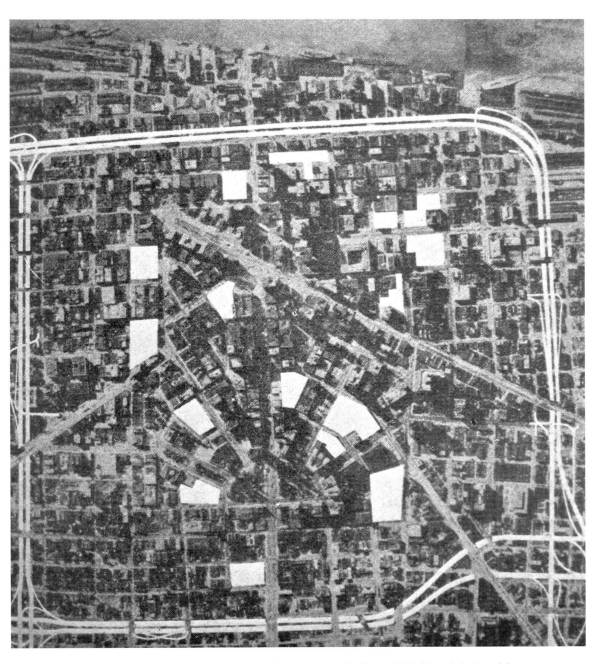

Figure 3.16. "Detroit Downtown Express Highway Loop" (Detroit, Michigan), in Harold Hammond, "Plans for Post-war Traffic Safety," in *1944 Proceedings of the Institute of Traffic Engineers* (New Haven, Conn., 1945), 107. Copyright 2012 Institute of Transportation Engineers, 1627 Eye Street NW, Suite 600, Washington, D.C. 20006, www.ite.org. Reprinted by permission.

and connected to through roads (Figure 3.17). For Mineola, New York, in 1946, planner Harold Lewis proposed the key elements of a remade system: one-way loops or "main traffic streets" connected to parking facilities in concert with small service streets. Also at the large scale, planners in Cincinnati, Ohio, proposed in 1947 a huge, abstracted ring plan with parking structures and parking lots linked to the highway system (Figure 3.18).[57]

From the smallest parking court to a regionalized movement and terminal system, the period witnessed myriad technical and design solutions to parking, movement, and merchandising. Chipping away at the street-wall conception of the typical city, composed of public fronts and service backs, the wealth of design ideas raised questions about the future performance of the elements of the city. Joining pragmatic

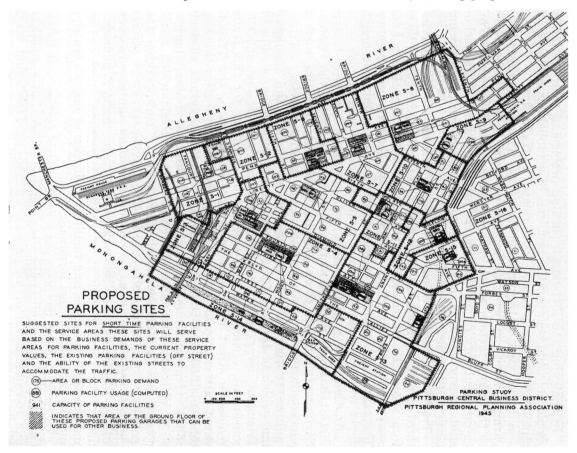

Figure 3.17. "Proposed Parking Sites" (Pittsburgh, Pennsylvania), in Donald McNeil, "Pittsburgh's Downtown Parking Problem," in *1946 Proceedings of the Institute of Traffic Engineers* (New Haven, Conn., 1947), 38. Copyright 2012 Institute of Transportation Engineers, 1627 Eye Street NW, Suite 600, Washington, D.C. 20006, www.ite.org. Reprinted by permission.

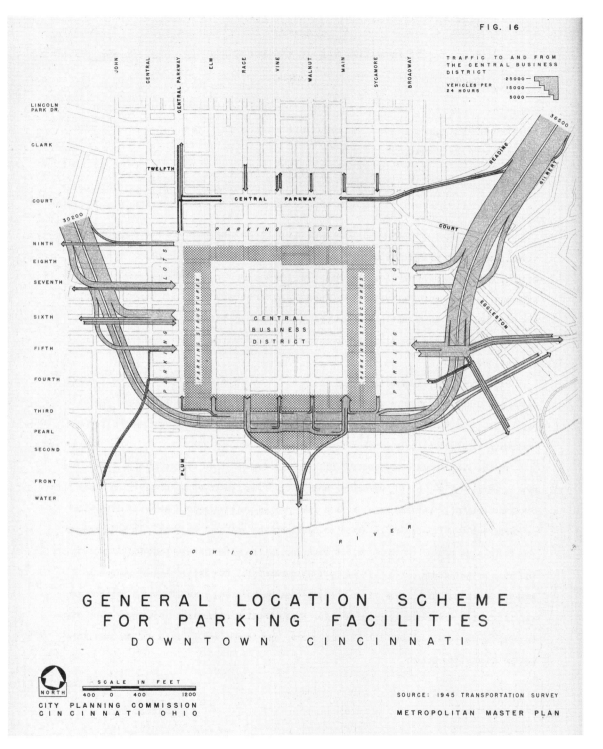

Figure 3.18. "General Location Scheme for Parking Facilities" (Cincinnati, Ohio), in *Parking: A Study of Present and Future Needs in Downtown Cincinnati* (Cincinnati City Planning Commission, 1947).

business concerns with a design and planning attitude that challenged historical urban patterns, parking the car pushed the language of urbanism to a breaking point. The historical and representational role of the street was no longer working particularly well.

Ken Welch and the Promise of Mobility

In addition to pursuing his interest in store furniture systems, Ken Welch made meticulous studies of automobile turning radii starting in the 1940s; the problem of cars became his obsession (Figure 3.19). For a wide array of commercial clients, Welch counted cars entering and leaving parking lots, plotted truck delivery times, and studied road systems with respect to income catchment areas for new store locations. In other words, beyond his role as a store consultant, architect, and salesman, Welch looked at retail problems far beyond the single store and researched trends in congestion, suburbanization, and new parking needs.[58] It is worth noting that Welch's 1929 store proposal with a ramp and basement garage shared the page in *Architectural Record* with Richard Neutra's Los Angeles Drive-In Market (see Figure 1.7), more than implying that both were serious research into the urban and architectural transformations wrought by the auto.[59]

Welch was active in national planning discussions and followed the changes in business and retailing patterns, discussing them with store owners, clients, and other businessmen. He joined the Grand Rapids, Michigan, Chamber of Commerce in the mid-1930s and was later chair of its Industrial Committee.[60] During these decades he kept an eye on the planning and legislative developments in Detroit, Chicago, and elsewhere.[61] In 1942, Welch had an opportunity to study this material more closely. During his convalescence after a heart attack, he later wrote, he read everything he could about city planning, then expanding greatly during the wartime hiatus. In 1943, he cofounded the Grand Rapids Planning Commission and helped start the advisory Metropolitan Grand Rapids Planning Association. Members included the presidents of Herpolsheimer's department store and the American Seating Company, major downtown employers. By the end of the year, the association hired the Cincinnati planner and land-use specialist Ladislas Segoe, with whom Welch directed planning, parking, and circulation studies based on a strong advocacy for the physical restructuring of the older core of the city for business and shopping purposes.[62]

Grand Rapids' introduction of a new planning initiative was typical of the civic-commercial initiatives of the time. During World War II, as Andrew Shanken has discussed, a broad discourse emerged across the country encouraging local planning and citizen participation (although inclusion in such initiatives was far less democratic in practice).[63] For example, a 1943 *Architectural Forum* program, "Planning with You," urged citizens and professionals to examine, debate, and improve their own towns and cities. In forming the Metropolitan Grand Rapids Planning Association,

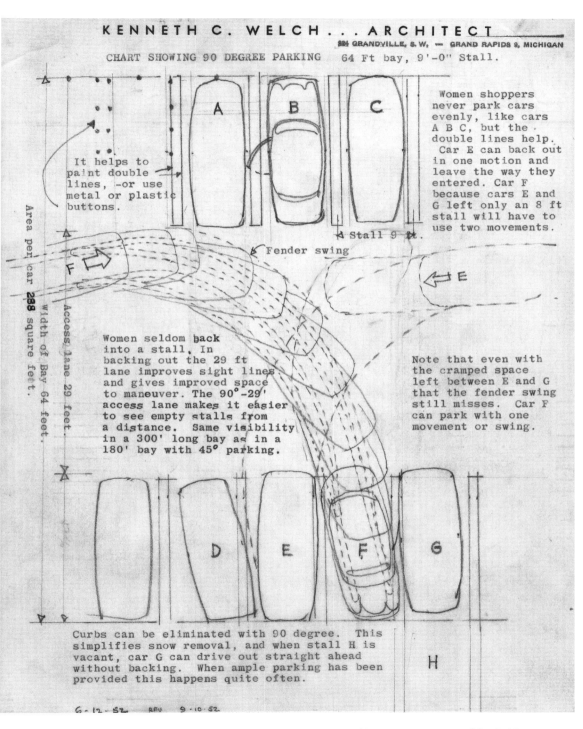

KENNETH C. WELCH ... ARCHITECT

804 GRANDVILLE, S. W. — GRAND RAPIDS 9, MICHIGAN

CHART SHOWING 90 DEGREE PARKING   64 Ft bay, 9'-0" Stall.

A   B   C

Women shoppers
never park cars
evenly, like cars
A B C, but the
double lines help.
Car E can back out
in one motion and
leave the way they
entered. Car F
because cars E and
G left only an 8 ft
stall will have to
use two movements.

It helps to
paint double
lines, -or use
metal or plastic
buttons.

Stall 9 ft.

Fender swing

F

E

Area per car 288 square feet.

Width of Bay 64 feet.

Access lane 29 feet.

Women seldom back
into a stall. In
backing out the 29 ft
lane improves sight lines
and gives improved space
to maneuver. The 90°-29'
access lane makes it easier
to see empty stalls from
a distance. Same visibility
in a 300' long bay as in a
180' bay with 45° parking.

Note that even with
the cramped space
left between E and G
that the fender swing
still misses. Car F
can park with one
movement or swing.

D   E   F   G

Curbs can be eliminated with 90 degree. This
simplifies snow removal, and when stall H is
vacant, car G can drive out straight ahead
without backing. When ample parking has been
provided this happens quite often.

H

6-12-52   REV 9-10-52

Figure 3.19. Kenneth Welch, "Chart Showing 90 Degree Parking," 1952. Box 3, Folder 3-22, Kenneth Welch Papers, Bentley Historical Library, University of Michigan.

Welch participated in this planning movement as well as fueled it. A *Grand Rapids Herald* article headlining Welch's work was shown in a later *Forum* article discussing the "Planning with You" series, and Welch was also listed among the notables ordering the *Planning with You* brochures.[64] Tactics to remake the city were bound up with the professional circulation of ideas and possibilities for cities in general.

In 1945, *Architectural Record* published a study and a proposal called the Grand Rapids Parking Plan. Welch—along with the Architects Civic Design Group of Grand Rapids, which he had organized and openly modeled on a similar Detroit organization under Eliel Saarinen—offered this master plan and architectural proposal for the "retail recentralization" of a section of Grand Rapids.[65] Published simultaneously in *Women's Wear Daily*—indicating that store work bridged different audiences—the plan solidified Welch's detailed observations and demonstrated the interventions many thought necessary for improvement. The *Record* editors had high hopes: "Though it starts as a 'parking plan' for the sake of better shopping terminals, it ends by opening the possibility of recreating the downtown area as a distinctive and coherent urban district." Welch promoted this urban intervention plan for the next five years in a variety of magazines and lecture halls.[66]

Paralleling the analyses of many urbanists, Welch and his staff found the downtown business district of Grand Rapids in dire need of reorganization. There were not enough spaces to park or enough streets to distribute traffic, many buildings were physically obsolete, sites and lots were underutilized, stores were suffering, and land values were dropping. Extensive research showed that the situation was "in the exact place where terminal parking is so badly needed." The Design Group's solution was less the tabula rasa remaking of wide swaths of urban land that would soon become standard urban renewal practice than a restructuring of the programmatic elements of the city, especially "auto storage," joining main street stores and institutions to parking to local roads to the regional road system.

The architectural demonstration of the parking plan was the Design Group's Grand River Court (Figures 3.20 and 3.21), which consisted of a continuous second-floor platform weaving together a newly formed superblock. Using "combination bridges and street level covered walkways" to form "an entire new level of terminal space," the superstructure allowed for parking on two levels—at grade at the center of the block and on the new upper level of the stores. Aesthetically, Welch wrote, the new strategy would "produce a long, quiet, restful horizontal in place of the restless sawtooth skyline." The resulting "collected, harmonious skyline" would re-create the walkable downtown shopping district and an "orderly framework for merchandising." Functionally and economically "repairing" the city core, the Grand River Court introduced a new urban tactic generated by a weave of new and old elements.[67]

For Welch, parking was the problem-solving urban glue to connect civic, pedestrian, community, and commercial functions. Before and after his own Grand Rapids

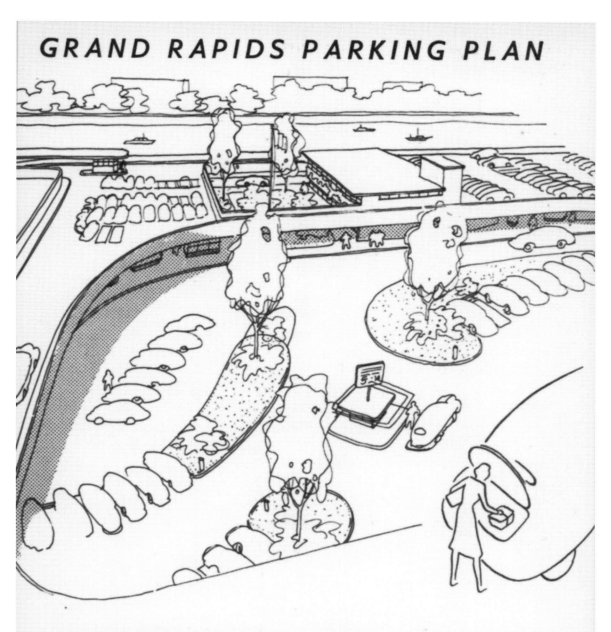

Figure 3.20. Kenneth Welch, "Grand Rapids Parking Plan" (Grand Rapids, Michigan), *Architectural Record* 97 (February 1945): 92.

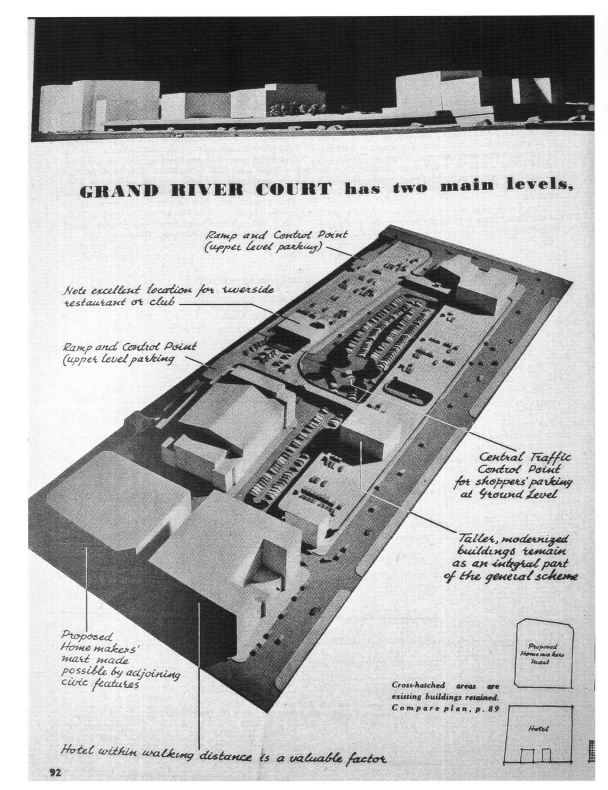

GRAND RIVER COURT has two main levels,

Ramp and Control Point
(upper level parking)

Note excellent location for riverside
restaurant or club

Ramp and Control Point
(upper level parking

Central Traffic
Control Point
for shoppers' parking
at Ground Level

Taller, modernized
buildings remain
as an integral part
of the general scheme

Proposed
Home makers'
mart made
possible by adjoining
civic features

Proposed
Home makers
mart

Cross-hatched areas are
existing buildings retained.
Compare plan, p. 89

Hotel

Hotel within walking distance is a valuable factor

Figure 3.21. Kenneth Welch, "Grand River Court" (Grand Rapids, Michigan), *Architectural Record* 97 (February 1945): 94.

work, Welch consistently advised store owners and civic leaders to acquire land for "terminal parking facilities" on peripheral lots or on rooftops to accommodate the four-wheeled "family package carrier."[68] The Grand Rapids Parking Plan and the Grand River Court were part of Welch's attempt to reorganize the workings of central business districts for the automotive age: the commercial and civic functions of the city would be fully accessible, Main Street would still have its stores, and the city would continue to prosper. The various elements of the proposals had long been discussed, but the Grand Rapids demonstration, heavy-handed though it might now appear, demonstrated how the city's shopping, movement, and accessibility needs fueled a new urban architecture even as more and more observers were looking solely to the periphery, as Welch soon would.[69]

Welch was increasingly aware that "decentralizing forces" were changing the postwar landscape. An indefatigable traveler, he visited many sites outside typical cities in his role as a consultant. In 1945, he worked on decentralization studies for a New York department store (unnamed), and the same year he joined the AIA's newly created Urban Planning Committee, formed specifically to demonstrate that the architect could uniquely participate in the discussions of store district and shopping groups outside the city.[70]

Welch also proposed reconfiguring the car-store relationship at regional and highway scales (Figure 3.22). In a June 1943 *American Builder and Building Age,* Welch discussed a shopping center fully integrated into the superhighways of the type many observers assumed would be implemented across the country. This site offered new trajectories of entry and movement and required new forms of "auto storage space." Welch's center comprised a regional department store at the core, with upper-level parking, and smaller, neighborhood-type, convenience stores at the edges, all joined by arcades and overhangs for pedestrians. Between the inner store and the outer ring of stores was a parking system designed for smooth one-way entry to and exit from the adjacent highway. The driver (typically depicted as female) would never have to back up. Welch's discussion included no mention of malls or greenways; it focused solely on moving the car through a complex architectural space as efficiently as possible. Although conceived at the large scale, the project was arguably a larger version of the drive-in shopping centers by Neutra, Wright, and others that had emerged in the 1930s. Continuing into the 1940s, such proposals offered, in effect, ever-longer sidewalks binding together more stores; the curbside paradigm remained the means to solve the problem of stores and congestion.[71]

Technical Challenges to the Curb

While Welch derived his raised urban platform from a study of parking needs and a broad awareness of urban thinking at the time, a similar architectural project by a less well-known architect and store expert offered a grander outlook on reorganizing

Figure 3.22. Kenneth Welch, "More Cars, Superhighways Will Set Post-war Pattern for Commercial Building," shopping center proposal, in *American Builder and Building Age* (New York: Simmons-Boardman Publishing, June 1943), 40.

the elements of the typical city. Louis Parnes, an architect and Ph.D. from Zurich, published his dissertation on the technical needs of stores in 1935—the dissertation's title translated into English as "Buildings of the retail trade and their circulation and organizational problems"—and cited Welch among his sources.[72] While in school, Parnes had worked briefly for Le Corbusier and subsequently practiced in Switzerland, winning several competitions. In 1940, he immigrated to New York, where he worked in the engineering departments of various manufacturers of war materiel. After the war, he completed projects in South America as well as Switzerland.[73] In 1948, Parnes published an English-language version of his dissertation on stores, adding a distinctly new section titled "City Planning Considerations" that addressed shopping design work. This section might have seemed strange to readers accustomed to specialized treatments of merchandising, or even compared to Morris Ketchum's aspirations for his *Shops and Stores* of the same year; in effect, Parnes's introduction was an urban design primer specifically based on the theories of Le Corbusier. Alongside photographs of congested, bottlenecked streets, Parnes placed diagrams and sketches of the Plan Voisin (1925) and Ville Radieuse (1929–35) and the plan for St. Dié, France (1945), and from these he concluded, quite polemically, that a "modern street is either a traffic street or a shopping street. It cannot be both."[74] A traffic street and a shopping street could, however, be stacked upon each other, and Parnes's proposed "elevated shopping avenue" consisted of a pedestrian platform above the automobile streets of the city (no longer echoing Le Corbusier's liberated ground plane). The raised promenade would be canopied and offer bridge lobbies to existing stores on either side of the existing avenue (Figure 3.23). The new shopping level would be a new "main floor" of the city, where shoppers and other pedestrians could move about undisturbed by the traffic below.

Parnes's raised pedestrian promenade expanded on modernist formal techniques, some of which had already been applied to store work. The arcades were cantilevered inward from triangulated supports at the edges of the platform; the platform itself was freestanding and partially open to the street below, so that the spaces of street and platform perceptually overlapped; and the promenade was lined with signage and floating display cases (one even curved) in the same manner that Gruen, Ketchum, and Lapidus had praised for storefronts. Even the bridge lobbies were treated as large display cases. Parnes's shopping avenue was a detailed demonstration of a modern urban intervention largely programmed for shopping.[75]

Parnes's shopping promenade in part echoed H. W. Corbett's 1925 elevated walkways (in the RPNYE) and a host of similar "visionary" projects of the period. Like many of them, it stretched economic credulity, but as a modernist sectional separation of uses to address the varied operations of the city, the project could also be linked to Rockefeller Center (started in 1929) or to many of the projects shown in José Luis Sert's 1942 *Can Our Cities Survive?*[76] Raised plazas and walkways were

Figure 3.23. Louis Parnes, elevated shopping avenue, in *Planning Stores That Pay* (Architectural Record Book, Dodge Corporation, 1948), 16.

already part of modernist discourse and would soon be proposed, and occasionally built, for many cities in the United States and abroad. In this sense, Parnes's project was notable because it specifically utilized the modernist urban platform to serve the merchandising functions of the city. It also introduced a pedestrian shopping area directly at the heart of the city, a hint of future proposals.

Parnes reframed mobility by separating pedestrian from auto, but, at about the same time, Chicago architect Howard T. Fisher proposed to unify the two. As an early advocate of a modernist position in architecture, Fisher explored the use of concrete for houses in the late 1920s and in 1932 started a fairly successful prefabricated housing company—General Houses—that exhibited a steel panel house at the 1933 Chicago Century of Progress International Exposition.[77] During World War II he worked on housing in Washington, D.C., and in 1946 he returned to Chicago and worked on conventional suburban housing. Fisher always saw modernism through a distinctly technological lens, and in 1948 he addressed the need for new shopping ideas in suburbanizing Chicago through a new "auto-shopping system" (Figure 3.24). Described as an extension of the drive-in concept that had floated through the professional and popular literature since the 1920s, the system, according to Fisher, would permit "a shopper to cash a check, buy groceries and drugs, pick up laundry and dry cleaning, leave shoes to be repaired, and perform other typical errands until an entire shopping tour has been completed by automobile, without need for finding parking space or carrying bundles to a distant car."[78] In a remarkably bold gesture, Fisher sought to completely short-circuit the car-to-store relation and dispense with the pedestrian altogether.

The extensive drive-through system could also be integrated into a larger shopping center so that goods could be invisibly sent from a store to a package pickup station. Fisher's 1948 proposal for the Lincoln Avenue shopping center utilized a sloping site to allow for a lower level—an "underground" drive-through system at which a customer could place an order, make a purchase, or pick up preordered goods. Fisher's "auto-shopping" was not implemented, but it was widely discussed, along with various other package-delivery systems (using a technology not unlike that employed for drive-through banking in later years). It demonstrated architects' continued fascination with technological means of addressing functional questions and showed the difficulty, still, of reconciling the consumer, the car, and the store.[79]

Testing the Curbside Paradigm Outside the City

Fisher and Welch were not the first to look beyond the city as a site and an organizational model for the relation between cars and stores. The spreading metropolis and the emerging suburbs offered new sites where programs planned according to

Figure 3.24. Howard T. Fisher, "Auto-Shopping," in Geoffrey Baker and Bruno Funaro, *Shopping Centers: Design and Operation* (New York: Reinhold, 1951).

the car could be tested, largely because land was cheaper than in the core of the city. From the early 1920s forward, and following the residential drift away from the city center, as detailed in depth by Richard Longstreth, store projects were often part of upper-class residential developments where one owner could control much of the building, leasing, and management process, if not the entire process. These new shopping projects outside the urban core experimented with some, but not all, of the design and siting of urban elements.

Perhaps the most widely published among the early shopping districts was Country Club Plaza in Kansas City, Missouri, developed by Jesse Clyde Nichols. The Plaza, which opened in 1923, was designed and managed as a unified "store group" even as it spanned its newly created streets.[80] The Plaza set a new standard in the literature on shopping center design by ensuring a broad sense of spatial and stylistic unity as well as keeping the car and the store in close proximity.

Particularly vital to the Plaza was attention paid to the details of traffic, parking, servicing, and loading. Almost 50 percent of the site was paved for streets (versus Manhattan, for instance, which is approximately 30 percent paved), which created small blocks and thus many intersections—that is, "100 percent locations" in the retailers' lexicon. Notably, many of the blocks had "interior service courts" for loading and store servicing but not for customer parking; garages were placed elsewhere in the district plan and were "discreetly" designed with walls, hedges, and sectional changes. The car-to-store ratio was untypically high compared with most shopping districts. Nichols also excluded office uses from the complex, because nonshopping workers' cars would, he said, merely clog the streets.[81] This approach, as Longstreth has pointed out, selectively intertwined the typical elements of the site plan for particular uses related to the mechanics of merchandising. The Plaza, in other words, was an improved and more profitable version of the sidewalk-facing store. Part suburban, part small town, and part urban, the Plaza was a design petri dish in which some elements were selected and others omitted, showing how a shopping district might function with more overtly commercial priorities and unencumbered by heterogeneous demographic and on-the-ground land-use histories. This was the freedom afforded by suburban development, albeit patterned on, and limited by, urban precedent.[82]

In the decentralizing process of American urban growth, other experiments attempted to adjust building and siting to the car, many of which have been detailed by Richard Longstreth. On the West Coast, projects such as the Palm Drive-In, the Plaza Market, and Richard Neutra's Los Angeles Drive-In (see Figure 1.7), all about 1929, provided parking space by setting back the buildings into the depth of the site or designed the center along the route of a car passing through the site. This latter format was perhaps epitomized by Neutra's Lexington, Kentucky, Drive-In project (1929). On the East Coast, the Radburn Plaza Building (1929) and the Munsey Park Business Center, both by Frederick Ackerman (1930), and Shaker Square

(1928) followed a similar method of locating buildings to the back of the site to provide for off-street parking. There are many others examples, including some that provided parking both in front of and behind the shopping building.[83] Sumner Gruzen's Jersey City Big Bear Shopping Center of 1934 offered entrances from rear and side parking lots as well as one from the street.[84] In much of this work, considerable changes to massing and siting were made, but the rule of the car remained paramount.

Several other suburban projects of the 1920s and 1930s worked within but also pushed against the limits of the curbside paradigm of the short walk from car to store.[85] Two representative developments in Texas, Dallas's Highland Park Village of 1930 (Figure 3.25) and Houston's River Oaks of 1937, demonstrate the state of store and site modernization in the interwar years. Both adopted unified management policies, used extensive local planning, street layouts, and marketing studies, and were designed as "store groups": single architectural and site plans organized

Figure 3.25. Fooshee and Cheek, Highland Park Shopping Center, Dallas, Texas, 1931, in Baker and Funaro, *Shopping Centers: Design and Operation*, 90.

around calculated amounts of parking and efficient circulation.[86] Highland Park (built out over a decade) consisted of one central and several perimeter shopping buildings—several with arcades—all separated by parking areas. The central building had a service alley and a small pedestrian courtyard, and the perimeter buildings contained separated service zones.[87] River Oaks, part of an older residential development begun in 1916, formed a semicircular symbolic gateway into a residential community and was unified by an arcade.[88] Both projects were praised as distinct advances in the shaping of modernized, large-scale, auto-based shopping centers. These and other projects indicate how nondowntown sites enabled experimentation with managed retailing beyond the scale of the single store. Yet while they demonstrated new forms of site planning, the design fulcrum remained the direct linkage of car to store. Setback siting was a pivotal design decision, but other than the arcade, one still had to walk from car to curb, from street to sidewalk; the relation of car to store was barely mediated.

A 1932 *Architectural Record* article on "neighborhood shopping centers" perhaps explains why shopping projects of the interwar period did not quite challenge the curbside paradigm. Buried in the "Drafting and Design Problems" section of the magazine were two juxtaposed images (Figure 3.26)—a typical Main Street with jumbled "Coney Island Architecture" and a "planned grouping" of stores set back to make room for parked cars. The former image implied congested conditions where parking was difficult, the buildings were "confused," and the street lacked design coherence. The latter image, by contrast, was designed so that order, coordination, "uniformity," and abundant parking were all evident.[89] The shopping center shown was the 1930 Connecticut Avenue Park and Shop in Washington, D.C., which Knud Lönberg-Holm had lauded as utterly rational in his 1931 *Record* article on stores. Set back from the road and making space for the by then technological "fact" of the car, the center appeared to rationalize and make more efficient the elements of the new metropolis. Merchandising was, in these terms, one among many social programs that could be made to function "better." Indeed, accompanying the 1932 article were automobile-based site plans drawn by *Record* editor Lawrence Kocher's occasional collaborator Albert Frey to demonstrate the reconfiguration of planning needed for smoother automotive access to shopping facilities.[90] Frey, Kocher, and Lönberg-Holm saw in this project a rational approach to the retailer's need to accommodate a new set of auto-borne customers—the shopper was a driver, not yet a pedestrian.[91]

Rethinking the 100 Percent Location?

In 1939, *Architectural Forum* editors worried about the typical downtown, organized around the retailers' "100 percent location," the busiest corner where the "customers are thickest."[92] If this urban shopping core was, as Morris Lapidus once

DRAFTING AND DESIGN PROBLEMS

NEIGHBORHOOD SHOPPING CENTERS

Keystone View

SHOPPING DISTRICT OF MAIN STREET CHARACTER. This unrelated "Coney Island Architecture" suggests the need for cooperative and unified planning by architects.

Underwood

A PLANNED GROUPING OF SHOPS with parking space that does not interfere with traffic of main thoroughfare. The design by one architect of buildings for a variety of uses results in uniformity.

Figure 3.26. "Drafting and Design Problems: Neighborhood Shopping Centers," *Architectural Record* 71 (May 1932): 325.

pronounced, a "national architectural expression,"[93] then, *Forum* editors intoned, the district needed a bigger and better plan. Downtown stores may have been "brilliant individual solutions," but sorely missing were district-wide policies and designs ensuring smooth operations into the future. As many observers had pointed out for quite some time, land use was "irregular," parking lots broke the unity of the street wall, and clogged streets caused multiple access problems. Only a "messiah on main" might bring regulation, order, "civic design," and action, all of which would enable Main Street to stay main.[94]

Modernist (or would-be modernist) architects in the 1930s and 1940s were eager to address the viability of Main Street's curbside model of commerce. Architects, planners, and other professionals worked from their respective forms of expertise, but they shared the view that cities needed to rethink and redesign the physical arrangement of urban parts to accommodate the car. In a process akin to urban bricolage, not yet urban renewal, they considered the turning radius of the car, raised platforms connecting older buildings to parking, ramps or lots squeezed into unexpected places, new technologies, alleys remade into walkways—in sum, they attempted to reimagine the older fabric as an integral part of something new. Through these various interventions, architects were able to position themselves as planners; they discussed the shop as part of a district or a store group, and they framed the shop or the car as only part of a *process* of shopping that unfolded across time and space. This working method of a many-scaled analysis of merchandising was also part of the modernist credo, worthy of Sigfried Giedion, and through it, the shape of the city was undramatically reconfigured. Larger-scale planning would soon be required.

FOUR

PEDESTRIANIZATION
TAKES COMMAND

The reconquering of the right of the pedestrian, the "*royauté du piéton*" as Le Corbusier put it, is the first requisite of the contemporary city plan.

> —SIGFRIED GIEDION
> "The Heart of the City: A Summing Up," 1952[1]

IN 1947, PRINCETON UNIVERSITY sponsored a conference titled "Planning Man's Physical Environment," with presentations by Frank Lloyd Wright, Walter Gropius, Richard Neutra, Sigfried Giedion, George Howe, Joseph Hudnut, and other notables.[2] The discussions about design, technology, education, and planning at the conference were high-minded, if general, and the participants framed the future of the city in broad and often dire terms. Giedion took a position that was cosmopolitan and represented the city as the highest of architectural syntheses, whereas others, such as the Boston architect William Roger Greeley, took the small town as a model. Shopping was never mentioned. In all cases, however, the participants agreed that good governance and an active citizenry were goals achievable only in planned, "organic" communities and not in cities of the ad hoc pattern typical of the American metropolis. This was not a new theme in architectural debate, but, fueled by the Depression and wartime experiences, growing Cold War tensions, and a call to reinvigorate democracy, the search for new American urban and design principles was a constant refrain.

133

One thread in the Princeton discussion was the "problem of the pedestrian"—at first glance, a rather pragmatic problem. The dangers of the traffic-clogged city, where pedestrians "hugged" the lampposts, had long been an issue. As *Forum* editors put it in 1944, "the pedestrian lost the right to do anything but dodge."[3] But the "right of the pedestrian" became a synecdoche for new and modern attitudes toward the urban condition and for polemics about change. Thus debates about the postwar metropolis framed the pedestrian as a literal reference as well as a social and political fulcrum. Addressing a broader idea of public life, Talbot Hamlin asked, "Would it not . . . be the part of true democratic planning to make the pedestrian circulation the chief element instead of, as it usually is, a mere secondary consideration?" Dean William Wurster of the Massachusetts Institute of Technology agreed but pointed out that pedestrian planning would be infeasible until the use, layout, and ownership of building sites could also be rethought.[4] At midcentury, "the pedestrian" offered a seemingly holistic lens for architectural, regional, and urban thinking and complemented debates about the nature of modernism.

Another participant at the Princeton conference felt compelled to add that new shopping centers and remodeled shopping districts were already taking the pedestrian as a starting point in design. This point was offered by Morris Ketchum, who was hard at work on site plans for both urban Main Streets and suburban shopping centers in which the pedestrian attained the status of civic actor, citizen, architectural and planning premise, and targeted consumer.[5] Based on an auto-free precinct or fixed area for the pedestrian, Ketchum's plans for shopping offered a concrete image of a new landscape, especially as consumption became the cultural undertow across the 1940s. The car had until then been the primary subject of analysis by architects and planners, but the protagonist of large-scale design concepts shifted to the person on foot.

More broadly, the pedestrian represented a subject without baggage, a citizen participant and icon of freedom. From Goethe, Thoreau, or even Rousseau to the *Wandervogel* of Germany, to E. B. White's or William H. Whyte's view of walking in the city, to Michel de Certeau's view of the liberative potential of walking—the well-trod footstep has long held a potent image of autonomy and enlightenment. That the wandering figures of Le Corbusier's 1929 Ville Radieuse sketches can be construed as walking in a radically different kind of city shows, among other things, that the pedestrian could be a trope in a variety of would-be modernist remakings of the city and its social life. "Le piéton," Le Corbusier later wrote, "est maitre du sol," the master of the soil.[6] Pedestrian-infused positions added meaning and content to architectural work—the person on foot was a legitimating figure as well as a reliable technical fact. Pedestrianism could invoke critiques of the industrial city, a need for renewal and rescaling of the "obsolete" city, and a logic for rebuilding inside *and* outside the city.

Units and Territories

In 1944, the editors of *Architectural Forum* took a firm position on the central tenets of modern planning and design. "The unit of manageable size must be the cell from which the city grows. Within such a unit, whether residential neighborhood or commercial center, man's two feet again become a pleasant and efficient means of getting around."[7] Only a controlled allotment of land, the neighborhood unit, could create the conditions for a properly functioning social realm. The design goals promoted were both discursive and pragmatic, as the editors sought to create a basis for thinking about a role for architects that complemented, for instance, the Pittsburgh planners who partitioned their city into districts served by parking lots (see Figure 3.17). Urban citizens, cowed and demoralized by congestion, could thrive once again only after the city had been reconfigured, and the grid made more flexible, by new delineations of territory remaking scale, movement, and spatial relations. Combining tactical utility with a progressive position, a "unit discourse" was the presumption that the spaces of the city could be classified and delimited areas, controlled. Setting edges to a particular urban space would give the planner-designer the authority and knowledge to program the use comfortably "within" a given area. The seeming stability, order, and rationality of units also filled out and legitimated modernist ways of replanning cities; the pedestrian set free within the logical unit of space became symbolic gesture as well as design principle. While typically *superblock* referred to an aggregation of lots and *unit* referred to larger combinations of social and settlement elements, the logic of parts suffused architectural and planning discourse on cities and regions and formed the discursive backdrop for an array of planning efforts. That unit discourse also shared the underlying logic for the rationalization of land exchange and development is one of its central paradoxes, symptomatic of the tensions of modernism in the United States, as elsewhere.

Unit ideas in the United States invariably lead back to Clarence Perry's canonical 1929 presentation of the neighborhood unit in the *Regional Plan of New York and Its Environs.*[8] As the end point of many years of urban improvement research reaching from garden cities to playgrounds, the unit also initiated a new discussion about the role of site planning in creating new forms of architectural and social organization.[9] After Perry's article, a veritable unit industry in city design and planning explored the ways in which new and existing communities could be subdivided and (re)assembled in a putatively objective manner to satisfy a full array of social "needs." The unit was presumed by its advocates to be physically and morally remediating, and it provided the discursive underpinnings as well as technical methods for what would become an international, if tendentious, language over the course of the twentieth century.[10]

Key to the durability of the unit idea was its explicit linkage between spatial and social control. Unit discourse reached back to urban theories of social groups and institutions that drew from Émile Durkheim and Ferdinand Tönnies as well as the observations about modernizing cities from Georg Simmel and hence to Chicago, where Robert Park and Ernest Burgess, among others, began to map the spatial implications of class and race onto the physical fabric of the city. Linking (perceived) social problems to locations and places within the city, the Chicago school provided the intellectual basis for delineating and planning territory, for a new type of "natural area" that would enable (or simulate) the identity, neighborliness, and familiarity that were seemingly absent from the anomie and brutality of the larger city.[11] In Perry's unit, and the many versions that followed, new physical and administrative borders would enable a neighborly refuge in which schools, churches, shops, and community spaces were now accessible by foot—as in a village—and thus were cohesive. Although the exclusionary practices implicit when not explicit in unit-based work had a profound effect on American urban change, the walking radius for the pedestrian also formed a key remediating image for progressive planning and design.

Pedestrian-based imagery linked to unit-based design thinking was shared among a variety of would-be urban reformers—from the myriad New Deal and wartime-era agencies to planning and architectural organizations such as the Regional Plan Association of America, the RPNYE, and CIAM, to the housing writings of Catherine Bauer (1934) and Henry Wright (1935), to images of community life at Greenbelt.[12] From Clarence Stein's "townless highway" linking groups of town units to Gropius and Wagner's unit agglomerations in suburban Boston, to Ludwig Hilberseimer's rationalistic and oddly bucolic "settlement units," to José Luis Sert's (and CIAM's) 1944 discussion of the scaling possibilities of the unit, not only was there a shared logic based on the reorganization of land divisions, but the proposals were also framed with respect to a pedestrian-citizen whose liberty would reactivate "normal social intercourse" and "neighborliness."[13] Walking, Sert wrote, was "one of man's natural functions," and in the replatted metropolis, pedestrians "would be able to walk freely among parks and athletic fields, or in front of shop windows, which they could examine at ease, without being disturbed by noise and dust."[14] In a 1943 issue of *Architectural Record,* planner Thomas Mackesey and landscape architect and Cornell University dean Gilmore Clarke wrote that the superblock—a conceptual cousin of the unit—would need to become the main method of redefining the city and would make possible the open spaces and "pleasant footways" that would make the city livable once again.[15] Walking was a representation of modernism's potential and served as a symbol of community and civic freedom; that it might also entail shopping was additional proof of its prosaic urbanity.

Emerging from a wide field of New Deal–era research, the 1939 *Supplementary Report of the Urbanism Committee to the National Resources Committee* (the original report was published in 1937) offers a good representation of urban ideas that unified these varied participants in unit discourse.[16] The report was based on the premise that the neighborhood unit and the superblock could and would produce "rational urban development" and peaceful social interaction. The space of the unit would be "self-sufficient," "fixed," "bounded," and without through streets. The unit would nurture social and financial "protection" and "stability" and would offer "completeness" as in a village, a "satellite," a suburb, or a section of any city; and it would be "integrated" into the larger "urban pattern" of similar units.[17] While the rhetoric and logic of unitization was framed with an eye toward social improvement, the rationalizing of land assembly and exchange was equally part of the process. The hallmark of the rationality prized by advocates of modernism was matched by the mechanics of modernization.

At a 1942 Harvard conference in which policy makers, planners, and architects debated how cities and regions would be altered to fit dramatically new conditions, central among the assumptions was the role of cells and units. T. T. McCrosky of the Chicago Plan Commission said that all future work, in or outside the city, needed to be in the form of the superblock or the neighborhood unit, a position seconded by Walter Gropius and Martin Wagner, just then embarking on Harvard's neighborhood unit studies in suburban Boston. In their essay added to the published collection, the unit, they wrote, would form the basis of the regional city, and in each, pedestrian distances would be the focus.[18]

The architectural magazines were consumed with the project of planning during the war years, as Andrew Shanken has shown, but the particular compartmentalized form of planning is also important.[19] For example, the dual threads of delineation and social improvement unified the work published in the two issues of *Architectural Forum*'s "Planned Neighborhoods for 194X," of 1943 and 1944.[20] One project for a "three-cell new town" consisted of three neighborhood units anchored by an irregular semicircular town center defined by perimeter parking and an arcaded "100 percent pedestrian" array of shops and civic facilities. The "100 percent" reference was a vital rhetorical connector of new forms of shopping with older forms of the city. Other studies in the *Forum* special issue specifically examined borders and edges. One article framed circulation and infrastructure as the way both to "bind the city and to separate it into development areas or neighborhoods," another framed the unit as a "continuous interior space," and yet another saw the unit—more than echoing Clarence Perry's canonical statements—as the proper administrative mechanism for the social life and politics of the city (Figure 4.1). All the projects framed the unit as an efficient, socially redeeming, and economically viable element of development. Discussions of schools, parks, parkways, and neighborhood dimensions revolved around the idea of a "complete" neighborhood made cohesive by the capacity of the residents to walk, undisturbed, within it. Richard Neutra's Channel Heights plan of 1942 used what he called "finger parks" to ensure walkable zones

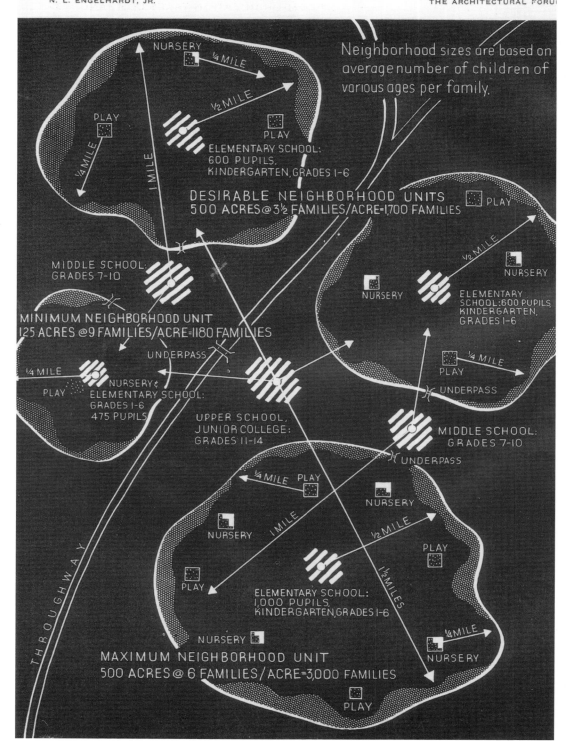

Figure 4.1. N. L. Engelhardt Jr., "Schools and Neighborhoods," *Architectural Forum* 79 (October 1943): 88.

within a "self contained neighborhood."[21] The pedestrian, the person walking to work, school, or store, was the symbolic core of a system of closed and safe semi-autonomous precincts.

Two publications of 1944 showed the potential progressive performance of the unit. That year, architects Oscar Stonorov and Louis Kahn published a pamphlet titled *You and Your Neighborhood* in a series sponsored by materials manufacturer Revere Copper and Brass, and the Museum of Modern Art opened its *Look at Your Neighborhood* exhibit and published the exhibit catalog. Both publications circulated widely and received considerable commentary. The Stonorov and Kahn book, in a didactic, how-to manner aimed at inspiring local participation, offered a vision of the unit as a part of a modern reweaving of the city into semiautonomous areas (Figure 4.2). Some streets were closed, loops for traffic were created, green space was inserted, and new community and shopping facilities were added. This was a flexible unit that, they wrote, would ensure that "you can reasonably safely walk from most of your neighborhood to school, to the common, the shopping center or to the swimming pool."[22]

At MoMA, architect Rudolf Mock curated the *Look at Your Neighborhood* show to demonstrate the community-making potential of the neighborhood unit. The impersonal "city of districts," Mock wrote, needed to become a nurturing, sociable "city of neighborhoods," with each neighborhood as the "basic unit." Key to the unit was its flexibility, and Mock pointed out that flexibility could be applied "from

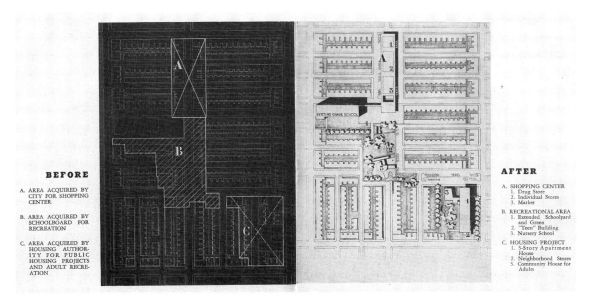

BEFORE

A. AREA ACQUIRED BY CITY FOR SHOPPING CENTER

B. AREA ACQUIRED BY SCHOOLBOARD FOR RECREATION

C. AREA ACQUIRED BY HOUSING AUTHORITY FOR PUBLIC HOUSING PROJECTS AND ADULT RECREATION

AFTER

A. SHOPPING CENTER
1. Drug Store
2. Individual Stores
3. Market

B. RECREATIONAL AREA
1. Extended Schoolyard and Green
2. "Teen" Building
3. Nursery School

C. HOUSING PROJECT
1. 3-Story Apartment House
2. Neighborhood Stores
3. Community House for Adults

Figure 4.2. Oscar Stonorov and Louis Kahn, "How to Look at Your Neighborhood," in *Why City Planning Is Your Responsibility* (New York: Revere Copper and Brass, 1943), 6–7.

scratch in the country or in the slum areas," and it could entail "gradual *re*development" in existing neighborhoods. The exhibit's photo panels, in several editions, traveled extensively across the United States—from planning agencies to Camp Fire Girls' meetings. The exhibit offered an image of a self-sufficient, democratic community based on the physical plan of the neighborhood in the city and outside it. In this new landscape, residents would "have a chance to become a REAL COMMUNITY OF RESPONSIBLE CITIZENS."[23]

In 1945, the MoMA show was displayed at the San Jose Civic Auditorium under the auspices of the city's Citizens' Planning Council and organized by planner Mel Scott.[24] In 1942 Scott had organized a citizens' introduction to Los Angeles planning called *Cities Are for People,* and central to the picture was the neighborhood unit. Such an approach would be orderly, attractive, and restful, and, if "self-contained," it could "satisfy" common needs and be so pleasant "that we should seldom be tempted to leave it."[25] Treatments of the unit such as Scott's, Mock's, and Stonorov and Kahn's displayed considerable faith in the ability for finite and walkable territory to generate social good.[26]

By the end of the 1940s, the neighborhood unit and the superblock became the normative core of modern urban discourse, undergirded by the logic of pedestrianization.[27] The editors of *Architectural Forum* sought for walking to become the new central parameter in design thinking. Distinctions between the unit and the superblock (and even new towns) remained considerable, and, despite the searing critiques initiated in 1948 by Reginald Isaacs and later by Jaqueline Tyrwhitt, the unit and superblock operated as the standard lens through which to view the "natural areas" of the city, as a "sampling technique" to examine the city, and as a prescriptive and easily circulated design tool among professionals.[28] Practices based on units aligned with and shaped modernist architectural practice and were adopted at many scales and for many programs. Unit planning was said to offer a democratic and neighborly social contract— unit-based planning and design, wrote Lewis Mumford, could be a "correlate of modern design."[29] But this planning also fused with the instrumentalities of economic rationalism as well as logics for large-scale housing and urban renewal, for which classification and distinction of parts often yielded problematic results.[30] Modernist tenets and the conditions of modernization were paradoxically joined in the figure of the pedestrian, made possible through the neighborhood unit. This logic of the unit, a delineated space containing a prescribed set of functions, was also integral to the shaping of shopping centers.

Pedestrianization: Beyond the Curbside Paradigm

Even as architects in the 1930s and 1940s adjusted their cities and buildings to the automobile, pedestrianization created a new set of priorities for site planning and organization, in the city and outside it. In a 1934 *Architectural Record* article titled

"Store Buildings and Neighborhood Shopping Centers," Clarence Stein and Catherine Bauer offered principles of rationalization for commercial siting processes (matching the utilitarianism of Lönberg-Holm) and explicitly targeted the emerging "strip" form of development through specific site planning limitations and possibilities. They highlighted the Radburn Plaza shopping building (Frederick Ackerman, 1929), which stepped back from the street to allow for parking and provided entry from a rear parking area for each store; but this did not go far enough. For Stein and Bauer, full access from a park adjacent to residences—that is, by pedestrians without their cars—was the next logical step. In the diagram they offered (Figure 4.3), parking was pushed to either side of the store building, service and deliveries were located at the street-facing front, and the wings of the store building formed a "child play space."[31] In other words, the building siting and organization were reversed: access was not from the street but from a new pedestrian zone. This was a radical change in what was considered a typical urban configuration, and other versions soon followed.

In a spirit of design reform entailing a reversal of previous siting norms, new pedestrian-based layouts were produced. The widely studied Greenbelt shopping

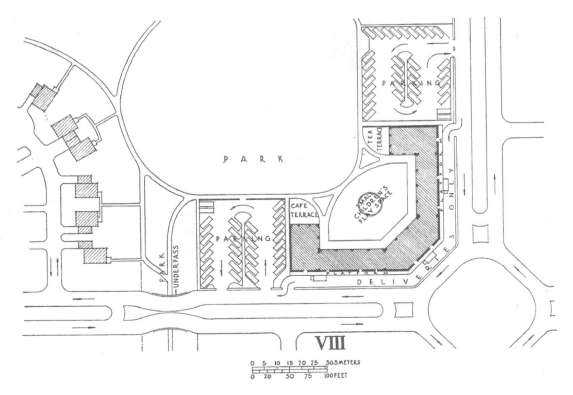

Figure 4.3. Clarence Stein and Catherine Bauer, "Neighborhood Shopping Center," *Architectural Record* 75 (February 1934): 181.

center (Wadsworth and Ellington, opened 1937) provided a plaza for shoppers and connected to a system of walkways, including an underpass to adjacent housing.[32] At about the same time, architect Albert Mayer, who had worked on Greenbrook, New Jersey, and written about and consulted on the Greenbelt program, proposed for a residential development a pedestrian "plaza" shaped by surrounding shopping and civic buildings.[33] In 1939, Carl Feiss proposed a similar shopping center that "turns its back on the road," and while he praised the Connecticut Avenue Park and Shop (see Figure 3.26), in which new space was provided for cars, he added that easy movement across a garden and under protected awnings would be a greater form of "civic beautification." His drawing of the proposed center for *House & Garden* (Figure 4.4) showed pedestrian access from a parking area and from a landscaped court, with a bucolic-looking pool and garden.[34] Such an attitude could also be displayed in the design of the city itself. In his 1937 *Shopping Districts,* Denver planner S. R. De Boer offered a hint of the future—even though the book was sprinkled with medieval and colonial images. De Boer encouraged lot owners to pay jointly for rehabilitation of obsolete commercial districts, proposed a district-wide "façade plan" for unifying a large area, and specifically praised the parking plan at Country Club Plaza. More important, De Boer showed his own plans for a commercial district, which included a "grass mall" for a town square as well as a back-alley servicing system and an arcade. Although none of these was attached directly to a pedestrian

Figure 4.4. Carl Feiss, "Shopping Centers," *House & Garden,* December 1939, 48–49. Illustration by Robert Harrer/House & Garden; copyright Condé Nast.

system, all were key ingredients for any reconfiguration of the shopping and urban realm. Yet De Boer stretched convention by suggesting that smaller streets, at certain times of day, could be closed for pedestrian uses only. "This is rather daring," he suggested, but if streets were "closed to traffic and beautif[ied] with flowers and fountains," such an urban strategy might revitalize whole districts.[35] These examples, often discussed with reference to older European cities and piazzas, show a form of site thinking in which shopping (or just strolling) in a pedestrian-specific area, not merely along a sidewalk, was a new lens through which to view the design of the city or suburb.

In the 1940s, experimentation continued, new designs were circulated in the magazines, and several projects became important references as the shopping center design field emerged. Morris Ketchum, so adamant at the Princeton conference that the pedestrian receive proper attention, devoted a chapter of his 1948 *Shops and Stores* to a survey of pioneering projects. His book was a somber and professional study of store design requirements, materials, and procedures, but the penultimate chapter, titled "Shopping Environment," looked beyond the needs of the single store and the problem of access and open space. Whether a store is in the city or not, he wrote, "the shopping traffic that reaches its doors will be chiefly pedestrian traffic."[36] Beginning with the small neighborhood center and moving up in scale through community and regionally sized centers, Ketchum reviewed selected projects showing a pedestrian-based unit as central to a modern approach to planning: the store was one piece of a larger civic puzzle. The projects illustrating the "Shopping Environment" chapter were evidence that planned commerce and unitized communities were integral threads of a modern environment.

Ketchum praised Pietro Belluschi's 1942 McLoughlin Heights shopping center (near the booming Kaiser Shipyard at Vancouver, Washington) as among the earliest innovations in separating the pedestrian and the car and, more important, in providing a green court (Figure 4.5). The semienclosed plan created a planted, pedestrian-only space bordered by arcades and walkways that linked the stores to local services and connected to new housing (reaching 100,000 by 1944) beyond the center. Ketchum described the project as an important strategy in which "rings of store buildings and parking spaces surround a pedestrian mall." The project was included in the 1944 Museum of Modern Art *Built in USA* exhibit and book, and it was praised for separating parking and servicing as well as for its "landscaped court."[37]

Ketchum described the 1943 Linda Vista Shopping Center (near defense housing in San Diego) by Earl Giberson and Whitney Smith as the "first well-organized" neighborhood center to use the planted mall shaped by an arcade, stores, and parking (Figure 4.6). *Forum* editors described the project as "the first full dress presentation of the Grass-on-Main-Street idea," and *California Arts & Architecture* editors put the project on the cover of their November 1944 issue. Ketchum also praised

Figure 4.5. Pietro Belluschi, shopping center, McLoughlin Heights, Washington, 1942.

Figure 4.6. Whitney Smith, Linda Vista, San Diego, California, March 1945. Photograph by Maynard L. Parker. Courtesy of The Huntington Library, San Marino, California.

the varied programming, which included a department store as well as smaller stores and services. The shopping center, planned as an integral part of a larger community, demonstrated the utility of good neighborhood unit planning.[38]

At a much larger scale, Eero Saarinen's 1943 Willow Run "town center" proposal for "Bomber City" near Henry Ford's new aircraft plant served as a model for postwar planning, Ketchum wrote, because it organized the pedestrian, the car, and five "neighborhood units" into an overall, unified system (Figure 4.7). Holding together five "sub-towns," the new center would provide for a full array of social needs—school, city hall, and so on. The informally composed complex consisted of an east–west pedestrian axis for the "business and shopping" blocks and a north–south pedestrian axis of civic functions, and, as if re-creating an old town green, it included a lake, a clock tower, and considerable landscaping—all with parking and roads behind. Pedestrian routes and underpasses linked the new center to the new neighborhoods. Willow Run's town center as well as its linked neighborhoods would have been a remarkable test of the applicability of unit-based, pedestrian planning for modern community design.[39]

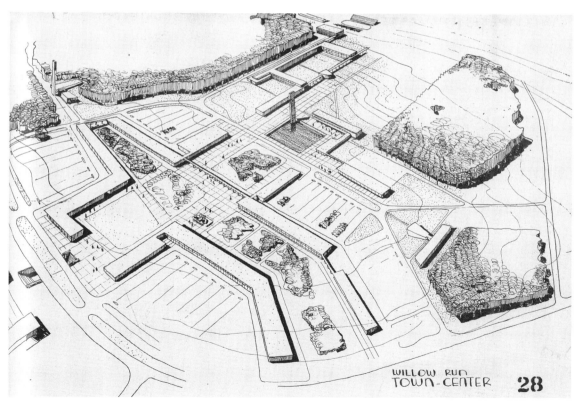

Figure 4.7. Saarinen and Swanson, "The Town of Willow Run," *Architectural Forum* 78 (March 1943): 37–54.

McLoughlin Heights, Linda Vista, and Willow Run were key projects in Ketchum's linkage of pedestrian planning, unit-based design principles, and commercial planning. They showed the overlap between the rationalism of modernist architectural thinking and the large-scale planning required of new commercial work. The projects showed a new organizational pattern of commerce that was inseparable from their role as modern social units.

The architectural journals also published other projects that integrated site planning, commercial planning, and community functions with various delineations of pedestrian space. A 1942 plan for the wartime community of Kingsford Heights, Indiana, included a community center with civic as well as shopping functions, the latter organized along a planted and landscaped spine leading to a "common" (Figure 4.8). Parking was located behind the stores next to the access roads. A 1943 sketch by Willo von Moltke (see Figure I.4 in the introduction) comparing a proposed pedestrian shopping area to an older congested commercial intersection—part of an article on housing by Harvard's architecture dean, Joseph Hudnut—showed that a distinctly pedestrian zone could connect other neighborhood institutions in a web of "civilizing" spatial relations. A 1945 design by architect Henry Churchill for a service station and shopping center provided a distinctive space for pedestrian usage similar to Feiss's design of 1939: a U-shaped block created semienclosed landscaped space, complete with small "pool" and playground, with parking out of sight,

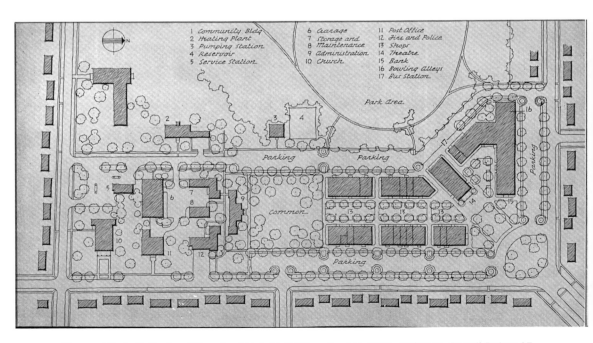

Figure 4.8. A. D. Taylor, "Kingsford Heights" (Kingsford Heights, Indiana), *Pencil Points* 23 (October 1942): 58–66. Copyright 2012 Penton Media, Inc., 90488:612SH.

behind the building.[40] At a larger scale (Figure 4.9), a pedestrian-based shopping center was proposed in 1947 by the firm of Loebl, Schlossman and Bennett, to be built at the center of a large planned suburban development (later named Park Forest) outside Chicago.[41] Several 1948 projects also showed a developing architectural language of the shopping center. One series by Clarence Stein shows a deep concern for "park" areas, as well as courts and promenades; another proposal by Matthew Nowicki and Stein used a tensile structure to create a series of open shopping spaces.[42] Another 1948 proposal by Kelly and Gruzen (Figure 4.10) for suburban New Jersey created a pedestrian core for a circular shopping complex.[43] Other projects offered fragments of pedestrian zones, such as the 1948 "ultra-modern" proposal by architect Howard T. Fisher for Lincoln Plaza (opened 1951), outside Chicago (see chapter 3). The project was designed more like a strip center, but the central area consisted of a pedestrian lane between blocks of stores, with "flowers and plantings," which was treated as "the mall" of the project.[44] The terms and strategies of shopping centers were gaining fluency and becoming clear: the insertion of the pedestrian zone stretched the curbside paradigm of shopping center thinking.

In shifting the commercial parameters from the car to the pedestrian, from parking space to walking space, the new designs for shopping areas, even when fragmentary, created a new spatial pattern represented as modern. That these pedestrian

Courtesy, American Community Builders, Inc.

FIGURE 11·47.   SKETCH OF PROPOSED SHOPPING CENTER FOR A SATELLITE TOWN NEAR OLYMPIA
FIELDS, ILLINOIS

Figure 4.9. American Community Builders, Inc., "Sketch of Proposed Shopping Center for a Satellite Town Near Olympia Fields, Illinois," in Harold M. Lewis, *Planning the Modern City,* vol. 1 (New York: John Wiley and Sons, 1949), 249.

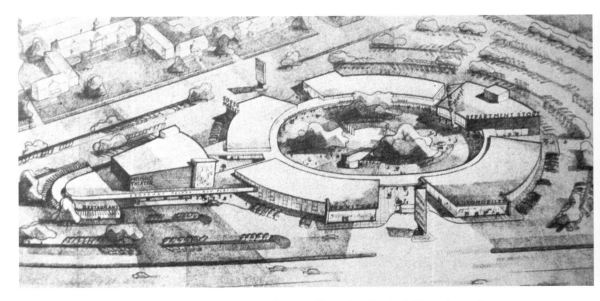

Figure 4.10. Kelly and Gruzen, "Bergen County Shopping Center" (New Jersey), *Architectural Record* 103 (June 1948): 10.

precincts were associated with large-scale planning projects—where the pedestrian precinct was integral to a broader area or neighborhood plan—further legitimated them as part of modernist discourse. Pedestrianization was a small yet integral part of a larger planning and design project that contributed to the social whole. This did not mean just a meander through the city; rather, it entailed the explicit shaping of territory that could be represented as a socially legible place—through a highly rationalized, modern architectural process.

George Nelson, City Planner

Perhaps the most developed demonstration of an integration of planning and pedestrianization was George Nelson's constellation of proposals for a new form of Main Street.[45] Following *Architectural Forum*'s 1941 editorial call for planning and action in a broadly framed, polemical set of articles titled "Post-war Pattern," Nelson and *Forum* editors led a detailed study of site and community design starting in 1943, the same year Nelson and Henry Wright Jr. became managing editors of the magazine under publisher Howard Myers.[46] Nelson organized and wrote several pieces aimed at professional and popular audiences on how pedestrianized Main Streets might address urban blight and congestion. His roles as editor, designer, planner, publicist, patriot, and advocate of modernism overlapped in profound ways.

The centerpiece of Nelson's project was a special issue of *Architectural Forum* titled "New Buildings for 194X," in which "Modern Architecture" was put to the test in a search for solutions to the problems of a "typical" American city, in this case,

Syracuse, New York: obsolete buildings, suburban competition, lack of movement systems, and congestion.[47] In late 1942, the Syracuse Chamber of Commerce began to consider postwar business planning, and *Fortune* magazine editors approached the city about participating in a "demonstration of over-all city planning."[48] This probably came about through the connections among the city's established industrialists—the heads of corporations such as Smith-Corona and Crouse-Hinds led the city's Post-War Planning Committee, along with the chancellor of Syracuse University—some of whom were likely acquainted with Henry Luce, the owner of *Fortune* and *Forum.* The committee work was supplemented by nationally known consultants, including the landscape architect and planner Russell Van Nest Black; Walter Blucher, president of the American Society of Planning Officials; and Hugh Pomeroy, president of the American Institute of Planners.[49] Reginald Isaacs, soon to be deeply involved in neighborhood unit planning critiques in Chicago, was on the Syracuse staff, but the role he played is unclear.[50] Also consulted on the project were two traffic experts, Donald Kennedy and Grant Mickle, both of whom had published widely on downtown congestion and parking questions. The Syracuse project, under the guidance of Nelson and *Forum,* was undertaken to show that modern architecture was the appropriate means of determining and expressing "the new concept of community," enabling "dignified and fruitful intercourse," and offering a renewed vision of society.[51]

The dramatic premise of Nelson's "194X" project was the creation of a pedestrian precinct in place of Syracuse's main street (Figure 4.11). This restructuring would reframe the uses, spaces, and perceptions of the entire downtown. While many of the published proposals were freestanding modernist works—including Mies van der Rohe's "Museum for a Small City"—the reorganization of the core of the city around a new green armature, the planted mall, was integral to the siting and articulation of several proposals. Oscar Stonorov and Louis Kahn (just then exploring pedestrianization in Philadelphia) proposed a hotel, Pietro Belluschi (who had recently completed McLoughlin Heights shopping center) proposed an office building (Figure 4.12), and Charles Eames proposed the new city hall; each was conceived as an extension of the city's main pedestrian "mall." The massing of each project created open spaces within the site as well as access routes and views across the mall. Belluschi's project included semisunken parking as well as an office building—not unlike Ketchum's 1940 "store block." The capacity to walk at the core of the city, and the design tactics such a project entailed, gave an image to a new urban possibility, a symbolically and pragmatically modern city, as formally complex as other American and European work of the time.[52]

Beyond the *Forum* project for Syracuse, Nelson's Main Street ideal was developed as an emblematic "Anytown" and circulated in several publications and in a pamphlet series sponsored by the construction materials supplier Revere Copper

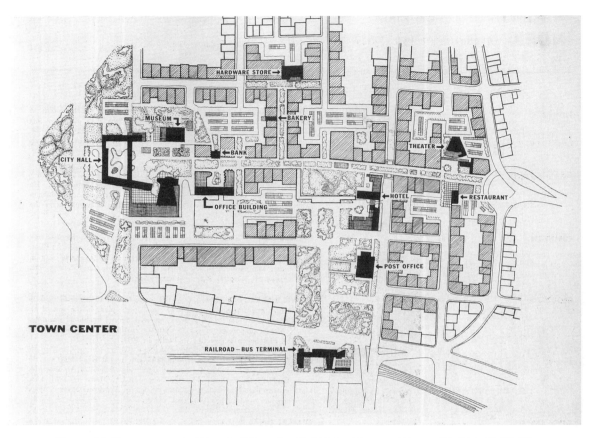

Figure 4.11. Town center, in "New Buildings for 194X," *Architectural Forum* 78 (May 1943): 71.

and Brass (Figure 4.13). In this more abstract version, the new city core was organized by a pinwheel plan of major and minor axes around a main intersection. Main Street formed the central armature, intermittently retaining its older street wall; a precinct was created through the siting of new buildings at either end of the ensemble. The now-pedestrianized street ran from a theater (with a small plaza) on one end to the new municipal plaza at the opposite end. The minor cross-axis led from a bus terminal to specialty shops, an office tower with a café, and a hotel. Two subsidiary arms led from each plaza, one to a wholesale commercial building and the other to local service shops. One side of Main Street was lined with department stores and the other with specialty shops. Both sides were linked with new, prefabricated "rust-proof" arcades to encourage "all-weather strolling," showing that older streets could be retrofitted. Between the buildings and a "greenbelt" ring road were large parking areas, ensuring that no one need walk more than five minutes to get to his or her destination. The new unitized town was concisely defined and smoothly functioning, yet it was not too new or unfamiliar.

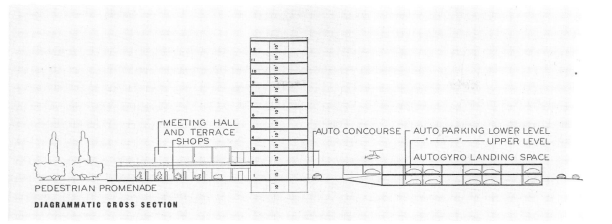

Figure 4.12. Pietro Belluschi, office building, in "New Buildings for 194X," *Architectural Forum* 78 (May 1943): 110.

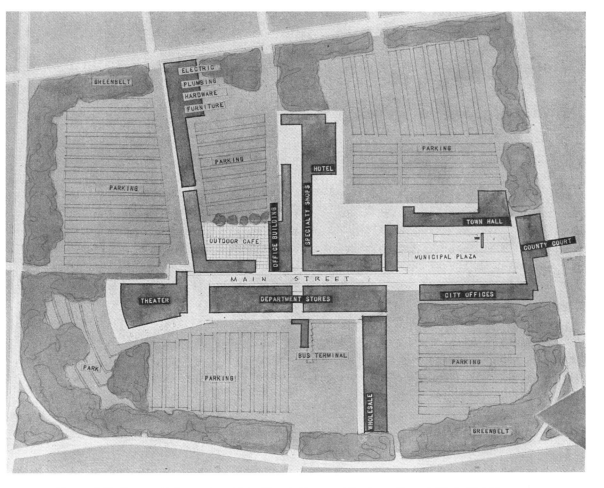

Figure 4.13. George Nelson, plan, *Main Street: Now and Postwar,* Revere Pamphlet 13 (New York: Revere Copper and Brass, 1943), 6.

Equally important to the various pedestrianization propositions was their circulation. For a general audience, Nelson published in *House & Garden* a version of his project that included a pedestrianized layout for a typical existing downtown, accompanied by an article on community planning by Richard Bennett.[53] To reach both popular and professional audiences, Nelson wrote a Revere pamphlet calling for pedestrianized Main Streets.[54] Finally, the project was featured in *Architectural Forum*'s "Planning with You" series, in which a pedestrian-based urbanism was the rallying point for "citizen participation" in the rebuilding of American cities and towns—more than 150,000 copies of the *Planning with You* booklet were eventually distributed.[55] The wide reach of the "194X" project was made possible, in part, by the project's lack of an overt radical program and its focus on urban change as an extension of the traditions of American pragmatism and on-the-ground action. Walking a fine line, the "194X" proposals were critical of the status quo but nevertheless were represented by *Forum* editors as reform, not revolution; they respected both property and capital.

Nelson's articles shaped a logic of pedestrianization by combining a populist appeal to precedent with the rhetoric of common sense. In "Planning with You," Nelson described the organic social life engendered by the medieval walled town (as did so many others, including Eliel Saarinen and Ludwig Hilberseimer) and the colonial town common (as did Clarence Stein and Walter Gropius) as models of planning fostering the social interaction to which cities could still aspire. In "New Buildings for 194X," he wrote that closing Main Street to provide a "park-like promenade for shoppers" was "far from Utopian" but could be based on known fiscal resources, existing technologies, and self-interested cooperation among merchants and politicians. Moreover, he wrote, "this kind of Main Street could be created right in your own town." Nelson portrayed this new pedestrian zone not as a "planner's dream" but as the logical unfolding of "natural" urban processes: as the inner city becomes congested and blighted, it becomes "ready" for pedestrianization.[56] This was a reformist, modern urbanism that looked to rehabilitate existing buildings, add to them, extend the pattern, and naturalize the process of development.

The features of this new pedestrian urbanism were nothing if not friendly (Figure 4.14). Nelson conjured up an irresistible imagery of "old pavement and trolley tracks" replaced by "long stretches of lawn, paved walks, benches, fountains, flowerbeds and trees." With tables, "splashing fountains," public sculpture, and small playgrounds for the kids of shopping moms, this new pedestrian form would be a better urbanism. "What were once side streets have become small squares where people can move about quietly and with complete comfort."[57] The images might have seemed strange to some readers, but Nelson pointed out that the shops and the department store were merely renovated buildings, saved by pedestrianization from decay. As a designed unit, the city core could be remade into a modern, walkable, urbane place.

Figure 4.14. George Nelson, view, *Main Street,* 11.

Pedestrianization was framed as a modernist solution, and an American and democratic solution as well, in which the reorganization of space and program for shopping gave a coherence and unity to change, working well within the expectations of real estate. To make sure Nelson's point was clear, captions such as "Grass Grows on Main Street" and "Your children could romp here while you shop" appealed to both professional and more popular audiences.

Victor Gruen: Pedestrianist

George Nelson's Main Street pedestrianization project cast a specific net within architectural culture: participants such as Mies, Charles and Ray Eames, and Pietro Belluschi indicated that vital work would come from the aesthetic, spatial, and planning inventions of an emerging group of modernist architects. Victor Gruen without a doubt wanted to be part of that group (although he often scoffed at their pretensions). Now relocated to Los Angeles, where population expansion and wartime industry proved a growth opportunity for his practice, Gruen participated in Nelson's project in two ways. Nelson published in the "194X" *Forum* piece one of Gruen's proposals for a small neighborhood shopping center, and, along the way, Gruen made clear his interest in a larger, pedestrian-based shopping center nearer to the highways then on the planning horizon.

In February 1943, Gruen was invited by *Forum* publisher Howard Myers to submit a "design for shops and stores" for a special issue on postwar building. At that point, the site was unstated. Gruen sent his acceptance the same day by telegram, responding that his firm would be happy to contribute a plan for a "post war suburban shopping center for which we have worked out ideas." (He also asked if expenses would be paid.) Myers had not used the term *suburban,* but neither had he given Gruen any other information. Ruth Goodhue, the *Forum* managing editor, responded with a clarification: the special issue would be devoted to projects for a "town of sixty or seventy thousand," and therefore a "small neighborhood shopping center" on a typical gridiron urban block would be preferable to a "larger" suburban center (and no, the magazine would not "underwrite expenses").[58]

An official letter from Myers explaining the "194X" project to all the participants arrived at Gruen's office a week later. A reformist position was emphasized over a radical approach. The special issue would show "buildings which might *reasonably* become part of the postwar construction activities in the average American city." But the city had not yet been selected. "At present we are studying air views of cities . . . with a view to preparing a general plan diagram with tentative locations for the various projects." Indicative of the underlying problems addressed by the study, sufficient parking space was the one common thread the magazine could then suggest to the participants.[59]

Myers described Gruen's particular assignment as a small building or complex embedded in a "typical" residential district and not on a busy commercial strip— already a leap from the normative commercial growth patterns in favor of planned facilities within a community. The program included a grocery store, a drugstore, a dry cleaner's shop, a hardware store, a variety store, and "perhaps" a small neighborhood movie theater. Gruen's project was also to provide the means for "moving from one store to another . . . under cover," and, Myers added, special attention "should be given to use by pedestrians, since all the homes are within walking distance."[60] This was to be a project about new forms of planned shopping, not mere real estate development. Gruen had other ideas.

On the same day Myers wrote to Gruen, Gruen sent in his proposal for a large-scale shopping center; his proposal and Myers's letter crossed in the mail. Gruen wrote that a small center would be inadequate for a town of sixty thousand, and a larger center ought to be located along major automotive routes. This, in early 1943, was among Gruen's earliest and clearest statements about a large-scale center. The postwar shopping center, he wrote,

> shall be built between highways in such a way that the stores are not directed towards these highways but towards a plaza, formed by the surrounding store buildings. Outside of these buildings and adjoining the highways and connecting roads is the huge parking area. The plaza is landscaped as a park, and contains a garden restaurant, milk-bars, music shell, and other recreational facilities. Surrounding buildings contain, in addition to the usual different kinds of stores, community buildings such as a post office, club building, day-nursery (where children can be left during shopping hours), library and so forth. . . . Thus we expect to make the shopping center at the same time the center of cultural activities and recreation.[61]

Gruen's proposal described a new type of shopping center, and his references were a mix of civic, market, and park elements. This was not a project at the neighborhood scale but an addition to the regional scale with broad social ambitions. Gruen also suggested the reorganization of the metropolitan region by including in each project "an office center" for municipal authorities, an auditorium for theatrical performances, and an exhibit hall for cultural organizations; this would be a modern architectural statement. In commercial terms, there would be stores rivaling the old downtown, with "specialty stores and a high-class department store," and while the new shopping centers would recentralize urban functions outside the city, they would also restore the viability of the existing core. Like many at the time, Gruen framed decentralization as a complement to the city, not a replacement. Last but not least, Gruen knew the business angle: the shopping center could not be too small, "lest it should not pay to erect the communal facilities."[62] Gruen's position on modernism was always complemented by the entanglements of building.

Nelson weighed in on the project, and while he supported the "scope" of Gruen's vision of distributed centers across the metropolis, he did not then want to embark on such a proposal. Reiterating the editorial framing of the invitation, Nelson saw the project not as a radical replanning of the city but as an extension of conventional urban development practices. A "realistic flavor" would be important for the "investors" who would be interested and thus willing to "improve" their communities.[63]

Crossed letters notwithstanding, Gruen followed up and accepted the smaller program for a center serving fifteen hundred families. His written design proposal (there are no sketches) described a single circular building 140 feet in diameter and surrounded by a "landscaped walk" and parking. This building would be set inside a circular roadway, which in turn would be connected to the street intersection, creating a "shopping island." The store layout, however, transformed into an interior condition the exterior pedestrian landscape of his larger proposal. Glass partitions would separate the stores but would be connected by aisles and movement patterns "so that the shopper may proceed from store to store without leaving the actual building.[64] Gruen revealed here his penchant for circular forms and, more important, used a bazaar-like, arcade condition of continuous and seemingly exterior space that some department store designers were starting to use, and that Morris Ketchum had proposed for his 1940 "store block" (see chapter 3).

Gruen's single-building project was not well received by Nelson, who "suggested" a center using a typical urban block system and a courtyard or plaza plan instead of a circular building. Nelson liked the plaza of Gruen's earlier proposal but not the massive scale or siting implications. Extant sketches show Gruen's study of the smaller store group. In one early sketch, Gruen illustrated a U-shaped plan in a gridded urban context with a main entry at the base of the U and smaller entries from each longer arm, all leading to an inner arcade and "park." Set back from the surrounding streets on all sides, the building was surrounded by parking. A more elaborate version of the proposal consisted of a larger oval-shaped complex with a "kiddie town" and an amphitheater in the enclosed park (Figure 4.15).[65] The published smaller U-shaped building consisted of a "landscaped patio" onto which the stores faced; parking was pushed to the ends of the project, leaving space only for a depressed service lane at the side street edges (Figure 4.16). The buildings turned away from the street, and a miniature scenic garden offered visual and physical respite from the gritty world beyond.[66]

Only in the *Forum* project introduction did the editors allow Gruen a reference to the greater scale he advocated for shopping center work: "Large centers could be built on the same principle, covering several blocks. Automobile traffic could be diverted around such centers or if necessary, under them." This was a grand claim in 1943. Grade separation had long been a key problem of urban design, and the overpass—from Central Park to Radburn to the highway interchanges of Frank Lloyd Wright and, later, to Kenneth Welch's Grand River Court (see Figure 3.21)—and Gruen's thinking for this proposal were prophetic. Another page of sketches, most likely from the same time, included a section locating automobiles in a tunnel running below the periphery of the buildings and creating a pedestrian zone faced by two-story retail buildings (Figure 4.17); another sketch showed a raised level above a parking structure.[67] Gruen's study of the section to address the car and shopping center operation showed his awareness of the technical hurdles of large-scale work, shopping or otherwise. The future shopping center would have to utilize these superblock or unit techniques to overcome the extant urban block system; the new shopping center would have to be a semiautonomous pedestrian territory.

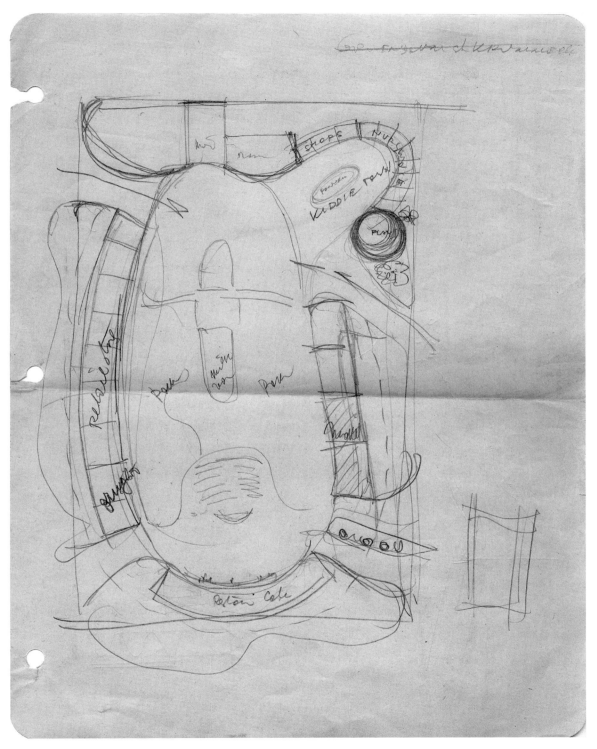

Figure 4.15. Victor Gruen, shopping center, sketch for *Architectural Forum* (1943). Box 54, Victor Gruen Collection, American Heritage Center, University of Wyoming.

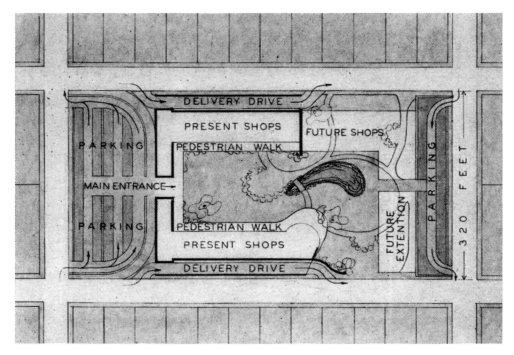

Figure 4.16. "Neighborhood Shopping Center, Gruen & Krummeck, Designers," *Architectural Forum* 78 (May 1943): 101. Box 54, Victor Gruen Collection, American Heritage Center, University of Wyoming.

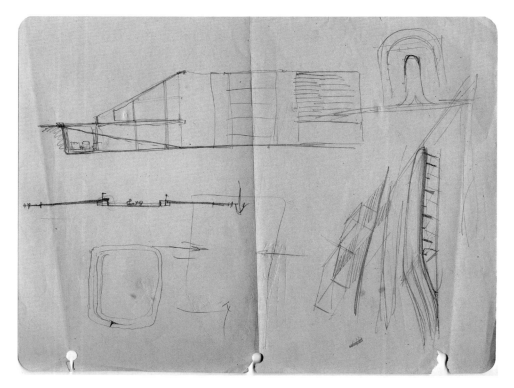

Figure 4.17. Victor Gruen, shopping center, sketch for *Architectural Forum* (1943?). Box 54, Victor Gruen Collection, American Heritage Center, University of Wyoming.

Gruen's "194X" work—proposals, sketches, and the published version (along with Nelson's catalytic input)—was an important thread in the making of the pedestrian realm. Gruen and other early experimenters considered the shopping center a new and modern architectural type, with large-scale urban and regional potential. "All necessities of day to day living can be found in the shopping center: post office, circulating library, doctors' and dentists' offices, and rooms for club activities, in addition to the usual shopping facilities. Shopping thus becomes a pleasure, recreation instead of a chore," with the shopping center a location of commercial *and* social activity.[68] While gendered safety, greenery, and "community" were never far from the representations of these new centers, an underlying logic of totality and control was implicit.

The newly designed provision of social and architectural functions could also look like the city itself. Gruen's 1947–48 shopping center project for Los Angeles recreated an urban scene (Figure 4.18). Arranged like a traffic intersection but without the cars, the two landscaped "shopping streets" were designed with kiosks, benches, flower beds, wading pool, city offices, a theater, and a trove of pedestrian furnishings that would "invite people to prolong their stay." Parking was located behind the store blocks, securing the safety of the pedestrian allées. At the center of the intersection, unlike in the typical city on which the shopping center was modeled, was a circular restaurant, or perhaps a department store, set in a pond and accessed by bridges. This new social complex would, Gruen wrote, become associated with "cultural enrichment and relaxation." In an associational reversal only he could muster, the Los Angeles project would not appear as a place for shopping but instead would have the "character of a large park surrounded by shopping facilities."[69] In his "194X" and Los Angeles projects, Gruen reconfigured the elements of the shopping

Figure 4.18. Gruen and Krummeck, shopping center, Los Angeles, California, *Chain Store Age* (July 1948): 22.

street by shifting the perception and status of the car. The auto was never absent, but it was in fact strategically hidden—through design and plan—so the pedestrian territory could attain the status of a modernist invention.

Ketchum's Pedestrian Plans

Morris Ketchum had already made a name for himself designing stores, and he too looked at the relation of the store to the larger city. In a 1940 *Forum,* Ketchum had published his "Store Block" proposal (see Figure 3.7), which created a mixed-use building with space for cars, pedestrians, and office workers.[70] More dramatically, Ketchum proposed (but did not illustrate) that the "store block" could work on *both sides* of the city's main street, enabling another far-reaching change. With parking accommodated and accessed from side streets, "paving can be torn up, gardens planted, and the citizens can enjoy open-air lounging and dining with their window shopping, with no traffic light to bother them." Thus the "store block" transformed traditional street-facing urban commercial forms by reprogramming the building to accommodate the car and by reorganizing the city itself with a pedestrianized ground plane at its core—the central idea of the "194X" project to follow shortly. *Forum* editors wrote that the building was "a fundamental contribution to improvement of the existing town plan."

In 1943, while Gruen and Nelson were hashing out their shopping center ideas, the city of Rye, New York, hired planner and educator Frederick J. Adams to examine the conditions of Rye's congested business core.[71] Over the next two years, Adams studied the town's subdivision standards, recreational needs, growth concerns, and traffic problems. In 1945, Adams was joined by planner and economist Homer Hoyt, who had just come from the Chicago Plan Commission, where he had been director of research for the city's early-1940s neighborhood studies.[72] Adams, Hoyt, and other analysts of the Rye Planning Commission described the key issue for the town as the redevelopment of the "blighted . . . drab, variegated" business district into a single and unified whole. Included in their recommendations were the provision of off-street parking, improvement of traffic arteries, and some unspecified "drastic . . . reorganization" of the business area.[73] Late in 1944, Rye officials hired Morris Ketchum to solve the Planning Commission's brief.

Joining together the various parking, shopping, recreational, and traffic needs, Ketchum provided a sweeping "vision" for Rye's business center by converting it into a pedestrian "island" (Figure 4.19).[74] Like many parking plans of the period, Rye's plan located off-street parking behind the main street buildings and connected to a traffic loop around the business district. Included in the plan was the reduction and concentration of business zoning to ensure a higher density of commerce in the core area. Ketchum also proposed the drastic step of closing and landscaping the main street. The planted, "grassed-over mall," which would intersect with crosswalks, would be lined by a continuous arcade designed for "weather protection," lighting, and space for unified signage and for the housing of "unsightly overhead electrical lines." The new arcade would, in other words, serve as infrastructure and allow the design of the pedestrianized street to "harmonize" the *existing* business properties, creating a "unified architectural effect."[75] Ketchum's "Rye Plan" entailed a complete restructuring of the relations among the town's central streets, stores, and parking and provided a new conception of a town center, even as it involved very little new building.

The Rye Plan renderings circulated widely—starting with the *Forum* cover in August 1946, and the plan's "park strip" in place of main street was widely noted. The *New York Times* editorialized that the "little city of Rye" had offered a forward-looking project from which all cities might learn. With the business district "island," stores could face both the grassed main street and tree-shaded parking behind. Others noted that the plan would be a turning point in addressing obsolete but still well-located town commercial centers. Redirecting the traffic-burdened slide of once-busy streets would enable a return to a more "leisurely day" in the annals of the business district; the project was represented as pragmatic *and* modern. Most important, the unit principles and tactics of the Rye plan could be "universally applied."[76]

In his 1948 *Shops and Stores,* Ketchum treated Rye as the ne plus ultra of design thinking because it examined the problems of an existing city, not a site on open land with few encumbrances. As with his "store block" of 1940, the extant fabric could be reconfigured for a new form of urban organization.[77] Ketchum was no romantic, however, and he saw the need for large-scale urban clearance as well. The time will come, he wrote, "when it will be economically possible to gradually replace our gridiron streets with superblocks, tear down or remodel our obsolete commercial buildings, and provide a city pattern adequate for both motor and pedestrian traffic." Aside from its explicit support of the broad-brush demolition that would soon become the norm, the role of the walking person remained a central trope. In fact, Ketchum offered high praise for Paul Lester Wiener and José Luis Sert's "Motor City" in Brazil (Figure 4.20). Designed at "the scale of the pedestrian citizen," the project was "proof" that "organized recentralization" could solve the problems of decentralization and that shopping and civic activities could be treated as a "single coordinated unit" linked to other parts of a modern city. The project was featured on the cover of *Progressive Architecture* in 1946 and was treated to an exhibit and conference at the Museum of Modern Art in 1947.[78] That Ketchum could invoke the "Motor City" project in his book on stores is symptomatic of his ambition for the new scale of planning for stores, which he equated with a form of modernist city planning.

All was not rosy for Ketchum's city planning, however, and the bond issue for the Rye project was rejected by voters who feared higher taxes more than they appreciated planning vision: "Withering Grass" was *Architectural Forum*'s wry headline about the failed financing.[79] But the vision did impress many, and soon Rye's neighbor

Figure 4.19. Ketchum, Gina, and Sharp, "Rye Plan" (Rye, New York), *Architectural Forum* 85 (August 1946): 78–79.

Mount Kisco sought to emulate it. In 1949, Henry Fagin, director of the Northern Westchester Joint Planning Program (and soon to be planning director of the RPA), pushed to convert his town's main shopping street into a "new shopping mall," closed to traffic, with extensive parking lots behind the store buildings. This plan met the same fate as Rye's and was cut back to a parking scheme.[80] The planned, modern, pedestrianized city—"Main Street minus auto traffic"—was circulating as a viable urban image, but it was having trouble getting built.

Ketchum and Welch in the Suburbs

Ken Welch's 1943 proposals for highway-based shopping centers were thoughtful if slightly simplified responses to retailing outside cities, and his 1945 proposal for Grand Rapids parking, perhaps a tinker's superblock, was a more finely tuned attempt

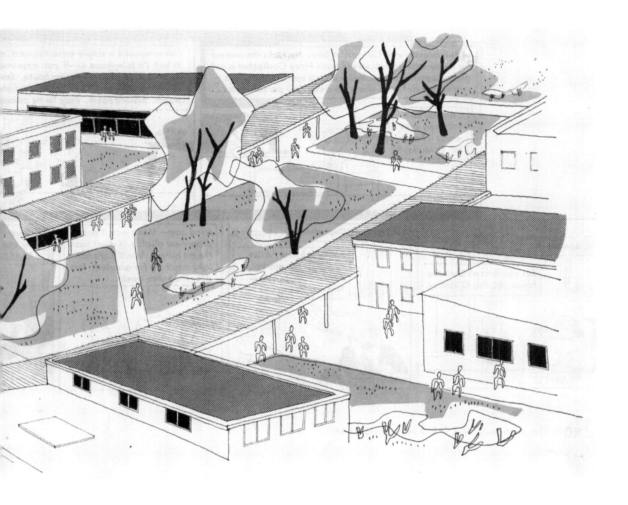

to reconcile the car with the older city fabric. Both proposals, however, remained within a curbside model; that is, they were quantitative propositions for improving automotive access, not new conceptions of city organization. In 1946, Welch took a different tack and focused on "constructive decentralization." In this model of urban expansion, new "outpost" shopping centers would offer "recentralized" places based on the separation of pedestrians and automotive traffic that he had studied in his earlier downtown work. In a 1946 *Planning and Civic Comment* and, a few months later, in *Women's Wear Daily,* Welch wrote that the new shopping center would be on a "pedestrianway" and "sheltered from traffic and noise."

It has grass where main street was, and the pedestrians are not asked to walk from store to store in the open weather amidst a confusing and ugly architectural environment.

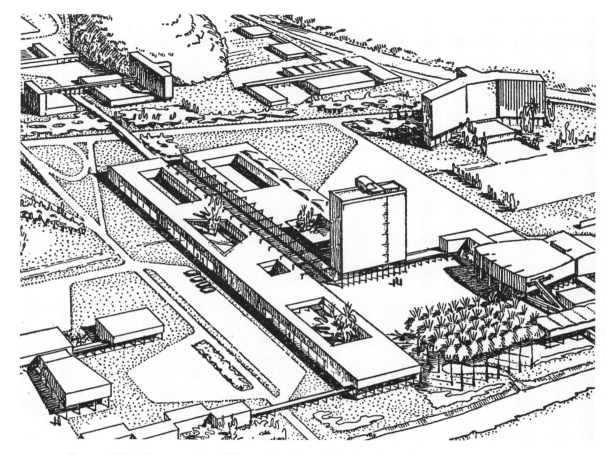

Figure 4.20. Wiener and Sert, "Motor City" (Brazil), in Morris Ketchum Jr., *Shops and Stores* (New York: Reinhold, 1948), 282.

This covered walkway is not a long, strung-out affair; it is more a circle. Then, there is ample parking. . . . It surrounds the shops rather than being "behind them" and, in this way, the walking distance from parked car to covered space is kept at a minimum. Thought is given to the safety of the pedestrian shopper at all times. . . . The shopping pedestrian does not even see an automobile when they are being subjected to the display of merchandise.

Elsewhere he wrote:

The shopper, before she realizes it, is sauntering along a covered walkway with greenery on one side and a continuous merchandise display on the other. She has not dented a fender, she does not get a crick in her neck, and she can concentrate completely on the display of things she has come to see.[81]

This soft-focus and highly orchestrated image of grass, trees, planting, and merchandising used a different kind of shopping imagery from the urban propositions Welch had previously discussed. The shopping center of the future was to be a grassed-over Main Street, perhaps borrowing the terms from *Architectural Forum,* and the organization was not to be linear but circular (predating Gruen). The organization and form were determined by the combination of shortened walking distances and the desire to alter the shopping experience. In other words, in a controlled orchestration of programs, the car was now invisible, access to goods was unfettered, and the environment of shopping was no longer the bothersome downtown. Aside from Welch's knowledge of the changing field of merchandising work, the reason for the new project was, perhaps, that Welch was moving into new terrain elsewhere. The *Women's Wear Daily* article described Welch as a consultant for a shopping center investment group called Suburban Centers Trust (SCT). Welch was expanding his repertoire to new locations.

As Rye's Main Street planting plan was headed to defeat, Ketchum, Welch, and Adams were working together on a project with almost the exact same pedestrianized site plan but proposed de novo in the suburbs: what was soon called a "regional shopping center." The regional center was conceived at a scale far larger than that of earlier branch stores or new districts.[82] Chief among the investors in these new projects were insurance companies and investment trusts returning to real estate after having moved the bulk of their assets into government bonds during the Depression. With underperforming retail outlets in the city, large investors looked for new ways to profit from what *Fortune* called the "lush new suburban market."[83]

A trendsetter in the expansion of the investment landscape called the Conant Real Estate Trust was formed in Boston in mid-1946. The trust was formed by a portfolio of other trusts, estates, and insurance companies to map out "a safe way to diversify holdings of downtown retail properties . . . for the right kind of suburban investments" and to "plan, build and provide equity financing" for a chain of shopping centers.[84] The trust was managed by Boston-based businessmen and led by William Coolidge, founder in 1940 of the National Research Corporation (NRC). The NRC financed and patented a commercially viable vacuum process used during World War II to produce penicillin. After the war, the company turned its expertise to consumer goods, in this case, to the production of freeze-dried coffee, television screen surfaces, and concentrated orange juice (the latter becoming the famous Minute Maid brand).[85] It is not surprising that a company whose products have come to epitomize the postwar rationalization of mass consumption would also engage in the mass-distribution apparatus of the suburban shopping center. Emblematic of the trust's catalytic role were the names of its chief operating subsidiaries, Retail Recentralization, Inc. (RRI), and National Suburban Centers, Inc. (NSC), the latter headed by well-known business promoter and investor Huston Rawls.[86] Not only was the new suburban landscape to be populated by dispersed shopping nodes, but also each node was to be understood as a singular, designed locus of activity.

The trust, operating through RRI, mapped out new regional markets with the assistance of Ken Welch, who conducted extensive studies throughout the northeastern United States of income, demography, time-distance measurements, site planning, and store design.[87] The location for the proposed Beverly Center showed the importance of automotive access and the role of the highway in reorganizing social life outside the city. Located eighteen miles north of Boston at an intersection of several major roads and the soon-to-be-finished circumferential Route 128, the new center would embrace a new "100 percent location" now defined by the car and truck. Anchored by Boston retailer Jordan Marsh, the center would be a node in a dispersed metropolis that included the core and its periphery.[88] In 1946, Welch and the developers put together a team of advisers for the new shopping center that included Ketchum, MIT dean William Wurster, Adams, and landscape architects Thomas Church (who was also working with Eero Saarinen on the early phases of the GM Technical Center) and the father-and-son team of Arthur and Sidney Shurcliff (the father having worked on parts of the Colonial Williamsburg restoration).[89]

The 1947 schematic Beverly renderings showed a large green precinct surrounded by parking (Figure 4.21).[90] One access road from the highway ran directly under the shopping center, as if the shopping center were a megastructure plugging into the transportation system. The single, saucer-shaped, department store was set off from the complex, creating an iconic, identifiable object at the scale of the moving car. Two one-story buildings shaped the "greenway" of the project—almost one thousand feet long. At the opposite end of the complex from the round department store were buildings described as a professional office building, a recreational facility, a theater, and an exhibition hall; these all created an open plaza with a "lake." The composition of the project, and especially its "civic" end, greatly resembled Nelson's and Saarinen's town center proposals of 1943, and the assemblage of social functions underscored the premise that the new modern center would function as a "recentralized development"—that is, a piece of the city—not merely as a shopping center.[91]

Ketchum's renderings of the Beverly proposal give a clear sense of the modernist organizational and formal affiliation (Figure 4.22). Under a long roof, the glass-paneled wall was continuous and interspersed by an occasional masonry or wood panel. Treated in the same plastic terms as Ketchum's Kawneer catalog work of 1944 and 1945, the two-story external perimeter of the store building was made of recesses, projections, and floating planes, and the impression of continuous space that characterized the work for individual store design was now expanded along the large building length. The one-story interior perimeter was also fully glazed and arcaded with a cantilevered extension of the roof. The project's exhibit hall and recreational buildings also demonstrated a modernist formal vocabulary: abstract, pared-down, panelized structures with deep cantilevered overhangs and glazed corners. One view of the greenway (Figure 4.23) showed an arcade bordering a serene open space, setting off the cantilevered seating block of a theater in the distance—the rendering and project could have come from any CIAM project. Another view of the exhibit hall (Figure 4.24) facing onto the reflecting pool could be mistaken for a modernist institutional design were it not for the prominently featured "home makers show"

Figure 4.21. Ketchum, Gina, and Sharp, "Beverly Shopping Center, Boston, Massachusetts," *Architectural Forum* 86 (June 1947): 84.

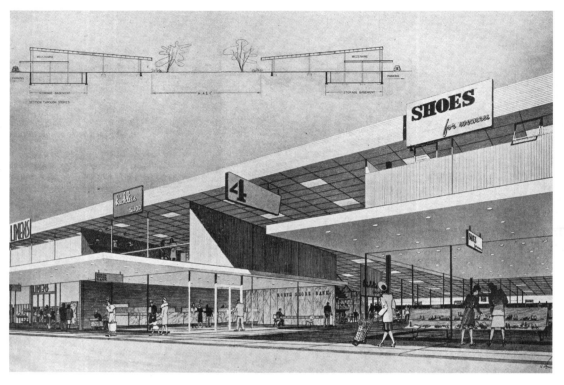

Figure 4.22. Ketchum, Gina, and Sharp, "Beverly Shopping Center, Boston, Massachusetts," *Architectural Forum* 86 (June 1947): 85.

sign—and the preponderance of women in most of the renderings. Beyond the modernist formal language that was, in the United States, already the norm, the larger planning and research of the shopping center also constituted a demonstration of a rational planning exercise, a modern undertaking, now directly in the employ of consumer capital.

But merchandising outside the city faced a variety of new obstacles. Another version of the center was split into two complexes—one commercial and one civic—most likely to avoid the need to excavate for a new road. Worse, however, and representative of the uncharted financial territory of the new suburban locations, title problems with the land and delays in the construction of Route 128 forced the developers to drop the Beverly project altogether and seek another location with another design. Operating through the SCT subsidiary, with Equitable Insurance as a major investor, the trust announced plans for a new center in Framingham, then called Middlesex Center.[92]

In 1948, the SCT published a new set of plans that internalized and reorganized the features of Beverly, and a version of the project was built (Figure 4.25). Instead of two retail stories facing parking and one arcaded story facing the grass mall, the

Figure 4.23. Ketchum, Gina, and Sharp, "Beverly Shopping Center, Boston, Massachusetts," *Architectural Forum* 86 (June 1947): 86.

new design flipped the section and put more of the merchandising face to the interior. A building of two stories now faced a smaller pedestrian mall, which was crossed at the upper level by three bridges. Further indication of an inward turn was the location of the sunken service areas immediately surrounding the building blocks and facing the parking, no doubt a cheaper solution than a tunnel. Ironically, this created a moat, requiring a bridge to enter the complex. The entire outside perimeter of the project facing the cars became the "back." This was a distinct shift from the double-faced store idea that had been part of the discussion—as at Rye and Beverly (although the double-entry store would still be used elsewhere, as at I. M. Pei's Roosevelt Field, which opened in 1955). The built "Shoppers' World" opened in 1951 and entailed a tighter but by no means intimate "midway"—measuring seventy-five by one thousand feet—less reminiscent of a bucolic landscape than of an urban park with vaguely naturalistic design effects.[93] Heightening the differences between the two versions of the project, the former turned outward and the latter inward, *Forum* editors called the new mall a "double-decked Main Street."[94] In broader terms, the Rye project and the Beverly/Framingham projects demonstrated a modernist architectural undertaking, both in expression and in planning, although their link to the pedestrian-citizen was slowly fading.

Pedestrian Priorities

In 1945, before his hotel work took off, Morris Lapidus described a "utopian" shopping center at the heart of the city (Figure 4.26). Alongside an image of the now-standard "tired" Main Street was a depiction of a superblock-scaled commercial

Figure 4.24. Ketchum, Gina, and Sharp, "Beverly Shopping Center, Boston, Massachusetts," *Architectural Forum* 86 (June 1947): 88.

district skewed from the urban grid, with a variety of large and small stores, parking and store servicing below grade, and landscape elements such as trees and paved courts, a pool, and children's play area, all held together by a continuous arcade. Lapidus waxed poetic:

> Some day perhaps, Main Street as we know it today, meandering across the continent, will disappear and its place will be taken by Shopping Centers which will be designed

to be just that—places to drive up to, park your car without any headaches, shop the various stores leisurely and under cover, with plenty of space for the children to play, and in general have all those amenities to which the planners of the future look forward. This Utopian arrangement is still a long way off.[95]

Car-free, planted shopping precincts based on the figure and meaning of the pedestrian were not as utopian as Lapidus put it. Nelson, Gruen, Ketchum, Welch,

Figure 4.25. Ketchum, Gina, and Sharp, "Middlesex Center, Framingham, Massachusetts," *Architectural Forum* 90 (March 1949): 124.

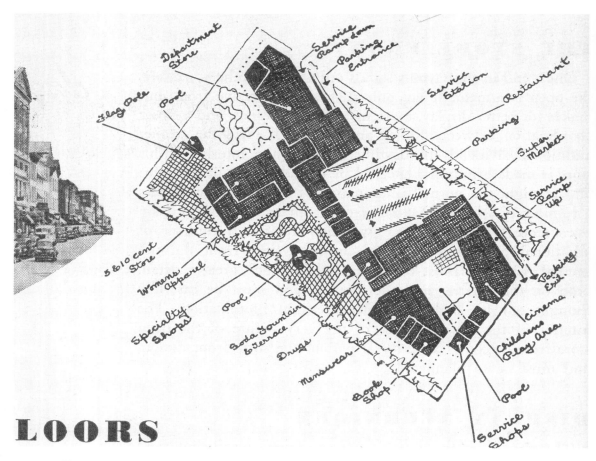

Figure 4.26. Morris Lapidus, shopping center plan, in "The Retail Store and Its Design Problems," Building Types Study No. 98: Shopping Terminals and Stores, *Architectural Record* 97 (February 1945): 96.

and many others across the 1940s worked out the parameters of the pedestrian precinct by drawing from and interpreting various threads of modernist planning and design theory. Quite simply, pedestrianization was, as Lewis Mumford later wrote, "an opportunity for architecture."[96] Moving beyond the curbside paradigm—an almost axiomatic reliance on the street—they saw their commercial work as one part of an expanding modernist practice. Distinctions between commerce and planning were not erased but were instead understood as complementary. Planned pedestrian precincts, like units and superblocks, were understood as modern architectural strategies, and through their use and representation, any discomfort with consumption could be subsumed within professionalized planning and urban design—almost.

FIVE

THE COLD WAR PEDESTRIAN

> Every slum clearance project, housing development, industrial plant,
> traffic artery or other public improvement should be scanned with a view
> to the military as well as the civic aspects of dispersal. This will not be
> difficult, since the basic criteria controlling each approach point so nearly
> in the same direction.
>
> —HAROLD HAUF, "City Planning and Civil Defense,"
> *Architectural Record*, 1950

IN THE UNITED STATES, after the atomic bomb was used on Hiroshima, widely circulated images of urban devastation elicited intense reactions and dire predictions and, as images are wont to be, were fully instrumentalized: deeply etched historical settlement patterns came into question and norms of professional practice were challenged. The bomb and its many representations altered the terms by which many Americans understood their cities. A *Saturday Evening Post* article of 1946 titled "Your Flesh Should Creep" concluded that atomic weaponry might impel the United States to dispense with the Constitution and forcibly abandon cities for the safety of the countryside. Physicist (and polemicist) Edward Teller warned in the *Bulletin of the Atomic Scientists* that big cities were "deathtraps."[1] Architect Ludwig Hilberseimer wrote that the concentrated city—in peace or war—had become obsolete, so "security, once provided behind walls, can only be found in the dispersion of cities and industries." In 1949, he sounded an even more chilling alarm: "City concentration can only be a preparation for man's suicide." From *Life* magazine to

Progressive Architecture, the threat of conflagration deeply affected debates about urban policy, building, and the very concept of the city.[2]

In the early Cold War years, urban dispersal, decentralization, and recentralization suffused professional discussion about the role and design of cities. At the same time, the place of this discourse in the making of buildings, plans, and policies is difficult to identify clearly. The power of atomic fear integral to Cold War tensions is undeniable: from Hiroshima to George Keenan's 1946 "long telegram" to the 1949 Russian nuclear test, to the McCarthy hearings and the Korean War, among many other links of a taut chain, a culture mobilized by fear suffused American professional (and popular) culture. However, given that they were everywhere, the effects of what historian Guy Oakes calls the atomic "imaginary" are difficult to render historically specific.[3] At the very least, a Cold War interpretation of settlement patterns and conceptions of urbanity added considerable legitimacy to arguments about historical patterns of suburbanization and decentralization, if it did not also give them additional weight. Dispersal advocate and planner Tracy Augur pointed out that dispersal was "good business" and good policy "anyway."[4]

Many planning and architecture professionals had long seen decentralization and suburbanization (in some forms) as a "healthy" process in which space, air, trees, and distance from neighbors were "normal" elements, and the bomb added another layer to this set of perceptions. Landscape architect Alfred Caldwell (an associate of Hilberseimer) combined pre- and postbomb discourse in 1945 when he called for a "ruralized" settlement pattern with a dispersed mix of agriculture, industry, and housing—not unlike the terms of Frank Lloyd Wright's Broadacre City—so an atomic attack would be fruitless and urbanites demoralized by congestion, revitalized. Atomic explosives would "undoubtedly" result in dispersal, wrote sociologist William Ogburn, but this had been "already under way" for some time. Clarence Stein in 1950 and planner Coleman Woodbury in 1952 both qualified the prefaces to their planning books, noting that defense added new urgency to a long-standing need for urban reorganization. Stein wrote that new defense concerns might finally initiate a "new era of nation-wide decentralization." Woodbury asserted that the growth patterns of industry matched the socioeconomic needs of the times. Dispersal, it seemed, was an answer to two forms of urban vision, one incremental and the other alarmist; "the bomb" left an indelible if also slightly unfocused mark in professional discussions of settlement units and urban organization.[5]

Dispersal discourse, or what Paul Edwards calls "closed world" discourse, enabled architects and planners to create a new subfield of work—they claimed (some said opportunistically) an expertise in survival.[6] In this role, principles of rational management integral to modernism were fruitfully if paradoxically joined with bomb-induced fears. The principle of a reorganized settlement unit system *inside and outside* the urban core confirmed that cities were newly dangerous, and an earlier language of the stability afforded by unit-based planning gained new weight in the professional imagination.

Morris Ketchum and Victor Gruen fruitfully navigated the dispersal discourse just before and after 1950. Each participated in various architectural and urban debates, organizations, and projects, the explicit and sometimes implicit logic of which used anxieties about the bomb to supplement an older language of prescribed units and delimited territories. In their work on shopping and large-scale design, Cold War tension was a key if also ambiguous touchstone. They both argued for far-reaching forms of design and control, and they claimed that modern architecture was best suited for such an enterprise; they participated in the civil defense culture that swept the architectural profession.

Architectures of Dispersal: Units, Satellites, Constellations

In 1946, John Hersey published *Hiroshima,* his famously dispassionate description of that city's destruction, and implicitly put the concept of the dense city into question. Hersey's narrative was among the earliest public representations of the devastating effects of the bomb, and among those professionals involved with planning and design, the fate of the city became a reasonable and logical question.[7] The concept of dispersal, the use of distance to ameliorate the effects of the bomb, placed a new item onto the agenda of the design professions: survivability. Political views on the world situation varied among the professionals, but specific design and planning prescriptions were now under scrutiny: How would the profession deal with the seemingly urgent need to break up cities, resettle populations, and move industry away from major urban centers in the crosshairs of Soviet bombers? In fact, dispersal proponents such as physicist Ralph Lapp mimicked the language of Hersey to drive home the point of the bomb's potential, but he also pointed out that planning could prevent disaster. The atomic bomb, he wrote, "is a truly powerful weapon; we do not wish to imply that it is not. On the other hand, it does . . . only *finite* damage and this fact must be appreciated."[8] "Life as we know it," he wrote, was possible only with a new type of city based on dispersed and separated services, industry, and settlements, all safe from the worst effects of the bomb.

Widespread dispersal discourse created a convincing context for policy thinking. Tracy Augur, who had carried the torch of the Regional Plan Association since the late 1930s, was among the strongest proponents of dispersal. He argued in 1946 that the dense industrial city was obsolete and offered an "inviting target" to enemy bombers, so a "dispersed pattern of small efficient cities" would improve the nation's security. He asserted that these "satellite" communities "clustered" around the older core but separated from it and from each other by "wide belts of open land" would also improve the quality of life and, he noted, in a revealing comment on the perceived state of the city, reduce the social unrest born of urban slums.[9] Echoing this position, architect Burnham Kelly wrote that space is a key defense against atomic weapons as well as against congestion, the latter a "hazard to good normal living."[10]

The tone and substance of the arguments for dispersal were legitimated by the U.S. Congress's creation of the National Security Resources Board (NSRB) in 1947. The role of the NSRB was to ensure uninterrupted government and production operations through nationally scaled planning and management. Augur became an NSRB planner in 1949. In 1951, the NSRB released a booklet titled *Is Your Plant a Target?*, which described the new "Industrial Dispersion Policy" as the "selective dispersal" and "strategic location" of key industries distant from each other as well as from central cities but all linked by communications, highways, and rail lines. In 1952, the Department of Commerce published the *Industrial Dispersion Guidebook for Communities* for the NSRB, the Office of Defense Mobilization, and the Defense Production Administration. This pamphlet—a how-to manual for surveying and identifying vulnerable target areas in cities—like most of the dispersal literature, identified a circular no-build zone (usually a ten-mile radius) and solidified the perceived danger of congested urban-industrial cores (Figure 5.1).[11] Amplifying this mode of thinking, *Business Week* noted a trend toward "garden-type" or suburban office buildings in the early 1950s, with Connecticut General Life Insurance Company scoping out suburban locations as early as 1952.[12] As the functions and institutions of urban social life continued their prewar migration to the periphery with an urgent sense of mission, the lineaments and language of the dispersed city took shape.

The American Institute of Architects (AIA) took a predictably strong interest in debates about the dispersed metropolis, especially with the escalation of global tensions in 1950. Mirroring broader debates, many members argued that there was "no defense" against a nuclear bombardment and that international regulations and diplomacy were desperately needed. Others argued that professionalism demanded action, and many architects participated in various ways in design and planning efforts.[13] The expertise of the architect was called for, ran the argument, and regionalized and decentralized systems of settlement, production, and movement would be the best defense against the bomb, and, in peace, would create a better social life. Space was a weapon and a much-needed medicine. At the May 1950 annual meeting of the AIA, Regional Plan Association president Paul Windels argued strongly for the breaking up of the city for security and long-term health. He called for the organized decentralization and redesign of extant cities with lower-density "separated" neighborhoods, each with "its own interior street layout . . . as though each were . . . a separate village." In his view, and using a term that was widely repeated, greenbelts could also be "firebreaks" in older cities and between new towns.[14] In August, AIA president Ralph Walker announced the formation of the institute's National Defense Committee, headed by past president Douglas Orr, to study how architects might contribute to security and dispersal plans.[15] In October, the committee issued

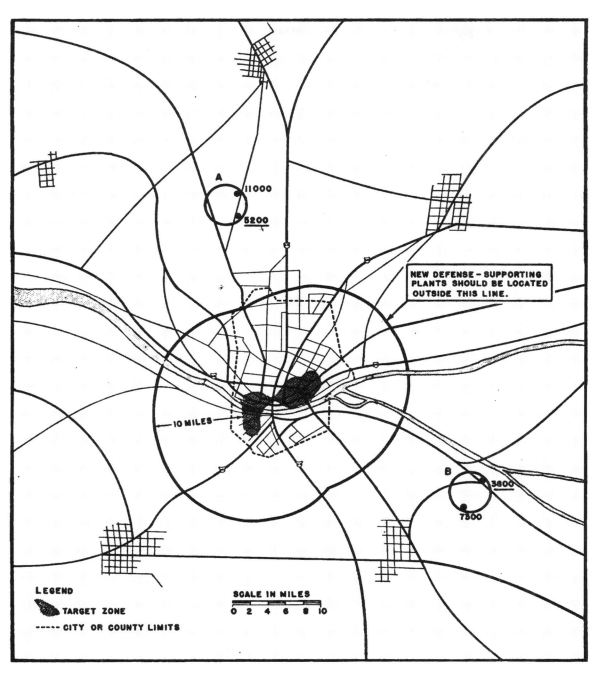

Figure 5.1. "The Outline of the Potential A-Bomb Target Zone," in U.S. Department of Commerce, Area Development Division, *Industrial Dispersion Guidebook for Communities* (Washington, D.C.: Government Printing Office, 1952), 11.

a call for a "comprehensive survey" of the profession to equip the AIA in aiding the looming defense efforts. The AIA was mobilizing, looking for work, asserting the central role of the architect, and the opened-up and dispersed city of units, parts, and precincts was the strategic representation of the designers' arsenal.[16]

The January 1951 issue of the *Journal of the American Institute of Architects* took up newly urgent defense and settlement questions. Coming on the heels of President Truman's declaration of a national emergency, the issue was titled "New Towns for American Defense," and the editorial introduction was signed by the AIA's National Defense Committee. Central to the committee's position was that older cities were now "inviting" targets and that "city patterns must now be guided by defense considerations."[17] Yet the introduction, titled "Long-Run, Short-Run," advocated a more pragmatic, dual strategy in which dispersal plans and funding might come from "existing" programs; in other words, the embrace of dispersal was not quite as radical as it might have seemed. For example, Harvard planner William Wheaton stated that "defense gives a new urgency to an already urgent peacetime need." Architect Albert Mayer, head of the AIA Urban Design Committee, noted that "self-containment in smaller concentrations" would offer "psychological and physical haven," but these dispersed patterns had long been needed to address the congested city.[18] Architect G. Holmes Perkins referred to the emerging military situation, but the bulk of his article described the role of the new town and a "galaxy of new towns" as a necessary result of congestion and unplanned expansion. Elsewhere, Catherine Bauer wrote that "self-sufficient communities with open space between" needed to be introduced and central areas "thinned out and larger open spaces introduced," all of which would not cost much since such changes were already under way.[19] At one of the pinnacles of Cold War tension just after 1950, the AIA's rhetoric of short- and long-term necessity affirmed the rethinking and reclassification of metropolitan territory.

Remade urban regions were described in professional circles as a system of dispersed nodes and dispersed centers of population and industry. The featured design work in the 1951 *Journal of the AIA* consisted of new town studies based on modernist tenets of rationalized planning and organization (yet also with distinct threads back to Clarence Perry) linking modernism to dispersal. Conducted by Harvard students between 1946 and 1949 under Walter Gropius, Martin Wagner, G. Holmes Perkins, John Harkness, Marcel Breuer, and William Wheaton, the work was the application to the urban periphery of precisely defined neighborhood units (Figure 5.2). The Harvard studies demonstrated the use of units in various iterations, but the larger principle of defense through precincts and satellites was evident. The modern metropolis—in peace or war—could be redefined as a collection of semiautonomous community units in the "countryside," supported by community centers—and shopping centers—enabling both survivability and a healthier way of life.[20]

Figure 5.2. "Detail of One Neighborhood, Showing School, Shopping Center, and Industry,"
in G. Holmes Perkins and Roger L. Creighton, "The Harvard Studies: The Design of New
Towns," *Journal of the American Institute of Architects* 15 (January 1951): 27.

The May 1951 AIA convention in Chicago was largely taken up with civil defense
issues, and the preceding months were full of debates and official resolutions under-
lining the organization's vision of a dispersed city made of settlement units, regionalized smaller cities, or new towns.[21] The organization established the Subcommittee
on Civil Defense, which was headed by AIA New York chapter president Harry
Prince, under whose supervision the AIA published the 1951 *Civil Defense: The
Architect's Part,* an informational report normalizing the architect's participation in
the postbomb planning and emergency procedures—from advising government to
exploring new construction techniques.[22] Alongside consideration of shelter types,
constructional and structural changes, material controls, and evacuation training,
the authors of *Civil Defense* endorsed the ongoing process of decentralization and
specifically called for the creation of "reception areas" for evacuees and the "breaking
up of obsolescent or congested city areas" and "fire-trap slums" with green or safety
zones to reduce dangerous urban density.[23] The language of de-densification, units,
and decentralization dominated the professional debates with new Cold War vigor.

Based on the discussions of the summer 1951 AIA meeting, a *Progressive Architecture* special issue titled "Pros and Cons of Architecture for Civil Defense" reexamined the architect's role in civil defense issues. The magazine published details about bomb shelters, bomb-resistant structures, and dispersal policies, in each case using the AIA convention texts or soliciting additional expert opinion.[24] While some, including editor Thomas Creighton, found "opportunistic" any planning to "survive" the bomb, and other contributors advocated political paths to peace, most took the position that it would be irresponsible not to be "prepared"—that is, to explore ways to mitigate the effects of an atomic attack.[25] And no matter where they stood on the larger political questions, most contributors envisioned a regionalized metropolis in which the older city as well as the periphery would house smaller, broken-up parcels linked by greenbelts and road systems. There was some disagreement between those who sought more fully autonomous satellite cities without a center (Clarence Stein, referring to MacKaye and Mumford's "townless highway") and those who sought an integrated or "constellated" region that included the central city (Jaqueline Tyrwhitt), but underlying the prescriptions was a dispersed articulation of sub-urban parts or units.[26] For most, the future of the city lay in variegated dispersal: a network of nodes, satellite cities, new towns, and old cities or production centers could constitute parts of the expanded, less dense, urban complex—an atomized and fully planned city-region.[27]

Coming as they did during the heated debates about housing and urban redevelopment laws in Congress—not to mention political "witch hunts" and loyalty oaths—the nuclear-fueled representations of clearance, slums, firebreaks, nodes, satellites, and new centers aided the centrifugal forces of the atomic imaginary. The fears and anxieties about nuclear destruction added yet another layer onto historic patterns of decentralization, aided in no small part by simmering racial conflicts and legislative battles, and helped steer capital in particular ways inside and outside most midcentury American cities. Concerns about the bomb also provided a mantle of patriotism and an image of action to strategies for parceling urban regions—that is, for safety and real estate development.

Architect as Good Citizen: Project East River

Morris Ketchum joined the AIA in 1942 and was deeply enmeshed in the professional apparatus as it went into high gear with the hostilities in Korea. In 1950, Ketchum chaired the New York AIA chapter's Committee on Civil Defense, chaired the Civil Defense Committee of the New York State Council of Architects, and was a vice president of the New York State Civil Defense Commission's subcommittee on building safety.[28] In 1951, he attended the Chicago AIA meeting and soon became head of the AIA's National Defense Committee.[29] Real and imagined, the nuclear threat created a vast network of organizations focused on the remaking of the city, and Ketchum placed himself deeply within these discussions.

Ketchum took a pragmatic, realpolitik position with respect to the need to protect cities and rethink American settlement patterns.[30] Like many of the professionals engaged with the institutions of building and planning, he pursued strategies incorporating extant planning and design tools with new needs. At the 1950 AIA convention and in the 1951 *Progressive Architecture* "Civil Defense" issue, Ketchum argued for small, "dual purpose . . . group [bomb] shelters" instead of massive shelters as others had proposed. For New York City, this meant that new shelters would be designed as part of an expanded subway system: "Small and decentralized" he wrote, "the subway shelter could become the core of future system expansion," such as the Second Avenue subway.[31] The "dual-use" position added a civil defense tenet to already proposed urban projects, but it just as often aroused suspicions of backdoor funding expediency. However, the need to provide protection in "critical [urban] target areas" was only half the problem presented by the bomb.

Ketchum also participated in the discourse of dispersal at the regional scale and wrote that cities needed to be "reorganized" and broken up into "dispersed fragments" through the redirection of existing programs. Echoing government and professional analyses, he advocated the "strategic decentralization of industry and population" into "compartmented . . . communities." Ketchum also sought to enlist *Architectural Forum* in the dispersal debates, trying to get editor Douglas Haskell to publish the AIA's positions on the civil defense issues.[32] Ketchum's attitude toward a remade city and his role in circulating the details and images of such a city are fully demonstrated in the small part he played in the famed Project East River.

Project East River (PER) was part of the Truman administration's attempts to control the effects on the home front of the perceived threat of nuclear destruction. The project was guided by a variety of engineers, social scientists, planners, architects, and bankers and was sponsored by a consortium of universities, all directed by Otto Nelson, a former general and a vice president of New York Life, which was then investing heavily in housing and stores.[33] While much of the report produced by PER focused on early warning systems and defense "in depth," the central tenet of the report's representation of cities was the problem of "vulnerability." The ten volumes of the report, released in 1952 and 1953, contained dire language alongside a rhetoric of science to bolster the claim that civil defense, like military defense, was immediately necessary and feasible. From among a thicket of observations, analyses, stipulations, and classifications, the report made sweeping land-use, administrative, and policy recommendations for all levels of government and commerce.

Several sections of the PER report related to the specifics of nuclear-inflected settlement patterns. Two subsections on the "reduction of urban vulnerability" were central in strengthening the logic of dispersal: William Wheaton wrote on reduced building density and "spacing," and Coleman Woodbury wrote on the problem of industrial "concentration." Both offered defense-derived proximity and adjacency requirements for viable dispersal. Wheaton noted that selective decentralization and satellites had been "long recommended by professional city planners" but that defense needs made explicit the autonomy and interdependence of regional nodes, any part of which was now subject to sudden destruction. His discussion of improved labor accessibility in a new landscape of highways and "sub-satellites" showed that distance from the core would not encumber development.[34]

Dispersal was made clear by the PER report in a concentric-ring map of a typical city diagrammed according to "degrees" of vulnerability. The layout of "vulnerable urban districts" (VUDs) was divided into Class I and Class II sectors (Figure 5.3), the former being the most congested, dense, industrial, and built-up and the most threatened by an atomic attack. For each sector, "density and dispersion standards" were established, and the general point was that the Class I districts needed immediate decongestion, even if partial. The key qualification to land use was that lot coverage needed to be reduced and "combustible roof coverings" banned. Lot coverage (floor area ratio) diagrams aimed at producing safe "open areas" around buildings and throughout threatened districts foreshadowed modernist urban ideas of buildings set in space, but here the logic was quite pointed: open spaces could act as firebreaks as well as parks; that is, the older city of dense blocks was no longer viable.[35]

PER carried out a "selected area study" of a "typical" older core to evaluate it against new vulnerability standards. Working under the establishment firm of Voorhees, Walker, Foley and Smith (Ralph Walker was then president of the AIA), the PER team examined simulated bombing damage in an east Midtown neighborhood of Manhattan whose density was, like that of many industrial cities, far in excess of standards that would reduce target vulnerability. Clearing much of the area was explicitly part of a "safety" program—as well as a strategy for some of the report sponsors to exploit a neighborhood ripe for development.[36] The PER report, like much of the dispersal literature, redefined urban elements such as streets, blocks, parks, boulevards, and greenbelts as part of nuclear-based techniques for breaking up the city in order to save it. The report and the areas study accomplished two things with respect to the design of cities: they reinforced existing decentralization trends, and they put the stamp of federal sanction on a policy framework that emphasized the breaking up of older urban settlements into clear and developable units. A metropolitan pattern of widely spaced communities around a core made of semi-isolated parts became standard language.

As head of the AIA Civil Defense Subcommittee, Morris Ketchum wrote a summary of PER findings for the *Bulletin of the AIA* in 1953 in which he described the new policies for cities as both new and old. In fact, the most "encouraging" aspect

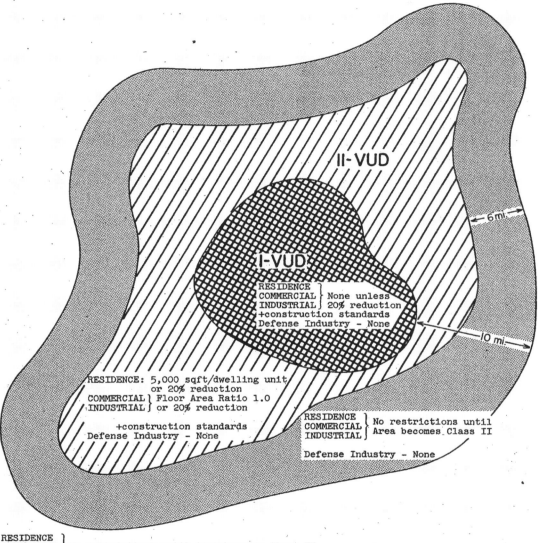

SCHEMATIC SUMMARY
OF URBAN DEFENSE STANDARDS
TO BE APPLIED TO NEW CONSTRUCTION IN WHICH THE FEDERAL GOVERNMENT HAS SOME INTEREST.

II-VUD

6mi.

1-VUD

RESIDENCE
COMMERCIAL } None unless
INDUSTRIAL } 20% reduction
+construction standards
Defense Industry - None

10 mi.

RESIDENCE: 5,000 sqft/dwelling unit
or 20% reduction
COMMERCIAL } Floor Area Ratio 1.0
INDUSTRIAL } or 20% reduction

+construction standards
Defense Industry - None

RESIDENCE
COMMERCIAL } No restrictions until
INDUSTRIAL } Area becomes Class II

Defense Industry - None

RESIDENCE
COMMERCIAL } No restrictions until Area becomes Class II
INDUSTRIAL

Defense Industry - allowed, until Area comes within 6 miles of
Class II or 10 miles of Class I.

Figure 5.3. "Schematic Summary of Urban Defense Standards," in Morris Ketchum, "Vulnerable Urban Districts, Civil and Industrial Defense: A Special Summary Report," *Bulletin of the AIA* 7 (March–April 1953): 37. Reprinted with permission from the American Institute of Architects, 1735 New York Avenue NW, Washington, D.C.

of the report, he wrote, was that none of the recommendations was new and all followed "well established contemporary trends." This is not to say that the PER report
did not raise serious land-use control issues—most notably the age-old American tension between home rule and regional or federal control—but it presumed the historical logic of breaking up the city. New, however, was the extent of risk. In his article,
Ketchum discussed the "vulnerable urban districts" of the PER report. He went on
to note, as an element of professional pride, that the 1952 AIA convention had offi-
cially adopted a similar agenda for reducing urban vulnerability, including calling
for firebreaks and new parks in cities as well as reduced densities for new construction and industrial and residential decentralization. Later that year, Ketchum introduced an AIA-sponsored case study on the industrial dispersal needs of Baltimore,
and at the 1953 AIA convention, he introduced a speaker on dispersal from the Federal Civil Defense Administration.[37] Project East River demonstrated the breadth
and depth of the professional machinery working to normalize the regionalized
metropolis of prescribed units, and Ketchum was a key participant in the circulation of images, information, and planning strategies concerning this new settlement
pattern. The "vulnerable urban districts" represented another rhetorical blow in the
move toward breaking the older city into a polynucleated metropolis, and Ketchum
was at the center of the action, writing about dispersal techniques as well as building
new shopping centers (see chapter 4) inside and outside the city.

Shopping Center as Wartime Tactic

In December 1950, *Life* magazine published "How U.S. Cities Can Prepare for
Atomic War," an article describing a regionalized, "bombproof" settlement pattern
suggested by MIT cybernetics founder Norbert Wiener and two colleagues. In strong
text and even stronger images—typical of the alarmist representations of Cold War
rhetorics—the magazine described how Wiener loosely applied to the metropolis the
systems and feedback ideas he had been developing (Figure 5.4). The plan involved
the selective dispersal and regional linkage of key elements of urban social and economic infrastructure. In the proposed reorganization, radiating roads provided routes
out of the targeted core and connected to a "life belt" system consisting of a circumferential highway ten miles out and a circumferential rail line fifteen miles out. A
system of such belts would bypass central cities, remove choke points of movement,
and seamlessly connect to the region and the nation. Hospitals, factories, shopping
centers, and warehouses—the social infrastructure—were located at the belt intersections and provided emergency destinations. With existing circulatory bottlenecks
near cities removed and urban functions dispersed throughout a regionalized, national
system, "no single point in the network would be worth the price of an A-bomb."[38]
The plan, *Life* optimistically reported, would bolster civilian defense and in peace it
would "accelerate the current trend" of urbanites moving to the suburbs and relieve

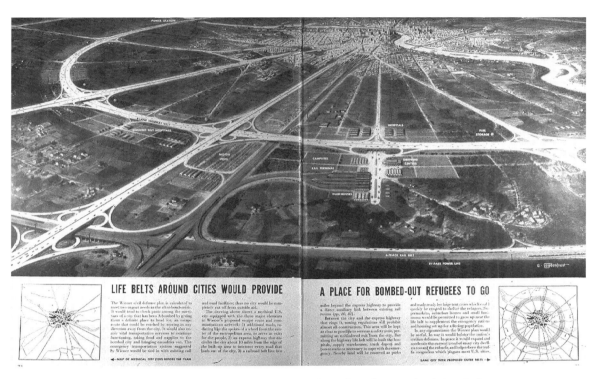

Figure 5.4. "Life Belts around Cities Would Provide a Place for Bombed-Out Refugees to Go," from "How U.S. Cities Can Prepare for Atomic War," *Life,* December 18, 1950, 78–79.

the traffic congestion plaguing American cities.[39] Thus Wiener endorsed the "dual-use" conception of urban elements, linking old needs with new conditions. And the clarity of the diagram and its presentation in the magazine made the urgency seem real.

At about the same time *Life* put its stamp of approval on dispersal, Victor Gruen spoke at the annual meeting of the National Retail Dry Goods Association (NRDGA), held in New York City, and told his audience that the future of retailing lay outside the city center in planned shopping centers. This was certainly not news to members of the NRDGA, who were well aware of and worried about the implications of the middle-class shift to the suburbs, but Gruen probably did shock some audience members out of their conference-chair naps when he concluded that civil defense was no small part of his thinking about shopping centers. In these times of "international unrest," he declared, the

> correctly planned regional shopping center could become the backbone of our civilian defense set-up, by providing fireproof buildings, basements, subterranean tunnels that can in emergencies provide air raid shelters, and emergency shelters; by providing all

human needs they will cut driving distance from residential areas and thus preserve gas, oil and cars, by providing medical buildings that can become first aid stations, by offering assembly rooms, auditorium club rooms, that become meeting places for defense committees, etc.[40]

Connecting the suburban shopping center to fears of nuclear destruction was both canny and a reasonable reading of the tenor of the times. The Soviets had tested a nuclear device in August 1949, and just a few days before the NRDGA meeting President Truman had responded to tensions in Korea by declaring a national emergency. Since a metropolitan region of semiautonomous settlements was increasingly the focus of planning efforts and discussion, it does not stretch credulity to imagine a planned shopping facility as part of the discourse of urban destruction.

At the "Architecture of Civil Defense" panel at the AIA convention in May 1951, a few months after his speech to the NRDGA, Gruen again described the shopping center as a key element of a defense strategy. His proposed Eastland Shopping Center for the Hudson Company would serve as an ideal "dual-purpose" project, serving peace- *and* wartime needs, and he focused most of his presentation on the latter.[41] He listed the qualifications for defense: built outside the core of a targeted industrial area, on a large site separated from adjacent residential communities, of fire-resistant materials and with space enough for storage and refuge, and—no small political advantage—built with private capital. He also made sure to point out that the AIA and other planning organizations had explicitly recommended dispersal as a defense strategy. In addition, Gruen circulated a booklet titled *Regional Shopping Centers and Civilian Defense,* which showed that after an atomic attack on the city, the shopping center could provide refuge for fleeing citizens and an emergency headquarters for rescue efforts. "If, against all of our hopes, peace should be interrupted," he wrote, "these centers will become one of the most important devices to safeguard the lives and morale of the civilian population." Suburban shopping centers would be massive "group shelters" with their own electrical and heating plants, bomb-resistant concrete basements and tunnels, Red Cross and "Defense Committee" meeting rooms, and plenty of parking lot space for a "temporary tent city." Gruen's engineer, Edgardo Contini, added an official-sounding note to the report concluding that Eastland was technically and structurally able to operate as a "self-sufficient entity."[42] As a peacetime community center and a wartime settlement refuge built without government assistance, the shopping center, in Gruen's hands, became a compelling civic actor.[43]

Many of the elements and systems of Wiener's "life-belt city" were planned or in place in 1950, but the force and clarity of Wiener's diagrams were grist for Gruen's mill (Figure 5.5). Gruen had the temerity to lift images from the *Life* magazine article about Wiener's plan for his AIA presentation and booklet about his proposed

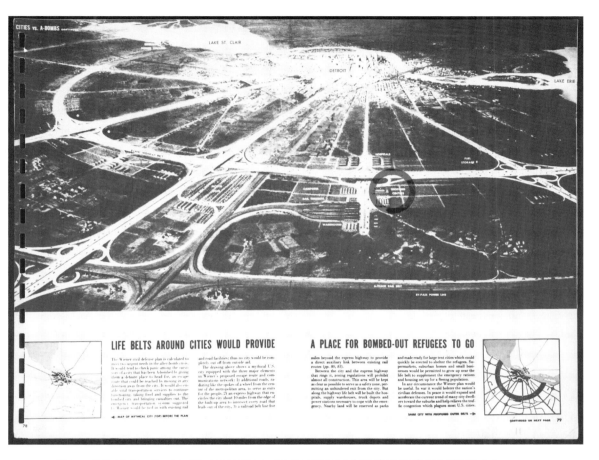

Figure 5.5. Victor Gruen, *Regional Shopping Centers and Civilian Defense* (1951), n.p. Library of Congress, Prints and Photographs Division.

Eastland. He cut and pasted, added Detroit's Lake St. Clair and other local land features, and, to drive home the point, circled the shopping center. Armed with this graphically powerful presentation, Gruen located his shopping center at the fulcrum of debate about the landscape of nuclear dispersal—as a key link in a newly rationalized and safe territory.

The civil defense logic for Hudson's Eastland Shopping Center reveals the enigmatic power of dispersal rhetoric and its intersection with historic processes of decentralization. During World War II, Hudson's hired the venerable Detroit architecture firm of Smith, Hinchman & Grylls to conduct studies for a downtown storage warehouse and affirmed the central-city model of social life, but wartime uncertainties put the project on hold.[44] The timing was auspicious and symptomatic of the weakening grip of central-city retailing. At about same time, Gruen (he later recalled) "cold-called" the company and made his first trip to Detroit, after which he developed a long-term strategy for a "ring" of Hudson's-owned regional shopping centers.[45] Hudson's was looking at ongoing demographic shifts, and local and national observers noted that with its new plans, the company had finally accepted that the periphery could not be ignored.[46] Just as likely, savvy Hudson's executives had studied the problem in depth, and in any case, their proposed ring of stores at the periphery of the city was a serious commitment to a regionalized shopping system, although, like many owners and merchants, they insisted that the suburban stores were to supplement, not replace, the main store. In fact, Hudson's executive Foster Winter was the director of the company's decentralization program—and Gruen's main contact—while at the same time he was proposing to demolish a Hudson's garage to build an even larger facility.[47] This was perhaps the last moment when such an ambivalence could be sustained, since the march to the periphery and the reshaping of the city were growing ever stronger.[48]

The Cold War tensions of 1950, however, cast doubt on proposals for "nonessential" new construction. The materials controls that loomed in the summer of 1950 put many senior-level business executives on high alert. The timing could not have been worse for Hudson's. The company intended to break ground for Eastland in late 1950 or early 1951, and Hudson's officials were worried about the prospect of having to apply to the National Production Authority for permission to construct their project. Thus they adopted a "dual" strategy for their publicity position. At a 1951 conference on war conditions and real estate valuations, Foster Winter spoke about the need for suburban shopping centers, and the *Detroit Free Press* real estate columnist, Henry H. Burdick, also claimed that regional shopping centers ought to qualify as "dual-purpose" facilities. After Winter's presentation, Burdick wrote that he was "impressed with the adaptability of the tunnels and basements as emergency bomb shelters." "This possible use," Winter said, "has interested the civil defense authorities."[49] The reframing of Eastland as a defense project was a creative if strained attempt at salvaging the project and symptomatic of the ways in which the discourse of dispersal entered into on-the-ground maneuvers of daily socioeconomic action. This was the kind of territory in which Gruen was unusually adept at navigating, but in this case Eastland was tabled by the Hudson Company by late spring because the National Production Authority was not convinced by the "dual-use" argument.[50]

Shopping Center as Social Place

The attempt to classify Eastland as an "essential" dual-use center is a revealing instance of the overlap between architectural discourse and the culture of the Cold War. Gruen's patriotic portrayal of the shopping center as urban node and refuge from nuclear attack fused his hopes for new public spaces, his penchant for publicity, and the marketing needs of an important client, and even the project's failure contributed to debates about urban reorganization—nuclear-fueled or otherwise.

Beyond the questions of vulnerability, Gruen's proposal that centers such as East-land serve as "crystallization points" in the regional landscape addressed long-standing perceptions of urban dysfunction and contemporary discussions about suburban social shortcomings. Typical suburbs lacked what Gruen and many observers of sub-urbs presumed was an appropriate cultural cohesion, so he characterized shopping centers with terms like "satellite downtown" and described them in civic terms through which they might satisfy the "primary human instinct to mingle."[51] In the newly dispersing region, new centers would offer points of recentralization. Eastland normalized the shopping center as part of a modern landscape now conceived as a field of new nodes, units, and better-organized social and cultural functions. The shopping center was a key point in the spreading out of the American landscape.

Alongside Eastland's role in the discourse of dispersal—the shopping center as a "good citizen"—the center's specific design and organization also offered an impor-tant lesson. The proposed design was overly concerned with parking, and the result would have been a congested mess.[52] Gruen's Eastland (Figure 5.6) did not fully sep-arate the car from the pedestrian as had been the emerging logic in shopping center design, to which Gruen himself had also contributed. Instead, the center's design

Figure 5.6. Gruen and Krummeck, Eastland Shopping Center, Detroit, Michigan, 1950, in Baker and Funaro, *Shopping Centers: Design and Operation*, 202–3.

appeared to derive from a traditional view of parking and shopping in which the distance from car to storefront was the singular qualification.[53] Eastland was, in other words, a throwback, a hyperbolic version of the curbside paradigm of store planning.

Eastland's design created neither a mall-like green nor piazza-like pedestrian space. The site plan was a ring composed of separate store buildings linked by inner-edge and outer-edge pedestrian colonnades and forming a vast, oval-shaped enclosure. Open spaces both outside and inside the ring of buildings were devoted to parking and lowered slightly in elevation so that the view from the car to the store was unimpeded. In addition, the center's access roads dipped in section so as not to interfere with pedestrian circulation through the colonnades. Thus these continuous inner and outer colonnades resembled nothing other than a diagram of arcaded storefronts facing onto a sidewalk and street with nearby parking: indeed, Gruen wrote, the goal was "to create a continuous, uninterrupted sidewalk."[54] Eastland was based on sidewalk model, but in this case the sidewalk was doubled to face two directions and, finally, curled into a loop. Gruen's 1950 Olympic Shopping Circle (see Figure 3.10) also offered a ring diagram of automotive access on the inside and outside of a building doughnut, with storefronts located on both inward and outward faces.[55] The Eastland and Olympic proposals are enigmatic because, as discussed in chapter 4, there were already experiments with pedestrian-based shopping centers that broke with the curbside model, including some of Gruen's own design. His 1943 *Forum* proposal made a precinct for the pedestrian, and his Los Angeles shopping center proposal of 1948 (see Figure 4.18) was based on intersecting pedestrian malls or greenways—similar in conception to projects discussed by Morris Ketchum.[56] So why the parking ring design retreat, which offered no open, pedestrian-only space— no space for the citizen afoot?

Before 1950, many developers and store owners may have been unwilling to experiment with untested design ideas and thus sought familiarity with an organization based on curb-facing stores—that is, the familiar "100 percent location"— and lots of nearby parking. In other words, like any good parking plan, Gruen's oval experiment at Eastland minimized the walking distance from the car and was therefore palatable to the perhaps wary Hudson Company executives. Nonselling spaces—like greenways—were considered unnecessary. Thus the National Production Authority's rejection of the project was a blessing in disguise and perhaps pushed Gruen to work with a new strategy.

The life of Eastland continued slightly beyond its official cancelation. In the 1951 *Progressive Architecture* feature on civil defense, the dispersal policies of the Hudson Company were discussed alongside images of the ill-fated ring plan of Eastland. The article was framed around the company's long-term, nuclear-inflected plan to build new centers far from vulnerable industrial and urban targets and that could act as emergency "defense warfare centers."[57] Yet, in another *Progressive Architecture* article only three months later, the same Hudson Company policies of decentralized shopping were illustrated with a different project site and a completely new design.[58]

Gruen's new 1951 Hudson's proposal, called Northland, dispensed with the ring parking plan of Eastland and utilized what he called a "cluster" strategy (Figures 5.7 and 5.8). Instead of buildings creating a vast open space for cars ringed by a singular pedestrian route, Northland consisted of a variety of pedestrian-only landscaped spaces and routes threading between the center's more than one hundred stores. In addition, landscape and planning names such as "Great Lakes Court," "Garden Terrace," and "East Mall" (among others) created a "pleasing . . . sense of density" and associations far from the center's shopping function.[59] These interlocking spaces were lined with stores as well as community spaces, post office, and meeting rooms, some of which were located on a lower level. A meandering route through quasi-public places, leading to the department store at the heart of the project, created what Gruen saw as a new and modern form of urbanity. If Eastland had been organized for the car, Northland was organized for the pedestrian.

Northland's site planning was integral to the center's image of social and physical complexity (Figure 5.9). A two-level site section (recall Gruen's 1943 site section

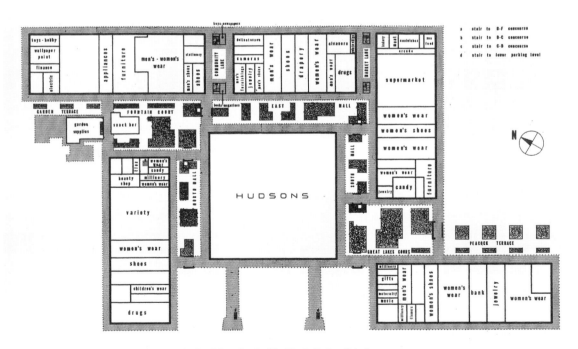

Merchandising plan for Northland Center, Detroit.
Architects: Victor Gruen Associates

Figure 5.7. Victor Gruen Associates, plan for Northland Shopping Center, Southfield, Michigan, 1954, in Victor Gruen and Larry Smith, *Shopping Towns USA: The Planning of Shopping Centers* (New York: Reinhold, 1960), 133.

Figure 5.8. Victor Gruen Associates, South Mall, Northland Shopping Center, Southfield, Michigan, 1954, *Architectural Forum* 100 (June 1954): 10x.

study) consisting of slopes and ramps enabled access to upper and lower levels of the center directly from the parking lots. The sectional split also enabled an all-important service tunnel and a bus drop-off area that, at the time, was considered necessary to ensure mass access to the center.[60] The service tunnel removed from view the messier side of merchandising operations—just those problematic aspects of stores that had characterized typical critiques of older city streets. Overall, the

Figure 5.9. Bus drop, West Side, Northland Shopping Center, Southfield, Michigan, 1954.

Figure 5.10. Albert C. Martin, Lakewood Shopping Center, Los Angeles, California, *Architecture Française* 15, nos. 145–46 (1954).

Figure 5.11. John Graham and Associates, Northgate Shopping Center, Seattle, Washington, 1950, *Seattle Post Intelligencer.* Reprinted by permission of Hearst Communications, Inc./Hearst Newspapers, LLC/Seattlepi.com.

cluster plan and the two-level section enabled what Gruen considered a properly urban sensibility—highly organized and controlled—for a "community center for the vast surrounding suburban area," that is, a civic center in the newly regionalized city. After it opened in 1954, the new Northland Center was professionally acclaimed as a triumph of site planning and pedestrian-based design.

Gruen's cluster plan was central to his staging (or simulation) of urbanity. It was also an explicit critique of the few pedestrian-based projects already in the works in 1951, including his own experiment at Eastland. Gruen found fault with the open spaces of Ketchum's Beverly project, published in 1947 (see Figure 4.21), early versions of Lakewood, also published in 1947 (Figure 5.10), and John Graham's

Northgate Shopping Center in Seattle, published in 1948 and built in 1950 (Figure 5.11), describing them as too linear and overscaled.[61] These projects did not offer an image of collective urban complexity, which was Gruen's key referent. He often cited his own experiences of Viennese social life as an important lesson for urbanity, and the cluster, with large and small lanes and gathering spaces, came closest to re-creating this atmosphere.[62] The cluster's planned informality, paradoxical though such an concept might be, was integral to making the shopping center into a new type of urban precinct.

Northland offered what Gruen and many others saw as a missing urbanity and civicness to the spreading American landscape. Like a city, and like many modernist projects, the new shopping center required a high level of design control and management; it drew from the expertise of many fields and entailed the resolution of complex technological and construction questions. In grander terms, however, Gruen described the social life provided by the spaces and programs of the shopping center as not merely like the city but better: an improved and modern city. Retailing provided a unique opportunity even if consumption was not quite as civic as it was presumed to be. Yet there were other ways the new precincts could become, and create, good citizens.

Art and Architecture

Throughout a career of navigating the muddy waters of design and merchandising, Victor Gruen argued that modern architecture could be both popular *and* serious. Gruen had a rather jaundiced view of what he saw as the elitist pretensions of the profession of architecture, and he framed the shopping center as uniquely suited to redirecting his colleagues' historically "high" architectural concerns toward a more broadly social and "popular" point of view. One of the ways he hoped to create an effective modernism was through the arts. Through art programs and institutions, Gruen hypothesized, the status of the shopping center—and that of its architect—could be improved. If the shopping center could be a home to art, it could become both urban and urbane. Gruen may have idealized the social place of art as somehow outside commodity culture, but he also claimed that art at the shopping center would reach more people than the art in any museum.

To stake out his position about the civic and professional value of shopping centers, Gruen submitted a grant application in 1952 to the American Federation of the Arts (AFA) for a traveling exhibit. The AFA, founded at the start of the twentieth century as part of a progressive enterprise to promote the arts and bring them to the "hinterlands" through traveling exhibitions, offered to circulate Gruen's exhibit provided he could find "financial sponsorship" (Figure 5.12).[63] With the title *Shopping Centers of Tomorrow,* Gruen had no trouble finding sponsors among his growing array of clients, including the Hudson Company, Dayton Company, Macy's, and

Figure 5.12. Page spread from Victor Gruen Associates, *Shopping Centers of Tomorrow*, 1954. Courtesy of Gruen Associates.

Carson Pirie Scott, and the exhibit opened in late 1952 in Roswell, New Mexico. The exhibit, which occupied about 2,500 square feet, was designed and built by Gruen's firm. It consisted of demountable four-by-eight-foot panels and frames holding photographs, drawings, and explanatory text. The show traveled for the next eighteen months to venues in Wichita, Louisville, Detroit, Minneapolis, Los Angeles, New York City, and many other locations in the United States and Canada. From Carson Pirie Scott department store in Chicago to the Museum of Natural History in New York to the Walker Art Center in Minneapolis, the exhibit was aimed at a wide and varied audience.[64] Attended by schoolchildren, professional and social groups, and civic organizations, the exhibit reached deeply into the world of the would-be shopping public with the message that new commercial environments required considerable planning, offered great pleasures, and served social needs and that modern architects were best equipped to create these complex places.

Gruen staged the *Shopping Centers of Tomorrow* exhibit as a pragmatic and rational project. Photographs, perspectives, plans, graphs, and accompanying text demonstrated how the planned shopping center would solve a host of social and physical problems. Overshadowing the civil defense terms that seemed so important just a few months previous, the shopping center was now represented as part of a historical trajectory of the loss and reclamation of an organic community life. Two familiar whipping posts gave coherence to this narrative: first was the congested industrial city, in which "the pedestrian world has dwindled to a ribbon of pavement on the banks of the traffic stream," and second were the "sprawling suburbs," created in response to the troubled city but equally problematic, lacking essential social functions and spawning commercial strips of no lasting value. Addressing both problems, the planned regional shopping center would offer the cohesion and "human scale" inherent in traditional marketplaces and act as a meeting place for "people afoot." The new shopping center would, Gruen wrote, "fill the vacuum created by the absence of social, cultural and civic crystallization points in our vast suburban areas."[65]

In the exhibit's renderings of spacious, organized, clean, and modern-looking shopping centers, all designed by Gruen's firm, pedestrian-based design principles were fully demonstrated. Shoppers trumped cars, open space was plentiful, and people unhurriedly shopped, met, gathered, and interacted.[66] Construction photographs of Northland were included in the exhibit as well as tempting renderings of the proposed Southdale Shopping Center. Both projects were portrayed as total and "complete living environments" with on-site community facilities. More broadly, both were shown as part of an expanded development with nearby housing, offices, schools, lakes, and playgrounds. Gruen transformed the shopping center into a community precinct that, in turn, lay at the core of an expanded settlement system. This was nothing less than a semiautonomous satellite, varieties of which were essential to the growing modernist examination of new settlement patterns in the postwar period. The pedestrianized core held it all together.

Discussions of *Shopping Centers of Tomorrow* showed how different audiences perceived the significance of the new building type. The mainstream press adored the depicted shopping centers' relief from the "noise and fumes" of the city, praising the comfort, convenience, order, greenery, and "splash of water" offered. Deeply integrated into the growing postwar hegemony of consumption as the central setting of social life, the new shopping centers were popularly framed as distinct and separated places, like downtown but much improved—that is, physically and socially cleansed.[67]

Positive but less exuberant, the architectural press looked more closely at the exhibit's examination of urban problems and planning provisions, treating consumption as only one part of a larger set of architectural issues about which the public could be educated. The *Progressive Architecture* reviewer noted that the exhibit "brings design to the public," and an *Arts Digest* reviewer wrote that the "simple pictorial form" of the material would appeal "to the layman." In the view of these observers, the problem of the shopping center was a part of a wider question of cities, planning, and architecture, and if the exhibit could raise these issues more broadly, then it was worth the dalliance with consumption.[68] This matched Gruen's view, and his ongoing and active participation in promotion—he often lectured at new exhibit locations—was just the sort of professional crisscrossing raised by architecture's engagement with shopping. In this way, the "educational" exhibit enabled Gruen to join consumption to planning and modern architecture.

With greater ambition than an exhibit *about* the shopping center, Gruen also proposed a role for art to complement and enhance the center as a new environment, as a "new architectural concept." Gruen convinced Hudson Company executives to fund a $200,000 art program at Northland as their "civic responsibility." Art, he wrote, would play an "organic role in the entire composition" and would consist of "sculptures, murals, fountains, mosaics on floors and mosaics on walls." Not only would the art ennoble the center, but, he noted, the added attractions would also cause people to slow down and linger, making each visit last longer than planned—the key to the merchandiser's success.[69]

Gruen ran the Northland art program himself. He selected both local and nationally recognized artists, he suggested themes, and he sited the work in the outdoor courts of the center. Gruen even organized a conference with the center's owners, several major tenants, and the artists in which ideas and proposals were vetted and finalized. Selected models and drawings were exhibited in a show titled *Architecture and Sculpture* at the establishment Jacques Seligmann Gallery in New York City in the spring of 1955. Gruen characterized the public debate that followed the installation of the work as both good publicity and "an expression of community life." Seeing in a Fifty-seventh Street gallery a model of the Northland Shopping Center and photographs of its installed sculptures must have raised (and lowered) a few brows. Like his clients, Gruen held a patronizing attitude toward his target audience, describing the typical suburban shopper as a woman with children for whom art should not portray "drama, heroism or tragedy . . . but humor, color, movement and lightheartedness."[70] It might be easy to chide Gruen for the fact that such terms all too easily described the middlebrow—the watered-down "ooze" of "midcult" described by Dwight Macdonald among others worried about "culture" or kitsch at midcentury—but Gruen was not alone in seeing the importance of art in social life.[71] That art in public places has historically been quite selective or that the shopping centers were not, in fact, public spaces does not mitigate Gruen's efforts to treat the shopping center as an almost new species of space, a modern urban realm, qualified as well as full of possibility. The art selected for Northland evidenced just such limits.

The artworks exhibited at Northland, mostly sculptures, were, for the most part, representational and figural yet always abstracted. In the work of Gwen Lux, Malcolm Moran (see Figure 5.8), Arthur Kraft, Richard Jennings, Marshall Fredericks, and Lily Saarinen, themes of nature and childhood were constant (Figures 5.13, 5.14, and 5.15).[72] Kraft, Moran, and Fredericks were known for sculptures of friendly-looking animals, usually for climbing on; Jennings for fountains of various scales; Lux for sunny interpretations of totem poles and wire-and-glass figures of birds. Saarinen's *Great Lakes* wall sculpture depicted the "wild life" of the region. The images of nature, the references to "Indians," and the appeal to childhood experience were intended to create an atmosphere of calm timelessness and appeal to a putatively universal ease, preadult and precivilized—that is, a world ready for the lures of shopping amid a hint of "culture."

In the larger context of art and architectural criticism of the period, the status of representational work was shifting, and several critics of the time weighed in on the relations of modern art and architecture. Henry-Russell Hitchcock in 1947 called for nonabstract forms of art to complement the abstraction of modernist architecture; realism and pictorialism were best suited for art placed in modernist settings. Noam Gabo's work, he pointed out, could be autonomous and too strong to complement a modernist building fruitfully. On the other hand, he praised the works of

Figure 5.13. Gwen Lux, *Bird Flight,* Northland Shopping Center, Southfield, Michigan, 1954, enameled copper mobile on painted wood, *Architectural Forum* 100 (June 1954): 118.

Figure 5.14. Arthur Kraft, *Baby Elephant,* Northland Shopping Center, Southfield, Michigan, 1954.

Figure 5.15. Lily Saarinen, *Great Lakes Group,* Northland Shopping Center, Southfield, Michigan, 1954. Photograph by Jeffrey Ligan—Belvair for Modern Living.

Bertoia, Calder, and Miró for their capacity to join with the architecture. Hitchcock went further by noting that the inevitable economies of modern building practice would produce lesser-quality architecture, which would need visual remediation of art.[73] In a 1952 survey of the relation of art and architecture, critic and *Architectural Forum* staff member Eleanor Bittermann wrote that architects had begun moving away from "purely architectural forms" to integrate art, imagination, and architecture more fully. The already established simplicity, sparseness, and utility of emerging modernist norms, she wrote, needed relief, and the right sculptures could "relieve the large expanses of plain brick wall."[74] Aline Saarinen, an art critic at the *New York Times,* frankly called for an art "willing to be architectural decoration, something which will make the emphasis, the dramatization, the vividization of the architecture." But even as she praised larger-scaled and semirepresentational work in principle because it related to the architecture, she specifically ridiculed wire sculpture, such as the work of Arthur Kraft at Northland, as overly "whimsical" and less than serious.[75] Terms such as *decorative* and an attitude that art should be recessive have historically described the debilitations of mass culture and consumption; in effect, such terms confirmed that the shopping center was a secondary place, with secondary art, and a place for women, who were only unheroic consumers, not producers.[76]

An *Arts & Architecture* reviewer took further the problem of audience. Northland politely alluded to the difficulties faced by the art selected for its lack of intellectual or artistic challenge. "The artists have legitimately incorporated as a necessary part of the function of the architecture . . . objects that not only handsomely and efficiently serve the needs of intelligent merchandising but also beguile and enchant the participating public."[77] By avoiding difficult themes and the complexities of abstraction, and by having the art "enchant" its audience—a hair's-breadth away from deception—Northland demonstrated that art could be seamlessly integrated into a total merchandising package; by providing undisturbed diversion or entertainment, the art could create an image of social texture and urbanity masking an otherwise totally controlled environment. This was a pedestrianized modernism, but it was not as unique or as unlikely as it might have appeared.

Gruen's embrace of art and his hopes for the joining of art and architecture echoed other discussions at midcentury. The Northland art program complemented debates among architects and critics looking for new meanings and roles for architecture to play in postwar social life, and, in the context of the Cold War, such a deployment of art was widely discussed. One of the most significant of midcentury discussions about art and architecture was the largely CIAM-based pursuit of a "new monumentality." In explicit rejection of what was described as the dogmatic, static, overly classicizing art and architecture under fascism (or under capitalism, for that matter) in the 1930s, a revitalized, even kinetic version of monumentality would enable art, symbols, and architecture to join and nurture democracy and community cohesion without prescriptions or proscriptions. Sigfried Giedion and José Luis Sert, along with artist Fernand Léger, proposed in 1943 that the collaboration of the planner, architect, painter, sculptor, and landscape architect could yield an architectural expression fostering freedom and creativity and satisfying the collective "aspiration for . . . joy, pride and excitement." These debates continued at the 1949 CIAM meeting in Bergamo, Italy, titled "Synthesis of the Arts," where discussions revolved around the ways in which art—with new materials, dynamic forms, and even temporary projects—could be part of an engaged cultural and public realm.[78] And if most of the CIAM monumentality and art discussions were explicitly anticommercial, the pursuit of community identification was an easily adapted pursuit.

While Gruen tended to distance himself from the debates of architectural circles, his pursuit of the integration of art and architecture to create community was the rhetorical realm in which Northland should be seen and judged.[79] For Gruen, the pedagogical exhibit and the symbolic role of "public" art and architecture enabled the shopping center to perform civic, cultural, and even psychological functions. The integration of art and commerce at the shopping center enabled a double sublimation of social tensions—that is, worries about consumption and the anxiety of the Cold War enabled the shopping center to become a fully modern architectural project.

Cold War Pedestrianism

American Cold War tensions injected a new urgency into architectural discourse. Older logics of decentralization and dispersal gained new weight. Remaking the metropolis into discreet yet connected autonomous units became the normative, modernist position of architects looking at regional change, and Gruen and Ketchum were important (although not the only) actors in this arena. The regional shopping center was a unique fixture in this new landscape; it appeared to address the potential and the problems of the dispersing city by creating a pedestrian precinct—that is, a tabula rasa urban node. This new center was without the dynamics—class conflict and racial strife—by which cities were increasingly understood by those in power, and the pedestrian realm was a refuge, or at least the image of one. But the pedestrian realm, of course, was also a landscape of consumption.

The postwar period was suffused with dreams and representations of consumption and, for some, new access to goods as well as homes. The pedestrian as a civic figure key to the architectural legitimacy of the shopping center was also central to an ever-expanding system of buying and selling goods. What *Fortune* magazine called the "lush new suburban market" merely hinted at the scale and reach of a new social and physical apparatus shaped by and for shopping.[80] Yet adding the civic to the commercial roles of shopping centers—and thereby transforming them—was central to Gruen's design strategies and especially to the arts program he initiated.

In bringing art to the shopping center, he tapped into the Euro-American legacy of "civic arts" and "new monumentality" as a representational project, through which the very idea of a modern city could be sustained. In this sense, the shopping center was merely another place of "public" gathering to be shaped and fitted out with the proper urban design and furniture. Art was conscripted to stabilize the pedestrian realm as a *public* and shared space, allowing the new realm to mediate the tensions of the Cold War with the joys of looking at and buying things.

SIX

THE LANGUAGE OF
MODERN SHOPPING

It is interesting to reflect that this challenging new building pattern is in
the hand of the modern architect: the architect who only several decades
ago recognized that movement—the simple traffic of a family through a
house—was the key to the plan. This vision of the importance of motion,
perhaps more than anything else, overrode yesterday's traditional space
allotment, which cut space into static cubicles. In the new building
pattern of the shopping center, today's architect is called upon to
understand and relate—not just the simple movement of a family
through a house—but a traffic complex composed of automobiles,
pedestrians, trucks, buses and merchandise.

—*Architectural Forum,* 1951

AT MIDCENTURY, the American shopping center outside the core of the
city was a new kind of architectural project whose form was undecided and
whose professional status was unclear. The shopping center was beginning
to reach beyond its "primer days," but the architectural value of the commission remained ambiguous.[1] *Architectural Forum*'s editorial position on
the transformation of midcentury modernism is symptomatic of the rhetorical balancing effected for the shopping center within architectural discourse: the central question for the "new building pattern" was to treat it
as an architectural concern first, a commercial problem second. Through
the treatment of the shopping center as a studied choreography of moving people, objects, and vehicles—as a "traffic complex"—the wiles of merchandising and economic calculation could be elided or, at the very least,
given a comfortably recessive position. Instead of a focus on the design of

individual buildings, the new program entailed the management of spaces, site, topography, and consultants, and thus the new center could be represented as a total problem worthy of the expertise of the modern architect.

In merchandising, with so many decisions made by teams of experts outside the architectural discipline, architects became increasingly interested in the site plan as their sphere of greatest knowledge and input. This attitude was echoed by Henry-Russell Hitchcock, who, in 1947, wrote: "Where imagination is required in the realm of bureaucratic architecture is in site planning."[2] Although secondary to iconic work such as the museum, the shopping center, it appeared, might attain a proper level of "amenity" and thereby be considered architectural. Morris Ketchum, like other architects doing shopping center work, seconded this point in his 1948 book *Shops and Stores* by treating the site plan as the key architectural contribution. While Ketchum's book dealt substantially with the architectural details of stores and the methods of selling, the trajectory of the story led to the programming of the shopping center as a complex urban problem, not merely a commercial one. In a 1949 *Architectural Record* piece on shopping centers, architects Geoffrey Baker and Bruno Funaro described the design possibilities of the shopping center with respect to municipal and transportation questions alongside commercial issues. The book version of their article, published in 1951 as *Shopping Centers: Design and Operation,* reiterated the importance not of particular building designs but of the new planning scale of work.[3] Baker and Funaro began frankly with economic, demographic, and marketing discussions and described the shopping center as a uniquely economic proposition among architectural commissions, but the bulk of the book bore out *Architectural Forum*'s conjecture of the shopping center as a site planning exercise for which modern architects were particularly qualified. Baker and Funaro emphasized the formal possibilities of the shopping center and richly illustrated their book with site analyses, project proposals, parking layouts, circulation diagrams, massing models, detailed photos with explanatory arrows, project photographs with extensive captions, and figure-ground plans redrawn by the authors (Figure 6.1). The book was a compilation of techniques and strategies, indicating that a formula for the design of the shopping center did not yet exist. In other words, the complexities of shopping center commission could still nurture experimentation and be part of a modern practice.

An *Architectural Forum* article of 1950 distinguished between a mere shopping center—"random suburban dispersal" akin to a strip development—and an "integrated suburban retail district," giving to the latter an affiliation with planning not unlike that of an urban district. In this guise, the shopping center had much more to offer the architect. To underscore the magazine's interest in a broad role for the architect, one section of the *Forum* article, "The Architect's Place in the Suburban Retail District," described the "shopping district" as requiring the architect to "coordinate the work of experts in a dozen fields," and placing him in "position of

FREIGHT HANDLING, SERVICE AREAS

SEPARATING FREIGHT AND CUSTOMER TRAFFIC
HOW TO INCLUDE SERVICE COURTS IN NEW STORE GROUPS
DIMENSION DATA FOR FREIGHT DOCKS
SUPERMARKET FREIGHT HANDLING. GARBAGE COLLECTION

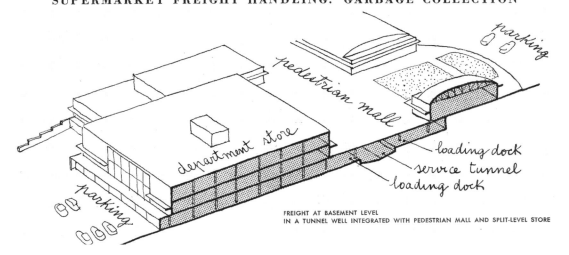

FREIGHT AT BASEMENT LEVEL
IN A TUNNEL WELL INTEGRATED WITH PEDESTRIAN MALL AND SPLIT-LEVEL STORE

Figure 6.1. "Freight Handling, Service Areas," in Baker and Funaro, *Shopping Centers: Design and Operation,* 51.

leadership . . . design freedom and . . . planning responsibility." In other words, the architect was represented as organizer and director, rather than a proxy for marketers, local officials, or real estate brokers. Once "in control" of traffic, zoning, and interior and exterior space, the architect would be in his disciplinary element.[4] Like the "orchestral cooperation" and team approach advocated most famously by Walter Gropius, this position rendered the architect simultaneously a team player and the leader of the team—what Pietro Belluschi called the "best man on the team."[5] Kenneth Welch was ambivalent, describing the new "regional shopping centers" as a new pattern of retail distribution and part of the "economic pattern of the entire metropolitan area"—giving to the project a clear financial image—but he was also quick to say that the shopping center was not a real estate problem but one that needed "the integrated team work of planners, architects, engineers, store and property managers, financial institutions and real estate organizations."[6]

Pursuit of leadership, status, and control over the shopping center entailed considerable research and publicity by the architects and the architectural press. A 1952 *Progressive Architecture* feature written by Gruen together with economist Larry

Smith and a 1953 *Architectural Record* article in one of the magazine's "building type" issues were densely packed manuals with massing studies and flowcharts not unlike Baker and Funaro's book, but they also added marketing charts, flow diagrams, even sample contracts and structural documentation.[7] Gruen and Smith insisted that their article in *Progressive Architecture* was neither a "handbook" nor a "recipe for cooking up the shopping center," but a reader would draw precisely the opposite conclusion. Their piece, which was printed on the special paper usually reserved for technical material and special supplements, contained sections such as "The Steps in Shopping Center Planning." One section of the 1953 *Record* article began with a list labeled "ingredients." Articles of the "how-to" genre were not unusual in the magazines, but in the case of the shopping center, the knowledge needed and specialties touched upon veered closer and closer to the edges of the discipline where financing was all too evident.

Gruen walked the razor's edge between the commercial and the architectural. First and foremost, his work with Smith stemmed from the failure of a proposal for a 1950 shopping center in Texas (proposed as an enclosed mall), after which Gruen said he realized marketing and financial analysis could make or break a project. It was best to have such knowledge *within* the firm's orbit, not outside it.[8] But this was just the tip of the discursive iceberg, and Gruen explicitly joined the architectural and the economic:

> The primary aim of a commercial project is realized profit. To arrive at such a realization, two factors must be present: the market potential and the correct tapping device. The analyst will detect, forecast and evaluate the potential. The architect will design the most efficient organic and economically sound environment for marketing—the most effective tapping device he can achieve for the given potential.[9]

In other words, the tapping device is transparent to the tapping potential, or, in modernist terms, rationality finds its equivalent in a finely tuned merchandising system. In joining merchandising and this view of modernism, Gruen worked in the seam between architecture and business, exposing the deep divisions between the two even as he wove them together. But even Gruen was not without his own idea of properly architectural territory, and he worried that in shopping center work the design could be circumscribed and "moved to the background." Already apparent to Gruen was that mechanistic design and the profit motive seemed to be gaining the upper hand—which in later years became his chief gripe—so a strategy to stake a claim of architectural expertise was essential.

Site planning offered the architect a specialized position and a secure place as coordinator of complex and large-scale processes. Gruen, with his usual bravado, wrote that the site plan of the new centers was an opportunity "not seen since the

Renaissance."[10] The cover image of the 1952 *Progressive Architecture* shopping feature consisted of several site plan alternatives in abstracted massing and "figure-ground" formats (Figure 6.2), privileging their importance and, more specifically, showing that the diagram of the site organization as a whole was more important than the design of individual buildings, much less their interiors.

The risks of the architect's role in shopping center work were echoed in the extensive 1953 *Architectural Record* "Building Types Study." Citing a "prominent architect who is actively engaged in shopping center work"—perhaps the well-traveled Kenneth Welch—the editors wrote that the key to success is the "architects' state of mind." "The architect must make every effort to approach the work as though he were the *owner* of the project—and design accordingly. This does not imply the giving up of high artistic and professional standards; on the contrary, they must simultaneously be held at the highest level."[11] In other words, the center must *first* be planned for successful financial operation, and within this disciplined framework the architect can then provide all the amenities and attractiveness possible.

That the editors insisted that aesthetics and standards must not be given up in shopping design work indicated that the opposite might in fact be the case. They appeared to say that the architect should work as if the money for the project was his own, and *after* being sufficiently humbled by this economic discipline might he add a veneer of "amenities and attractiveness." Architecture, in the parlance of building contractors, is "an extra." This was a startling admission that threatened the deeply ingrained professional conception of the architect as the central interpreter of the design process. This new definition implied that the professional status of shopping commissions was or would soon be problematic.

The ambiguous professional status of the architect of shopping centers was amplified in the 1953 *Architectural Record* feature also by virtue of its source. Almost the entire article was a reprint of a report issued a few months earlier by the Urban Land Institute (ULI)—the realtors', builders', and developers' lobbying organization.[12] Founded in 1939, the ULI had published a study of shopping center development in 1944, and by 1953 the organization had already issued several widely used "technical bulletins" on the subject.[13] These publications reflected the marketing and building concerns of shopping center developers, and it is logical that other professionals seeking to learn about the new building type might turn to the ULI as a source. In fact, the *Record* editors acknowledged their use of the ULI study, although they also went to great lengths to distinguish the architectural discussion from the developers' (and the ULI, in turn, cited Gruen).

Differences between the architectural and real estate languages heightened a sense that the architectural role in shopping center work was not resolved. First, the *Record* editors demonstrated dissatisfaction about borrowing from the ULI report by noting that "additional material" from other sources would be inserted in "different type face

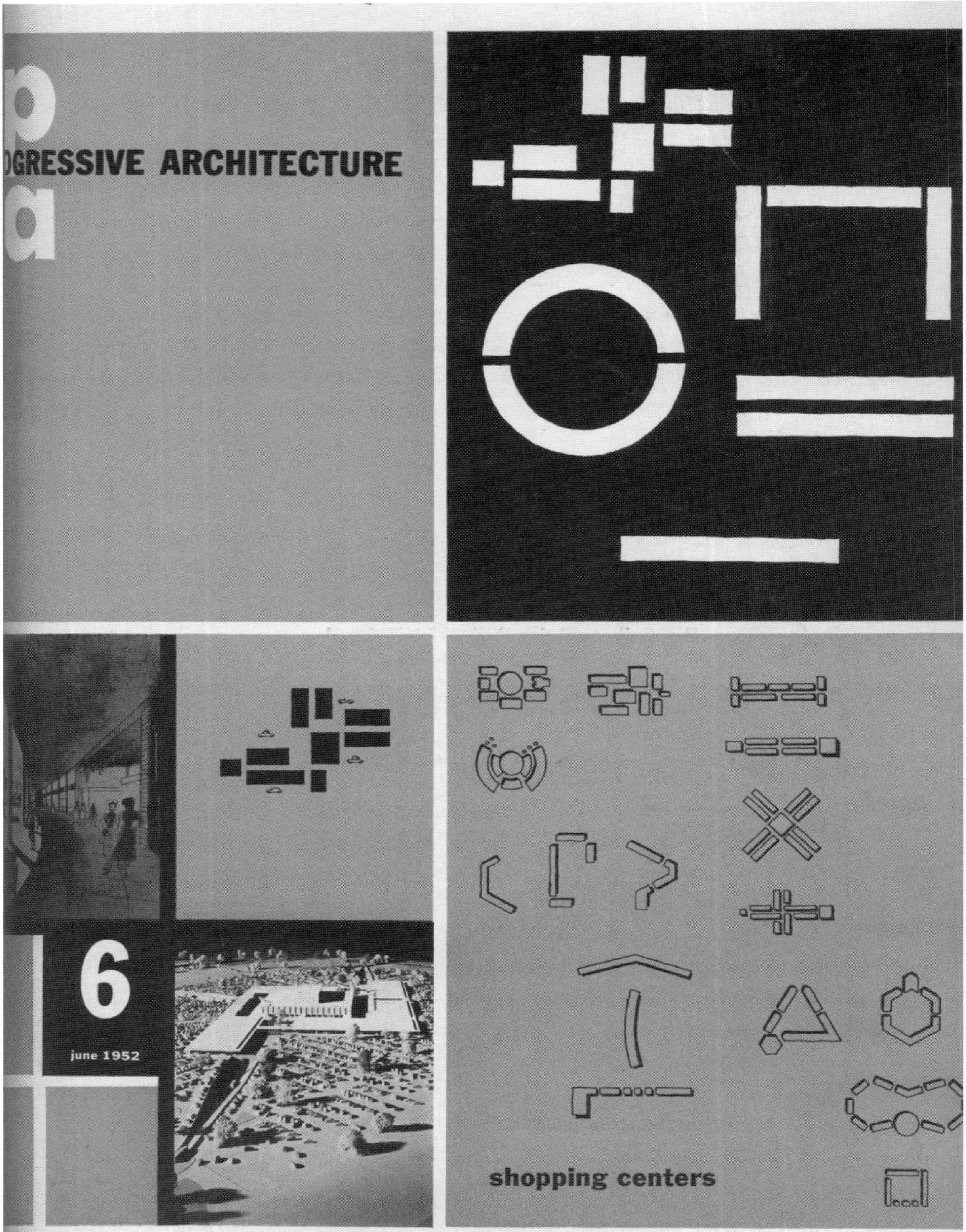

Figure 6.2. Cover of *Progressive Architecture* (June 1952).

to amplify certain points." These points were not mere details but efforts to translate the ULI's financialized language into "strictly architectural terms."[14] Editorially dramatic, the *Record*'s illustrations were different from those for the same projects in the ULI bulletin—the former featuring more sketches and experiments—and the captions used were entirely rewritten for those projects the *Record* editors borrowed.[15] This representational split between text and image is revealing: the *Record* editors apparently considered the ULI examples, chosen for their economic success or the track records of their developers, less worthy of architectural endorsement. Instead, they substituted more formally innovative proposals and thus refashioned the architectural meaning of the essay. The proper design of the shopping center was framed as a planning and architectural project, not the passive transcription of pedestrian economic data. Finally, the *Record* editors resisted the financialization of their work by omitting most of the ULI market analysis section, depicting such work as outside architectural practice and expertise. To resolve the tension between finance and design and to bolster the architectural claim to a key role in the design process of the shopping center, the editors wrote:

> Too often the architect is not consulted early enough in the selection of the site when his advice to the owner might be invaluable. Such considerations as shape, orientation, access, slope, drainage, soil condition, etc. should be his direct concern from the beginning.[16]

Writing as if the architect's role in shopping center work was already in question, the editors stressed the site work, which the architect should lead. In effect, they were trying to wrest from the developer a more formative role for the architect in shopping center design. If the literal control was not to be had, there was another representational arena in which the architects could play a key role.

To the Architect Belongs the Symbolism

In their 1951 book, Baker and Funaro portrayed the shopping center as an architectural project "still in the stage of groping and experiment."[17] At midcentury, designers and planners of shopping centers did not share referents or models with which to approach what they considered a new type. There were few full and demonstrated precedents for the design of large shopping centers—most examples were small, partial, or fragments of other kinds of work, as described in chapter 4, so there was wide latitude for design interpretation and invention. The influence of the visual and site strategies of Mies van der Rohe's Illinois Institute of Technology, published in 1939, or Eero Saarinen's General Motors Technical Center, first published in 1945, is not discussed in the shopping literature, although Ketchum worked with Thomas Church, landscape architect for Saarinen.[18] Of course, the shopping center was also an economic engine for which many builders and investors sought (and soon found) formulas of financing, structure, or organization, but the notable feature of the midcentury shopping center was not its design uniformity, as is suggested in many popular conceptions, but the opposite. A heuristic sketch of several models for shopping center design shows the malleability of the emerging type and how these varied models functioned in architectural representation and rhetorics.

The most popular model for shopping centers, or the most easily disseminated in diagrammatic form, was a linear boulevard or Main Street. The referent was, Morris Ketchum wrote, "Main Street minus auto traffic."[19] A populist Main Street and a cosmopolitan Fifth Avenue were persistent corollaries, joined by their association with the bustle and activity of a mythic, preautomotive street, where interaction and informality were created by pedestrian usage. Early examples of the street model included architect John Graham's Northgate Shopping Center (see Figure 5.11), organized by a "miracle mall," fifty feet wide and fifteen hundred feet long, that was treated more as a street than as a lawn. This was closely followed by architect Welton Becket's Stonestown Shopping Center (San Francisco, 1949–51) (Figure 6.3). Described as "a city street for pedestrians only," the main section of Stonestown

Figure 6.3. Welton Becket and Associates, Stonestown Shopping Center, San Francisco, California, 1952. San Francisco History Center, San Francisco Public Library.

consisted of two blocks of stores facing each other across a sixty-foot, minimally landscaped walkway. Architect Albert Martin's Lakewood Center (Los Angeles, 1949–51) (see Figure 5.10) was organized around a "shopping walk lined with stores" but was considered rather long at a quarter of a mile.[20] Just outside New York City, Lathrop Douglass's Cross County Center (Yonkers, 1950–54) was organized by an L-shaped plan with two arcaded, informally planted lanes less than fifty feet wide, like two city blocks meeting at a corner (Figure 6.4).[21] Some of these centers, such as Cross County and Ketchum's Shoppers' World, also contained a second story of smaller stores and offices, further sustaining the image of a busy street, and Cross County included a ten-story office building, lending to the center a sense of complexity, as if the tall building signified an urban place. The Main Street model was also visually familiar, resembling closed pedestrian streets and projects of the 1940s. As collections of urban elements, not unlike Disneyland's "Main Street," which opened in 1954, the street model offered reassuring images of urban life.[22]

Figure 6.4. Lathrop Douglass, Cross County Shopping Center, Stamford, Connecticut, 1954. Library of Congress, Prints and Photographs Division, Gottscho-Schleisner Collection, LC-G613-73745.

Refinement of the street model was also a possibility. *Architectural Forum* editors described a 1951 shopping center proposal by Morris Ketchum not only as a street but also as a pleasing series of linked and "modulated plazas" (Figure 6.5). For a competition by the Chicago retailer Marshall Field, Ketchum continued to work with Kenneth Welch, and they were joined by landscape architect Thomas Church and the local firm Perkins and Will to design the proposed Skokie Center in the city's emerging suburbs. Their proposal was composed of a semiregular array of linear buildings and open spaces, with no single focal point or formal core. The spaces of the center were broken up and bookended by large stores, creating two smaller "intimate" courts, as well as a variety of access allées—some of which were bridges over the open service road.[23]

A "modulated plaza" design was, perhaps, Ketchum's critique of the scale of the single-space designs (by him or others) of the time: the massive open space of Beverly, the slightly less grand space of Shoppers' World, the elongated spaces at Northgate or Lakewood perhaps seemed homogeneous or static to a designer looking to restage the complexities of the city. Equally important, Ketchum's plan for Marshall Field offered a version of social interaction not unlike that sought by Gruen in his "cluster" plan for Northland, the first version of which was published in late 1951, at the same time as the Marshall Field competition.[24] In his 1952 *Progressive Architecture* article on shopping centers, Gruen went to great lengths to show that the cluster was superior to the linear mall or the street models, since, he wrote, the latter tended to create long walking distances and were monotonous and overbearing.

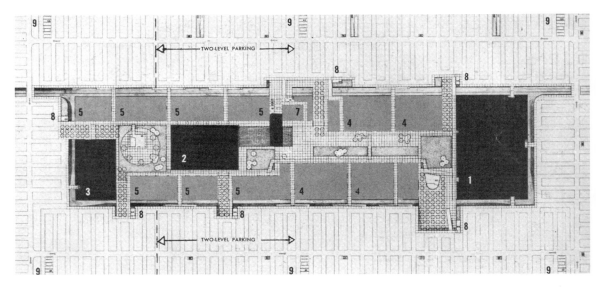

Figure 6.5. Ketchum, Gina, and Sharp, Marshall Field Shopping Center competition, *Architectural Forum* 95 (December 1951): 189.

Ketchum and Gruen came to share the pejorative view of single-space site plans in favor of a mixed-scale array of spaces, which sought urbanity as a constellation of experiences and routes.[25] The imagined intricacies of the historic city remained an ever-present motive in early shopping center work.

In contrast to urban models, or taking further the idea of complexity, was an explicitly picturesque design strategy. This entailed setting up a series of views, referring more to "nature" than the city, and typically using "informal" or nonorthogonal organizations (Figures 6.6 and 6.7). For the 1951 Marshall Field Skokie competition, architect Howard T. Fisher manipulated the section as well as the plan to form what he described as a "series of vistas which flow into each other." These "inviting" views were modulated by plan shifts, angles in the building layout, and the slope of the site, which combined to lend the project an air of "charm and informality" even if it was undergirded by a highly controlled system of technologies of the sort that had long fascinated Fisher. The design formed a complex landscape that Fisher described as having "the varying effect of a group of northern lakes."[26] With multiple orientations, varied masses to move between, near and far views, and compositional surprises, the project gave to the pedestrian the status of privileged observer of a landscape to be traversed, by foot and by eye.

Picturesque planning principles such as varied materials, irregular spaces, composed views, and a "succession of visual images" also informed Richard Bennett's design for Park Forest Plaza (Park Forest, Illinois, 1947–52) (see Figure 4.9) and his design for Marshall Field's Old Orchard Shopping Center (Skokie, Illinois, 1954–56), the

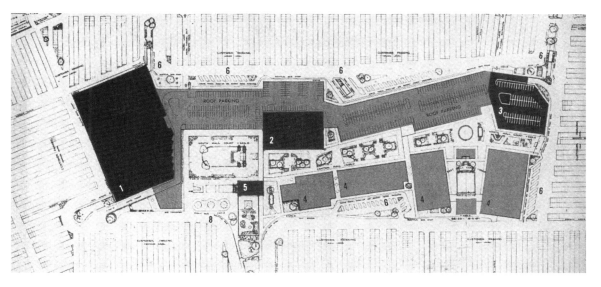

Figure 6.6. Howard T. Fisher, Marshall Field Shopping Center competition, *Architectural Forum* 95 (December 1951): 198.

TERRACE LEVEL *(above) overlooks the mall on the south. Sketch of mall level (below) shows informal landscaping, resting benches for shoppers, and office building in background.*

Figure 6.7. Howard T. Fisher, Marshall Field Shopping Center competition, *Architectural Forum* 95 (December 1951): 199.

latter with landscape architect Lawrence Halprin.[27] A 1954 shopping center design proposal for Los Angeles by architect Paul Laszlo shows a similar sensibility at work (Figure 6.8). Park Forest was organized by an "informal" arrangement of irregularly shaped courts with the building masses broken into smaller groups allowing multiple access points from the surrounding housing and parking lots.[28] In a later *Architectural Record* article, Bennett described his interest in giving architecture a sense of adventure and anticipation, and he cited the influence of British architect and town planner Thomas Sharp, whose town planning proposals in Britain utilized "curvature" to stress experience over abstraction (echoing Camillo Sitte as well). A mix of views and elements, like the winding streets of medieval cities, Bennett wrote, maintained a sense of ritual, a desire to wander and linger.[29] Architectural journalist James Hornbeck wrote that the "informal" plan makes the shopper "pleasantly aware of a scene that changes refreshingly—he finds a change of pace, of scale, of direction, of

Figure 6.8. Paul Laszlo, shopping center, Los Angeles, California, *Arts & Architecture* (October 1954). Copyright David Travers. Reprinted with permission. Photograph by Robert C. Cleveland.

shape, of surface."[30] The picturesque referent lent to the shopping center the calm of an individual's walk through nature's charm and variety—not a public sense—and a reassuring experience in which visual satisfaction elbowed aside any troubling social questions, especially about consumption; this was a pastoral design in the simple sense—in the terms of Leo Marx, a use of nature as wish image.[31]

A civic model shifted emphasis from the informal to the monumental and brought to shopping center design thinking a sense of gravitas and overt political symbolism. The civic emphasis was an echo of the wartime and postwar architectural debates about a "new monumentality" that explored the role of built form in fostering a community-minded, democratic polity.[32] Skidmore, Owings & Merrill (then completing the drawings for Lever House in New York City) designed a "great square" for their version of the Marshall Field Skokie project (Figure 6.9). Their project was organized by an abstract set of gridded masses and spaces, including a community building, an office building, and a system of smaller courts and pedestrian ways, all leading the visitor to a vast open plaza, a spatial crescendo. With an iconic (if almost de rigueur) reflecting pool, the plaza was treated as a forum in which social and civic life would unfold, able to hold ten thousand people for "carnivals, concerts, Easter sunrise services." Monumentally scaled, the plaza was complemented by informally planted allées bordering the stores and smaller courts. To ensure an unclouded civic image for the project, the SOM designers placed considerable emphasis on locating the parking lots below grade, with different sections served by a system of escalators and ramps. Even the renderings gave a sense of the gravity and seriousness sought by the designers.[33]

Victor Gruen's version of the civic model can be characterized by his penchant for monumental, sometimes heavy-handed gestures. Such projects were less spatial compositions than defined through sculptural mass and iconic elements. In this category were his 1948 shopping center proposal for Los Angeles (see Figure 4.18), with a round department store at the center of two pedestrian allées; his first Eastland proposal (see Figure 5.6), with a round department store at the head of the oval-shaped store complex; and his 1952 cluster plan at Northland (see Figure 5.7), where the store was at the center of the plan. In these projects a central figural mass, the department store, was approached by prominent axes as well as minor routes, and, although Gruen described the sequence of spaces as "informal," the planning and massing endowed his projects with a visual legibility and power he felt appropriate to the shopping center as a newly pivotal social institution. Complementing the use of a figural mass, Gruen's 1950 Olympic Shopping Circle project (Figure 6.10; see also Figure 3.10) used a monumental circular form and central space—but only for cars—and perhaps refers to Sumner Gruzen's 1948 shopping center proposal (see Figure 4.10). Gruen was deeply interested in symbols and icons, spatial

Figure 6.9. Skidmore, Owings & Merrill, Marshall Field Shopping Center competition, *Architectural Forum* 95 (December 1951): 196.

or sculptural, as catalysts of community formation. The architect in these cases was equipped not only to organize the complex programming of the center but also to ensure its visual coherence and cultural vitality.

Gruen's use of monumental masses or spaces was an afterimage of the symbolism he valued in the culture of his beloved Vienna, often his comparative touchstone and to which he later returned. Many observers have commented on Gruen's interest in streets as places fostering informal sociability, but the civic spaces and monumental buildings of the Ringstrasse—the site of his first store designs—were anything but informal, instead offering the lesson that symbolic and visually expressive forms were a necessary part of the social fabric of urban life. For Gruen, grand public gestures were part of the substance and ideal of a pedestrian promenade. This was complemented by his early stores and his participation in the 1939 World's Fair, where the pedestrian was incorporated into the spectacle of business and art. From early on, Gruen (like Lapidus) embraced the communicative and theatrical gesture, as seen in his Grayson's chain store (1944) (see Figure 2.4) and Wynn Furniture Store (1947), among many others. That Gruen, like others, thought the new shopping

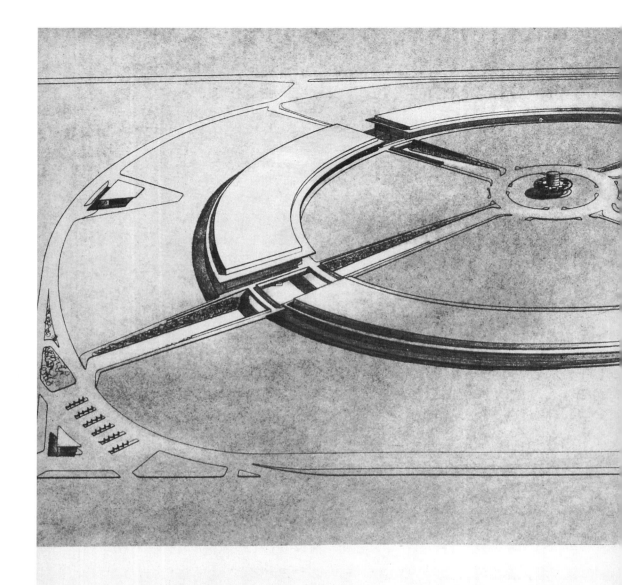

OLYMPIC SHOPPING CIRCLE

In this bird's eye view, looking from Whittier Boulevard towards Olympic, the organization of the circle is dramatically clarified. The circular mall on both sides of the stores bridge the automobile underpasses, which lead into the inner parking circle, flows around the department store, and guides the customer smoothly and uninterruptedly from store group to store group. The circular path provides the customer with continuous new points of interest without any interference from automobile traffic. The parking circle is depressed two feet so that all the stores around the center are visible from the inner mall.

Figure 6.10. Victor Gruen Associates, Olympic Shopping Circle, Los Angeles, California, 1950. Box 12, Victor Gruen Collection, American Heritage Center, University of Wyoming.

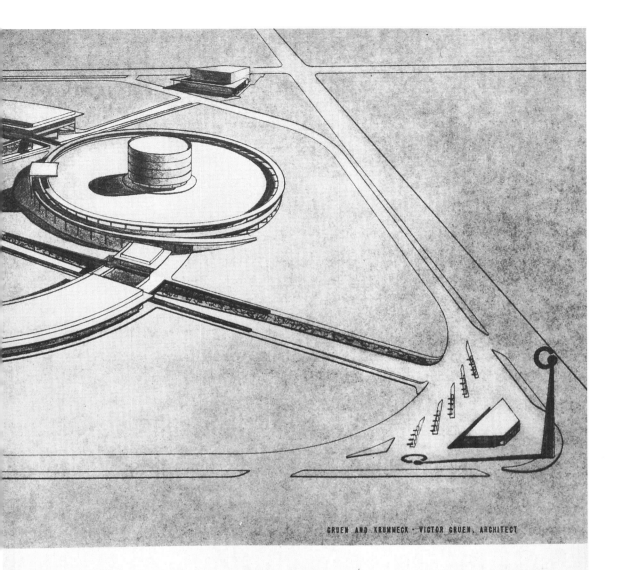

On the right is the department store. Its roof parking for 300 cars is fed by ramps which furnish additional shelter for the pedestrians below and accent the entrance from the inner parking circle. The service core, which towers over the store and landmarks the center, houses air-conditioning, freight elevators, escalators and other storage and customer facilities. The department store loads and receives in a basement, which is reached by an underground road leading from the automobile underpass. The basement storage areas in the other building groups are served by truck loading platforms located out of the traffic lanes in each of the underpasses.

The building group in the upper center is two stories high with the upper floor opening on the inner parking circle and the lower floor opening on the Olympic parking area. The 1,500 seat theatre is in the upper right, and on the far left is the nursery building and playground. In the foreground, to the extreme right and left, are gas stations, and in the center, at the hub, is the drive-in restaurant. Landscaping and planting are used to break up the monotony of the extensive parking areas. Architectural control provides the unity which eliminates anarchy and breathlessness which characterizes typical, deteriorating shopping areas.

centers would unproblematically combine civic and the commercial social spheres remains one of the more paradoxical aspects of the form.[34]

Strongly complementing the urban and civic models for shopping center design, the model of a "town green" or commons tapped into a cultural vein of republican idealism, an ever-present element in American affairs given new life during World War II and the Cold War. Part park, part public assembly space, and part religious meeting place, the commons supplied the image of a preindustrial town square as a refuge from the complexities of the *urbs* and a rosy view of a small, organic community. During the war, George Nelson published admiring discussions of idealized organic communities, such as European medieval towns or American colonial towns, demonstrating that a social glue and shared identity—building on Van Wyck Brooks's "usable past"—could be manifested in physical and planned form. In one drawing, a memorial obelisk at the heart of a town green represented a timeless social life, one not far from the Mumfordian vision polemically demonstrated in the film *The City,* shown at the 1939 New York World's Fair.[35]

In the shopping center, the commons found expression in generous lawns, planted areas, and open green space, beyond the civic or picturesque models. Such spaces were not to be mistaken for streets without cars but were seen as honored open and social spaces that, according to architect Pietro Belluschi, would guide and shape the proper community spirit.[36] Early iterations of the town green were his McLoughlin Heights shopping center (see Figure 4.5), organized around a "landscaped court," and Whitney Smith's Linda Vista Shopping Center (Figure 6.11; see also Figure 4.6), which *Forum* editors praised for its "quiet lawn" and "pedestrian park." Morris Ketchum also experimented with the town green image in his early centers. Despite their rather large size, his proposals for the 1947 Beverly Shopping Center (see Figure 4.23), the 1951 Shoppers' World, and the Clearview shopping center in Princeton of 1952 were all organized by planted "malls" offering a visual fantasy of a bucolic American community, a new town green, visually aided in that association by modern interpretations of clock towers.

Suburban shopping center designs around 1950 were characterized by many typal affiliations because the site planning considerations yielded no immediate or distinct expression. Constant, however, was the perceived need to provide the shopper with associations beyond commerce and closer to an ennobling if not also leisurely citizenship. Redirecting the image of shopping as a component of modern social life also held out the possibility that the shopping center might have greater legitimacy in architectural discourse. The monumentality and arts debates of the 1940s and 1950s showed that architects were deeply interested in the problem of meaning, and in the shopping center the representational possibilities were widely explored. Thus the architectural literature around 1950 legitimated the shopping center as a new kind of social institution and a recognizable architectural-urban type.

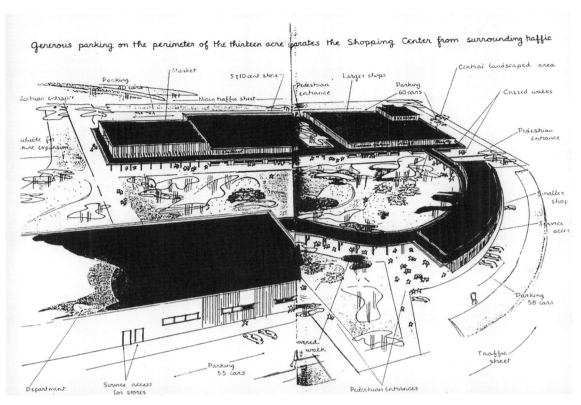

Figure 6.11. Earl F. Giberson and Whitney Smith, Associated Architects, Linda Vista Shopping Center, San Diego, California, in "'Grass on Main Street' Becomes a Reality," *Architectural Forum* 81 (September 1944): 86–87.

Ranging from urban surrogate to civic catalyst to republican town green, the associations for the design of midcentury shopping centers were tested by on-the-ground revision. Shoppers' World owners later sought to narrow the outdoor mall by making the stores deeper to shape a more street-like sensibility.[37] Ketchum's wide mall at Clearview shopping center made infeasible the roofing and enclosure that many malls underwent in later years. In effect, Ketchum's wide mall, like Gruen's first Eastland Shopping Center "necklace," proved unsustainable as the formulaic economics, layout, and site design of shopping centers emerged from the more experimental phases of the late 1940s. The associations and images of shopping center literature showed the breadth of possibility but quickly evaporated as the built versions of such ideas were tested. Nevertheless, the varied design strategies for the shopping center entailed a broad vision and a high level of technological and spatial control. The new shopping centers, Gruen wrote, could "serve as testing and proving grounds of ideas for the renewal of our city cores."[38] The crowning glory of the suburban shopping center appeared to be a modern urban design project.

Modern Pedestrian Tactics

Victor Gruen's career took a fateful turn after the highly public success of Northland Shopping Center in late 1954. A new urban commission gave him the opportunity to show that his design ideas were not derived from the particulars of the suburbs but instead grew from an analysis of program and organization—a modern approach to any design question. In an ambitious 1955 proposal to reshape entirely the older downtown core of Fort Worth, Texas, he set his sights beyond the suburban shopping center, its culture, and its design limits. Turning shopping center techniques "back" onto an ailing city would affirm the importance of his work as a planner-architect by reinforcing his view that shopping center design principles were not tied to suburbanization or merely an efficient commodity distribution system; rather, in the most expansive of visions, pedestrian planning strategies were an integral part of modern urban design and architecture.

Gruen's Fort Worth Plan entailed a transformation of three hundred acres at the heart of the old downtown into a pedestrian precinct and would have involved the complete restructuring of services, infrastructure, streets, and connections to the region (Figure 6.12).[39] As extreme an intervention as it might have seemed, Gruen was adept at telling the chilling story of the alternative. Fort Worth, he warned, was doomed to play second fiddle to fast-growing Dallas because of outmoded land use, buildings and infrastructure, complex ownership patterns, underaccessed businesses, and a dearth of integrated social and cultural activities. It followed, therefore, that the city could be saved only with the large-scale planning and organizational thinking that the shopping center architects, using what they considered a modernist approach, had succeeding in implementing.[40]

Gruen's plan created a fully serviced pedestrian "reservation"—a perfected urban precinct. The shopping and business core was surrounded by six strategically placed parking garages, similar to Detroit's 1945 plan (see Figure 3.16), each holding several thousand cars and accommodating the city's daytime traffic load. The garages connected the urban core to a ring and regional highway system seamlessly leading to the growing suburbs. Commentators boasted of the ease of walking from one's car to any destination and called it the "three minute plan."[41] Gruen's study was paid for by the Texas Electric company, whose chief executive was worried about a city in which investments in extant infrastructure might, with continued congestion and suburbanization, have to be written off. Thus the plan would guide the formation of an up-to-date city with increasing land values and run like the efficient machine Northland and other early shopping centers were designed to be (Figure 6.13).[42] This dream of the smoothly operating mechanism of urban capital was dramatically demonstrated through Gruen's renderings of a pedestrian realm of comfort and culture, walking and browsing, where civic life and shopping merged seamlessly.

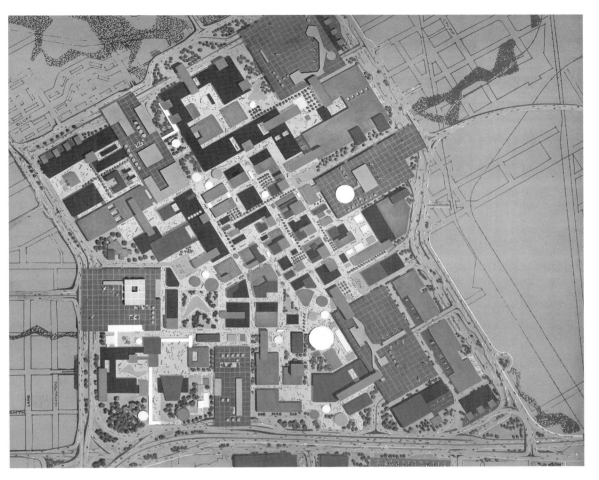

Figure 6.12. Victor Gruen Associates, Fort Worth Plan (Fort Worth, Texas), *A Greater Fort Worth Tomorrow* (Greater Fort Worth Planning Committee, 1954).

Gruen's remade pedestrian precinct and urban system offered an easygoing image of a city for newly liberated drivers. With pedestrian-only streets and open spaces home to continuous festivals and arts exhibitions, all essential services hidden from view and even the garages and their tenants treated as participants in a cosmopolitan, urbane life (Figure 6.14), the new Fort Worth staged the new modernist city. That it was also something of a consumerist paradise did not deter many from praising it. In a 1957 piece, Jane Jacobs called the Fort Worth Plan an "exception" to the already dead-looking plans on the urban renewal horizon, the design's liveliness and variety providing the necessary complexities of urbanity. "Intricate, pluralistic, flexible," she later added, noting that the plan's most radical element was its mix of new and existing elements (not unlike earlier urban "tinker" plans; see chapter 3), bringing both meaning and efficiency to bear on the problem of the existing

Figure 6.13. Victor Gruen Associates, Fort Worth Plan (Fort Worth, Texas), *A Greater Fort Worth Tomorrow.*

city.[43] And although the plan was widely acclaimed and followed by local and national news, it nevertheless proved too "visionary" for downtown business and civic and state stakeholders, and the project was consigned to paper.[44]

The Fort Worth Plan played a key role in shaping the discourse of designing and redesigning cities based, it was widely claimed, on the lessons of the suburbs. Gruen's plan was widely lauded for its introduction into the city of suburban shopping center strategies that designers had borrowed and transformed so, as Gruen put it, they could repay their "debt" to the city. This trope was a constant in Gruen's rhetoric and was common in the professional and popular literature. *Business Week* and *Fortune* announced that Gruen's suburban shopping centers offered design elements that could solve the problems of the city.[45]

Older shopping districts were also "ripe" for what were sometimes called suburban lessons. *Architectural Forum* editors in 1953 presented a rehabilitation plan for an older Chicago district (Figure 6.15) in the same issue as a discussion of Gruen's proposed Southdale Shopping Center. The "Chicago Plan," also called the "perimeter

Figure 6.14. Victor Gruen Associates, Fort Worth Plan (Fort Worth, Texas), *A Greater Fort Worth Tomorrow.*

plan," applied "suburban shopping center lessons" in which traffic was diverted around a congested shopping district and the overrun streets were turned into "pedestrian malls."[46] Gruen's 1953 proposal for the core of the small Wisconsin town of Appleton (Figure 6.16) used the same strategy and suburbanization rhetoric: a series of reorganized superblocks were accessed by a one-way circumferential-regional road and organized around a "landscaped pedestrian mall" created by closed streets.[47] The shopping center came to represent the perfectibility of large-scale designed environments.

Building on the idea of a coherent, modern precinct-based city, Gruen wrote in 1954 that older city centers, like suburban shopping centers, should be "organized into various land usage elements, each with its own parking area, its own green area and with its own surrounding traffic arteries." Alongside images of his Appleton plan, Gruen continued: each separated area would be "restricted in size to make it useful and enjoyable to the pedestrian." Suburban "islands of order" needed to be carved from the dense and obsolete urban fabric.[48] In the city, this would entail multilevel parking facilities, pedestrian zones, and tall buildings. The city and the entire metropolitan region could be reorganized and made into a series of units and

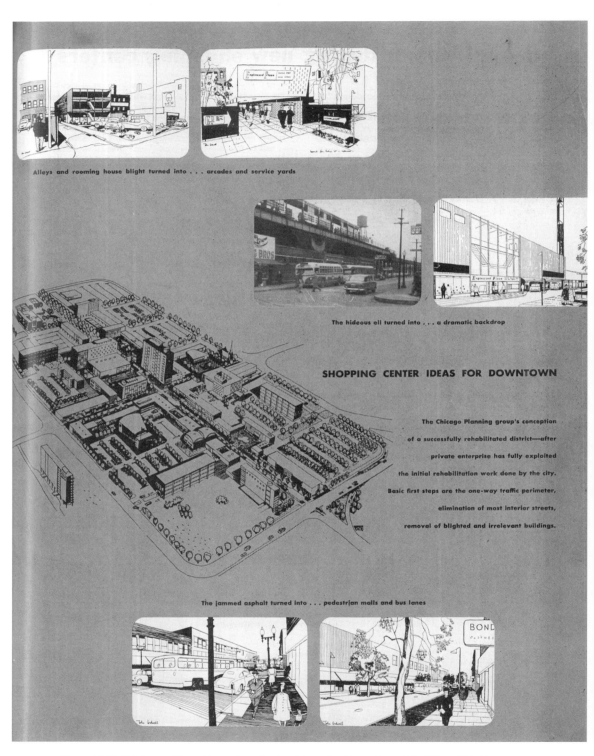

Alleys and rooming house blight turned into . . . arcades and service yards

The hideous el turned into . . . a dramatic backdrop

SHOPPING CENTER IDEAS FOR DOWNTOWN

The Chicago Planning group's conception
of a successfully rehabilitated district—after
private enterprise has fully exploited
the initial rehabilitation work done by the city.
Basic first steps are the one-way traffic perimeter,
elimination of most interior streets,
removal of blighted and irrelevant buildings.

The jammed asphalt turned into . . . pedestrian malls and bus lanes

Figure 6.15. "Chicago Plan: Shopping Center Ideas for Downtown," in "New Thinking on Shopping Centers," *Architectural Forum* 98 (March 1953): 122.

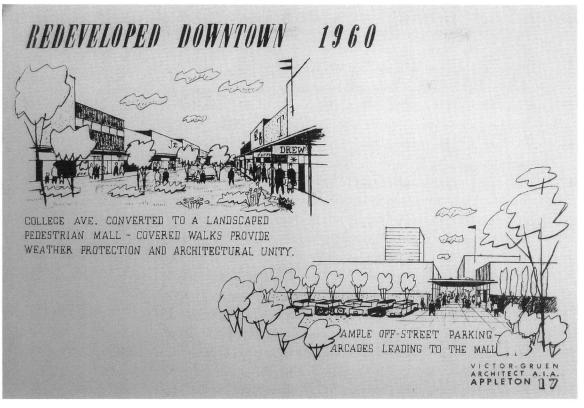

Figure 6.16. Victor Gruen Associates, Appleton Plan (Appleton, Wisconsin), *Downtown Appleton: Its Future?* (September 1953). Box 21, Victor Gruen Collection, American Heritage Center, University of Wyoming.

precincts, directly picking up the unit discourse that had shaped urban and planning ideas since the 1930s.

Gruen demonstrated a remarkable fluidity in the ways urban and suburban problems could be addressed, and in one presentation, he showed how Northland and Fort Worth offered nearly identical solutions to planning problems.[49] The problem in both was to "unscramble" various traffic, use, and spatial overlaps so the entire complex, in the city or not, could function frictionlessly. The guiding design principle was the seamless perambulation by the citizen underpinned by massive servicing and control. However, this perfected machine was based on neither urban nor suburban locations but on modernist architectural and urban tenets. In other words, Gruen and many other observers often described pedestrianization as the product of the suburban shopping center, and the trope has become utterly axiomatic. However, the vision of a smoothly run, pedestrian social complex joining visual, technical, and infrastructural elements of a city was also a decidedly modernist idea.

Hearts of the City

Alongside rationalist and scientific threads of American urban improvement since the early 1900s, the dream of the perfected city was also integral to the discourse of the garden city movement and especially CIAM-based modernism. The city as a well-functioning machine was central to the narrative of the 1942 CIAM *Can Our Cities Survive?*, organized around a quasi-scientific rendering of the "four functions": dwelling, work, recreation, and transportation. A decade later, CIAM's *The Heart of the City*, an edited compilation of statements and projects from the 1951 CIAM meeting in Great Britain, dramatically demonstrated a strategic realignment of priorities, techniques, and terms. The book's theme of "the core" and a pedestrian, precinct-based urbanism was a remarkable turnabout, even as it maintained an underpinning of highly planned systems. Laced with discussion and images of older urban streets and people-filled piazzas—Venice's Saint Mark's being the most prominent, alongside Rockefeller Center—*The Heart of the City* made more than evident a new view of the culture of the city. Architecture could and should create unmediated, unscripted, and "humanized" encounters between citizens as the first step to a revitalized society. Gone were the critiques of overmechanization and unguided property development of CIAM's earlier years, and in their place were discussions of vitality, complexity, and the layers of history that shaped older and new urban cores. In such places, "secure from traffic, where the pedestrian can move about freely," there could be a return to democratic process, "collective emotion," and an enriching culture. At various scales and locations, the new core would create and nourish a sense of community through a mix of urban functions, and the "right of the pedestrian" would restore dignity to the citizen, whose cars would be "on the periphery."[50] The apparent retreat from the hyperrationalism of prewar CIAM policies was substantial, and it did not go unnoticed.

Arthur Comey, a landscape architect and planner, praised the CIAM book as "inspiring" because its "central thesis" calling for the use of pedestrian plazas provided a clear "cause to plead for." In fact, he wondered why Ketchum's 1946 plan for pedestrianizing Rye's main street was not included (see chapter 4). In a similar vein, architect Robert Weinberg was less than sanguine about battling automobiles and mass communications but nevertheless found in his review of *The Heart of the City* that the "core" approach provided a satisfying "perception of the spirit of a city" rather than a mere quantitative reorganization and, furthermore, that the "pedestrian plaza" could take its proper community-making place alongside the village greens of "old England and New England." Weinberg illustrated his review with the CIAM members' plans for Stevenage, Great Britain (Figure 6.17) (Gordon Stephenson et al.), and Tumaco, Colombia (Wiener and Sert), and while he worried that the illustrated projects might be homogeneous, he praised the pedestrian-based

logic of the new approach to cities.[51] Most telling, however, is that Weinberg explicitly examined the logic of the CIAM proposals, and hence of the emerging norms
of modernism, favorably comparing their urban core projects to new shopping centers in the United States and, in effect, placing Gruen and CIAM on the same disciplinary page.

In *The Heart of the City,* José Luis Sert and Sigfried Giedion made a few references
to American shopping centers as communal places. Sert praised the shopping center's
capacity to "protect pedestrian circulation," to "recentralize" social life, and to utilize landscape to foster social interaction and for offering "new opportunities to
reassert an urban culture unmolested by the car." Giedion went further and wrote
that the new shopping centers in the United States offered a necessary dose of genuine human contact and could create important gathering places. American shopping centers, he later wrote, provide "points of crystallization for the social life of
the people" and "give evidence of the newly realized need to provide some space

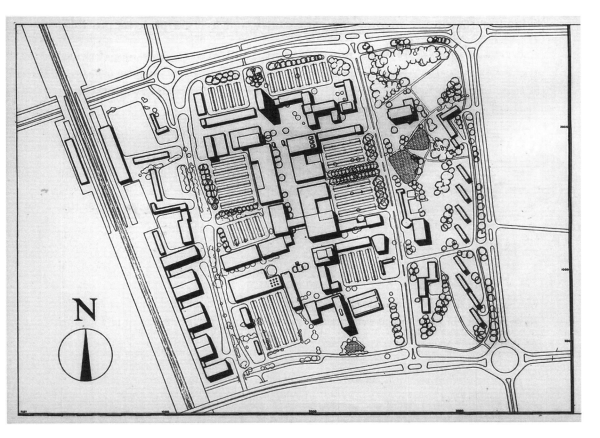

Figure 6.17. Gordon Stephenson, Stevenage, 1950, in *The Heart of the City: Towards the
Humanisation of Urban Life,* edited by J. Tyrwhitt, J. L. Sert, and E. N. Rogers (New York:
Pellegrini and Cudahy, 1952), 122.

where long neglected contacts between the inhabitants can take place." As an example, Giedion praised I. M. Pei's Roosevelt Field Shopping Center, then nearing completion in 1955 outside New York City (see Figure I.5).[52] None of this was news to Gruen, who had developed his position about pedestrian zones as early as 1943. Pedestrian "landscaped places" would not only aid sales, he wrote in 1948, but would also be places to engage "matters of public interest." In 1952, Gruen expanded his view and wrote that the shopping center "offers again, to modern man, the values of informal order, well-scaled environment and relaxed activity that were characteristic of the old-time plaza or the country market, lost to the chaos of downtown development."[53]

Rose-colored though his view on "old-time" urbanism might have been, one cannot miss Gruen's CIAM-like tone and aspirations, or the shared term "crystallization," which seemed to join the various threads of a new urbanity, made possible by a modern approach. While Gruen often made a show of disaffection from the "elite" realm of urban theory, his own theorization of the shopping center as urban node, in or outside the city, paralleled and staked his claim within modernist urban discourse. Most simply, however, the formal attributes of the projects that filled the CIAM book matched Fort Worth in detail—a pedestrian precinct was a technological and social construction of modernism.

Among the many claims one might make for *The Heart of the City* is that the illustrated projects, as noted by various reviewers at the time and since, shared a formal architectural and urban language.[54] Many of the proposals—for cities such as Stevenage, Lausanne, Oslo, and Liège—were remarkably similar in site planning, massing, connections to existing or new city fabric, program organization, and spatial scale. The projects were based on units, precincts, and a shared pedestrian realm, fed by hidden (or gleaming) infrastructures, peripheral access roads, and regional connections. They were modernist visions designed to revitalize their respective urban cores or create new ones far from the city. Just as important, they were demonstrations of the capacity and knowledge of the modern architect to lead such massive interventions. In this sense, *The Heart of the City* echoed and reinforced Gruen's perceptions of his own role and of his approach to architecture. When he cited the CIAM book in his 1954 article on shopping centers, it was to show that his work arrived at the same conclusions as CIAM about the nature of modern architecture in the city and in the suburb. Fort Worth was his contribution to this discourse, and it was no accident that his 1964 book on the "cure" for troubled cities was titled *The Heart of Our Cities.*[55]

Urban or Suburban or Modern?

Among Victor Gruen's papers is a page from a 1953 issue of the Dutch magazine *Bouw* about the Lijnbaan, an urban reconstruction project at the center of Rotterdam.

The page shows details of the project, which had just opened to the public, and is inscribed "To Mr. Gruen" although the signature is illegible.[56] That an official or another architect thought the widely discussed project would be of interest to Gruen shows the scope of his reputation in the making of commercial spaces as well as his place in a story of modernism.

Designed by CIAM members J. H. van den Broek and Jaap Bakema, the Lijnbaan was a central feature of the rebuilding of Rotterdam after wartime destruction (Figure 6.18).[57] Consisting of stores, offices, and housing, the project was organized around a central spine created by several long, shallow buildings housing the shops. The typical section of the project was a fifty-foot-wide paved pedestrian street faced on both sides with two-story, concrete frame buildings divided into commercial spaces. A continuous 1.5-meter overhang on both sides of the street linked the store-fronts, and covered walkways crossed the pedestrian areas at various points. Small streets running behind the store blocks enabled all servicing needs. These streets also provided automotive access to a series of three- and ten-story residential slabs behind the commercial buildings, which wove the project into the fabric of the city beyond. At the ground plane along the pedestrian allée, storefronts—in ways that Morris Ketchum or Morris Lapidus would have lauded—receded from and projected into space that was taken up with display cases, kiosks, planters, seating, trees, and other amenities. As a small part of a larger urban intervention, the Lijnbaan stood out as a "sparkling" gem that, critics noted, augured well for an urban future.[58] The reception of the project in the United States yields important insight into the thinking of postwar architects and urbanists.

American critics uniformly praised the Lijnbaan for bringing pedestrian, auto-free space to the city's core. Featured on the cover of a 1954 issue of the ULI's journal *Urban Land* with the caption "Europe's Fifth Avenue," the project was widely discussed and circulated. The Lijnbaan, the ULI wrote, was a "practical" demonstration of the "rehabilitation" of downtown shopping areas, which could nicely counter the suburban shopping center's increasingly powerful allure. Gruen lauded the design, saying that American downtown shopping districts might "take a lesson from Lijnbaan's setup."[59] Catherine Bauer compared the Lijnbaan favorably to Edmund Bacon's pedestrian-friendly plans for Penn Center in Philadelphia, and Lewis Mumford gave an unusually strong endorsement of the project, saying, "Here is a sound urban form that could be adopted anywhere."[60] That Gruen would be asked to comment on such a project was further evidence that he was perceived as uniquely capable of combining commerce and modern urban design.[61]

The examination of urban structure and spatial organization was a massive project in the postwar years in the United States (as elsewhere), and the pedestrian continued to be an icon for remediating (not always successfully) perceived urban ills. Fueled by selective federal largesse, the remaking of American downtown districts

EUROPE'S FIFTH AVENUE
Lijnbaan-Rotterdam Testifies to Success of the Downtown Shopping Center
By ROBERT KIEK, Consultant to the Lijnbaan Association

Figure 6.18. Robert Kiek, "Europe's Fifth Avenue," *Urban Land* 13 (October 1954): 6.

gained momentum after 1949, even as approaches and strategies were still under considerable debate.[62] In 1953, *Architectural Forum* sponsored an "Urban Traffic Forum," and in 1955 (*before* Gruen's Fort Worth Plan was announced) it cosponsored a conference, "How to Build Cities Downtown," with the National Retail Dry Goods Association.[63] The first conference stressed the technical question of the city in the guise of movement and parking, and the latter examined a more regional version of urban congestion; both focused on the restructuring of the city. Participants included department store organizations, transportation and parking experts, and government planners as well as planners and architects Oscar Stonorov, Carl Feiss, Kenneth Welch, Frederick Adams, and Morris Ketchum. Presentations at both events stressed tactics that were becoming familiar: in-town garages, off-street loading, new transit systems, closed streets, inner and outer loop roads, radial freeways, and, of course, pedestrian-friendly (although not always pedestrian-only) city cores.[64] These conferences detailed an array of hurdles as well as opportunities in urban redevelopment and were part of a much broader examination of the state of the city by professionals. Most notable was that the participating architects worked under the mantle of modern architecture and brought to the problem of the city their experience with pedestrian and merchandising work.

Continuing the growth of a modern urban discourse, "urban design" was given status, a framework, and vocabulary at a 1956 conference held at Harvard's Graduate School of Design. The discussions that took place there, which were published in *Progressive Architecture,* were based on the theories and applications of modernist principles at a new scale. The conference was represented as the culmination of the entire CIAM project, with a new American tenor and direction.[65] Gruen's Fort Worth project was treated in the proceedings as one of many urban projects, such as proposals for Pittsburgh, Philadelphia, and Boston, among others. Most pointedly, all the work shared particular tactics, including pedestrian zones, open spaces, and highway connections, none of which appeared to need reference to suburban design experiments. Jane Jacobs, for instance, praised the urbanity of Fort Worth, and Carl Feiss examined at length several urban design projects, including Fort Worth, and argued in support of modern urban intervention without reference to suburbs.[66] The conference sought to formulate a coherent body of modernist urban design principles, and the Fort Worth Plan easily fit this program. Merchandising and stores were part of the discussions, but neither the suburb nor shopping played a central part in this project.

Other contemporary urban restructuring projects of the early 1950s also inform the context of Gruen's Fort Worth Plan. Oscar Stonorov and Louis Kahn offered a vision of incremental urban change in the late 1940s (see Figure 4.2), inserting into Philadelphia's older gridded fabric new pedestrian zones, reoriented streets, and rescaled movement patterns. In 1953, Kahn's Philadelphia studies, published in *Perspecta* (Figure 6.19), demonstrated a dramatic rethinking of the scale and flow of the city. These now-famous drawings demonstrated parking "harbors" inside remade blocks, hierarchical movement systems, and monumental parking structures and pointed to a system supporting the pedestrian experience of the city.[67] These techniques were presaged in urban tinkering projects in the 1940s (as discussed in chapter 3), and while not identical to Fort Worth, more than evident among them is a shared set of urban ideas based on units and precincts, largely derived from modernist principles—from garden city to CIAM.

After 1954, when federal legislation codified particular forms of urban intervention, many cities embarked on projects that would socially and physically reshape their downtowns in pursuit of new housing, new jobs, and new civic and commercial development.[68] Through new urban plans and "urban renewal," cities such as Sacramento, Pittsburgh, Detroit, Kansas City, and St. Louis, among many others,

Market Street as a dock

Chestnut Street as a pedestrian way

Figure 6.19. Louis Kahn, pedestrian way, "Toward a Plan for Midtown Philadelphia,"
Perspecta 2 (1953): 18.

erased and restructured large sections of their downtown cores and shopping districts.[69] These projects often depended on exclusive, if not racist, assumptions about power, economic development, and decision making, and they also actively employed the formal tools of modernist urbanism, especially an urbanism based on the unitized block, the precinct, the pedestrian, and the movement and storage of the car. That such tactics became part of a regime of urban restructuring that served decidedly narrow political and economic interests raises questions, ultimately, about other ways such modernist tools might have been (or were yet to be) utilized.[70] Putting stores and shopping centers back into modernist discourse increases the necessity of such scrutiny.

Total Pedestrian Pastoral

Careening across the American wilderness, the monumental steam engine was naturalized, as Leo Marx described it, through imagery that rendered the machine as part of a metaphoric garden and thus muted the dissonance a viewer might have registered. The accommodation of the machine in the garden undergirded the modernization of the American landscape, capturing it for use by the machinery of capital and nation building. The naturalizing of conflicting elements, the trope of pastoralism, can also be read in reverse. The regional shopping center (or perhaps any large-scale modernist building complex) was a garden in a machine. The pedestrian precinct, made logical by the neighborhood unit and the superblock, with sympathetic art and music, "milk bars," and, of course, "nature" in the guise of shrubs, bushes, fountains, and metal birds, was, it seemed, as close to paradise as one can imagine. This was a perfected garden, Edenic and serene, held in place by a vast social, economic, and technical machinery—symbolized by the cars sited safely outside the precinct. The shopping center offered pleasure and community enabled by a highly qualified set of physical and social circumstances. Adding to what Tim Mennel calls the "technological substrate" for such large-scale undertakings, the shopping center was perhaps the strangely fulfilled dream of modernism.[71] The role of the shopping center, in the city and outside it, was to demonstrate that modern methods were technically, professionally, and representationally coherent and logical, even if the architects were placed in the unenviable position of revealing the profession's all-too-close ties to capital. No matter; the best was yet to come.

Victor Gruen's fully air-conditioned Southdale Shopping Center outside Minneapolis opened in 1956 and was breathlessly praised in popular and professional media (Figure 6.20). *Architectural Forum* editors described the protected, regulated, and sedate interior as "more like downtown than downtown itself."[72] Compact yet uncongested, technically yet invisibly innovative, roofed but skylighted for natural light, and severing the auto from the shopper completely, the center offered an image of a frictionless modern social life. Gruen described the new environment through various paradoxes indicating the ironies, if also the potential, of the shopping center: "variety without confusion, colorful appearance without garishness, gaiety without vulgarity."[73] In the "garden court," serendipity and informal gathering were part of the program and fashion and art shows were regular events. Harry Bertoia's *Golden Trees* sculptures (installed at the same time as his work in Chase Bank in New York City) endowed the garden court with a bucolic referent and offered art as balm and legitimacy for a space controlled by consumption.[74] In Southdale, the total package of aesthetic, formal, spatial, administrative, marketing, engineering, and planning controls evidenced a mature and fully instrumentalized modernism. The project was not about the suburbs but about modernity; cities and suburbs would never be the same.

Figure 6.20. Victor Gruen Associates, Southdale Shopping Center (interior), Edina, Minnesota, 1956. Sculpture by Harry Bertoia in background. Courtesy of the Minnesota Historical Society.

Southdale was not the first enclosed shopping center proposed. Gruen had proposed such a project for a suburban Houston shopping center in 1950.[75] An early 1951 proposal by Pietro Belluschi (assisted by Ken Welch, among others) for Baltimore's Mondawmin Shopping Center entailed an enclosed, air-conditioned shopping space, but the project was built as a two-story outdoor mall, only later enclosed.[76] At about the time of Southdale's opening, Ketchum wrote that new shopping centers would, eventually, contain all of the typical downtown under one roof. Based on the emerging trend of a "merchandising island surrounded by parking space," he wrote, full enclosure was the logical next step. The result will be a "varied, interesting and attractive pattern of indoor shopping streets with no feeling of either monotony or claustrophobia."[77] Ketchum's optimism, like Gruen's and that of many others, for the total design control of such a project remains the troublesome heart of the shopping center, not unlike modernist design thinking of the mid-twentieth century.

Long before Southdale, Walter Benjamin observed the frisson created by the pedestrian realms of the Parisian arcade. The tension, he found, was that interiorization was never complete, and despite its comforts, there was always a teasing hint of an outside to experience and to consciousness that would interrupt the easy containments of consumption. The charms of the world of goods could never quite close the deal. That the shopping center operated in the same way, and perhaps continues to operate in the same way—that is, as a *not quite* totalized environment—indicates that the pedestrian modern, like the broader lens of modernism in America, was, and is, an unfinished story.

CONCLUSION

PEDESTRIAN MODERN
FUTURES

Arcades are houses or passages having no outside—like the dream.
—W A L T E R B E N J A M I N , *The Arcades Project,* 1999

WALTER BENJAMIN wrote that Eugène Atget's images of deserted Parisian streets were comparable to crime scene photographs in which action is suspended and all hints of human presence are elided (Figure C.1).[1] In particular, Atget's 1920s store windows may have been empty of subjects, but they were bursting with signs of active consumption. This absent presence was a sign of modernity—the window became a flat screen onto which the world was projected, and, at the same time, it joined interior to exterior, the space of the store to the city beyond. The images document the world of commodities not merely as the outcome of mass production but also as a libidinal prompt made possible by the social system, which worked more efficiently with plate-glass windows. Yet Benjamin was ambivalent about the role of goods, and Atget's images, he wrote, "stir the viewer" and raise questions, perhaps nudging the viewer toward an understanding of the reach of modernity and its material correlate, goods.

Notable here is that Kenneth Welch took a keen interest in shopwindow lighting, glass angles, reflection parameters, and views.[2] If Gruen and Lapidus fixed upon the shopwindow as almost a comedy, Lönberg-Holm saw it as a transparent plan, and Frederick Kiesler understood it as

Figure C.1. Eugène Atget, *Avenue des Gobelins,* 1925. Ford Motor Company Collection, Gift of Ford Motor Company and John C. Waddell, 1987. Image copyright The Metropolitan Museum of Art/Art Resource, New York.

liberative, Welch's technical expertise in the "science" of glass fills out a picture of a complex modernity in which the store was an active site of change.

So, too, the infamous Parisian arcades that fascinated Benjamin presaged another trajectory of modernity. Inserted into the hidden cores of the city's residential blocks, the arcades were made possible by skylights of iron and glass, and the stores were stocked with upper-class goods provided by the humming engines of mass production. Yet the space and atmosphere of the arcade were hard to describe, and Benjamin was uneasy, finding in the always-even, dimmed lighting an awkward pleasure in being almost lost but always comfortably managed. The arcades defied categories of time as well as the cues of inside and outside, street and courtyard, and created a space of possibility despite, or alongside, what Sigfried Giedion called their "lascivious" extractive function.[3] As an unknowable and liminal space lined with display windows and goods, the arcade was a strange piece of urban design. Like their spectacular descendants, the department stores, the arcades were glimpses of a designed and planned urban future, an almost totalizing condition—witness the attraction they held for Charles Fourier and other utopianists. As a fragment of a city made modern, in which ever-greater mechanisms of control and oversight were implicit, the arcade remained, somehow, prosaic and pedestrian. This was how the store and the shopping center, in the city or not, could be modern. Southdale, Gruen's enclosed mall, and his subsequent Midtown Plaza in Rochester, New York (which opened in 1962), showed that complete containment might yet be the central design legacy of modernism and shopping.[4]

In this book, I have posited that designs for shopping, rather than being a secondary part of the architectural practices of the modern movement in the United States, were deeply embedded in that movement's discourse. Quite simply, we can understand modernism better if we see stores as sites of historically specific architectural experimentation, and, conversely, we can better grapple with the design of spaces for shopping if we understand them as modern architecture, not merely as the products of economic modernization or suburbanization. But perceptions continue to change.

Walking Back to the Future?

In the summer of 2008, the New York City Department of Transportation proposed "Broadway Boulevard," a length of the famed street between Times Square and Herald Square substantially closed to automobiles, with expanded space for pedestrian movement and café furniture. Months later, the department announced more street closings in the area and an intention to implement the pedestrianization program in other parts of the city.[5]

The overlooked fact in the debates that have surrounded the city's new program is that street closing is a recurring idea in the conception and implementation of the modernist American city. Since the 1930s, as noted throughout this book, the transformation of the street has been an explicit part of a modern program for a new social life. In 1948, New York architect Simon Breines proposed closing parts of Fifth Avenue to create "pedestrian islands" for shopping and walking (Figure C.2). A few years later, Victor Gruen told the *New York Times* that much of Thirty-Fourth Street near Herald Square should become a pedestrian mall.[6] Following on his well-regarded 1955 Fort Worth Plan as well as his suburban shopping centers, Gruen embarked on a new set of projects for downtown shopping districts. After the opening of his Kalamazoo Mall in 1959 (Figure C.3), countless similar, if less ambitious, projects were planned—and some carried out. In 1959, the *Washington Post* reported that one hundred cities were already working on permanent and temporary pedestrian malls.[7] Evident in projects such as Fresno's Fulton Mall (Gruen, 1964) and Brooklyn's Fulton Mall (NYC Urban Design Group and Lee Harris Pomeroy, 1975), the perception among planners, architects, public officials, and store owners was that urban congestion, urban "problems"—often involving racial and ethnic succession—and suburban competition had to be addressed if the downtown retailing function was to survive. The pedestrian mall seemed like a perfect and simple solution to failing shopping districts; the only problem was that the larger system of loop roads, parking, and regional connections were often implemented halfheartedly at best. Gruen and others warned that pedestrianization needed to be part of a regional plan, a broad enterprise beyond adding more customers.[8]

At the same time, the growth of an architectural literature about pedestrian malls showed that the malls were not merely commercial resolutions to congestion or failing downtowns but also part of a critique of the ways in which modernism had transformed the city. A 1965 *Architects' Year Book* organized by the theme "The Pedestrian in the City" included work by Gruen alongside that of a very mixed group including Archigram, Eduardo Paolozzi, Candilis-Josic-Woods, and Maxwell Fry. The contributors utilized a variety of approaches to cities, but they shared a strong focus on the role of the pedestrian.[9] In 1969, Bernard Rudofsky, longtime advocate of an "unregimented modernism," published *Streets for People,* a paean to the informal life of the street, in which only three or four contemporary works were shown, one of which was Gruen's plan for Fort Worth. With its many layers of movement, Rudofsky wrote, Gruen's plan "made architectural history."[10] As a renewal and extension of modernism, pedestrianization would enable architects to continue to shape the city in progressive ways. In fact, pedestrianization became a critique of modernism.

As an emerging engagement with the tenets of established modernism, more focus on the street (perceived or real) continued. In 1972, architect Roberto Brambilla organized an exhibit titled *Against the Automobile, for the City* and brought the project to Jacquelin Robertson, then head of the New York City Office of Midtown Planning and Development (Figure C.4).[11] Robertson was trying to implement the

EASTER SUNDAY: PEDESTRIAN HEAVEN

FIFTH AVENUE

EVERY DAY: PEDESTRIAN HELL

Figure C.2. "Fifth Avenue," in Simon Breines and John Dean, "City People on the Move: A Policy for Guided Urban Growth" (unpublished manuscript, New York, April 1948), following page 39.

city's (ultimately unsuccessful) proposal to pedestrianize parts of Madison Avenue. Encouraged by Robertson, Brambilla formed the Institute for Environmental Action and published *More Streets for People* in 1972.[12] The book is dedicated to Rudofsky, who contributed to it alongside Jane Jacobs, William H. Whyte, Louis Mumford, and others. Subsequently, Brambilla and the architect Gianni Longo published five detailed volumes on pedestrianization procedures and an abridged compilation of these volumes in their 1977 survey as *For Pedestrians Only,* with an introduction by Rudofsky.[13] The trajectory of the pedestrian as a catalyst of urban debate continued in the observations of Whyte, whose book *The Social Life of Small Urban Places* (1980) initiated a new wave of examinations of, and projects for, the streets and pedestrian zones of the city.[14] Whyte's mantle has been taken up by Danish architect Jan Gehl, who served as New York City's consultant leading to the recent Times Square plan for pedestrians. Despite the failure of many 1960s and 1970s pedestrianization projects in the United States—with many torn up after only a decade of use—this short lineage shows that designers' and urbanists' fascination with the re-making of urban space through the figure of the pedestrian is an important modernist legacy—as critique *and* advocacy—although the results were uneven.[15]

Yet, for some, suburbanization lurks behind pedestrianization. In 2009, the *New York Times* architecture critic Nicolai Ouroussoff wrote about New York's pedestrian

Figure C.3. The Mall, Kalamazoo, Michigan, 1960.

Figure C.4. Van Ginkel Associates, Forty-eighth Street and Madison Avenue, New York, "New Patterns for a Metropolis," *Architectural Forum* (October 1971): 28.

zones: "If the city decides to keep the plazas, it will have to design the spaces in a way that genuinely reflects the urban toughness of the city that feeds into them. It can't simply recreate an image of a medieval European park. Or a mall in Southern California."[16] A warning that such planned public, outdoor spaces will form an impoverished social space, without grit or character, requires examination. Ouroussoff reported that the Department of Transportation's plan was partly inspired by recent streetscape redevelopments in Copenhagen, which enjoys its historical buildings, programmed outdoor plazas, and an urbane culture, whereas in New York, somehow, the pedestrian plaza runs the risk of an association with a suburban—that is, less than urban—landscape. Other writers have expressed the concern that the transformation of automobile streets into pedestrianized zones is a part of the "suburbanization of the city," a creeping sanitization or insipidity fueled by overdevelopment.[17] In this book, I have shown that pedestrianization is a hallmark of *modern* architecture, proposed for urban and suburban sites in equal measure. New York City's planning experiments are not always typical, but turning over precious, "100 percent location" urban asphalt to pedestrians has become part of the tactical toolbox that planners employ when they rethink the use of city streets. If there is room for complaint, as there always is, the shift to or from the suburb is not the issue; rather, the issue is that modernist pedestrianization has also been embedded in the transformations wrought by social and economic modernization.

Dead Malls

In 1960, the Republican candidate for the U.S. presidency, Vice President Richard Nixon, stopped at seven shopping centers in one of his campaign swings through the Midwest. In his speeches Nixon referred to shopping centers and freeways as signs of progress and prosperity for all Americans.[18] Both the choices of sites for his campaigning and his descriptions indicate that by 1960 the aims of many modern architects—Victor Gruen hardly alone among them—had been met: the shopping center had become a stage where consumerism and citizenship actively supported each other. Even if citizenship was highly qualified and (sometimes violently) contested, pedestrianization appeared to be the architectural means to modernist ends.

The success of shopping centers has also been their weakness. In recent years, the American landscape has been "overstored" and "overmalled," so that inner-ring and older suburbs today suffer from empty malls (Figure C.5). Although exceptionally profitable and celebrated, shopping malls were (and remain) subject to ever-changing growth patterns and to the unique financial structures that enabled them. In the past half century, as middle-class whites moved up the real estate ladder into newer, more exurban residential developments, inner suburban communities often moved down the same ladder. This was not without some benefits, since the smaller houses of older communities became affordable for less affluent and often marginalized

Figure C.5. Dixie Square Mall, Harvey, Illinois.

groups aspiring to single-family homes with backyards and barbecues. However, the older shopping centers and their business models were inflexible. Typical development patterns, where builders seek cheaper land farther and farther from the city core, have usually meant that "today's" shiny, attractive new mall often becomes "tomorrow's" boarded-up or empty mall.[19] Abandoned, boarded-up, or still in their death throes, these malls no longer generate profits and no longer serve their communities; they become visible evidence of narrowly defined design and planning.

In recent years, the social and economic values of these moribund sites have been recognized, and some malls have been rebuilt, with added functions such as housing and office uses. Others have become more community-based places, often straddling profit and nonprofit status, providing sites for community centers, schools, or outpatient health care facilities.[20] Proposals have sought to place malls back into the local social systems from which they were removed. By extracting malls from the flow of capital that created them and setting up a more broad-based idea of community that the malls might serve, planners might yet create malls that fulfill the dreams of Gruen and other modern architects.

Total Publics

There were no reports of protesters at Vice President Nixon's shopping center campaign stops, but one wonders how the right to exercise free speech would have been interpreted at these political rallies held on private property. Malls since 1960 have become contested spaces in large part because they have come to act as de facto public spaces for so many people.[21] In some states, mall owners are required to provide space for peaceful speech on their premises, but these are exceptions to the general rule of authority over private property. Indoor or outdoor, malls have been subject to the interests of their owners, for whom any "disturbance," no matter how trivial, is grounds for removal. There is little if any adjudication or appeal in this mixing of public and private social roles, and this condition contributes to conceptions of the mall as an "interiorized" place, that is, a place where references and connections to the larger world are muted, if not erased.

Southdale's central atrium took to the extreme the modernist notion of control, order, and rationality. In the United States, malls and, more generally, atriums have housed escalators, art, skating rinks, food courts, post offices, mobile kiosks, and amusement parks, as well as all sorts of events—or none at all. Despite this seeming variety, atriums have come to dominate a variety of building types, where they create something akin to a floating signifier of "the public" even as the term has grown more vague and misrecognized. Fredric Jameson saw in the hotel atriums of John Portman a new space of placelessness produced by capital.[22] Late-modern architectural works used atriums extensively: Kevin Roche's Ford Foundation headquarters (1967) (Figure C.6), HOK's Houston Galleria (1970), and I. M. Pei's East Wing of

Figure C.6. Roche-Dinkeloo, Ford Foundation headquarters, New York, interior, *Progressive Architecture* 49 (February 1968): 95.

the National Gallery (1976) were all organized around atriums and were discussed as retreats from the urban (or suburban) condition; Pei's East Wing was directly compared to the suburban mall.[23] The atrium, now seen everywhere and suiting any program, is proof that the mall was deeply if problematically effective in normalizing modernist forms of space making—a place apart, cleansed and distant from selected aspects of the social realm.

And the controlling, modernist impulse of the mall and atrium have, remarkably, unenclosed counterparts in some American cities: privately owned public spaces (POPS). Such spaces have become part of the pedestrian landscape. In several American cities, planning agencies since the 1960s have offered bonuses to builders in exchange for building "public" amenities on their properties. In New York City, the awarding of additional buildable square footage to developers in return for including pedestrian plazas resulted in a mix of public space and the marketplace.[24] POPS have become integral parts of urban life in some cities, and they have also been contentious. In the 1980s and 1990s, various art and architectural projects examined the policing, exclusions, and regulation of indoor and outdoor POPS that were administratively approved as public, and most found the concept honored in the breach.[25] These spaces have been surveyed, rated, taken over by the homeless or by cafés (or both), "improved," and, in 2011, "occupied." Many of these uses have challenged the institutions of power and governance to regulate what many perceive as functionally, and *necessarily,* public. These pedestrianized realms, heirs to the trajectory of modernism and merchandising, have been at the very center of design, politics, and economics, hiding in plain sight and waiting for their paradoxes to emerge on a wider stage.

NOTES

Introduction

1. "The Splashiest Shopping Center in the U.S."

2. The Valley Fair Shopping Center in Appleton, Wisconsin, opened in 1955 but was considered a partial enclosure. The term *shopping mall* was not used until the mid-1960s; until then, shopping centers were said to have malls—that is, green or landscaped areas for walking.

3. Accelerated depreciation dramatically altered the financial calculus of commercial construction. See Hanchett, "U.S. Tax Policy and the Shopping-Center Boom of the 1950s and 1960s."

4. Gillette, "The Evolution of the Planned Shopping Center in Suburb and City."

5. Timothy Mennel insightfully discusses this tension of total planning in "Victor Gruen and the Construction of Cold War Utopias."

6. Marx, *The Machine in the Garden,* 220.

7. Sert, "Centres of Community Life." See also Mumford, *The CIAM Discourse on Urbanism, 1928–1960.*

8. On Macy's "interior display managers," see Leach, *Land of Desire,* 319; Ferry, *A History of the Department Store.* Standard reference merchandising texts rarely included any discussion of architects. Not until about 1940 was the architectural profession considered in, for instance, Duncan and Phillips, *Retailing Principles and Methods.* See also Clausen, "The Department Store"; Siry, *Carson Pirie Scott,* 119–28; Bruegmann, *The Architects and the City.*

9. The Parsons School of Design began as the New York School of Fine and Applied Arts, with programs such as "advertising display" and "commercial design." See "Frank A. Parsons, Art Educator, Dies," *New York Times,* May 27, 1930, 25. See also Richards, *Art in Industry,* 251–310.

10. Meikle, *Twentieth Century Limited,* 50–51; Wilson, Pilgrim, and Tashjian, *The Machine Age in America, 1918–1941*; Leach, *Land of Desire,* 307–8. Although many in the architectural profession saw the industrial designers as competition, others in architecture culture did not reject the designers; see Reid, "Walter Dorwin Teague." See also Marcus, *The American Store Window.* In the 1920s, Raymond Loewy worked as a "displayman" for Macy's, and Bel Geddes

255

was the display director of New York City's Franklin Simon store. See "Window Display by Bel Geddes," *New York Times,* August 29, 1927, 20. In Sheldon and Arens, *Consumer Engineering,* the term *consumer engineer* is attributed to the famed advertising executive Earnest Elmo Calkins.

11. Woods, *From Craft to Profession*; Larson, "Emblem and Exception"; Gutman, *Architectural Practice.*

12. Lebhar, *Chain Stores in America.*

13. Typical of store treatment was a dispassionate tone and language. See, for instance, Abbott, "The Store Building." Hunley Abbott was president of Abbott, Merkt, a well-known engineering and architecture firm that took on many commercial projects.

14. See Longstreth, *The American Department Store Transformed,* 49–59. There were exceptions to the opaque box, such as SOM's store project for Phoenix, with indoor/outdoor spaces worthy of a study by Theo van Doesburg. See Owings, "Economics of Department Store Planning." Frederick Kiesler's 1928 department store was an opaque box on massive piers, but Kiesler also proposed a glass-enclosed continuous sales ramp. Perhaps most radical, Louis Parnes invented a system of alternating storage and display floors. Parnes, "Intermediate Floors for Greater Efficiency in Storage and Service," 95–97 and cover image. See also "Department Store, Houston, Texas."

15. Hamlin, "Some Restaurants and Recent Shops," 495.

16. There is a wide literature on evaluations of consumption, much of it American. For example, see Horowitz, *The Morality of Spending*; Jackson Lears, "From Salvation to Self-Realization"; Agnew, "Coming Up for Air"; Fiske, *Reading the Popular*; Baudrillard, "Consumer Society." Cultural theory in recent years has looked at shopping and consumption as an enactment of legitimate desires and a means of forming a coherent and even shifting identity within an environment largely shaped by capital. While most understand this "agency" as still highly circumscribed, many observers no longer view consumption as the subterfuge that is the legacy of the harshest critiques—from the Frankfurt School, Stuart Hall, Daniel Bell, or Dwight Macdonald—and now take a more ambivalent view.

17. Leach, *Land of Desire*; Miller, *The Bon Marché*; Laermans, "Learning to Consume." On "theaters of goods," see Ewen and Ewen, *Channels of Desire,* 45.

18. Barth, *City People*; Boyer, *Manhattan Manners,* 86–129; Bowlby, *Carried Away,* 30–78.

19. See the discussion in chapter 4.

20. *Flâneurie* and its pleasures and tensions are described in Baudelaire's *The Painter of Modern Life* (1863) and in, among others, Walter Benjamin's "Paris, Capital of the Nineteenth Century" (1935). See de Certeau, *The Practice of Everyday Life,* 91–103; Adorno, *Minima Moralia,* 162; Huyssen, "Mass Culture as Woman."

21. Macauley, "Walking in the Urban Environment."

22. Gillette, "Film as Artifact."

23. Passanti, "The Skyscrapers of the Ville Contemporaine"; Moos, *Le Corbusier.*

24. Giedion, *Space, Time and Architecture.* Giedion presents the "many-sidedness" of the Bauhaus Building in Dessau and Rockefeller Center in New York City as best perceived by a viewer in motion. This is not to say that Giedion and CIAM did not also idealize the movement of the car and the image of the highway, but these were distinct from the spaces of the pedestrian, and their separation was part of the polemic.

25. Hudnut, "The Art in Housing," 62.

26. Hamlin in Holden, *Planning Man's Physical Environment*; these conference proceedings were revised and republished in 1949 as *Building for Modern Man,* edited by Thomas H. Creighton.

27. "Main Street, USA," 73.

28. Ibid. (italics added).

29. "Forty Stores," 93–94.

30. "Main Street, USA." The subtitle of the article was "Where Design and Dollars Interlock." See also Esperdy, *Modernizing Main Street*; and Isenberg, *Downtown America.*

31. "Markets in the Meadows." See also Lowenthal, "The Suburban Branch Department Store."

32. Sert, "Centres of Community Life," 4, 11.

33. "Roosevelt Field Shopping Center."

34. Giedion, "The Humanization of Urban Life," 126.

35. Ockman, "Toward a Theory of Normative Architecture"; Martin, *The Organizational Complex.* See also Goldhagen and Legault, *Anxious Modernisms.*

36. See Fox and Lears, *The Culture of Consumption.*

37. Longstreth, *City Center to Regional Mall*; Longstreth, *The Drive-In, the Supermarket, and the Transformation of Commercial Space in Los Angeles*; Longstreth, *The American Department Store Transformed.*

38. Esperdy, *Modernizing Main Street*; Shanken, *194X*. See also Castillo, *Cold War on the Home Front*; Monteyne, *Fallout Shelter.*

39. Rowe, "Introduction," 5.

40. Upton, *Architecture in the United States*; Wright, *USA*; Bruegmann, *The Architects and the City.* The positioning and role of the architect can also be sociologically placed via the work and tradition of Pierre Bourdieu, especially his *Distinction.* Beauregard, *Voices of Decline*; Boyer, *Dreaming the Rational City*; Crawford, "The World in a Shopping Mall"; Fishman, *Urban Utopias in the Twentieth Century.* See also Ciucci et al., *The American City.*

1. The Store Problem

1. Kimball, "What Is Modern Architecture?"

2. Esherick, "Architectural Education in the Thirties and Seventies." See also Stern, "The Thirties"; Solomonson, *The Chicago Tribune Tower Competition.*

3. Walker, "Architecture of Today"; Adams, "Recent European Architecture"; Hopper, "Twentieth Century European Architecture"; Harbeson, "Design in Modern Architecture"; Hitchcock, "Architectural Education Again"; Howe, "What Is This Modern Architecture Trying to Express?"; Watkin, "The Advent of the New Manner in America"; Paris, "Modernism."

4. Hitchcock, "Review of *Wie Baut America* by Richard J. Neutra." Compare, for instance, Lönberg-Holm, "Two Shows"; and Kimball, "Modern Architecture."

5. Woltersdorf, "Carnival Architecture"; Haskell, "Mixed Metaphors at Chicago."

6. Mumford, "Machinery and the Modern Style." See also the following of Mumford's writings, all of which appeared in his *New Yorker* architecture column "The Sky Line": "What Might Have Been"; "The Modern Restaurant"; "The Laundry Takes to Architecture"; "The New York Lunchroom," in which he cites Walter Curt Behrendt's praise of New York's "simple eateries"; and "Two Restaurants and a Theater."

7. Mumford, "Modern Design." Mumford met with architect Ernst May and historian/critic Walter Curt Behrendt in New York in 1925. Samson, "'Unser Newyorker Mitarbeiter.'" See also Striner, "Art Deco."

8. Boyd, "The Art of Commercial Display, Part I," and "The Art of Commercial Display, Part II." Longstreth, *The American Department Store Transformed,* 21–23.

9. The earlier German use of the term *Sachlichkeit* was framed as design fitness, appropriateness, or matter-of-factness and revealed as much about taste as it did rationality. See Schwartz, *The Werkbund.*

10. Kahn, "Essential Details in Store Designing"; Kahn, "The Modern European Shop and Store," 804.

11. "A Fifth Avenue Pipe and Tobacco Shop," 60.

12. "Innovations in Small Store Design."

13. "Shop Fronts," 383; Trowbridge, "New Shop Fronts, 1," 136.

14. Burford, "The Design of the Shop Front from Ancient to Modern Times," 15.

15. Boyd, "The Newer Fifth Avenue Retail Shop Fronts," 468.

16. Eberlein, "Shop Fronts in Country Towns and Smaller Cities," 875, 878.

17. Coolidge, "The Problem of the Store Front," 77.

18. Pugin did his own structurally and visually rational designs. See Scalzo, "All a Matter of Taste." See also Dan and Willmott, *English Shop-Fronts Old and New,* 16.

19. "The Architecture of the Small Shop, Part I," 102; Boyd, "The Newer Fifth Avenue Retail Shop Fronts," 468.

20. Walters, "Modern Store Fronts," 155.

21. "Shop Fronts," 385.

22. Trowbridge, "New Shop Fronts, 2," 161.

23. Chain stores increased in number almost fourfold between 1920 and 1930. Lebhar, *Chain Stores in America,* 48; Nystrom, *Chain Stores,* 31.

24. Boyd, " The Newer Fifth Avenue Retail Shop Fronts," 459.

25. March, "The Problem in Designing Modern Shop Fronts," 783.

26. Boyd, " The Newer Fifth Avenue Retail Shop Fronts," 462.

27. Sexton, *American Commercial Buildings of Today,* 156–58.

28. Boyd, "Milgrim—a Fashion Shop for Women," 523; Hagopian, "The A. S. Beck Shoe Store," 543. See also Stern, Gilmartin, and Mellins, *New York 1930,* 293–328, 361, 364. Wright, "The Art and Craft of the Machine," 89.

29. Boyd, "The Newer Fifth Avenue Retail Shop Fronts," 487.

30. Meikle, *Twentieth Century Limited*; Eidelberg, *Design 1935–1965.*

31. "New York's Shopping District and the Shifting of Trade Centers," 386.

32. Boyd, "The Newer Fifth Avenue Retail Shop Fronts," 485; Burford, "Design of the Shop Front from Ancient to Modern Times," 18. See also Stern et al., *New York 1930.*

33. Dan and Willmott, *English Shop-Fronts Old and New,* 17–22; Walters, "Modern Store Fronts"; "Shop and Store Reference Number," 234. See also "Recessed Shopfronts"; Trowbridge, "New Shop Fronts, 2," 161.

34. The Avedon shop was completed in 1921. "New Fifth Avenue Shop Fronts"; "The Avedon Building," *New York Times,* April 24, 1921, RE1.

35. Kahn, "Essential Details in Store Designing," plate 84; Somes, "Recent Shop Fronts in New England," with a discussion of the "deep entrance" vestibule; Stern et al., *New York 1930,* 296.

36. "The Adler Shoe Store, New York City."

37. Jacobs's plan appears to have preceded similar proposals, more precisely conceived to improve traffic flow, by the Regional Plan of New York and Its Environs. "Plan to Relieve Fifth Avenue Congestion by Widening Roadway and Decking Sidewalks," *New York Times,* January 22, 1922, 104; "Has Arcade Plan to Relieve 5th Ave.," *New York Times,* April 24, 1925, 7. See also Bibbins, "Traffic-Transportation Planning and Metropolitan Development"; Knowles, "City Planning as a Permanent Solution to the Traffic Problem," 57; Adams, "Fitting Streets to Buildings." Adams praised the arcade-based design of the Barclay-Vesey Building in Lower Manhattan, by Ralph Walker of McKenzie, Voorhees & Gmelin, 1926. See Johnson, *Planning the Great Metropolis.*

38. Black, "The Spectacular in City Building," 56.

39. "The Development of the Arcaded Shop Front." A Parisian arcade, La Galerie du Palais, graced the introductory page of the special issue. Other American projects, such as The Arcade in Providence, Rhode Island (1827), were not widely discussed. See also Geist, *Arcades.*

40. Somes, "Recent Shop Fronts in New England," 249.

41. "Shop and Store Reference Number," 249; "The Architecture of the Small Shop, Part II," 98.

42. Vogelgesang, "Architecture and Trade Marks"; North, "A Modern Store Alteration"; "Walker at Opening of Bedell Store," *New York Times,* March 10, 1929, 16. See Stern et al., *New York 1930,* 319.

43. Longstreth, *The Drive-In, the Supermarket, and the Transformation of Commercial Space in Los Angeles.* See also Marquis, "The Spanish Stores of Morgan, Walls & Clements."

44. Welch, "The Department Store," 6.

45. Mikkelsen, "Two Problems of Architecture." Mikkelsen was a real estate writer, then worked for the Dodge Corporation, owner of the *Architectural Record* and *Sweet's Catalog,* and served as editor of the *Record* from 1914 to 1937. Lichtenstein, "Editing Architecture," 53. See also Pai, *The Portfolio and the Diagram,* 148–59.

46. Mikkelsen had changed the magazine to a smaller, more easily produced size the previous year. Mikkelsen, "Two Problems of Architecture." See also Mikkelsen, "Expansion of the *Architectural Record* for 1930"; Mikkelsen, "A Word about the New Format."

47. Hitchcock, who arrived in 1928, had already been an advocate of the "New Architecture"; Haskell arrived in 1929 and also wrote for *Creative Art* and *The Nation*; Kimball was already a well-known historian of American architecture; and Theodore Larson and Robert Davison were "technical" specialists, both of whom went on to do research in housing, prefabrication, and information organization. Howard T. Fisher was a contributing editor in 1929. Kocher became editor in 1937. "Professor Kocher Joins the *Architectural Record* Staff." See also Tomlan, "Architectural Press, U.S.," 281–83.

48. Kocher received his bachelor's degree in architecture from Stanford University in 1909 and his master's degree in architecture from Penn State College; he was department chair at Penn and then taught at the University of Virginia and, later, at Black Mountain College.

49. One of Kocher's earliest *Record* articles consisted of measured drawings of colonial architecture. Kocher, "Early Architecture of Pennsylvania." The series ran for two years. See Kocher, "The Country House"; Kocher and Dearstyne, *Colonial Williamsburg, Its Buildings and Gardens.* See also Stiverson, *Architecture and the Decorative Arts.*

50. "Sunlight Towers"; "Sunlight Towers, an Apartment House"; Rosa, "A. Lawrence Kocher, Albert Frey"; Kocher and Frey, "Real Estate Subdivisions for Low-Cost Housing"; Kocher, "Low-Cost Farmhouse."

51. Walter Gropius, Berlin, to A. Lawrence Kocher, March 25, 1934, A. Lawrence Kocher Papers, Special Collections, Williamsburg Colonial Foundation Library. Cited in Lichtenstein, "Editing Architecture," 124.

52. Boyd, "Milgrim—a Fashion Shop for Women," 523. See also "Modernism and Tradition."

53. The "Store Buildings" issue was preceded by "Swimming Pools" in January 1929, "Garages" in February 1929, "Apartment Houses" in March 1929, and "Airport Design and Construction" in May 1929.

54. "Store Buildings," 584.

55. Ibid., 603–6.

56. Ibid., 603.

57. Woods, *From Craft to Profession.*

58. Dessauce, "Control lo Stile Internazionale."

59. Lönberg-Holm, "Planning the Retail Store," 497.

60. Chamber of Commerce of the United States, Domestic Distribution Department, *Small Store Arrangement*; Progressive Grocer, *Better Grocery Stores.*

61. The terms *flow* and *friction* are reminiscent of Alexander Klein's diagrams, as noted in Evans, "Windows Doors Passages."

62. Lönberg-Holm, "Planning the Retail Store," 501.

63. On the Co-op Vitrine, see Hays, "Picturing Collective Consumer Culture." Mendelsohn, 1929, cited in Stephan, *Erich Mendelsohn,* 108. Lönberg-Holm's photographs were used by Mendelsohn in his *Amerika* of 1926. See also Gropius, "Principles of Bauhaus Production," 95.

64. Lönberg-Holm, "Architecture in the Industrial Age."

65. Kiesler, *Contemporary Art Applied to the Store and Its Display,* 66–68.

66. Kiesler, "On Correalism and Biotechnique," 65.

67. Kiesler said that Theo van Doesburg introduced himself to Kiesler backstage after the second performance of Karel Čapek's science fiction play *RUR,* the sets for which Kiesler had designed. Creighton, "Kiesler's Pursuit of an Idea," 109.

68. In 1925, Josef Hoffmann asked Kiesler to organize the theater exhibit for the Austrian section of the Paris Exposition. Lesak, "Visionary of the European Theater." See also "Says Aerial Cities will Rise in Future," *New York Times,* July 5, 1925, 9; "Design's Bad Boy"; Held, "Endless Innovations."

69. Kiesler, "Manifesto of Tensionism," 95.

70. Banham, *Theory and Design in the First Machine Age,* 197–98.

71. Kenneth MacGowan, "Stagecraft Shows Its Newest Heresies," *New York Times,* February 14, 1926, SM9; "Exposition Reveals New Theater Ideal," *New York Times,* February 28, 1926, 16; J. Brooks Atkinson, "Bourgeois Laughter," *New York Times,* March 14, 1926, X1; Held, "Endless Innovations," 102; Johnson, *America Modern, 1925–1940,* 17–18. Kiesler was involved with various theater projects, including one in Brooklyn and another in Woodstock; see Held, "Endless Innovations," 110–22.

72. The recommendation that Saks hire Kiesler might have come from Harvey Wiley Corbett, for whom Kiesler claims to have worked; cited in Creighton, "Kiesler's Pursuit of an

Idea," 104. On window designs, see "Display Window Design," *New York Times,* November 25, 1928, N18; Kiesler, "Shop Window Displays, Saks and Company, New York City." Kiesler would go on to do set design for opera and to teach courses at the Juilliard School and Columbia University on design and materials. "Ultra-modern Sets for American Opera," *New York Times,* October 13, 1934, 10; "The Architect in Search of . . ."; "Columbia to Give Course in Design," *New York Times,* July 11, 1937, 162. See also Goodman, "The Art of Revolutionary Display Techniques." Kiesler was a member of Fuller's Structural Studies Associates.

73. Walter Rendell Storey, "New Modes Capture Our Shop Windows," *New York Times,* April 29, 1928, SM9.

74. "4-Screen Theater Being Built Here," *New York Times,* December 9, 1928, N1.

75. Kiesler, "Space House." The "Design Correlation" series ran in the *Record* monthly during the first half of 1937 and included his research on theater, glass, "folk spectacles," and photography. See Phillips, "Toward a Research Practice."

76. "Union of Artists Meets," *New York Times,* June 1, 1928, 28.

77. "Local Items," *New York Times,* March 10, 1929, 136. Frank Lloyd Wright spoke at an October 1929 meeting of AUDAC; see "City Brevities," *New York Times,* October 12, 1929, 26; "Twelfth Annual Home Show Opens Tomorrow," *New York Times,* March 30, 1930, RE2; Byars, "What Makes American Design American." Indicative of AUDAC's integration into the business of American design were the organization's efforts in lobbying Congress to pass antipiracy and copyright legislation. "Bills Aimed at the Fashion Design Pirates," *New York Times,* March 30, 1930, X16. On the Brooklyn show, see Walter Rendell Storey, "Arts and Crafts Attuned to the Hour," *New York Times,* May 3, 1931, SM7. See also Wilson, Pilgrim, and Tashjian, *The Machine Age in America,* 288–95.

78. Kiesler, *Contemporary Art,* 3.

79. Ibid., 39, 42.

80. Ibid., 68.

81. Kiesler called the department store the "interpreter" of the new art.

82. Kiesler, "On Correalism and Biotechnique."

83. Frederick Kiesler, "Putting Merchandise on the Spot," 1931, Kiesler Archives.

84. Kiesler, *Contemporary Art,* 79–84.

85. The Reimann School, begun by Albert Reimann early in the twentieth century, was a successful art and design school; it moved to London in the mid-1930s. The Arundell School of Display in London was started in the 1920s. On the Reimann School, see Suga, "Modernism, Commercialism and Display Design in Britain"; Aynsley, *Graphic Design in Germany,* chap. 3.

86. Haskell, "Review, *Contemporary Art Applied to the Store and Its Display*"; Walter Rendell Storey, "Newark Museum Exhibition . . . ," *New York Times,* May 18, 1930, SM8.

87. Walter Rendell Storey, "Peasant Crafts That Live in This Age," *New York Times,* October 29, 1933, SM12; "Architect Designs a Space House for Modernage Furniture Company"; Kiesler, "Space House"; Kiesler, "The Space House: Annotations at Random," 293. See also Safran, *Frederick Kiesler 1890–1965*; Braham, "What's Hecuba to Him?"; Linder, "Wild Kingdom"; Colomina, "Space House."

88. Kiesler singled out for critique Bel Geddes's Franklin Simon store in New York City. Kiesler, *Contemporary Art,* 134.

89. Ibid., 78–81.

90. "Design's Bad Boy," 88. See also "Ten Miles High" and the obituaries for Kiesler in the February 1966 issue of the *Architectural Record* and the April 1966 issue of *Architectural Design.*

91. Stowell, *Modernizing Buildings for Profit.*

92. Cheney and Cheney, *Art and the Machine,* 16–18, 146. See also Platt, "Sheldon Cheney."

93. See also Lawrence, "Declaration of Function."

94. Smith, *Making the Modern,* 385–404.

2. Machines for Selling

1. McAndrew, *Guide to Modern Architecture,* 15–16.

2. "Main Street, USA," 86.

3. Bach, "Common Faults in Store Front Design"; "New Arrangement for Bringing the Inside Outside."

4. Gruen's almost antimodern self-representation was a constant trope. See, for instance, "The Influence of Architecture on Home Furnishings," speech presented at a meeting of the National Retail Dry Goods Association (NRDGA), Arizona Biltmore, May 31, 1950, box 27, Victor Gruen Papers, American Heritage Center, University of Wyoming (hereafter cited as VGPAHC). See also Guzzardi, "An Architect of Environments," 80.

5. See Crawford, "The World in a Shopping Mall."

6. Victor Grünbaum was born in Vienna in 1903. He studied at the State University School of Architecture and the Vienna Academy of Fine Art, graduating in 1925. He worked in Vienna for the firm of Melcher and Steiner. Among his residential clients and indicative of his *bildungsburgertum* circle was Paul Lazarsfeld, later of the Frankfurt School and head of the Bureau of Applied Social Research at Columbia. See Gruenbaum, "Wohnung eines geistig arbeitenden Ehepaares"; Neuhardt, "Licht im Landhaus," 40; "Ein Portalumbau von Arch. Viktor Grünbaum," *Österreichische Kunst* (April 1936): 27; all in box 11, VGPAHC. See also the 1928 Lazarsfeld apartment in "Roster of Works . . . 1937," translated by Executive Service Corporation, Los Angeles, 1951, 75-10, 77-12, Victor Gruen Papers, Library of Congress (hereafter cited as VGPLOC). Grünbaum was also called Gruenbaum in the English-language press. According to the entries in the *Art Index,* Gruenbaum became Gruen in late 1941. See Hardwick, *Mall Maker,* 8–15.

7. Augenfeld, "Modern Austria," 171; "Parfumerie et magasin a Vienne," box 12, VGPAHC.

8. Viktor Grünbaum, "Die Grosstadt von Morgen," 1930, 78-10, VGPLOC.

9. On Wittbold, see "General Motors Special Showing"; "It's a Hit!"; "Wood Panels Designed by George Wittbold for Setting of Exhibition of General Motors Products." See also Greenberg, "Victor Gruen"; Hardwick, *Mall Maker,* 18. Through the 1939 World's Fair, Gruen met Elsie Krummeck, who would become his first partner and his wife; Krummeck also worked at the 1933 Chicago World's Fair. "Victor Gruen, Obituary"; McCallum, *Architecture USA,* 104–6; "Contributors," *Architectural Forum* (April 1947): 54; Cohen, "Victor Gruen and the Regional Shopping Center," 25–26.

10. Gruen later recalled that he worked "with" Bel Geddes; "General Book Plan," 1977, 5, 77-2, VGPLOC. A letter of recommendation from George Wittbold is more humble: the letter states that Gruenbaum was employed as draftsman under Bel Geddes; see "Letter of Recommendation from George Wittbold Inc—Exhibit Engineering," February 3, 1939, 77-2, VGPLOC.

11. Loewy, cited in Miekle, *Twentieth Century Limited,* 197. See also Smith, *Making the Modern,* 405–24.

12. McAndrew, *Guide to Modern Architecture,* 78. *Women's Wear Daily* noted the "pleasing modern feeling" of the Lederer arcade, and the editors were impressed by the extensive glass showcases for "unbroken merchandise display." "Entry with a Pleasing Modern Feeling," *Women's Wear Daily,* June 9, 1939; "Lederer de Paris Front Is New Departure," *Women's Wear Daily,* June 16, 1939; both in OV-11, VGPLOC. Ciro and Lederer sat directly adjacent to each other.

13. Hamlin, "Some Restaurants and Recent Shops," 495; "Stores." Also included in these discussions was work by Alexander Girard, Hamby and Nelson, Louis Friedland, Gilbert Rohde, and Alfred Alschuler of Raymond Loewy.

14. "Design Decade," 289. On Gruen's Canterbury, see Walter Rendell Storey, "Styling with Paint," *National Painters Magazine,* January 1941; Altman-Kuhne, *Store of Greater New York,* December 1939; Altman and Kuhne, interior rendering, in "Hotel, Store and Apartment Properties Figuring in Manhattan Real Estate Activity"; Gruenbaum and Krummeck, "Face to Face"; all in OV-11, VGPLOC.

15. Mumford, "The Sky Line: New Faces on the Avenue."

16. Hardwick, *Mall Maker,* 8–23. See also "And Now 'From Vienna,'" *New York Times,* June 18, 1939, 114; "News of the Stage," *New York Times,* July 11, 1939, 26; "From Jobless Refugee to Stage Manager," *Christian Science Monitor,* May 10, 1940, 10.

17. Gruenbaum and Krummeck, "Face to Face"; "The Arcade Front," OV-11, VGPLOC.

18. "Recent Work by Gruenbaum, Krummeck and Auer"; Gruenbaum, "Some Notes on Modern Store Design."

19. Rachel Bowlby describes the passerby as "indeterminate," passive, and suggestible. Bowlby, *Carried Away,* 49–78. The coining of the neologistic "Gruen effect" contributed to Gruen's image as the icon of manipulative modern shopping. Crawford, "World in a Shopping Mall."

20. Grayson's, cover of *Chain Store Age* (February 1941); advertised in *Evening Outlook,* Santa Monica, California, November 29, 1940, OV-11, VGPLOC.

21. "General Book Plan, Historic Development," 77-10, VGPLOC; Hardwick, *Mall Maker,* 48–71. While the percentage of unmarried women in the U.S. workforce remained steady during the 1940s, the percentage of married women in the workforce rose. May, *Homeward Bound.*

22. "Recent Work by Gruenbaum, Krummeck and Auer"; Gruenbaum, "Some Notes on Modern Store Design"; "Getting Twenty-Four Hour Service from Store Fronts," box 11, VGPAHC.

23. "Commercial Remodeling," 88. See also, regarding Grayson's Hollywood, "Women's Specialty Shop . . ."

24. Storey, "Styling with Paint"; "Novel Design Proves to Have Customer Pulling Power," *Women's Wear Daily,* February 24, 1941; "The Case of the Displayman vs. the Store-Designer," *Display World* 39 (September 1941); "First Step in Selling," *Display World* 39 (December, 1941); all in box 11, VGPLOC.

25. On architects and advertising, compare the negative "Selling Architecture" and the more sympathetic Kyson, "Architecture." See also Kyson, "Blades of Grass"; and Kyson, "Advertising and . . . Advertising."

26. Hugh Ferris, Wallace K. Harrison, George Howe, Edward Durell Stone, Howard Myers, and George Nelson were all on the review committee for the *40 under 40* exhibit. Letter from Hugh Ferris, no date, OV-11, VGPLOC; photo of *40 under 40* exhibit, OV-11, VGPLOC.

27. McAndrew, *Guide to Modern Architecture,* 15–16, 17, 77–83. Gruen's work is by Gruen and Krummeck. McAndrew was meticulous in crediting Gruen's and Ketchum's work, which was no small task since authorship remains murky. According to McAndrew's citations, the Lederer store was designed by Gruen "in association with" Ketchum, Ciro was by Ketchum, Steckler was by Ketchum "in association with" Gruen, Paris Decorators was done by Ketchum with Gruen as "associate," and Strasser Studio was designed by Gruen.

28. One trade magazine featured the two stores on its August 1939 cover and more than hinted at their uniqueness *and* their replicability; see "Symphony in Stores."

29. "Stores," 427.

30. "General Book Plan," 5; "General Book Plan, Historic Development," 5. See also Hardwick, *Mall Maker,* 23.

31. The "delineator," R. I. Hoyt, has not been researched.

32. Ketchum's grandfather was a successful New York City banker in the mid-nineteenth century. Ketchum spent the latter part of 1928 at the School of Fine Arts in Fontainebleau. Some of his drawings are in the archive of the Avery Architectural and Fine Arts Library; see Bletter, "Modernism Rears Its Head," 106. On Ketchum's marriage to Isabella Stiger, see *New York Times,* April 26, 1934, N4.

33. Information about Ketchum's employment history comes from his application for membership in the American Institute of Architects (AIA): Morris Ketchum Application for Membership, AIA, July 1, 1942, AIA Archives, Washington, D.C. See also Walter H. Waggoner, "Morris Ketchum Jr., 80," *New York Times,* November 27, 1984, B7.

34. Keally's projects ranged from colonial restaurant interiors to moderne suburban homes to proposals for airports, windowless buildings for factories, and all-glass buildings for banks. Keally was vice president of the Architectural League (under Ralph Walker), an executive of the New York chapter of the AIA, and one of several advisers to Mayor Fiorello LaGuardia. Keally, "How Airports Will Affect Zoning Laws"; "Factory Building with No Windows," *New York Times,* December 14, 1929, RE4; "Plans Blank Edifice with Glass Walls," *New York Times,* March 29, 1931, RE5; Keally, "A New Effect with Stucco"; "Architects Induct Officers," *New York Times,* May 21, 1937, 17.

35. "Clock Tower, Amboise"; "Jacques Coeur House, Bourges."

36. Gordon Bunshaft later recalled that "there was another man . . . using Ed Stone's office. I guess they had a few little puttery jobs. . . . He was called Morris Ketchum." *Oral History of Gordon Bunshaft,* 91.

37. All of Ketchum's former employers—York and Sawyer, Francis Keally, and Mayers, Murray & Phillip—worked on various pavilions and exhibits. York and Sawyer designed the U.S. Steel Subsidiaries building; Keally designed the Communications Building; and Mayers, Murray & Phillip designed the Medicine, Public Health, and Science and Education Pavilions. Appelbaum, *The New York World's Fair,* 44, 87; *Official Guide Book of the New York World's Fair, 1939,* 71, 109, 168.

38. This building was also known as Food Building #3. "Three Building Awards for Fair Are Made," *New York Times,* April 23, 1937, 23; Appelbaum, *New York World's Fair,* 66, 102; *Official Guide Book,* 103; Ketchum, *Morris Ketchum Jr., Architect.*

39. "Dining-Kitchens"; "Win $1,000 Prizes for Post Offices," *New York Times,* July 13, 1938, 19.

40. "Service Men's Centers." Edward Durell Stone designed Myers's apartment on Fifty-seventh Street. On the architectural culture of the time, see Stone, *Evolution of an Architect,* 32–37, 93–94.

41. Ketchum's future partner Stanley Sharp also worked with and for Stone in 1939. "Planning for Economy and Flexibility."

42. "Linen Shop."

43. "Skillful Enlargement"; "House for Mr. Charles Mitchell Bliss." On the preference of the clean lines of Greek Revival and colonial, see, for example, Tuttle, "To Stimulate Renovization." See also Gowans, *Styles and Types of North American Architecture,* 232.

44. "Productive Home Architectural Competition," *New York Times,* April 12, 1939, 43; "Productive Home Architectural Competition," *Pencil Points*; "Winners of Productive Home Competition Are Announced," *Architectural Forum*; "Winners of Productive Home Competition Are Announced," *Architectural Record.* Department stores often mediated the relations between consumers and architecture professionals, especially in house design and in home furnishings; see Smiley, "Making the Modified Modern."

45. "Design Decade," 287; "Glamour in Glass"; "Flower Market"; "Three Small Shops."

46. Ketchum, "The Open Faced Shop." The "open faced shop" was also claimed by architect José Fernandez; see "The Year's Work." On the use of glass at Ketchum's Wallach's store, see "Men's Store Remodeled for Modern Merchandising."

47. "Artek-Pascoe Furniture Shop, New York City." See also "Artek Exposed." Artek was founded by Aalto in 1937 and, with the help of Wallace Harrison, opened in New York in 1941. Clifford Pascoe was a designer who managed the New York store.

48. Quoted in Newhouse, *Wallace K. Harrison, Architect,* 30.

49. Bannister, *The Architect at Mid-century,* 185–210; Esherick, "Architectural Education in the Thirties and Seventies." The BAID was founded in 1914. Stern, Gilmartin, and Mellins, *New York 1930,* 115.

50. Teegan, "Here Stands the B.A.I.D."

51. BAID members included Goodwin, Ely Jacques Kahn, Fouilhoux, Abramovitz, Stone, Walter Gropius, William Muschenheim, Gordon Bunshaft, William Wurster, Eero Saarinen, and Donald Deskey. See *Bulletin of the Beaux-Arts Institute of Design,* various mastheads. On Gruen's arrival, see *Bulletin of the Beaux-Arts Institute of Design* 16 (November 1949): 10, 12.

52. Ketchum, "A Mural for a Handicraft Shop"; Ketchum, "A Merchandise Display Window."

53. Ketchum, "A Decorators Accessory Shop"; Ketchum and Reisner, "Master Room." Richard Bennett, friend of Ketchum and later a shopping center designer, wrote the program for the BAID drugstore project.

54. Gina, "A Costume Jewelry Shop." Sharp is listed as a codesigner with Stone and Cope Walbridge for a prefabrication proposal in 1942; "Planning for Economy and Flexibility," 117. On Gina, see *Bulletin of the Beaux-Arts Institute of Design* 20 (1944): 45; Telchin and Gina, "Retail Fronts, Comparative Details"; Telchin and Gina, "AR Time Saver Standards."

55. It is unclear how Kawneer was introduced to Ketchum or the BAID. "A Small Stores Development"; "Designs for Suburban Stores."

56. Ketchum, "A Shopping Group and Motion Picture Theater Entrance."

57. Reid had a unique propensity for masculine images of strength and power, later calling for leaders with "undeniable maleness" to control necessary social and architectural change. Reid, "New Beginnings," 242.

58. Reid, "The Modernist from Wainscott," 65. Ketchum also wrote on the principles of transparency and "dramatizing" the shop for urban and suburban services such as drive-ins and laundries. Ketchum, "Services for Sale."

59. Sheumaker and Wajda, *Material Culture in America,* 391.

60. The Welch-Wilmarth Corporation figures prominently in retailing specialist Paul Nystrom's *Bibliography of Retailing,* 18. Welch's father started the company in Vermont with the manufacture of folding beds; see 1-1, Kenneth C. Welch Papers, Bentley Historical Library, University of Michigan (hereafter cited as KWPBHL).

61. Welch received his architecture degree from the University of Pennsylvania in 1916, after which he joined the U.S. Air Force and was stationed in Texas. He then set up a small architectural practice in Grand Rapids with Charles Hugget before joining the family furniture business about 1920. See "Profile"; Jenny Zukowski, "Introduction," KWPBHL.

62. Welch appears to have consulted on a 1929 store for Strawbridge and Clothier in Ardmore, Pennsylvania, but other references to the project are less clear; see box 1, KWPBHL.

63. Others consultants were Frank Gaertner of Starrett & Van Vleck; C. A. Wheeler of C. A. Wheeler, Inc., Store Designers; William Foulks, assistant chief engineer, Curtis Lighting, Inc.; and Anthony McCabe, chief engineer, Erikson Electric Co. "Store Buildings," 585.

64. Welch, "The Logic of Layout."

65. Ibid., 351. The GRSEC was consultant to Hutzler Brothers in Baltimore; the GRSEC provided only the images for the furnishings of the Strawbridge and Clothier Store in Jenkintown, Pennsylvania, and the Frederick Loesser and Company in Brooklyn.

66. Welch, "Planning a Small Men's Shop." The local architect was Lancelot Sukert. See also Sukert, "The Retail Shop." Later in 1934, the GRSEC provided information for a "checklist" article on store work, part of another *Record* "Technical News and Research" feature on store work. "Checklist for New Construction and Modernization of Stores."

67. Pawley, "The Retail Store"; see Welch, "The Apparel Store"; Woodburne, "The Drug Store."

68. Pawley, "The Retail Store," 55.

69. On modernization, see Esperdy, *Modernizing Main Street.* See also "To Discuss Modernizing Drive," *New York Times,* June 14, 1935, 43.

70. Other jurors included Melvin Copeland, a professor of marketing at Harvard, and Frank R. Walker, a well-known construction estimator and consultant. Walker's 1915 *The Building Estimator's Reference Book* became an industry standard. "Modernize Main Street."

71. "John Wanamaker Men's Store, New York City"; "Building Types"; "Men's Shops."

72. "Department Stores," *Architectural Record* 81. Other GRSEC commissions shown were Meyer Jonasson, Pittsburgh; Rosenbaum Department Store, Pittsburgh; R. A. Freed Shop, New York; and Weber and Heilbroner Shop, New York. Longstreth, *The American Department Store Transformed,* 42–46.

73. See, for example, "The Lighting of Merchandise"; "Portfolio," with furnishing by the GRSEC, in "Building Types."

74. Welch, "Plan Fundamentals for the Men's Shop." "Merchandising Goes Modern," 1938, 12-1, KWPBHL; Welch, "Modernizing for Wartime Efficiency," 12-2, KWPBHL; Welch,

"Self-Selection Is Sensible," 12-4, KWPBHL; "Kenneth Welch of the GRSEC takes you over the hurdles of open stock selling and effective store layout," "1943 Study of Parkchester," 10-18, KWPBHL.

75. Lapidus, "Basic Plans and Profiles of Store Front Construction." Lapidus was born on November 25, 1902, in Odessa, Russia; his family settled in Brooklyn in 1903. Lapidus studied drama at New York University before attending Columbia.

76. For his 1934 Swank Jewelry store, Lapidus said he was affected by Mies's Tugendhat dining area semicircle. While at Columbia, he worked for Wallace Harrison, Warren and Wetmore, and Bloch and Hesse. Lapidus, *Architecture,* 194–98; Lapidus, *Too Much Is Never Enough,* 59–101. See also Box 1, 2, Morris Lapidus Papers, Special Collections Research Center, Syracuse University.

77. Evan Frankel, also trained as an architect, was Sidney Mangel's first cousin. See information on Mangel's store in "Supplement," NRDGA, *Planning the Store of To-morrow*; "Bulova Watch Company Offices, Rockefeller Center"; Box 1, Morris Lapidus Papers, Special Collections Research Center, Syracuse University. Ross-Frankel was also active at the 1939 World's Fair.

78. "Doubleday Doran Bookshop"; "Postman's Makes the Most of a Narrow Frontage." On other work by Lapidus, see "Executive Bar for Seagram Distillers, Chrysler Building"; "Regal Shoes"; "Wallach's New York." *Architectural Forum*'s 1937 "Planning Techniques" study included a page of Lapidus's and Ross-Frankel's entryway display systems; "Planning Techniques No. 2," 95.

79. Lapidus, "Store Design." Lapidus experimented with glass in his work on his own home. See "The Year's Work," 33.

80. Lapidus, "Store Design," 132, 113; "Where Sales Depend on Economic Health."

81. Lapidus's 1934 Eimer & Amend Apothecary was an early interpretation of the stripped down, austere form of modernism, just two years after the Museum of Modern Art show. See also Lapidus, "Planning Today for the Store Tomorrow"; "Inside Out, Ross-Frankel, Inc.," in which the firm is credited with "creating the open space front"; Lapidus, "The Retail Store and Its Design Problems"; Lapidus, "Free Flow Plan in Tight Areas."

82. Kawneer ad, *Pencil Points* 23 (July 1942). See Shanken, *194X*; Friedel, "Scarcity and Promise."

83. William Lescaze also served as an adviser for the 1935 Libby-Owens-Ford competition.

84. "Store Fronts of Tomorrow," *New Pencil Points* 23. Other jurors were planner Frederick Bigger and architects Samuel E. Lunden and Roland Wank; Wank was the site planner for the Tennessee Valley Authority. The "Store Fronts of Tomorrow" competition was organized in late 1942 and judged in January 1943.

85. "Store Fronts of Tomorrow," *New Pencil Points* 24. Whitney Smith, then working on the Linda Vista shopping center (see chapter 4), received a "special mention" for completely opening the store to the exterior. Other winners included Ralph Rapson, Stanley Sharp, and Jedd Reisner. Although unpremiated, probably because of its massive sign, Morris Lapidus's proposal was praised for its intricately composed exterior entry.

86. "Stores of the Future." As noted in chapter 1, Ken Stowell had pushed for modernization in the mid-1930s. "Store Designers Don't Suffer from Tradition Fixations." See also "Commercial Remodeling."

87. "Remodeling Main Street, Niles Michigan," 82. See also issues of Kawneer's employee newsletter, the *Kawneer Front,* for August, October, and December 1945.

88. Walter Dorwin Teague made a similar proposal for Montclair, New Jersey. See Austin, "New Life for an Old Shopping Area." A Kawneer detailing catalog also of 1944 showed these were not mere fantastic images but were ready for installation; Kawneer Company, *Kawneer Sales-Building Store-Fronts.* For an evaluation of the program almost a decade later, see "Who Did What for Niles, Michigan."

89. "Machines for Selling," Kawneer ad, *Architectural Forum* (July 1944): 15; "Millions of People Will Be Attracted by Store Fronts"; Kawneer Company, *Machines for Selling.*

90. Introduction in Kawneer Company, *Machines for Selling.* On sales and the store, see Bowlby, *Carried Away,* 30–48.

91. Ketchum retained the rights to six window system patents and was rewarded by Kawneer with the commission for the company's Berkeley factory offices in 1947; Morris Ketchum Files, Vertical Files, AIA Archives, Washington, D.C. The project received an honorable mention in the 1948 Progressive Architecture Awards and was the subject of a *Progressive Architecture* feature presentation. See "Factory Administration Building"; "Factory Offices."

92. "Machines for Selling."

93. Libbey-Owens-Ford Glass Company, *Visual Fronts.* Ketchum was not included because he had been hired by Kawneer. However, his 1940 (or 1941) portfolio contained a full-page advertisement taken out by Libbey-Owens-Ford. In 1941, Gruen's designs had been featured in publicity materials for the company; "LOF Glassic," July 1941, OV-11, VGPLOC. On the 1935 Libbey-Owens-Ford competition, see Esperdy, *Modernizing Main Street,* 265–79.

94. Pittsburgh Plate Glass Company, *There Is a New Trend in Store Design.*

95. Eero Saarinen's proposal was part of a quasi-megastructural shopping and community center and requires further research. Ibid., 32.

96. The PPG *Design of the Month* series has been popularized in Heimann, *Shop America,* with an essay by Steven Heller. The book does not, however, offer provenance for the work. On Lundberg, see "Architects Offer Ideas for Stores," *New York Times,* June 1, 1947, R3; "Caravan Displays Modernized Store," *New York Times,* March 16, 1948, 41; "Store Modernizations"; "Lundberg."

97. "Modern Architectural Design for Sacramento"; "Sacramento: Joseph Magnin New Store"; "Sacramento, California"; "California Department Store for Women"; "Joseph Magnin Store, Sacramento"; Ross, "Magnin's New Store, San Mateo." On other Gruen stores, see "Barton's Bonbonniere"; "Gallen Kamp's Shoe Store, Los Angeles."

98. Nicholson, *Contemporary Shops in the United States,* 11. The second edition, published in 1946, included new work by Gruen, among others. Nicholson was himself a textile and furniture designer.

99. Nelson, "Foreword," 8.

100. Burke and Kober, *Modern Store Design,* 8. Burke and Kober had done commercial work since late 1930s and were also called industrial designers; see "Planning Techniques No. 2," 185–96. For a later book with more images and less polemic, see Fernandez, *The Specialty Shop.*

101. "Program: Store Modernization Show Clinics," July 1947, Victor Gruen Papers, Manuscript Division, Library of Congress, Washington, D.C.; "Architects Offer Ideas for Stores." The NYU School of Retailing was founded in 1921 and was later incorporated into the School of Business.

102. Remarks of José Fernandez, Victor Gruen, and Morris Ketchum in "Modernized Store Fronts," in "Transcript of the Two Clinic Sessions, Store Modernization Show, Inc.," New York,

1947, 5, 7, 10, 11; all in KWPBHL. Other speakers included Elmer Lundberg (of PPG) and Charles Telchin. Ken Welch attended the session as well, and his marginal notes to his program are extensive.

103. A second Store Modernization Show followed in 1948, with similar themes and speakers. *1948 Store Modernization: Clinics and Forums.*

104. An adapted excerpt of the book appeared at the same time. Ketchum, "Current Trends in Store Design."

105. "Book Review, *Shops & Stores*"; and reviews in *Architectural Record* 104 (November 1948): 28; and *Architectural Forum* 89 (November 1948): 220. The *Forum* review was almost too glowing, praising "our country's best known and most productive store designer" for producing a book that "surpasses all expectations." The book was dedicated to *Forum*'s Howard Myers, who had died suddenly in 1947, and who had helped boost Ketchum's career.

106. Ketchum, *Shops and Stores,* 9–10.

107. An unpublished work by Gruen, aimed at businessmen instead of architects, demonstrated his perennial concern to look past the discipline and to sell the expertise of the architect. See Gruen, "How to Live with Your Architect," 78-15, VGPLOC; Hardwick, *Mall Maker,* 145.

108. "What Makes a 1940 Store Obsolete?," 63. The article consultants were Victor Gruen, Morris Ketchum, Morris Lapidus, Kenneth Welch, and department store architect Daniel Schwartzman.

109. "Commercial Remodeling," 81–82, with work by SOM, José Fernandez, Gruen and Krummeck, Morris Lapidus, and Gardner Dailey; see also "Forty Stores," 93–94, 97–144. Even among the architects, one could be "too" modern: an article by Gruen criticized the overused glazed front and the recipe-like use of odd shapes and elements, perhaps a swipe at Lapidus or Ketchum; "Is the open front getting out of hand?" Gruen asked. Gruen, "Somewhere in Claustrophobia."

3. Park and Shop

1. Instructions, Park & Shop (Allentown, Pa.: Traffic Game, Inc., 1951).

2. "Campe Euwer, 88, Inventor of 'Park and Shop' Game," *Morning Call,* March 24, 1997. Euwer was president of Traffic Game, Inc., and had done artwork for the Container Corporation of America. The first patent application for Park & Shop was dated July 1951. WikiPatents, "Improvements in parking and shopping traffic board game—Patent Review GB19520016557 19520701," http://www.wikipatents.com/gb/70954.html, accessed December 1, 2008.

3. Jakle and Sculle, *Lots of Parking,* 69–72.

4. Davidson, "Untangling the Traffic Snarl."

5. LeCraw, "Allentown Saves Its Shopping Area"; McGavin, "Teamwork Can Solve the Downtown Parking Problem."

6. Instructions, Park & Shop. The game insert notes "1600 car spaces on 20 Lots within two blocks of the Main Business Center," serving one million parkers per year and more than eighty stores participating.

7. Clarke, "Transportation," 43.

8. Lefferts, "Should Business Provide Off-Street Parking for Patrons?"; Smith, "Business Aids Traffic Problems"; "Traffic Problems Told to Engineers," *New York Times,* January 21, 1927, 14.

9. Phillips," The Traffic Problems in Detroit and How They Are Met," 243; Nolting and Oppermann, *The Parking Problem in Central Business Districts,* 1.

10. Ballard, *A Survey in Respect to the Decentralization of the Boston Central Business District,* 34; U.S. Department of Commerce, *Retail Store Design Problems,* 111; Smith and LeCraw, *Parking,* 3.

11. See Fogelson, *Downtown*; Norton, *Fighting Traffic.*

12. Special issues of the *Annals of the American Academy of Political and Social Science,* one in November 1924 and another in September 1927, were devoted entirely to the problem of the automobile and traffic.

13. Ihlder, "Coordination of Traffic Facilities"; "Parking in Retail Area Downtown," *Boston Daily Globe,* March 11, 1924, 9A; "Report Made on Ordinances," *Los Angeles Times,* October 18, 1925, G3; "Motor Parking Big City Problem," *New York Times,* November 1, 1925, XX17; Hubbard and Hubbard, *Our Cities To-Day and To-Morrow,* 212–23; "Parking Regulations and Reactions in Several Large Cities."

14. See, for instance, Reeder, "City Planning and Traffic Surveys"; a one-way street plan and bypass roads for Schenectady, New York, in Moot, "Directional Traffic Engineering"; Mitchell, "What Can Be Done about Traffic Congestion"; American Automobile Association, *Parking Manual*; "Pedestrian Protection," in Erskine Bureau for Street Traffic Research, Harvard University, *A Traffic Control Plan for Kansas City,* 3; Eno, "The Storage of Dead Vehicles on Roadways."

15. The conference proceedings were published by the International City and Regional Planning Conference as *Planning Problems of Town, City and Region* and included a preface by President Calvin Coolidge. Also attending the conference were Louis Mumford, Clarence Stein, and Alfred Bettman. See in that volume Morris Knowles, "City Planning as a Permanent Solution to the Traffic Problem"; and August Bruggeman and Jacques Gréber, "Circulation et Transports." See also "City Plan Experts of World Coming," *New York Times,* April 15, 1925, 7; Orrick Johns, "New Layout for City Urged by Planners," *New York Times,* June 14, 1925, XX10.

16. "To Park or Not to Park." Consultants for the article included Harland Bartholomew, George B. Ford, Robert Whitten, and Miller McClintock.

17. Lewis, *Highway Traffic,* 94–103, 139–42; Adams, *The Building of the City,* 275–331. See also MacDonald, "Parking Facilities Outside the Traffic Zone"; Simpson, "Downtown Storage Garages"; Ihlder, "Coordination of Traffic Facilities"; Erskine Bureau for Street Traffic Research, *A Traffic Control Plan for Kansas City,* 3; "Traffic Congestion, Parking Facilities and Retail Business"; "Vehicular Traffic Congestion and Retail Business," in U.S. Department of Commerce, *Retail Store Design Problems.*

18. Adams, *The Building of the City,* 309. A conception of a multisectioned street (a popular theme in urban fantasy and professional discourse) included projects by Ernest Flagg, Nelson P. Lewis, Cass Gilbert, V. Hagopian, and, most famously, Harvey Wiley Corbett; the work of Eugene Hénard of Paris was noted as early as 1907 in the American press; see "Congestion in Paris Streets," *Washington Post,* May 19, 1907, M7. Hénard met Daniel Burnham in London in 1910; see "Cities of Future Will Be Beautiful," *New York Times,* October 16, 1910, C4. See also "To Relieve Traffic Congestion in New York."

19. Buttenheim, "The Problem of the Standing Vehicle."

20. Adams, *The Building of the City,* 259.

21. "To Have Garages for Customers," *New York Times,* January 1, 1922, 36; "Has Garage for Patrons," *Washington Post,* September 10, 1922, 64; "St. Louis Now Has Downtown Garages,"

New York Times, September 14, 1924, XX11; Longstreth, *The American Department Store Transformed,* 83–109.

22. "Commonwealth Garage, New York, Herbert Lippman, Architect"; "The Durgin Garage, Brookline, Mass., Harold Field Kellogg, Architect"; "Long Span Concrete Arches Used in Garage"; "Fisher Building Garage, Albert Kahn, Inc., Architects"; "Hill Garage, Los Angeles, Kenneth MacDonald, Jr. & Company, Architects." The Hill Garage used "turntable" elevators.

23. "The Ramp Garage." On Kent garages, see "Skyscraper Garage to Rise 28 Stories," *New York Times,* June 29, 1927, 44; "Kent Automatic Parking Garage, New York, Jardine, Hill and Murdock"; "Skyscraper Garages Offer Solution to City Parking Problem"; Stern, Gilmartin, and Mellins, *New York 1930*; Leon Dickinson, "Skyscraper Garages," *New York Times,* December 22, 1929, XX8.

24. Davison, "Garages," 178.

25. Goodrich, "The Place of the Garage in City Planning." Other styles included the Italianate Chapman Garage and the neoclassical May Company Garage, both in Los Angeles. "Chapman Park Garage"; "May Company Garage." For an example of a deco garage, see Shepley, "Park Square Garage, Boston, Ralph Doane, Architect."

26. "Under One Roof"; "Fisher Building Garage, Albert Kahn, Inc., Architects."

27. Davison, "Garages," 178.

28. Hough, "Experience with Off-Street Parking in Pittsburg"; Locke, "The Use of Parking Facilities in the CBD of Baltimore, May, 1931"; Baker, "Parking Facilities and Habits in the CBD of LA." One publication noted in 1946 that 280 cities had built or acquired off-street parking lots. Yocum, *Municipal Provision of Parking Facilities.* See Isenberg, *Downtown America,* chap. 4.

29. Shepley, "Park Square Garage, Boston."

30. Abbott, "Low Cost Off-Street Parking"; Wolfe, "Shoppers Parking Deck, Detroit, Smith, Hinchman & Grylls"; "Parking Deck, Smith, Hinchman & Grylls, Inc., Architects"; Abbott, "Metropolitan Store Parking."

31. See, for instance, Frank Sturdy, "Traffic's Vital Need Here: More Parking Spaces," *Chicago Daily Tribune,* July 18, 1946, 5; "Parking 1,000 Cars"; "Parking Garage"; "Garages Grow Up"; "Parking Deck"; "Nine Garages for City of Chicago Make a Frontal Attack on Parking Problem."

32. Weinberg, "For Better Places to Park." On Arthur A. Shurcliff, see Longstreth, "The Neighborhood Shopping Center in Washington, D.C., 1930–1941," 16; National Register of Historic Places, *Merchants Square and Resort Historic District.*

33. Mayer and Whittlesey, "Horse Sense Planning, 2."

34. Sears, Roebuck & Company, Los Angeles, 1938–39, John Stokes Redden, architect. See "Store Building for Sears"; Mock, *Built in USA,* 110.

35. Hale, "New Haven's Post-war Plan."

36. "Store Block." See also Clausen, "Shopping Centers," 410. For the store interior, all partitions were made of glass to create a bazaar-like, quasi-free plan of shops, departments, or "islands" arranged for browsing—"Main Street brought indoors." Longstreth, *City Center to Regional Mall,* 188.

37. "Something New in Stores"; "Milliron Department Store." See Hardwick, *Mall Maker,* 96–97; Longstreth, *American Department Store Transformed,* 156–57.

38. "Olympic Shopping Circle"; "Store-on-Stilts."

39. Regional Plan Association, "Parking Facilities Found Inadequate in Communities of the Region," 7. On proposals in Los Angeles, see Longstreth, *City Center to Regional Mall,* 176–218. See also "Providing Parking Spaces in Downtown Business Districts."

40. Stetson, "From Municipal Lots to Complete Parking Program"; Knight, "Parking Headache Gone in Montclair." On Quincy, see Welch, "The Department Store," 5. See also Baker and Funaro, *Shopping Centers,* 57–59; Jakle and Sculle, *Lots of Parking,* 84–85.

41. "Finds 45% of Stores Give Parking Service," *New York Times,* July 13, 1939, 31; "Cities Studying Parking Problem," *New York Times,* January 21, 1940, 135; "Oakland Free Parking Plan Outlined Here," *Washington Post,* December 8, 1940, 16; Fisch, "Meeting Parking after the War"; "In Oakland There Is No Traffic Problem"; "A Community Shopping Center, Glendale California."

42. Nolting and Oppermann, *Parking Problem in Central Business Districts,* 5. See also the Regional Plan Association's *Information Bulletin* 46 (September 18, 1939): 6; Rogers, "Model Off-Street Parking Provided, Garden City, N.Y."; Rogers, "Municipal Parking Lots Set Pattern for Business Districts of Future."

43. See Rogers, "A New Solution to the Parking Problem"; Nolting and Oppermann, *Parking Problem in Central Business Districts,* 6; "City Tests Parking Ban," *New York Times,* January 1, 1939, 110; McCrosky, "Decentralization and Parking"; "Anticipating Problems of Postwar Traffic"; Mickle, *Solutions to Local Parking Problems*; Hurd, "Holding Customers in the Central District"; "Main Street Malady Plagues Municipalities."

44. "Parking Plan Wins in Greenwich," *New York Times,* October 7, 1941, 21; Longstreth, *City Center to Regional Mall,* 186, 196, 218; Regional Plan Association, "Parking Facilities Found Inadequate," 8; "Parking Facilities Relieve Traffic Congestion"; "Municipal Off-Street Parking Systems in the NY Metropolitan Region"; Hurd, "Holding Customers in the Central District"; Public Administration Clearing House, "Public Parking Facilities"; Kennedy, "The Parking Problem Can Be Solved"; "Kalamazoo Keeps Her Customers"; American Automobile Association, *Parking Manual,* 92; Smith and LeCraw, *Parking*; Saul Pett and William Conway, "31 Million Autos Want to Park!," *Washington Post,* January 26, 1947, B2; Miller, "Pasadena Tackles Its Parking Problem"; National Conservation Bureau, Traffic Division, "Street and Off-Street Parking Study."

45. "Parking Facilities Relieve Traffic Congestion."

46. Buttenheim, "Problem of the Standing Vehicle"; LeCraw, "Interior Block Planning"; National Conservation Bureau, Traffic Division, "Demonstrating to Retail Businessmen the Relative Unimportance of Curb-Parked Vehicles," 95; Evans, "Planning Off-Street Parking Lots."

47. Behrendt, "Off-Street Parking"; "Planning for Parking in Buffalo."

48. Nolting and Oppermann, *Parking Problem in Central Business Districts,* 6; for an illustration, see Jakle and Sculle, *Lots of Parking,* 84.

49. Skinner, "Parking Lots—and 30-Minute Meters to Encourage Their Use"; "Kansas City Flanks Business District with Six Modern Parking Lots."

50. Taylor, "Hollywood Tackles the Parking Problem."

51. Longstreth, *City Center to Regional Mall,* 216–18. See also Downtown Business Men's Association, *Downtown Los Angeles Parking Study.*

52. Smith and LeCraw, *Parking,* 84–85; Wall, "Unique Community Planning Follows Expansion of Defense Industries"; LeCraw, "City-Owned Parking Lot Experience in Miami Beach, Florida."

53. "Parking 1,000 Cars"; Nolting and Oppermann, *Parking Problem in Central Business Districts,* 9; Koch, "Parking Facilities for the Detroit Central Business District"; "Traffic Jams Business Out"; Hammond, "Plans for Post-war Traffic Safety"; Steinbaugh, "Underground Parking for Detroit"; Urban Land Institute, *Automobile Parking in Central Business Districts.* See also extensive Detroit materials compiled by Ken Welch, 4-2, KWPBHL.

54. Bartholomew, *Report upon Streets, Parking, Zoning, City of Beverly Hills, California*; "Traffic and Parking in Beverly Hills."

55. Kincaid, "Chicago Plans."

56. National Interregional Highway Committee, *Interregional Highways,* 75–77. See also Willier, "Parking Needs of a Modern City"; Lovejoy, "What Can Be Done about Traffic Congestion"; Mickle, "Traffic Planning"; McNeil, "Pittsburgh's Downtown Parking Problem"; Marsh, "Parking and Terminal Problems."

57. Barnes, "Flint Merchants Provide Downtown Parking Lot"; Buttenheim, "City Highways and City Parking"; Farr, "Parking Clinic in Kansas City"; McNeil, "Pittsburgh's Downtown Parking Problem"; "Municipal Programs for Off-Street Parking Facilities"; Nolting and Oppermann, *Parking Problem in Central Business Districts,* 6; Hammond, "Plans for Post-war Traffic Safety"; "Parking Lots for Mineola." See also Cincinnati City Planning Commission, *Parking,* 49, in which planners stated that all persons should "become pedestrians" at the end of their trip.

58. Welch conducted what he called an "isochron" analysis for time and road systems. See Baker and Funaro, *Shopping Centers,* 32–33.

59. "Store Buildings," 585, 606.

60. Among Welch's papers was a 1927 Detroit publication called *Planning the Future of Your City,* which contained suggestions about citizen involvement, planning procedures, surveys, and cooperative action. Welch used the brochure as a checklist, noting in the margins "Done" and "Should do" for his hometown of Grand Rapids. *Planning the Future of Your City,* Detroit, 1927, 5-11, KWPBHL.

61. Other items in the Welch archives include a marked-up copy of the 1943 California law allowing government to build, tax, bond, and run garages, 3-21, KWPBHL; City Plan Commission, *Planning Detroit 1944,* Detroit, 1944, 4-1, KWPBHL; City of Detroit, Traffic Engineering Bureau, "Detroit's Parking Needs: Central Business District," August 1946, 4-2, KWPBHL; City of Detroit, "Proposed System of Trafficways," December 1946, 1-14, KWPBHL.

62. The commission got the advice of Walter Blucher, executive secretary of the American Society of Planning Officials. Welch, "Urban Planning." See also Kenneth C. Welch, Speech to the Detroit Chapter, American Institute of Architects, February 16, 1944, 6, 12-5, KWPBHL. Welch edited the City Planning Commission's 1947 "Parking Study," 5-18, KWPBHL.

63. Shanken, *194X,* 15–58. See also Hanchett, "Federal Incentives and the Growth of Local Planning, 1941–48"; Bauman, "Visions of a Post-war City."

64. See "Planning with You," *Architectural Forum* 80; "Planning with You," *Architectural Forum* 79.

65. Welch followed the urban design and especially the parking propositions for Detroit in great detail. Folders 4-1, 4-2, KWPBHL.

66. "Grand Rapids Parking Plan to Rehabilitate Shopping at the Urban Center"; "Grand Rapids Retail Center Acclaimed as Model." In a letter to *Record* editor Kenneth Stowell, Welch noted that he had received dozens of reprint requests. Kenneth Welch to Kenneth Stowell, May 18, 1945, 5-17, KWPBHL.

67. "Grand Rapids Parking Plan," 95. See also Welch, *The Effect of Retail Distribution on the City Plan,* 22, 24. A new "parking authority," Welch wrote, should be able to "contract for roof space" to ease parking. "Parking Study," Staff of the CPC, January 1947, with marginal notes by Welch, 5-17, KWPBHL.

68. No town was too small for Welch to accept a speaking engagement there; see "Says Parking Is Key to Increased Business," *Emporia Gazette,* July 12, 1945, KWPBHL.

69. Welch also cited a proposal for an "upper level vehicular circle throughout [the] central business districts." Welch to Stowell, May 18, 1945. He also thanked Stowell for the publication of the Grand Rapids Parking Plan in *Architectural Record.*

70. Kenneth C. Welch to W. E. Conley, General Electric Company, August 14, 1945; Welch to J. V. Gregory, Traffic and Parking Committee, New Rochelle, June 22, 1945; both in 5-17, KWPBHL.

71. "More Cars, Superhighways Will Set Post-war Pattern for Commercial Building."

72. Parnes's doctorate (title as published in German, *Bauten des Einzelhandels und ihre Verkehrs- und Organisationsprobleme*) was supervised by noted Swiss architect Otto Salvisberg. It included no introductory words about city design.

73. "Dr. Louis Parnes, Obituary"; "Community Building, Zurich, Switzerland"; Louis Parnes, "Centro de recreación para el personal de los laboratorios Hoffmann La Roche," *Revista de Arquitectura* 31 (April 1946): 138-140.

74. Parnes, *Planning Stores That Pay,* 13.

75. Equally polemical was Parnes's department store with cantilevered storage floors, a tour de force of modernist programmatic and formal invention. Parnes, "Intermediate Floors for Greater Efficiency in Storage and Service."

76. For a modernist reading of Rockefeller Center, see Giedion, *Space, Time and Architecture,* 845–56.

77. "New Elements in House Design"; "General Houses, Inc., Chicago."

78. Quoted in "Chicago Will Get 2 Store Centers," *New York Times,* September 12, 1948, R10.

79. Emile Tavel, "Marketing in the Future," *Christian Science Monitor,* April 3, 1948, 7; "Zoners Hear Bid for New Shop Center," *Chicago Daily Tribune,* August 15, 1948, N1; "Advance Type Shopping Center to Be Built in Chicago," press release, William R. Harshe Associates, Chicago, December 13, 1948, Papers of Howard T. Fisher, Harvard University Archives; Al Chase, "Plan Center for Shopping from Autos," *Chicago Daily Tribune,* December 15, 1948, C5; Fisher, *The Impact of New Shopping Centers upon Established Business Districts*; "Can Main Street Compete?"

80. Edward Buehler Delk and, later, Edward Tanner, architects, but Nichols takes credit for most of the planning. Jesse Clyde Nichols, "The Development of Outlying Shopping Centers," National Conference of City Planning, Buffalo, May 1929, KC106, J. C. Nichols Company Records, Western Historical Manuscript Collection, Kansas City; Longstreth, "J. C. Nichols, the Country Club Plaza and Notions of Modernity."

81. Nichols later recalled he did not want bypass roads (soon to be integral to planning discourse) because on such roads drivers would move too fast, preventing visual engagement with stores. "Planning and Management of Nichols Shopping Centers," 48; "Advocates Neatness in Shopping Areas," *New York Times,* February 7, 1937, 186.

82. Richard Longstreth describes Nichols's modernism as split between "expression" and "convenience," which he also calls "two compatible urges" in American architecture. Longstreth, "J. C. Nichols"; Longstreth, "The Diffusion of the Community Shopping Center Concept during the Interwar Decades."

83. "Munsey Park, Business Center"; Longstreth, "Neighborhood Shopping Center."

84. Gruzen, "Automobile Shopping Centers." The first branch was in Elizabeth and another was in Paterson; "Super-servicenter for Jersey City Shopping Center." See also "Food Market," which describes an infill project without auto considerations. On the supermarket, see Bowlby, *Carried Away,* 134–51.

85. Earlier examples were not widely cited at the time: Riverside, Chicago, 1870; Roland Park, Baltimore, 1910.

86. On early markets, see Longstreth, *City Center to Regional Mall,* 273–83; Longstreth, "Diffusion of the Community Shopping Center Concept"; Longstreth, "River Oaks Shopping Center." See also Rowe, *Making a Middle Landscape.*

87. Highland Park: Hugh Prather, developer; Fooshee & Cheek, architects. See "Suburban Shopping Centers," 30–32; "A Model Shopping Village in Texas"; "Highland Park Shopping Village," National Historic Landmark Nomination, U.S. Department of the Interior, National Park Service, 1986. Highland Park's developer called it a transformed "Court House Square," inscribing into the project American traditions of public and civic space, yet this image was flexible enough to be organized around cars instead of green or monumental elements.

88. River Oaks: Hugh Potter, developer. "No. 1: Shopping Center at River Oaks, Houston"; "A Long Considered Scheme Develops"; Longstreth, "River Oaks Shopping Center"; Baker and Funaro, *Shopping Centers,* 69–70.

89. "Drafting and Design Problems"; "A New Model Shopping Center Developed by Realtor Firm."

90. The article was without byline, but Richard Longstreth cites a personal conversation with Albert Frey concerning his role; Longstreth, *The Drive-In, the Supermarket, and the Transformation of Commercial Space in Los Angeles,* 151–52n33.

91. Longstreth, "Neighborhood Shopping Center." See also Stoever, "No. 3"; "Park and Shop."

92. "Main Street, USA," 74.

93. Lapidus, "Store Design."

94. "Main Street, USA," 74, 75, 79, 86, 88. See also "100 Per Cent Locations."

4. Pedestrianization Takes Command

1. Le Corbusier also wrote, in 1948: "Le Piéton pourra donc retrouver sa royaute et sa dignite." Le Corbusier, "L'Habitation moderne," 431. See also Giedion, "Historical Background to the Core," 18; Sert, "Centres of Community Life"; Sert, *Can Our Cities Survive?,* 190.

2. Arthur C. Holden (Princeton, 1912), of Holden, McLaughlin Associates in New York City, organized the conference and edited the first published version of the proceedings. Holden, *Planning Man's Physical Environment.* The proceedings were revised and republished in 1949 as *Building for Modern Man,* edited by Thomas H. Creighton.

3. "'Grass on Main Street' Becomes a Reality," 83. See also Baldwin, *Domesticating the Street,* 214–24.

4. Hamlin cited in Wurster, "The Need for Change," 176; ibid., 175.

5. Ketchum, cited in ibid., 175.

6. Le Corbusier, "L'Habitation moderne," 432.

7. "Planned Neighborhoods for 194X," *Architectural Forum* 80.

8. Perry, "The Neighborhood Unit."

9. Perry's plan had antecedents in the Chicago City Club competition of 1913. Johnson, "Origin of the Neighborhood Plan." See also Perry, *The Extension of Public Education.*

10. Mumford et al., "The Planned Community." See also Gillette, "The Evolution of Neighborhood Planning from the Progressive Era to the 1949 Housing Act"; Banerjee and Baer, *Beyond the Neighborhood Unit*; Patricios, "The Neighborhood Concept"; Larsen, "Cities to Come"; Larsen, "The Radburn Idea as an Emergent Concept."

11. Park, Burgess, and McKenzie, *The City*; Zorbaugh, "The Natural Areas of the City." See also Fairfield, "Alienation of Social Control."

12. The literature is broad. See, for example, Eckbo, "Site Planning"; "A Technique for Accelerated Planning." See also Hise, *Magnetic Los Angeles,* 86–116.

13. Stein, "City Patterns . . . Past and Future," 53; Gropius, *Rebuilding Our Communities,* 18; Pommer, "'More a Necropolis than a Metropolis'"; Sert, *Can Our Cities Survive?,* 68–72; Sert, "The Human Scale in City Planning."

14. Sert, *Can Our Cities Survive?,* 190.

15. Mackesey and Clarke, "Planned Communities."

16. National Resources Committee, Research Committee on Urbanism, *Supplementary Report of the Urbanism Committee to the National Resources Committee*; Light, "The City as National Resource."

17. Wirth and Shils, "Urban Living Conditions," 215; Comey and Wehrly, "Planning Communities," 8.

18. Greer, *The Problem of the Cities and Towns,* 26, 103, 111.

19. Shanken, *194X,* 15–58.

20. "Planned Neighborhoods for 194X," *Architectural Forum* 79; "Planned Neighborhoods for 194X," *Architectural Forum* 80.

21. "A Satellite Town for the Detroit Area," project architect George Hellmuth at Smith, Hinchman & Grylls; codesigned by Earl F. Giberson, who would shortly join Whitney Smith to design the shopping center at Linda Vista. Engelhardt, "School-Neighborhood Nucleus." See also Herrey, Herrey, and Pertzoff, "An Organic Theory of City Planning"; Dowling, "Neighborhood Shopping Centers." Dowling worked on Met Life's Parkchester (1938–42) and Stuyvesant Town (1945–47). Neutra, "Peace Can Gain from War's Forced Changes," 29.

22. Revere Copper and Brass produced a multiyear series of pamphlets starting in 1941 arguing for planning and architecture as well as promoting the company's products. See Shanken, *194X,* 111–34; Stonorov and Kahn, *Why City Planning Is Your Responsibility*; Stonorov and Kahn, *You and Your Neighborhood.* Stonorov and Kahn's work on the *Better Philadelphia Exhibit* of 1947 was sensitive to context while closing streets and providing alternative transportation routes; see "Philadelphia Plans Again." See also "Philadelphia Slum Modernization by the Block."

23. Museum of Modern Art, *Look at Your Neighborhood,* panel 10. Clarence Stein was credited as consultant for the project.

24. Letter from Mel Scott, *Look at Your Neighborhood* (1944) exhibit 256, 1945, Museum of Modern Art Archives.

25. Scott, *Cities Are for People,* 62; Scott, *Metropolitan Los Angeles.*

26. A proposal by architect Carl Troedsson for closing and planting streets in Los Angeles was exhibited at Bullock's department store. Troedsson, "Plan for Pedestrians"; Troedsson, "The City-Town."

27. The application of the unit could take on absurd proportions and hinted at the overuse of the concept in later years; see Sanders and Rabuck, *New City Patterns*; Justement, *New Cities for Old.*

28. Crane, "Analyzing Obsolescent Neighborhoods"; Isaacs, "Are Urban Neighborhoods Possible?"; Isaacs, "The 'Neighborhood Unit' Is an Instrument for Segregation"; Tyrwhitt, "The Size and Spacing of Urban Communities." See the defense of the unit by Adams, Riemer, Isaacs, Mitchell, and Breese, "The Neighborhood Concept in Theory and Application."

29. Mumford, "The Modern City," 815.

30. Bauman, "Visions of a Post-war City."

31. Stein and Bauer, "Store Buildings and Neighborhood Shopping Centers"; Longstreth, "The Neighborhood Shopping Center," 11.

32. Longstreth, *City Center to Regional Mall,* 292; "Greenbelt, MD, Ellington and Wadsworth, Architects"; Stein, *Toward New Towns for America,* 127–32.

33. Mayer, "A Technique for Planning Complete Communities, Parts 1 and 2."

34. Feiss, "Shopping Centers." Feiss also wrote a piece on commuter train stations for *House & Garden* and proposed a series on "community planning." Carl Feiss to Arthur McK. Stires, *House & Garden,* December 18, 1939, #2635, Box 9, Folder 35, Carl L. Feiss Papers, Division of Rare and Manuscript Collections, Cornell University Library.

35. De Boer, "Accommodations for Parked Automobiles a Main Requirement, Boulder City, Nevada," in *Shopping Districts,* 37, 39; De Boer, *Shopping Districts,* 46.

36. Ketchum, *Shops and Stores,* 241.

37. Ibid., 267; "Commercial Facilities for 4,500 Families"; Mock, *Built in USA,* 106–7; Belluschi, "Shopping Centers." See also Clausen, *Pietro Belluschi*; Longstreth, *City Center to Regional Mall,* 291, 296–98.

38. "'Grass on Main Street' Becomes a Reality"; "Commercial Center, Linda Vista, California"; Smith, "No Cars on Main Street"; Longstreth, *City Center to Regional Mall,* 296–98. A 1941 version of the Linda Vista "shopping and administrative center" was most likely designed by Spencer Sanders and C. David Persina (and "consulting architect" Gilbert Stanley Underwood). On Linda Vista, see Cameron and Beckman, "Linda Vista."

39. "The Town of Willow Run." The architects for the subtowns included Mayer and Whittlesey; Skidmore, Owings & Merrill; and Stonorov and Kahn. Tracy Augur was the Federal Public Housing Authority site plan consultant. The plan for Willow Run as a whole was whittled down as it met resistance from local property owners, realtors, and Henry Ford himself. "What Housing for Willow Run?"

40. Taylor, "Kingsford Heights." Little of the shopping area was built. Hudnut, "The Art in Housing," 62; "A Station for a Shopping Center, Henry S. Churchill, Architect." Clarence Stein is listed as a contributor to the "community planning" aspects of the project. "Shopping Center Designed to Attract Shoppers."

41. Rendering published in Lewis, *Planning the Modern City,* 249.

42. Longstreth, *City Center to Regional Mall,* 312–22, also shows a plan by Robert Alexander for alternating pedestrian malls, vehicular service roads, and parking areas.

43. "Bergen County Shopping Center"; "Triangular Site Suggests Circular Mall."

44. See chapter 3, note 79; see also Howard T. Fisher, "The Development of Planned Shopping Centers," in "Regional Shopping Centers," Chicago Region Chapter of the American Institute of Planners, Chicago, June 1952 (Conference September 1951), Harvard University Archives; Nicholas Veronico, "Lincoln Village Park and Shop to Open Sept. 15," *Chicago Daily Tribune,* August 16, 1951, W4.

45. Nelson began working at *Architectural Forum* in 1936. See Abercrombie, *George Nelson.*

46. "Post-war Pattern." The series continued for two years and included letters and comments from readers as well as special features such as "Building's Post-war Pattern, No. 1"; "Building's Post-war Pattern, No. 2"; and "Building's Post-war Pattern, No. 3."

47. "New Buildings for 194X"; Buttenheim, "Citizen Interest and Participation in City and Regional Planning and Housing," 617. See Shanken, *194X,* 94–96; Longstreth, *City Center to Regional Mall,* 269–71; Hardwick, *Mall Maker,* 72–76.

48. Greer, "Syracuse Plans Its Future," 182; Greer, *Your City Tomorrow. Your City Tomorrow* was a compilation of Greer's *Fortune* articles of 1943 and 1944.

49. The committee's work was directed locally by Sergei Grimm, a "city engineer" and head of the Syracuse City Planning Commission.

50. On the organization of Syracuse planning, see *The Post War Report, 1945,* Syracuse-Onondaga Post-War Planning Council, Syracuse, 1945, Series 1, 4, Reginald R. Isaacs Papers, Archives of American Art, Smithsonian Institution.

51. Nelson, "Stylistic Trends in Contemporary Architecture," 575.

52. Sert, *Can Our Cities Survive?,* 229–30. Nelson, having traveled to Europe in 1935, was likely aware of the British work on town planning. *Architectural Forum* noted the County of London Plan in "End of the Great WEN?"

53. "Grass Grows Green on Main Street"; Bennett, "Nobody Lives in a House." See also Bennett, "How to Fit Your Home to Your Family"; and Bennett, "Our Town—It's Up to Us." Bennett worked for Edward Durell Stone from 1936 to 1938, worked with Caleb Hornbostel from 1938 to 1943, and taught at Vassar and Yale; in 1946, he joined Loebl and Schlossman in Chicago.

54. Nelson, *Main Street;* see also "Grass on Main Street"; Shanken, *194X,* 111–34.

55. "Planning with You." The series ran through 1944.

56. Ibid., 66–67, 75; "New Buildings for 194X," 70; Nelson, *Main Street,* 6.

57. "Planning with You," 74, 75.

58. Telegram from Howard Myers to Victor Gruen, February 8, 1943; telegram from Gruen to Myers, February 8, 1943; telegram from Ruth Goodhue to Gruen, February 10, 1943; all in box 54, VGPAHC.

59. Letter from Howard Myers to Victor Gruen, February 16, 1943, box 54, VGPAHC.

60. Ibid.

61. Letter from Victor Gruen to Ruth Goodhue, February 16, 1943, box 54, VGPAHC.

62. Ibid.

63. Letter from George Nelson to Victor Gruen, March 3, 1943; letter from Nelson to Gruen, March 9, 1943; both in box 54, VGPAHC.

64. Letter from Gruen to Goodhue, February 26, 1943, box 54, VGPAHC.

65. Letter from Nelson to Gruen, March 3, 1943; letter from Nelson to Gruen, March 9, 1943; Gruen, undated sketches; letter to Nelson from Gruen, March 22, 1943; all in box 54, VGPAHC.

66. Longstreth, *City Center to Regional Mall,* 302–4; Hardwick, *Mall Maker,* 72–87.

67. "Shopping Center," in "New Buildings for 194X," 101. Gruen, undated sketches, box 54, VGPAHC.

68. "Shopping Center," in "New Building for 194X," 101–3.

69. Gruen, "What to Look for in Shopping Centers"; Longstreth, *City Center to Regional Mall,* 323–25.

70. "Store Block."

71. Adams, "A Planning Program for the City of Rye."

72. Hoyt was a respected real estate researcher and writer who, at the time of his Rye work, lived in the neighboring town of Larchmont. A founding member of the Urban Land Institute, he conducted analyses of more than two hundred shopping centers; his publications about shopping center standards were required reading. Joan Cook, "Homer Hoyt, Early Planner of Urban Shopping Centers," *New York Times,* December 1, 1984, 28. See also Beauregard, "More than Sector Theory."

73. Rye, New York, *On Our Way*; Adams and Langloh, *A Master Plan and Capital Outlay Program for the City of Rye,* 8.

74. "Replanning in Rye, N.Y." Ketchum associate Vincent Furno completed the much-circulated renderings and claims a substantial role in the Rye project. Vincent Furno, personal communication, December 15, 2004.

75. Rye, New York, *On Our Way,* 19–24. Also part of the Rye Plan was the creation of recreational fields, swimming facilities, a school program, storm sewer improvements, and a scenic trail.

76. "Shopping Center," *Architectural Forum* 85. See also Harrison, "Rye Aims at City Planning Leadership"; "Rye Gets Plan for Improvements at Cost of $4,000,000 in 25 Years," *New York Times,* June 26, 1946, 26; Longstreth, *City Center to Regional Mall,* 325–26; Ketchum, *Shops and Stores,* 281, 284.

77. Ketchum's comments echo those of *Forum* editors: without "disrupting" the existing city, they wrote, "convenience could be achieved . . . by diverting traffic and using the street proper as a planted area." "'Grass on Main Street' Becomes a Reality," 85. Similarly, Whitney Smith wrote that existing shopping districts might be planted and turned into a "parklike promenade for shoppers." Smith, "No Cars on Main Street."

78. "Brazil Plans a City"; "Brazil Plans Entire New City"; Museum of Modern Art, *Two Cities*; Lee Cooper, "Brazil Is Building a Modern City," *New York Times,* September 8, 1946, W1.

79. "Withering Grass."

80. The early versions of Mount Kisco with its Main Street converted into a "shopping mall" were published in 1949 in Funaro and Baker's "Shopping Centers," 115. The scaled-back version without the mall was published in the authors' subsequent book, Baker and Funaro, *Shopping Centers,* 12–13. See also Northern Westchester Joint Planning Program, "Appendix A," 76–84, 116–20.

81. Welch, "Neighborhood Shopping Centers and Parking Problems"; Welch, "Convenience vs. Shopping Goods," 82. See also "Transcript with minor corrections and additions

to article appearing in 12/26/46 WWD," and untitled typed manuscript; both in 12-28, KWPBHL. Welch first presented this material at a September 1946 planning meeting of the Grand Rapids Local Planning Institute. See also Welch, *The Effect of Retail Distribution on the City Plan.*

82. "New Beverly Trading Center to Have Space for 3,000 Cars." Some branch stores were "stand-alone" projects in wealthier suburbs (on the East Coast) or new urban districts (on the West Coast), and others were built as part of outer urban housing projects, such as New York's Parkchester Houses (1938–42), where Morris Ketchum designed a midsize store in 1944. "Wide Store Space with Open Front." See Longstreth, *The American Department Store Transformed,* 109–35, 183–86.

83. Hanchett, "Financing Suburbia"; "The Lush New Suburban Market."

84. "Suburban Retail Districts," 108. The connection of the Conant Trust to James Conant, then president of Harvard, is unclear but one of the Trust advisers, William A. Coolidge, was on Harvard's Board of Overseers at the time. "Trust Rides Shopping Center Boom."

85. "Florida Foods Offering," *New York Times,* July 31, 1945, 22; "New Device Spurs Output: High Vacuum Machine Steps Up Television Mirror Production," *New York Times,* July 17, 1947, 34. Bing Crosby appeared in Minute Maid ads and was a stockholder in a Florida-based NRC subsidiary. "Investors Guide, Citrus Concentrates," *Chicago Daily Tribune,* October 18, 1949, A7.

86. Rawls had invested in furniture stores and Great Lakes shipping companies, and, most notably, his firm helped to capitalize and franchise the "Piggly-Wiggly System" of self-service retailer Clarence Saunders. See "20,000 Units, Clarence Saunders Stores, Inc.," *Chicago Daily Tribune,* November 5, 1928, 29. The NSC letterhead subtitle was also revealing: "A national service in recentralizing retail business districts—Planning, Financing & Building." 1-14, KWPBHL.

87. Baker and Funaro, *Shopping Centers,* 196–98. Welch used an "isochron" analysis (a sectoral model based on driving times) to map out the potential trading areas for proposed stores.

88. Welch, "Convenience vs. Shopping Goods," 82–83. At the same time, Jordan Marsh's new store in Boston was to be designed by Perry, Shaw and Hepburn of Boston; the firm also designed a new headquarters for the NRC. "Jordan Marsh, Boston, Perry, Shaw and Hepburn, Architects," cover. See also Judt, "Reshaping Shopping Environments."

89. According to Ketchum, Rawls first contacted Welch, who contacted him. Ketchum, *Blazing a Trail,* 11. The team included Anderson and Beckwith as associate architects.

90. The Beverly proposal appeared in *Women's Wear Daily* in an article by Welch. The same plan was dated July 1946 in Welch's papers, 9-30, KWPBHL. "Modern Theory Is Used in Beverly Mass to Design the North Shore Shopping Center"; "Shopping Center," *Architectural Forum* 86; "Retail Center Planned," *New York Times,* June 6, 1947, 36.

91. A similar design was proposed for sites sought by NSC, including Purchase and White Plains in New York and in Livingston, New Jersey. See MacGregor, "The Shopping Center"; "A Mammoth New Shopping Center."

92. "Framingham Picked as New Shopping Site"; "Markets in the Meadows"; "Awards Contract on Store Center," *New York Times*, February 6, 1949, R3; "Start First Unit of Store Centers," *New York Times,* May 22, 1949, R10; "Shoppers' World at Framingham Applies New Ideas"; "Shoppers' World"; "Suburban Retail Districts." See also Broomer, "Shoppers' World and the Regional Shopping Center in Greater Boston."

93. Shurcliff, "Shoppers' World."

94. "Shoppers' World," 181.

95. Lapidus, "The Retail Store and Its Design Problems," 96. Fifteen years later he would design Lincoln Road pedestrian mall in Miami: "What Makes a Mall Plan Practical?"

96. Mumford, "The Highway and the City," 186. Lapidus, in fact, proposed several unbuilt, car-based shopping centers in the early 1950s: Falls Shopping Center, Fallsington, Pennsylvania, and "The Hub," Hicksville, Long Island. See "Shopping Centers," *Architectural Record* 114: 185, 187.

5. The Cold War Pedestrian

1. Alsop and Alsop, "Your Flesh Should Creep"; Teller, Marshak, and Klein, "Dispersal of Cities and Industries," 13; Boyer, *By the Bomb's Early Light,* 3–27, 107–30.

2. Hilberseimer, "Cities and Defense," 93; Hilberseimer, *The New Regional Pattern,* 188; Hilberseimer, *The New City,* 40, 51. Fears of conventional bombing had long existed; see "Civilian Defense Reference Number," 1–68; Monteyne, *Fallout Shelter.*

3. Donovan, *Tumultuous Years,* 99–102; Whitfield, *The Culture of the Cold War,* 101–26; Mason, *The Cold War, 1945–91,* 1–23; Oakes, *The Imaginary War,* 10–32; Hales, *Atomic Spaces,* 71–114.

4. Augur, "Decentralization," 132; Augur, "Dispersal Is Good Business."

5. Caldwell, "Atomic Bombs and City Planning," 299; Ogburn in discussion in "The Politics of Atomic Power," in Wendt and Geddes, *The Atomic Age Opens,* 211; Stein, *Toward New Towns for America,* i; Woodbury, *The Future of Cities and Urban Redevelopment,* iv. See also Farish, *The Contours of America's Cold War.*

6. Edwards, *The Closed World.* For a parallel and prehistory of dispersal logic, see Easterling, *Organization Space.*

7. Hersey, *Hiroshima*; Boyer, *By the Bomb's Early Light,* 203–10. See also Masters and Way, *One World or None.*

8. Lapp, *Must We Hide?,* 74.

9. Augur, "The Dispersal of Cities as a Defense Measure"; Augur, "Planning Cities for the Atomic Age," 75; Augur, "Decentralization Can't Wait," 32; Augur, "Security Factors in the Planning of Urban Regions." See also Dudley, "Sprawl as Strategy"; Dimendberg, "City of Fear"; Parsons, "Shaping the Regional City."

10. Kelly, "The Necessity for Dispersion," 108.

11. "Factory Dispersal for National Security and Rational Town Planning," "Presidential directive, August 10, 1951: Industrial Dispersion Policy," and Jack Gourrie, "NSRB Dispersion Policy Statement: Is Your Plant a Target?," all reprinted in "Defense through Decentralization"; National Security Resources Board, *National Conference on Industrial Dispersion*; U.S. Department of Commerce, *Industrial Dispersion Guidebook for Communities.* See also Scott, *American City Planning since 1890,* 368–471.

12. "Offices Move to the Suburbs," 79; "Rural Insurance Plant"; Tobin, "The Reduction of Urban Vulnerability"; Mozingo, *Pastoral Capitalism.*

13. Boyer, *By the Bomb's Early Light,* 47–106; Bradley, *No Place to Hide,* xvii, 149, 167.

14. "To Prevent the Utter Destruction of Urban Civilization"; Windels, "How Should Our Cities Grow?," *Journal of the American Institute of Architects,* October, November, and December 1950. See also Lear, "Hiroshima, USA"; "Preview of the War We Do Not Want."

15. Walker, "Alert." Walker served on the Construction Advisory Committee of the National Production Authority. National Defense Committee, "Shortages Are Opportunities." Earlier, Walker supported dispersal not as a defense strategy but merely as good settlement policy. "Forget Bombs, Architect Says," *Washington Post,* May 10, 1950, 8.

16. National Defense Committee, "Architecture and War"; *Memo from the Octagon* (AIA newsletter), September 25, 1950, 1. In July 1950, the *Bulletin of the American Institute of Architects* included a mail-in insert titled "Be Prepared," which asked architects to supply their professional information to federal agencies.

17. National Defense Committee, "Short-Run, Long-Run."

18. "Partial" decentralization, Mayer wrote, as had been proposed for federal office workers in Washington, would be "timid" and dangerously incomplete. Mayer, "A New-Town Program," 9. See also Mayer, "The Need for Synchronized Dispersal."

19. Perkins, "New Towns for America's Peacetime Needs"; Bauer, "Redevelopment," 24. Perkins also wrote that the new metropolitan region would consist of a "galaxy of new towns," and the "old city with congestion eliminated." Perkins, "The Regional City."

20. Perkins and Creighton, "The Harvard Studies."

21. *Memo from the Octagon,* various, 1949–51; American Institute of Architects, "Proceedings, Eighty-Third Convention," Chicago, May 8–11, 1951, 58–135, AIA Archives.

22. Prince worked for the New York City Housing Authority and other city housing organizations; he was involved with civil defense issues as early as 1939. "Defense Architect"; "Planning Is Urged for Defense Areas."

23. American Institute of Architects, *Report of the 83rd Convention,* Washington, D.C., May 1951, 11–20, AIA Archives; American Institute of Architects, *Civil Defense,* 19–20. The book was followed by *Defense Measures in Multistory Buildings* (1951), *Defense Measures in Industrial Plants* (1952), *Defense Measures in Schools* (1953), and *Defense Measures in Hospitals* (1953). "Convergence on Chicago," *Memo from the Octagon,* May 1951, 1, AIA Archives.

24. "Pros and Cons of Architecture for Civil Defense." Respondents included architects— Morris Ketchum, Albert Mayer, Lawrence Perkins, Harry Prince, Eugene Klaber, and Thomas Creighton—as well as engineers, civil defense officials, planners (such as Tracy Augur), and journalists.

25. Henry Wright attacked efforts to plan for survival of the bomb as well as the "witch hunts" that had taken control of politics. Wright, letter to the editor, *Progressive Architecture.*

26. Clarence Stein in "Pros and Cons of Architecture for Civil Defense," 75; Jaqueline Tyrwhitt in ibid., 76. Tyrwhitt illustrated a mixed dispersal with an image from Gyorgy Kepes's then forthcoming *The New Landscape.*

27. See also Winkler, *Life under a Cloud.*

28. "Named by Architects," *New York Times,* September 5, 1950, 46; "Planning Is Urged for Defense Areas," *New York Times,* February 9, 1951, 46; "Architects Aid Defense," *New York Times,* March 2, 1951, 27; "Architects Urge Balanced Defense," *New York Times,* April 22, 1951, 23.

29. American Institute of Architects, *Press Book: Eighty-Third Convention,* Washington, D.C., May 1951, 2, AIA Archives.

30. Ketchum was perceived as a figure of balance and leadership. As one observer put it in 1951 (reminiscent of Kenneth Reid's adulation earlier), Ketchum was "a tower of strength to all." Harry Prince, in American Institute of Architects, "Proceedings," 103.

31. Morris Ketchum, "Group Shelters," in American Institute of Architects, "Proceedings," 80–85; Lee Cooper, "Architects Warn of Building Delay," *New York Times,* May 9, 1951, 57; *Memo from the Octagon,* January 1, 1951, AIA Archives; "Can Group Shelters Save Lives?" New York City spokesmen, such as Robert Moses, lobbied to use subway stations as shelters. Charles G. Bennett, "134,500,000 Ask for Queens Transit," *New York Times,* June 22, 1950, 1.

32. Ketchum, "Group Shelters," 78, 86; memo from Douglas Haskell to staff, *Architectural Forum,* February 27, 1951, Douglas Putnam Haskell Papers, Drawings and Archives, Avery Architectural and Fine Arts Library, Columbia University. Later in 1951, Haskell presided over a conference on dispersal, "Ninth Ann Arbor Conference on Changing Community Patterns as a Result of Industrial Location," University of Michigan, November 1951, KWPBHL.

33. Project East River was sponsored by a consortium called Associated Universities, Inc., which included Columbia, Cornell, Harvard, Johns Hopkins, Massachusetts Institute of Technology, Pennsylvania, Princeton, Rochester, and Yale. New York Life Insurance, typical of insurance companies during and after the war, engaged in extensive building projects, including Fresh Meadows, on Long Island, in 1949 and Manhattan House in New York City in 1952. See Hanchett, "Financing Suburbia"; Grossman, *Neither Dead nor Red,* 41–67; Oakes, *The Imaginary War,* 47–71.

34. [William Wheaton], "Minimum Density and Spacing for Metropolitan Dispersion," in Associated Universities, Inc., *Project East River,* 39b–45b; [William Wheaton], "Forces Making for Concentration in the Cores of Metropolitan Areas," in Associated Universities, Inc., *Project East River,* Appendix V-B to Part V (July 1952). The land-use project was headed by C. McKim Norton (son of Charles Dyer Norton of the RPNYE), planner and vice president of the RPA, and Burnham Kelly, head of the Bemis Foundation, an industry-funded housing research organization. See Norton, "Report on Project East River" and "Report on Project East River, Part II"; McLean, "Project East River"; Monson, "City Planning in Project East River."

35. Associated Universities, Inc. "Federal Leadership to Reduce Urban Vulnerability," in *Project East River,* Part II-B (June 1952), 10; repeated and revised in *Project East River,* Part V (July 1952), 27.

36. Participants included New York Hospital, the Rockefeller Institute (soon Rockefeller University), City and Suburban Homes Company (a well-known limited-dividend builder), and New York Life Insurance (whose vice president was one of the leaders of the study). Associated Universities, Inc., "General Report, Part 1 of the Report of Project East River," in *Project East River* (October 1952); and "Selected Area Study, Appendix V-A to Part V of the Report of Project East River," in *Project East River* (September 1952), 7a.

37. Ketchum, "Civil and Industrial Defense"; Larkin, "A Pilot Study of Planned Industrial Dispersion in the Baltimore Area."

38. "How U.S. Cities Can Prepare for Atomic War," 79, 81. Political scientist Karl Deutsch and MIT historian Giorgio de Santillana collaborated with Wiener on the plan. Deutsch amplified dispersal ideas at an MIT conference in 1951. See Alfred Farwell Bemis Foundation, *Housing.* Reinhold Martin has placed the Wiener project into a history of organizational and communications theory; see his "The Organizational Complex" and *The Organizational Complex.*

39. "The Planners Evaluate Their Plan," in "How U.S. Cities Can Prepare," 79, 85.

40. Victor Gruen, "New Trends in Branch Store Design," address to National Retail Dry Goods Association, New York, December 12, 1950, box 27, VGPAHC.

41. Victor Gruen, "Defense on the Periphery," May 8, 1951, 5, A5, VGPLOC.

42. Victor Gruen, *Regional Shopping Centers and Civilian Defense: A Memorandum with Special Reference to the Eastland Shopping Center in Detroit,* 1951, AIA Library; Gruen, "Defense on the Periphery," box 81, Speeches, vol. A, VGPLOC; Edgardo Contini, "Additional Notes . . . ," in Gruen, *Regional Shopping Centers and Civilian Defense.*

43. American Institute of Architects, *Press Book.*

44. Holleman and Gallagher, *Smith, Hinchman & Grylls,* 147. The firm served as Eero Saarinen's associated architect for the GM Technical Center.

45. Victor Gruen, "Notes on Trip to Detroit," November 1949, 66, 4, VGPLOC. That Gruen wrote to the company out of the blue is plausible, since he was an inveterate self-promoter and routinely sent copies of his speeches to executives. See also Feinberg, "Hudson's No. 1, 2, 3, 4 in Detroit," in *What Makes Shopping Centers Tick,* 52; Hardwick, *Mall Maker,* 106–11.

46. "Hudson's to Build 102 Acre Shopping Center," *Detroit News,* June 4, 1950, 1; "Hudson's First Branch to Be Ready in Fall, 1952," *Women's Wear Daily,* June 5, 1950; "Hudson's Finally Goes Suburban," *Business Week,* June 10, 1950; "Hudson Throws Weight around Detroit," *Women's Wear Daily,* July 13, 1950; "Detroit Department Store Subsidiary to Develop New Shopping Center"; all in OV-44, VGPLOC.

47. Winter later became vice president of Hudson's, and he was a vice president of the Urban Land Institute's Business District Council. See *Urban Land Institute Bulletin* 1 (November 14, 1941); *Urban Land Institute Bulletin* 2 (January 1943); *Urban Land Institute Bulletin* 5 (January 1946). On the Hudson's garage, see McGavin, "Teamwork Can Solve the Downtown Parking Problem."

48. The period during which many cities hovered between an urban past and a suburbanized future is discussed in Johns, *Moment of Grace.*

49. Introduction, "Notes for a Regional Conference on the Effect of Current War Conditions on Real Estate Market and Valuation Problems: Notes for the Introduction of Mr. Foster Winter by the Chairman"; and Foster Winter, "Controlling Factors in the Establishment of Suburban Shopping Centers"; both in Associated Merchandising Corp., New York, April 1951, box 27, box 81, speeches, VGPLOC; also in box 27, speeches, VGPAHC. Burdick, "Realty Rostrum." The shopping-center-as-shelter was entertained by observers from the *New York Times* and the National Association of Real Estate Boards, among others. Another firm proposed an underground department store as a bomb shelter. "Store Centers Eyed as Air Raid Shelters," *New York Times,* June 20, 1951, VIII.5; "Triple-Threat Store." See Oakes, *The Imaginary War,* 105–44.

50. On the delay of Eastland, see "Hudson's Store Project Plans Will Be Delayed," newspaper item (probably *Detroit Free Press*), April 24, 1951; "When Controls End—More New Stores than Ever"; *Hudsonian,* December 1951; "Hudson Shifts Its Shopping Center Plans," *Women's Wear Daily,* December 26, 1951; all in OV-44, VGPLOC. See Monteyne, *Fallout Shelter,* 1–34.

51. Sigfried Giedion also used the term "crystallization points" in 1954, but the term was not uncommon. Gruen and Smith, "Shopping Centers," 68.

52. Longstreth, *City Center to Regional Mall,* 330.

53. Gruen's rationale for the parking solution for Eastland was that no car would be more than 350 feet from a store. See American Institute of Architects, Southern California Chapter, *News,* June 6, 1950, box 27, VGPLOC. Walking distances from car to store were widely debated.

54. Victor Gruen, "New Trend in Branch Store Design," NRDGA Convention, New York City, December 1950, box 27, VGPAHC; "Shopping Center Round Up," box 22, VGPAHC.

55. "1951 Design Survey"; "Big New Shopping District Planned," *Los Angeles Times,* September 22, 1950, 18; see also Longstreth, *City Center to Regional Mall,* 328–30. In 1950, the developer published a version of the Olympic project with an added circular department store; see "Olympic Shopping Circle: Los Angeles Hot Spot," Olympic Shopping Circle, Inc., 1950, box 12, VGPAHC.

56. See chapter 4, note 67. See also Gruen, "What's Wrong with Store Design?"; Longstreth, *City Center to Regional Mall,* 323–26.

57. "Does Safety Lie in Dispersal?," in "Pros and Cons of Architecture for Civil Defense."

58. "Shopping Near a Defense Center."

59. Gruen and Smith, "Shopping Centers," 90; Gruen, *Shopping Centers of Tomorrow,* 22. The rest of the outdoor spaces at Northland were named Fountain Court, South Mall, North Mall, Peacock Terrace, and Market Lane.

60. Howard T. Fisher used the elevational split at Evergreen Park Shopping Plaza; see Baker and Funaro, *Shopping Centers,* 118–21; Fisher, "Traffic Planning Opportunities in Shopping Center Design," 383–92.

61. "Lakewood Park, Los Angeles County." Some observers noted that Northgate's forty-eight-foot-wide mall was "oppressively narrow." "New Towns," 141. See also Clauson, "Northgate Regional Shopping Center."

62. Victor Gruen, "Executive for a Night or Making a Decision," address to Junior Section of Engineering Society of Detroit, February 2, 1951, box 27, VGPAHC. On Gruen's preference for the cluster over the mall, see Gruen and Smith, "Shopping Centers," 68–72.

63. Thomas M. Messer, AFA assistant director, to Victor Gruen, February 10, 1953; *AFA Presents Shopping Centers of Tomorrow: A Group of Architectural Studies by Victor Gruen Associates,* advance press material, 1953; both in OV-1, VGPLOC. On the AFA, see Cahill, "Forty Years After"; "50th Anniversary." It was perhaps no coincidence that Richard F. Bach, who was instrumental in bringing commercial design into the Metropolitan Museum of Art in the 1920s and 1930s, was a trustee and vice president of the AFA during the 1950s.

64. Department store exhibits were not new, but the *variety* of venues that hosted Gruen's exhibit was telling. "Traveling Exhibition Brings Design to the Public," 74.

65. Gruen, *Shopping Centers of Tomorrow,* 6, 8, 9.

66. Ibid., 15. The exhibit formed the basis of Gruen's more professionally aimed book *Shopping Towns USA,* which he coauthored with Larry Smith.

67. "The Splashiest Shopping Center in the U.S.," 61; later discussion in Guzzardi, "An Architect of Environments." See also Hardwick, *Mall Maker,* 141–45.

68. "Traveling Exhibition Brings Design to the Public"; "Shopping Centers of Tomorrow Exhibition, prepared by V. Gruen"; *AFA Presents Shopping Centers of Tomorrow.* See also "Exhibit of Shopping Centers," *New York Times,* October 19, 1954, 42.

69. Gruen and Smith, "Shopping Centers," 69; Gruen, "Sculpture and Architecture," 11. Gruen also lectured on arts and architecture; see, for instance, "Speakers to Discuss Public Building Art," *Los Angeles Times,* December 6, 1955, 41.

70. "Northland's Sculpture in a Gallery, Models at the Jacques Seligmann Galleries"; "Exhibition at Seligmann Gallery"; Gruen, "Sculpture and Architecture," 33.

71. Macdonald, "Mass Cult and Midcult." Also implicated here is the problem of kitsch and the role of mass-produced goods; see Greenberg, "Avant Garde and Kitsch"; Lynes, "High-brow, Lowbrow, Middlebrow."

72. The list of works at Northland: Gwen Lux: "Totem Pole, Bird Flight"; Lily Saarinen: "Noah, Great Lakes Group"; Malcolm Moran: "Giraffes," and "Fish"; Arthur Kraft: "The Cat," "The Turtle," "The Peacock," and "The Elephant"; Richard H. Jennings: "The Mobile Pool"; Marshall Frederick's: "Bear and Boy."

73. Hitchcock, "The Place of Painting and Sculpture in Relation to Modern Architecture"; Hitchcock, "The Architecture of Bureaucracy and the Architecture of Genius." See also Ock-man, "Art, Soul of the Corporation."

74. Bittermann, *Art in Modern Architecture,* 2, 6, 81. Mumford offered a brief nod to Bittermann's book; Mumford, "The Sky Line: Preview of the Past," 75.

75. Saarinen, "Art as Architectural Decoration," 133.

76. Huyssen, "Mass Culture as Woman."

77. "Architecture and Sculpture."

78. Giedion, Sert, and Léger, "Nine Points on Monumentality"; Giedion, "The Need for Monumentality"; Mumford, "Monumentalism, Symbolism and Style." See also Mumford, *The CIAM Discourse on Urbanism,* 150–53.

79. Many of the CIAM books were in his library, and he soon began to cite them; see Gruen, "Dynamic Planning for Retail Areas."

80. "The Lush New Suburban Market."

6. The Language of Modern Shopping

1. "New Thinking on Shopping Centers," 122.

2. Hitchcock, "The Architecture of Bureaucracy and the Architecture of Genius," 5.

3. Funaro and Baker, "Shopping Centers"; Baker and Funaro, *Shopping Centers.* Baker and Funaro produced several how-to book in the 1950s, normalizing modernist forms and methods: *Windows in Modern Architecture*; *Motels*; and *Parking.*

4. "Suburban Retail Districts," 106, 110.

5. Gropius, "Gropius Appraises Today's Architect," 112; response by Pietro Belluschi, 113. See also Giedion, *Walter Gropius,* 13–16.

6. Welch, "Regional Shopping Centers," 122.

7. Gruen and Smith, "Shopping Centers"; "Shopping Centers," *Architectural Record* 114.

8. "Memorandum Concerning the Retail Trade Opportunities at Montclair in Suburban Houston," 1950, box 47, VGPAHC; Jones, "109-Store Houston Shopping Center of 1952 to Feature Pedestrian Mall," box 47, VGPAHC; Gruen and Smith, "Shopping Centers," 90. See also Hardwick, *Mall Maker,* 111–17.

9. Gruen and Smith, "Shopping Centers," 73–74.

10. Ibid., 84, 90.

11. "Shopping Centers," *Architectural Record* 114: 179.

12. McKeever, *Shopping Centers.*

13. "Shopping Centers: A Neighborhood Necessity." The institute's "technical bulletins" included no. 11, Mott and Wehrly, *Shopping Centers*; and no. 12, Hoyt, *Market Analysis of Shopping Centers.* See also Community Builders Council, *Community Builders Handbook.* On the ULI, see Weiss, *The Rise of the Community Builders.*

14. "Shopping Centers," *Architectural Record* 114: 179, 189.

15. Seventeen out of twenty of the ULI published centers were either built or in construction in contrast to only six out of eighteen of the projects in *Record*. The two articles shared only one-third of their illustrated projects.

16. "Shopping Centers," *Architectural Record* 114: 180–81.

17. Baker and Funaro, *Shopping Centers,* 110.

18. "General Motors Technical Center."

19. Ketchum, "What to Look for in Shopping Centers," 23.

20. Priaulx, "Northgate"; Clausen, "Northgate Regional Shopping Center"; "New City within a City"; "San Francisco's Stonestown Shopping Center"; "New Thinking on Shopping Centers"; "Un Example de centre commercial aux Etats-Unis." See Baker and Funaro, *Shopping Centers,* 210–11, 214–21; Longstreth, *City Center to Regional Mall,* 333–40.

21. Cross County Center, Sol Atlas developer. The L-shaped site plan resulted from constrained site conditions. An earlier plan by Harris and Brown was a biaxially symmetrical project with a monumental grand court for cars. See Funaro and Baker, "Shopping Centers," 128–29. Atlas built North Shore Mart, designed by Douglass, in 1950, and Miracle Mile, which opened in the late 1940s, both on Long Island.

22. Findlay, *Magic Lands,* 52–116; Avila, *Popular Culture in the Age of White Flight,* 106–44.

23. "Marshall Field's New Shopping Center." In 1949, Marshall Field began buying land in Skokie and had already opened branches in Lake Forest, Oak Park, and Evanston. "Field's Plans 15 to 20 Million Shopping Center for Skokie," *Chicago Daily Tribune,* August 5, 1950, 1; "More State Street Stores Eyeing Skokie Center," *Chicago Daily Tribune,* November 1, 1951, D6; *Oral History of Norman J. Schlossman,* 69–71; *Oral History of Richard Marsh Bennett,* 66-67. See also Wendt and Kogan, *Give the Lady What She Wants!,* 372–74.

24. Northland was announced in *Women's Wear Daily* and the Hudson Company newsletter. "Hudson Shifts Its Shopping Center Plans," *Women's Wear Daily,* December 26, 1951; and *Hudsonian,* December 1951; both in OV-44, VGPLOC.

25. Gruen and Smith, "Shopping Centers," 66–74. Ketchum used the basic Beverly layout for proposals in New Jersey and New York. "A Mammoth New Shopping Center"; MacGregor "The Shopping Center."

26. "Marshall Field's New Shopping Center," 197. Kenneth Welch proposed an informal design for a Toledo, Ohio, developer. Welch, "Regional Shopping Centers," 122.

27. Marshall Field decided not to build the center itself and instead leased facilities from a builder, American Community Builders (which had built Park Forest); the builder hired Loebl, Schlossman and Bennett. Al Chase, "Field Shifts Old Orchard Building Plan," *Chicago Daily Tribune,* December 16, 1953, C5. Old Orchard was the outcome of the Skokie competition.

28. "Shopping Center for a Satellite Town near Olympia Fields, Illinois"; Lewis, *Planning the Modern City,* 249. See also Randall, *America's Original GI Town.* Park Forest Plaza was the core of the vast eight thousand–unit community made famous by William H. Whyte.

29. Bennett, "Random Observations on Shopping Centers"; Sharp, *Town Planning*; Silver, *Design for Better Living.*

30. Hornbeck, "Shopping Can Be a Pleasure," 221.

31. Marx, *The Machine in the Garden.*

32. See chapter 5, note 78.

33. "Marshall Field's New Shopping Center," 194–96; "Atom City."

34. "Wynn Furniture Store in LA Is Designed for Motorist Attention and Minimum Cost."

35. Brooks, "On Creating a Usable Past." Nelson, like Saarinen, Hilberseimer, and many others, praised medieval town plans for their supposed integration of design and social life. "Town common" sketch in "Planning with You," *Architectural Forum* 79: 67.

36. Belluschi, "Shopping Centers," 129; Longstreth, *City Center to Regional Mall,* 293–94.

37. Feinberg, "On the High Road to Success," in *What Makes Shopping Centers Tick,* 43.

38. Victor Gruen, "Planning for Shopping," Boston Conference on Distribution, October 18, 1955, box 27, VGPAHC.

39. The Fort Worth Plan would have transformed an area about the size of midtown Manhattan, from Forty-second to Fifty-seventh Streets and from Third to Seventh Avenues.

40. Gruen, "Planning for Shopping"; Victor Gruen Associates, "Master Planning Study for the Central Business District of the City of Fort Worth, for the Harvard Conference on Urban Design," April 19, 1956, box 27, VGPAHC; Gruen Associates, *A Greater Fort Worth Tomorrow.*

41. "Typical Downtown Transformed"; "Fort Worth Plan Excludes Autos"; Tanner, "Closed to Traffic," 89. See also Hardwick, *Mall Maker,* 162–92; Browning, "Legacy of a Planning Legend."

42. J. B. Thomas, head of the Texas Electric Company, read Gruen's article in the 1954 *Harvard Business Review.* Gruen, "Dynamic Planning for Retail Areas." Hardwick, *Mall Maker,* 186–92; Longstreth, *The American Department Store Transformed,* 227–28; Wall, *Victor Gruen,* 126–30.

43. Jacobs, "Downtown Is for People," 162; Jacobs, "Two Projects," 109–10. Jacobs favorably compared the Fort Worth Plan to what she saw as the single-minded devotion to traffic needs in Gruen's proposal for Roosevelt Island.

44. Tanner, "Closed to Traffic," 89; Lowe, "What's Happening in Fort Worth"; Hardwick, *Mall Maker,* 186–92.

45. "New Thinking on Shopping Centers," 122; "Downtown Needs a Lesson from the Suburbs."

46. "Chicago Plan," in "New Thinking on Shopping Centers," 122–23; Nelson and Ashman, *Conservation and Rehabilitation of Major Shopping Districts.*

47. Victor Gruen Associates, "Downtown Appleton: Its Future?," September 1953, box 21, VGPAHC. Another plan for the town center of Warwick, Virginia, also called for a "pleasant suburban atmosphere," traffic separation, landscaping, and arcades similar to Appleton. The project date is unclear. Victor Gruen Associates, Warwick Shopping Center, 1950?, box 47, VGPAHC.

48. Gruen, "Dynamic Planning for Retail Areas," 57; Gruen, "Planning for Shopping"; Gruen, speech at Memorial Art Galleries, Rochester, New York, September 30, 1955, box 27, VGPAHC.

49. "Architect Says Suburb Center Can Aid Loop," cited in Hardwick, *Mall Maker,* 263n49.

50. Tyrwhitt, "Cores within the Urban Constellation," 103; Sert, "A Short Outline of the Core," 164.

51. Comey, "Review, *The Heart of the City*"; Weinberg, "The Spirit of a City."

52. Sert, "Centres of Community Life," 4, 11; Giedion, "The Humanization of Urban Life," 126; Giedion, "Historical Background to the Core," 20; Giedion, "The State of Contemporary

Architecture II," 188; Giedion, "Marginalia, Introducing Part 6," in *Architecture You and Me,* 156.

53. Gruen, "What to Look for in Shopping Centers," 22; Gruen and Smith, "Shopping Centers," 67, 68, 104.

54. See Mumford, *The CIAM Discourse on Urbanism,* 201–14; Gold, *The Experience of Modernism,* 210–30.

55. Gruen, "Dynamic Planning for Retail Areas," 57; Gruen, *The Heart of Our Cities.*

56. *Bouw,* October 1953, box 11, VGPLOC.

57. Rotterdam had been leveled by Nazi bombing on May 14, 1940. Van den Broek and Bakema designed the Lijnbaan between 1948 and 1951, and it opened in 1953.

58. Others also offered high praise for the Lijnbaan; see Johnson-Marshall, "Rotterdam," 562; Grebler, "Post-war Rebuilding in Western Europe," 132; Grebler "New City Centers in Europe"; "The Lijnbaan at Rotterdam."

59. Kiek, "Europe's Fifth Avenue"; see also Bakema, "Dutch Architecture Today."

60. Bauer, "Central City," 118–19; Mumford, "A Walk through Rotterdam," 174.

61. For reaction to the Lijnbaan in the popular press, see "The Shopping Center Back Where It Started." One author suggested that it was time to "give the city back to the people" and praised the pedestrianization of the Lijnbaan *and* Northland as models of ways to "create downtown centers for foot traffic only" and for city leaders to "set aside whole city blocks and streets as pedestrian malls during the daytime." "Retailers' Problem."

62. There is a broad literature on postwar urban change. See, for example, Teaford, *The Rough Road to Renaissance*; Bauman, "The Paradox of Post-war Planning."

63. "Urban Traffic Forum"; "How to Build Cities Downtown."

64. By the early 1950s a boom in garage construction was under way. "Garages Grow Up"; "Nine Garages for City of Chicago Make a Frontal Attack on Parking Problem." See Longstreth, *The American Department Store Transformed,* 83–107.

65. "Urban Design." See also Krieger and Saunders, *Urban Design*; Mumford and Sarkis, *Josep Lluís Sert.*

66. "Urban Design," Jane Jacobs's comments, 102–3; Feiss, "The Architecture of Redevelopment in USA."

67. Kahn, "Toward a Plan for Midtown Philadelphia"; "Philadelphia Slum Modernization by the Block." See also Brownlee and De Long, *Louis I. Kahn,* 20–49; Reed, "Philadelphia Urban Design."

68. Between 1940 and 1948, half of all U.S. states passed redevelopment legislation enabling condemnation of land for new scales of intervention. Bauman, "The Paradox of Post-war Planning," 235. See also Hirsch, *Making the Second Ghetto*; Weiss, "The Origins and Legacy of Urban Renewal."

69. "Sacramento, a Model for Small City Redevelopment"; "Pittsburgh in Progress." Richard Neutra and Robert Alexander's proposal for Kansas City sited parking in new inner-block sunken courtyards; see "In Kansas City, a Framework for the Future"; "Special Design Award"; "Cities Not for Dying." See also Teaford, *The Rough Road to Renaissance,* 145–62.

70. Montgomery, "Improving the Design Process in Urban Renewal."

71. Mennel, "Victor Gruen and the Construction of Cold War Utopias."

72. "Southdale"; "A Breakthrough for Two-Level Shopping Centers"; "A Controlled Climate for Shopping." See Hardwick, *Mall Maker,* 142–61; Wall, *Victor Gruen,* 92–100; Gillette, "The Evolution of the Planned Shopping Center in Suburb and City."

73. Gruen and Smith, "Shopping Centers," 69.

74. "New Thinking on Shopping Centers"; Gruen, "Planned Shopping Centers"; "A Controlled Climate for Shopping"; "A Breakthrough for Two-Level Shopping Centers"; "Brisk Business for a Bright Shopping Center."

75. See "Memorandum Concerning the Retail Trade Opportunities at Montclair in Suburban Houston"; Jones, "109-Store Houston Shopping Center of 1952 to Feature Pedestrian Mall"; Gruen and Smith, "Shopping Centers," 90. See also Hardwick, *Mall Maker,* 111–17.

76. "New Thinking on Shopping Centers," 134–39; "60 Stores Open in Big Baltimore Shopping Center," *New York Times,* October 5, 1956, 46. Mondawmin began with Rouse seeking designers and ideas in 1952; Ken Welch and Pietro Belluschi were on the team. See also Longstreth, *The American Department Store Transformed,* 211–12.

77. Ketchum, "An Architect Looks at the Shopping Center of the Future."

Conclusion

1. Benjamin, "The Work of Art in the Age of Mechanical Reproduction."

2. See, for instance, Welch, "Reflection Factors in Store Windows"; and Welch, "New Concepts in Store Lighting."

3. Giedion, *Building in France, Building in Iron, Building in Ferroconcrete,* 16.

4. On Midtown Plaza, see "Center for Rochester." Hardwick, *Mall Maker,* 193–208; Wall, *Victor Gruen,* 143–49.

5. William Neuman, "2 Lanes to Close on Broadway, Making Way for Bikes and Lunch," *New York Times,* July 11, 2008, A1; William Neuman, "Mayor's Plan for Broadway as a Walkway," *New York Times,* February 27, 2009, A1.

6. Breines, "We Won't Cure Billion Dollar City Traffic Jams until We Make Room for the Pedestrian"; Gutheim, "Pedestrian Millennium Sighted"; Breines and Dean, "City People on the Move"; "Merchants Lose Downtown Blues," *New York Times,* February 27, 1955, F7.

7. Damon Stetson, "Kalamazoo Mall Gathers Acclaim," *New York Times,* October 4, 1959, 78; "Shopping Malls," *Washington Post and Times Herald,* February 8, 1959, B4; Edmond J. Barnett, "Shopping Malls Proving Success," *New York Times,* November 15, 1959, R1; "Pedestrian Malls Tried in Toledo, Kalamazoo." Planners in Peekskill, a small city in upstate New York, proposed a closed main street in 1958 (not implemented), designed by Raymond & May Associates with architect Richard Klein. See "Plan to Revamp Peekskill Filed," *New York Times,* October 17, 1958, 41. In other cases, pedestrian malls were temporary affairs and portrayed as tests.

8. On Fresno, see Gruen, "Retailing and the Automobile"; "Fresno Mall"; "Heart of Gruen's Fresno Plan." See also Wall, *Victor Gruen,* 151–54. On Brooklyn, see "Ghirardelli Square in Brooklyn"; Robert E. Tomasson, "City Plans Fulton St. Mall in Brooklyn," *New York Times,* October 29, 1973, 1; *Camminare a Brooklyn* = People-oriented Mall in Brooklyn." See also Barnett, *Urban Design as Public Policy.*

9. Lewis, *The Pedestrian in the City.*

10. Rudofsky, *Streets for People,* 114, 197, 259. See Scott, "Allegories of Nomadism and Dwelling."

11. The Italian Art and Landscape Foundation, of which Brambilla was vice president, sponsored an exhibit titled *Contro l'automobile, per la citta* and brought to New York's Metropolitan Museum a show produced by Brambilla titled *Art and Landscape of Italy: Too Late to Be Saved?* See Rudofsky, "Foreword," in *Streets for People,* 10–13.

12. Italian Art and Landscape Foundation, *More Streets for People.*

13. Brambilla, Longo, and Dzurinko, *American Urban Malls.* See also Breines and Dean, *The Pedestrian Revolution*; Brambilla and Longo, *For Pedestrians Only.*

14. Whyte, *The Social Life of Small Urban Spaces.*

15. Cheyne, "No Better Way?"; Robertson, "The Status of the Pedestrian Mall in American Downtowns."

16. Nicolai Ouroussoff, "Lose the Traffic. Keep That Times Square Grit," *New York Times,* May 25, 2009, A1.

17. Hammett and Hammett, *The Suburbanization of New York.*

18. "Remarks of Vice President Nixon, Hillside Shopping Center, Chicago, IL," the American Presidency Project, http://www.presidency.ucsb.edu/ws/index.php?pid=25508, accessed November 3, 2011. See also Randall, *America's Original GI Town.*

19. Smiley, *Sprawl and Public Space*; Kotler and Armstrong, *Principles of Marketing,* 388.

20. See Dunham-Jones and Williamson, *Retrofitting Suburbia.*

21. The "functional equivalent" argument stems from a 1968 Pennsylvania court case—*Amalgamated Food Employees Union v. Logan Valley Plaza.* In a 1980 case, *Pruneyard v. Robins,* the U.S. Supreme Court ruled that each state had the right to decide free speech rules at shopping centers. See Staeheli and Mitchell, "USA's Destiny?" See also Kohn, *Brave New Neighborhoods.*

22. Jameson, "Postmodernism, or the Cultural Logic of Late Capitalism."

23. "Stores in Urban and Suburban Shopping Centers."

24. Kayden, *Privately Owned Public Space.*

25. Bolton, "Figments of the Public"; Chung et al., *Harvard Design School Guide to Shopping.*

BIBLIOGRAPHY

Abbott, Carl. "Five Strategies for Downtown: Policy Discourse and Planning since 1943." *Journal of Policy History* 5 (1993): 5–27.

Abbott, Hunley. "Low Cost Off-Street Parking." *Architectural Concrete* 4 (January 1938): 6–8.

———. "Metropolitan Store Parking." *Architectural Concrete* 7 (1941): 32–34.

———. "The Store Building: Its Modernization through the Years." In *Twenty-Five Years of Retailing.* New York: National Retail Dry Goods Association, 1936.

Abercrombie, Patrick. *Greater London Plan 1944.* London: HM Stationery Office, 1945.

Abercrombie, Stanley. *George Nelson: The Design of Modern Design.* Cambridge: MIT Press, 1994.

Adams, Frederick J. "A Planning Program for the City of Rye." Rye, N.Y., September 1, 1943.

Adams, Frederick J., and Edward J. Langloh. *A Master Plan and Capital Outlay Program for the City of Rye.* Rye, N.Y.: City of Rye, March 28, 1945.

Adams, Frederick J., Svend Riemer, Reginald Isaacs, Robert B. Mitchell, and Gerald Breese. "The Neighborhood Concept in Theory and Application." *Journal of Land Economics* 25 (February 1949): 67–88.

Adams, Rayne. "Recent European Architecture." *Architectural Forum* 50 (January 1929): 41–52.

Adams, Thomas. *The Building of the City,* vol. 2 of *Regional Plan of New York and Its Environs.* New York: Regional Plan of New York and Its Environs, 1931.

———. *The Design of Residential Areas: Basic Considerations, Principles, and Methods.* Cambridge, Mass.: Harvard University Press, 1934.

———. "Fitting Streets to Buildings." In *The Building of the City,* vol. 2, 275–324. New York: Regional Plan of New York and Its Environs, 1931.

"The Adler Shoe Store, New York City." *Architecture* 46 (July 1922): 226.

Adorno, Theodor W. *Minima Moralia: Reflections from Damaged Life.* Translated by E. F. N. Jephcott. London: Verso, 1974.

Agnew, Jean-Christophe. "Coming Up for Air: Consumer Culture in Historical Perspective." In *Consumer Society in American History,* edited by Lawrence Glickman, 373–98. Ithaca, N.Y.: Cornell University Press, 1999.

"Airport Design and Construction." *Architectural Record* 65 (May 1929): 490–515.

Albrecht, Donald, ed. *World War II and the American Dream: How Wartime Building Changed a Nation.* Washington, D.C.: National Building Museum and Massachusetts Institute of Technology, 1995.

Alfred Farwell Bemis Foundation. *Housing: A National Security Resource; A Conference and Exhibition, Held January 19 and 20, 1951, Massachusetts Institute of Technology.* Cambridge, Mass.: N.p., 1951.

Alofsin, Anthony. "Broadacre City: The Reception of a Modernist Vision, 1932–1988." *Center* 5 (1989): 5–43.

Alsop, Joseph, and Stewart Alsop. "Your Flesh Should Creep." *Saturday Evening Post,* July 13, 1946, 9, 47–50.

American Architect. *Time-Saver Standards: A Desk Manual of Architectural Practice.* New York: American Architect, 1935.

American Automobile Association, Traffic Engineering and Safety Department. *Parking Manual.* Washington, D.C.: American Automobile Association, 1946.

American Institute of Architects. *Civil Defense: The Architect's Part.* Washington, D.C.: American Institute of Architects, 1951.

———. *Defense Measures in Hospitals.* Washington, D.C.: American Institute of Architects, 1953.

———. *Defense Measures in Industrial Plants.* Washington, D.C.: American Institute of Architects, 1952.

———. *Defense Measures in Multistory Buildings.* Washington, D.C.: American Institute of Architects, 1951.

———. *Defense Measures in Schools.* Washington, D.C.: American Institute of Architects, 1953.

———. *National Community Fallout Shelter Design Competition Awards.* Washington, D.C.: American Institute of Architects, 1964.

"Anticipating Problems of Postwar Traffic: Suggestions for Handling the Return of Congestion." *Regional Plan Bulletin* 61 (August 27, 1943).

Appelbaum, Stanley, ed. *The New York World's Fair.* New York: Dover, 1977.

"The Arcade Front." *Apparel Arts* (June 1940).

Archer, John. *Architecture and Suburbia: From English Villa to American Dream House, 1690–2000.* Minneapolis: University of Minnesota Press, 2005.

"Architect Designs a Space House for Modernage Furniture Company." *House & Garden,* December 1933, 8–10.

"The Architect in Search of . . ." *Architectural Record* 81 (February 1937): 1.

"Architect Says Suburb Center Can Aid Loop." *Minneapolis Morning Tribune,* June 18, 1952, 12.

"Architecture and Sculpture." *Arts & Architecture,* May 1955, 21.

"The Architecture of the Small Shop, Part I." *Architectural Forum* 43 (February 1925): 97–120.

"The Architecture of the Small Shop, Part II." *Architectural Forum* 43 (August 1925): 97–112.

"Artek Exposed." *Interiors* 102 (August 1942): 58–59.

"Artek-Pascoe Furniture Shop, New York City." *Architectural Forum* 77 (August 1942): 86–88.

Associated Universities, Inc. *Project East River,* 10 vols. New York: Associated Universities, Inc., 1952–53.

"Atom City." *Architectural Forum* 83 (October 1945): 103–17.

Augenfeld, Felix. "Modern Austria: Personalities and Style." *Architectural Review* 83 (April 1938): 165–74.

Augur, Tracy B. "Decentralization: Blessing or Tragedy?" In *Planning 1948: Proceedings of the Annual National Planning Conference.* Chicago: American Society of Planning Officials, 1948.

———. "Decentralization Can't Wait." In *Planning 1948: Proceedings of the Annual National Planning Conference,* 32–35. Chicago: American Society of Planning Officials, 1948.

———. "Dispersal Is Good Business." In "Civil Defense against Atomic Attack." *Bulletin of the Atomic Scientists* 6 (August/September 1950): 243–46.

———. "The Dispersal of Cities as a Defense Measure." *Bulletin of the Atomic Scientists* 4 (May 1948); reprinted in *Journal of the American Institute of Planners* 14 (Summer 1948): 29–36.

———. "Planning Cities for the Atomic Age: Mere Survival Is Not Enough." *American City* 61 (August 1946): 75–76.

———. "Security Factors in the Planning of Urban Regions." *Planning and Civic Comment* 18 (September 1952): 9–14.

Austin, Cleland. "New Life for an Old Shopping Area." *American City* 63 (October 1948): 106–7.

Avila, Eric. *Popular Culture in the Age of White Flight: Fear and Fantasy in Suburban Los Angeles.* Berkeley: University of California Press, 2004.

Aynsley, Jeremy. *Graphic Design in Germany: 1890–1945.* London: Thames and Hudson, 2000.

Bach, Alfons. "Common Faults in Store Front Design." *Interiors* 104 (September 1944): 54.

"The Back Bay Center." *Architectural Forum* 99 (November 1953): 104–15.

Bacon, Mardges. *Le Corbusier in America: Travels in the Land of the Timid.* Cambridge: MIT Press, 2001.

Baer, Sidney. "Central City Planning: The Next Step." *Stores* 35 (April 1954): 15–16.

———. "The Political Problems of Downtown Reconstruction." *Stores* 36 (November 1954): 38–39.

Bakema, Jaap B. "Dutch Architecture Today." In *Architects' Year Book 5,* 67–82. London: Elek Books, 1953.

Baker, Geoffrey, and Bruno Funaro. *Motels.* New York: Reinhold, 1955.

———. *Parking.* New York: Reinhold, 1958.

———. *Shopping Centers: Design and Operation.* New York: Reinhold, 1951.

———. *Windows in Modern Architecture.* New York: Architectural Book Publishing, 1948.

Baker, William H. "Parking Facilities and Habits in the CBD of LA." *Proceeding of the Institute of Traffic Engineers* (1932): 39–47.

Baldwin, Peter C. *Domesticating the Street: The Reform of Public Space in Hartford, 1850–1930.* Columbus: Ohio State University Press, 1999.

Ballard, William H. *A Survey in Respect to the Decentralization of the Boston Central Business District.* Chicago: Urban Land Institute, 1940.

Banerjee, Tridib, and William C. Baer. *Beyond the Neighborhood Unit: Residential Environments and Public Policy.* New York: Plenum Press, 1984.

Banham, Reyner. *Theory and Design in the First Machine Age.* New York: Praeger, 1960.

Bannister, Turpin C., ed. *The Architect at Mid-century: Evolution and Achievement.* Washington, D.C.: American Institute of Architects, 1954.

Barnes, Henry A. "Flint Merchants Provide Downtown Parking Lot." *American City* 59 (November 1944): 115.

Barnett, Jonathan. *Urban Design as Public Policy: Practical Methods for Improving Cities.* New York: McGraw-Hill, 1974.

Barrett, Paul. *The Automobile and Urban Transit: The Formation of Public Policy in Chicago, 1900–1930.* Philadelphia: Temple University Press, 1983.

Barth, Gunther. *City People: The Rise of Modern City Culture in Nineteenth-Century America.* New York: Oxford University Press, 1980.

Bartholomew, Harland. "The Neighborhood: Key to Urban Redemption." In *National Conference on City Planning: Proceedings,* 212–16, 230–34. Washington, D.C.: American Planning and Civic Association, 1941.

———. *Report upon Streets, Parking, Zoning, City of Beverly Hills, California.* St. Louis: Harland Bartholomew & Associates, January 1948.

"Barton's Bonbonniere." *Architectural Forum* 84 (February 1946): 119.

Baudrillard, Jean. "Consumer Society." In *Jean Baudrillard: Selected Writings,* edited by Mark Poster, 29–56. Stanford, Calif.: Stanford University Press, 1988.

Bauer, Catherine. "Central City: Concentration versus Congestion." In "By 1976: What City Pattern?" *Architectural Forum* (September 1956): 103–37.

———. "Good Neighborhoods." *Annals of the American Academy of Political and Social Science* 242 (November 1945): 104–15.

———. *Modern Housing.* Boston: Houghton Mifflin, 1934.

———. "Redevelopment: A Misfit in the Fifties." In *The Future of Cities and Urban Redevelopment,* edited by Coleman Woodbury, 7–25. Chicago: University of Chicago Press, 1953.

Bauman, John F. "The Paradox of Post-war Planning: Downtown Revitalization versus Decent Housing for All." In *Two Centuries of American Planning,* edited by Daniel Schaffer, 231–64. Baltimore: Johns Hopkins University Press, 1988.

———. "Visions of a Post-war City: A Perspective on Urban Planning in Philadelphia and the Nation, 1942–1945." In *Introduction to Planning History in the United States,* edited by Donald A. Krueckeberg, 170–89. New Brunswick, N.J.: Center for Urban Policy Research, 1983.

Baxandall, Rosalyn, and Elizabeth Ewen. *Picture Windows: How the Suburbs Happened.* New York: Basic Books, 2000.

Beauregard, Robert A. "More than Sector Theory: Homer Hoyt's Contributions to Planning Knowledge." *Journal of Planning History* 6 (August 2007): 248–70.

———. *Voices of Decline: The Postwar Fate of U.S. Cities.* New York: Blackwell, 1993.

———. *When America Became Suburban.* Minneapolis: University of Minnesota Press, 2006.

Behrendt, Walter Curt. "Off-Street Parking: A City Planning Problem." *Journal of Land and Public Utility Economics* 14 (November 1940): 464–67.

Bel Geddes, Norman. *Magic Motorways.* New York: Random House, 1940.

Belluschi, Pietro. "Shopping Centers" (1948). In *Forms and Functions of Twentieth-Century Architecture,* edited by Talbot Hamlin, vol. 4, 114–39. New York: Columbia University Press, 1952.

Benjamin, Walter. *The Arcades Project.* Edited by Rolf Tiedemann; translated by Howard Eiland and Kevin McLaughlin. Cambridge, Mass.: Belknap Press, 1999.

———. "Paris, Capital of the Nineteenth Century" (1935). In *Reflections: Essays, Aphorisms, Autobiographical Writing.* Edited by Peter Demetz, 146–62. New York: Schocken, 1978.

———. "The Work of Art in the Age of Mechanical Reproduction" (1936). In *Illuminations: Essays and Reflections.* Edited by Hannah Arendt, 217–51. New York: Schocken, 1968.

Bennett, Richard. "Confident Idealist." *House & Garden,* May 1943, 20–23.

———. "How To Fit Your Home to Your Family." *House & Garden,* June 1943, 16–19, 90.

———. "Nobody Lives in a House." *House & Garden,* July 1943, 28–31, 66–69.

———. "Our Town—It's Up to Us." *House & Garden,* August 1943, 41, 64.

———. "Random Observations on Shopping Centers." Building Types Study No. 250. *Architectural Record* 122 (September 1957): 219–20.

Benson, Robert. "Douglas Haskell and the Modern Movement in Architecture." *Journal of Architectural Education* 36 (Summer 1983): 2–9.

"Be Prepared." *Bulletin of the American Institute of Architects* 4 (July 1950).

"Bergen County Shopping Center." *Architectural Record* 103 (June 1948): 10, 174.

Berman, Marshall. *All That Is Solid Melts into Air: The Experience of Modernity.* New York: Simon & Schuster, 1982.

Bibbins, J. Rowland. "Traffic-Transportation Planning and Metropolitan Development: The Need of an Adequate Program." *Annals of the American Academy of Political and Social Science* 116 (November 1924): 213–14.

Bittermann, Eleanor. *Art in Modern Architecture.* New York: Reinhold, 1952.

Black, Russell Van Nest. "The Spectacular in City Building." *Annals of the American Academy of Political and Social Science* 116 (November 1924): 50–56.

Bletter, Rosemarie Haag. "Modernism Rears Its Head: The Twenties and Thirties." In Richard Oliver, ed., *The Making of an Architect, 1881–1981: Columbia University in the City of New York,* edited by Richard Oliver, 103–18. New York: Rizzoli, 1981.

Bolton, Rick. "Figments of the Public: Architecture and Debt." In *Restructuring Architectural Theory,* edited by Marco Diani and Catherine Ingraham, 42–47. Evanston, Ill.: Northwestern University Press, 1989.

"Book Review, *Shops & Stores.*" *Progressive Architecture* 29 (December 1948): 108, 110, 112.

"Boston's Back Bay Center." *Architectural Record* 114 (October 1953): 143–53.

Bottomly, William Lawrence. "The Architecture of Retail Stores." *Architectural Forum* 40 (June 1924): 233–38.

Bourdieu, Pierre. *Distinction: A Social Critique of the Judgment of Taste.* London: Routledge, 1984.

Bowlby, Rachel. *Carried Away: The Invention of Modern Shopping.* New York: Columbia University Press, 2001.

Boyd, John Taylor, Jr. "The Art of Commercial Display, Part I." *Architectural Record* 63 (January 1928): 59–66.

———. "The Art of Commercial Display, Part II." *Architectural Record* 63 (February 1928): 169–77.

———. "Milgrim—a Fashion Shop for Women: Louis H. Friedland, Architect." *Architectural Record* 65 (June 1929): 523–33.

———. "The Newer Fifth Avenue Retail Shop Fronts: An American Contribution to Modern Art." *Architectural Record* 49 (June 1921): 459–88.

Boyer, M. Christine. *Dreaming the Rational City: The Myth of American City Planning.* Cambridge: MIT Press, 1983.

———. *Manhattan Manners: Architecture and Style, 1850–1900.* New York: Rizzoli, 1985.

Boyer, Paul. *By the Bomb's Early Light: American Thought and Culture at the Dawn of the Atomic Age.* New York: Pantheon Books, 1985.

Bradley, David. *No Place to Hide.* Boston: Little, Brown, 1948.

Braham, William W. "What's Hecuba to Him? On Kiesler and the Knot." *Assemblage* 36 (August 1998): 6–23.

Brain, David. "Discipline and Style: The Ecole des Beaux-Arts and the Social Production of an American Architecture." *Theory and Society* 18 (1989): 807–68.

Brambilla, Roberto, and Gianni Longo. *For Pedestrians Only: Planning, Design, and Management of Traffic Free Zones.* New York: Whitney Library of Design, 1977.

Brambilla, Roberto, Gianni Longo, and Virginia Dzurinko. *American Urban Malls: A Compendium.* New York: Institute for Environmental Action, 1977.

"Brazil Plans a City." *Progressive Architecture* 27 (September 1946): 52–74.

"Brazil Plans Entire New City." *American City* 62 (April 1947): 97.

"A Breakthrough for Two-Level Shopping Centers: Two-Level Southdale." *Architectural Forum* 105 (December 1956): 114–26.

Breines, Simon. "We Won't Cure Billion Dollar City Traffic Jams until We Make Room for the Pedestrian." *Architectural Forum* 88 (May 1948): 13.

Breines, Simon, and John P. Dean. "City People on the Move: A Policy for Guided Urban Growth." Unpublished manuscript, New York, 1948.

Breines, Simon, and William J. Dean. *The Pedestrian Revolution: Streets without Cars.* New York: Vintage, 1974.

"Brisk Business for a Bright Shopping Center." *Fortune,* February 1957, 141.

Brooks, Van Wyck. "On Creating a Usable Past." *Dial,* April 11, 1918, 337–41.

Broomer, Kathleen Kelly. "Shoppers' World and the Regional Shopping Center in Greater Boston." *Society of Commercial Archeology Journal* 13 (Fall–Winter 1994–95): 2–9.

Browning, David L. "Legacy of a Planning Legend: The Victor Gruen Plan for a Greater Fort Worth Tomorrow." *Crit* 12 (Winter 1983): 5–9.

Brownlee, David B., and David G. De Long, eds. *Louis I. Kahn: In the Realm of Architecture.* New York: Rizzoli, 1991.

Bruegmann, Robert. *The Architects and the City: Holabird & Roche of Chicago, 1880–1918.* Chicago: University of Chicago Press, 1997.

"Building's Post-war Pattern, No. 1: Planning." *Architectural Forum* 75 (September 1941): 139–51.

"Building's Post-war Pattern, No. 2: Standardization." *Architectural Forum* 75 (November 1941): 353–64.

"Building's Post-war Pattern, No. 3: Integrated Industry." *Architectural Forum* 76 (October 1942): 77–81.

"Building Types: Retail Stores—A Reference Study." *Architectural Record* 83 (February 1938): 101–34.

"Bulova Watch Company Offices, Rockefeller Center." *Architectural Forum* 72 (February 1940): 86–88.

Burdick, Henry H. "Realty Rostrum: J. L. Hudson Shopping Center Plans Progress; 3rd One Due; Burdick Envisions Them as Possible Bomb Shelters." *Detroit Free Press,* January 21, 1951, 11, 14.

Burford, James. "The Design of the Shop Front from Ancient to Modern Times." *Architects' Journal* 55 (January 4, 1922): 15–18.

Burke, Eugene, and Edgar Kober. *Modern Store Design: A Practical Study of the Influence of Store Style on Modern Merchandising.* Los Angeles: Institute for Product Research, 1946.

Buttenheim, Harold S. "Citizen Interest and Participation in City and Regional Planning and Housing." In *New Architecture and City Planning,* edited by Paul Zucker, 607–23. New York: Philosophical Library, 1944.

———. "City Highways and City Parking: An American Crisis." *American City* 61 (November 1946): 116, 117, 123, 139.

———. "The Problem of the Standing Vehicle." *Annals of the American Academy of Political and Social Science* 133 (September 1927): 147–55.

Byars, Mel. "What Makes American Design American." In *Modern American Design,* edited by R. L. Leonard and C. A. Glassgold, v–xviii. 1930. Reprint, New York: Acanthus Press, 1992.

Cahill, Holger. "Forty Years After: An Anniversary for the AFA." *Magazine of Art,* May 1949, 169–78, 189.

Caldwell, Alfred. "Atomic Bombs and City Planning." *Journal of the American Institute of Architects* 4 (December 1945): 289–99.

"California Department Store for Women." *Architectural Record* 101 (February 1947): 98–100.

Cameron, Donald, and Gerald Beckman. "Linda Vista: America's Largest Defense Housing Project." *Pencil Points* 22 (November 1941): 696–708.

"*Camminare a Brooklyn* = People-Oriented Mall in Brooklyn." *Domus,* October 1976, 30–31.

"Can Group Shelters Save Lives?" *Progressive Architecture* 32 (September 1951): 66–67.

"Can Main Street Compete? Automobile Age Has Brought Shopping Center as Rival." *American City* 65 (October 1950): 100–101.

Cannell, Michael T. *I. M. Pei: Mandarin of Modernism.* New York: Carol Southern, 1995.

Castillo, Greg. *Cold War on the Home Front: The Soft Power of Midcentury Design.* Minneapolis: University of Minnesota Press, 2010.

"Center for Rochester." *Architectural Forum* 116 (June 1962): 108–13.

Chamber of Commerce of the United States, Domestic Distribution Department. *Small Store Arrangement.* Washington, D.C.: Chamber of Commerce of the United States, 1931.

"Chapman Park Garage." *Architectural Digest* 6, no. 4 (1930): 54.

"Checklist for New Construction and Modernization of Stores." *Architectural Record* 76 (December 1934): 435–46.

Checkoway, Barry. "Large Builders, Federal Housing Programs, and Postwar Suburbanization." In *Marxism and the Metropolis,* 2nd ed., edited by William K. Tabb and Larry Sawers, 152–73. New York: Oxford University Press, 1984.

Cheney, Sheldon, and Martha Candler Cheney. *Art and the Machine: An Account of Industrial Design in Twentieth-Century America.* New York: Whittlesey House, McGraw-Hill, 1936.

Cheyne, Michael. "No Better Way? The Kalamazoo Mall and the Legacy of Pedestrian Malls." *Michigan Historical Review* 36 (Spring 2010): 103–28.

"Chicago Plans." *New Pencil Points* 25 (March 1943): 34–63.

Chung, Chuihua Judy, Jeffrey Inaba, Rem Koolhaas, and Sze Tsung Leong, eds. *Harvard Design School Guide to Shopping.* Cambridge, Mass.: Harvard Design School, 2001.

Churchill, Henry. "What Shall We Do with Our Cities?" *Journal of the American Institute of Architects* (August 1945): 62–64.

Cincinnati City Planning Commission. *Parking: A Study of Present and Future Needs in Downtown Cincinnati.* Cincinnati: City Planning Commission, 1947.

"Cities Not for Dying: Redevelopment Boom." *Architectural Record* 115 (May 1954): 170–77.

Ciucci, Giorgio, Francesco Dal Co, Mario Manien-Elia, and Manfredo Tafuri. *The American City: From the Civil War to the New Deal.* Translated by Barbara Luigia La Penta. Cambridge: MIT Press, 1979.

"Civilian Defense Reference Number." *Architectural Forum* 76 (January 1942).

Clarke, Gilmore. "Transportation: An Expanding Field for Modern Building." *Architectural Record* 90 (October 1941): 43–47.

Clausen, Meredith L. "The Department Store: Development of the Type." *Journal of Architectural Education* 39 (Fall 1985): 20–29.

———. "Northgate Regional Shopping Center: Paradigm from the Provinces." *Journal of the Society of Architectural Historians* 43 (May 1984): 144–61.

———. *Pietro Belluschi: Modern American Architect.* Cambridge: MIT Press, 1994.

———. "Shopping Centers." In *Encyclopedia of Architecture: Design, Engineering and Construction,* edited by Joseph A. Wilkes, vol. 4. New York: John Wiley, 1989.

"Clock Tower, Amboise." *Pencil Points* 12 (August 1931): 52.

Cohen, Diane. "Victor Gruen and the Regional Shopping Center." Master's thesis, Columbia University, 1984.

Cohen, Lizabeth. *A Consumer's Republic: The Politics of Mass Consumption in Postwar America.* New York: Alfred A. Knopf, 2003.

———. "From Town Center to Shopping Center: The Reconfiguration of Community Marketplaces in Postwar America." *American Historical Review* 101 (October 1996): 1050–81.

———. "The New Deal State and the Making of Citizen Consumers." In *Getting and Spending: European and American Consumer Societies in the Twentieth Century,* edited by Susan Strasser, Charles McGovern, and Matthias Judt, 111–25. New York: Cambridge University Press, 1998.

Colean, Miles. "Fundamentals of Land Planning." In "Planned Neighborhoods for 194X." *Architectural Forum* 79 (October 1943): 66–68.

Colomina, Beatriz. "The Lawn at War: 1941–1961." In *The American Lawn,* edited by Georges Teyssot, 134–53. New York: Princeton Architectural Press, 1999.

———. *Privacy and Publicity: Modern Architecture as Mass Media.* Cambridge: MIT Press, 1994.

———. "Space House: The Psyche of Building." In *Intersections: Architectural Histories and Critical Theories,* edited by Iain Borden and Jane Rendell, 59–69. New York: Routledge, 2002.

Colomina, Beatriz, Ann Marie Brennan, and Jeannie Kim, eds. *Cold War Hothouses: Inventing Postwar Culture, from Cockpit to Playboy.* New York: Princeton Architectural Press, 2004.

Colquhoun, Alan. "The Superblock." In *Essays in Architectural Criticism: Modern Architecture and Historical Change,* 83–102. Cambridge: MIT Press, 1981.

Comey, Arthur C. "Review, *The Heart of the City.*" *Landscape Architecture* 43 (July 1953): 187–88.

Comey, Arthur C., and Max S. Wehrly. "Planning Communities." In *Urban Planning and Land Policies,* vol. 2 of *Supplementary Report of the Urbanism Committee to the National Resources Committee,* 3–162. Washington, D.C.: Government Printing Office, 1939.

"Commercial Center, Linda Vista, California." *California Arts & Architecture,* November 1944, 26–29.

"Commercial Facilities for 4,500 Families." In "Shopping Facilities in Wartime." *Architectural Record* 92 (October 1942): 66–67.

"Commercial Remodeling." *Architectural Forum* 81 (October 1944): 81–151.

"Commonwealth Garage, New York, Herbert Lippman, Architect." *Architecture and Building* 54 (February 1922): 20, plate 27.

Community Builders Council. *Community Builders Handbook.* Washington, D.C.: Urban Land Institute, 1947.

"Community Building, Zurich, Switzerland." *Pencil Points* 26 (June 1945): 73–79.

"A Community Shopping Center, Glendale California." *Architectural Record* 75 (March 1934): 240–41.

Conroy, Marianne. "Discount Dreams: Factory Outlet Malls, Consumption, and the Performance of Middle-Class Identity." *Social Text* 54 (Spring 1998): 63–83.

Constant, Caroline. "Hilberseimer and Caldwell: Merging Ideologies in the Lafayette Park Landscape." In *Hilberseimer/Mies van der Rohe, Lafayette Park Detroit,* edited by Charles Waldheim, 95–111. New York: Prestel, 2004.

"A Controlled Climate for Shopping: Minneapolis' Southdale Shopping Center by Victor Gruen." *Architectural Record* 120 (December 1956): 193–95.

Cook, Joan. "Homer Hoyt, Early Planner of Urban Shopping Centers." *New York Times,* December 1, 1984, 28.

Coolidge, J. Randolph, Jr. "The Problem of the Store Front." *Architectural Review* (Boston) 8 (July 1901): 77–80.

Crane, William P. "Analyzing Obsolescent Neighborhoods." In "Planned Neighborhoods for 194X." *Architectural Forum* 79 (October 1943): 121.

Crawford, Margaret. "The World in a Shopping Mall." In *Variations on a Theme Park: The New American City and the End of Public Space,* edited by Michael Sorkin, 3–30. New York: Hill and Wang, 1992.

Creighton, Thomas H., ed. *Building for Modern Man.* Princeton, N.J.: Princeton University Press, 1949.

———. "Kiesler's Pursuit of an Idea." *Progressive Architecture* 42 (July 1961): 104–23.

Dahir, James. *The Neighborhood Unit Plan.* New York: Russell Sage Foundation, 1947.

Dan, Horace, and E. C. Morgan Willmott. *English Shop-Fronts Old and New.* London: Batsford, 1907.

Davidson, Bill. "Untangling the Traffic Snarl." *Collier's,* July 1, 1950, 32–33, 71–72.

Davison, Robert. "Garages: Standards for Construction and Design." *Architectural Record* 65 (February 1929): 177–98.

De Boer, S. R. *Shopping Districts.* Washington, D.C.: American Planning and Civic Association, 1937.

de Certeau, Michel. *The Practice of Everyday Life.* Translated by Steven Rendall. Berkeley: University of California Press, 1984.

"Defense Architect." *Architectural Forum* 75 (July 1941): 4.

"Defense through Decentralization: A Symposium on Dispersal." *Bulletin of the Atomic Scientists* 7 (September 1951): 242–79.

"Department Store, Houston, Texas." *Progressive Architecture* 29 (July 1948): 49–59.

"Department Stores." *Architectural Record* 81 (January 1937): 3–12.

"Department Stores." Building Types Study No. 95. *Architectural Record* 96 (November 1944): 91–108.

"Design Decade." *Architectural Forum* 73 (October 1940): 217–300.

"Design's Bad Boy." *Architectural Forum* 86 (February 1947): 88–91, 138, 140.

"Designs for Suburban Stores." *Architectural Record* 93 (February 1943): 67–70.

Dessauce, Marc. "Control lo Stile Internationale: 'Shelter' e la stamp architectonical Americana [Against International Style: 'Shelter' and the American architectural press]." *Casabella* 57 (September 1993): 46–53, 70–71.

"Detroit Department Store Subsidiary to Develop New Shopping Center." *American City* 31 (October 1950).

"The Development of the Arcaded Shop Front." *Architectural Forum* 40 (June 1924): 269–72.

Dimendberg, Ed. "City of Fear: Defensive Dispersal and the End of Film Noir." *ANY: Architecture New York* 18 (1997): 14–17.

"Dining-Kitchens." *Better Homes and Gardens* 23 (November 1944): 19.

Dixon, John Morris, Suzanne Stephens, and Martin Filler. "P/A on Pei: Roundtable of a Trapezoid." *Progressive Architecture* 59 (October 1978): 50–57.

Dobriner, William M., ed. *The Suburban Community.* New York: Putnam, 1958.

Donovan, Robert. *Tumultuous Years: The Presidency of Harry S. Truman.* New York: W. W. Norton, 1982.

"Doubleday Doran Bookshop." *Architectural Record* 79 (March 1936): 211–13.

Douglass, Lathrop. "New Departures in Office Building Design." *Architectural Record* 102 (October 1947): 119–23.

Dowling, Robert. "Neighborhood Shopping Centers." *Architectural Forum* 79 (October 1943): 76–78.

Downtown Business Men's Association. *Downtown Los Angeles Parking Study.* Los Angeles: Downtown Business Men's Association, 1945.

"Downtown Needs a Lesson from the Suburbs." *Business Week,* October 22, 1955, 64, 65, 68.

"Drafting and Design Problems: Neighborhood Shopping Centers." *Architectural Record* 71 (May 1932): 325–32.

Dreier, John. "Greenbelt Planning: Resettlement Administration Goes to Town." *Pencil Points* 17 (August 1936): 401–19.

"Dr. Louis Parnes, Obituary." *Architectural Record* 110 (October 1951): 292.

Dudley, Michael Quinn. "Sprawl as Strategy: City Planners Face the Bomb." *Journal of Planning Education and Research* 21 (2001): 52–63.

Duncan, Delbert J., and Charles F. Phillips. *Retailing Principles and Methods.* Chicago: D. Irwin, 1941.

Dunham-Jones, Ellen, and June Williamson. *Retrofitting Suburbia: Urban Design Solutions for Redesigning Suburbs.* Hoboken, N.J.: John Wiley, 2009.

"The Durgin Garage, Brookline, Mass., Harold Field Kellogg, Architect." *American Architect* 132 (July 5, 1927): 69–70.

Easterling, Keller. *Organization Space: Landscapes, Highways, and Houses in America.* Cambridge: MIT Press, 1999.

Eberlein, Harold Donaldson. "Shop Fronts in Country Towns and Smaller Cities." *Architectural Forum* 50 (June 1929): 869–84.

Eckbo, Garrett. *Landscape for Living.* New York: Dodge, 1950.

———. "Site Planning." *Architectural Forum* 76 (May 1942): 263–68.

Editors of Fortune, ed. *The Exploding Metropolis.* Garden City, N.Y.: Doubleday, 1958.

Edwards, Paul. *The Closed World: Computers and the Politics of Discourse in Cold War America.* Cambridge: MIT Press, 1996.

Eidelberg, Martin, ed. *Design 1935–1965: What Modern Was.* New York: Harry N. Abrams, 2001.

"End of the Great WEN?" *Architectural Forum* 79 (August 1943): 51–52.

Engelhardt, N. L., Jr. "School-Neighborhood Nucleus." *Architectural Forum* 79 (October 1943): 88–90.

Engelhardt, Tom. *The End of Victory Culture: Cold War America and the Disillusioning of a Generation.* New York: Basic Books, 1995.

Eno, William P. "The Storage of Dead Vehicles on Roadways." *Annals of the American Academy of Political and Social Science* 116 (November 1924): 169–74.

Erskine Bureau for Street Traffic Research, Harvard University. *A Traffic Control Plan for Kansas City.* Kansas City, Mo.: Chamber of Commerce, 1930.

Esherick, Joseph. "Architectural Education in the Thirties and Seventies: A Personal View." In *The Architect: Chapters in the History of the Profession,* edited by Spiro Kostof, 238–79. 1977. Reprint, Berkeley: University of California Press, 2000.

Esperdy, Gabrielle. *Modernizing Main Street: Architecture and Consumer Culture in the New Deal.* Chicago: University of Chicago Press, 2008.

Evans, Henry K. "Planning Off-Street Parking Lots." *Traffic Engineering* 15 (February 1945): 169–76.

Evans, Robin. "Windows Doors Passages." *Architectural Design* 48 (1978): 267–78.

Ewen, Stuart, and Elizabeth Ewen. *Channels of Desire: Mass Images and the Shaping of American Consciousness.* Minneapolis: University of Minnesota Press, 1982.

"Un Example de centre commercial aux Etats-Unis: Stonestown." *Architecture Française* 15, nos. 145–46 (1954): 7–10.

"Executive Bar for Seagram Distillers, Chrysler Building." *Architectural Record* 87 (January 1940): 90–91.

"Exhibition at Seligmann Gallery." *Art News* 54 (June 1955): 59.

"Factory Administration Building." *Progressive Architecture* 29 (June 1948): 56–57.

"Factory Dispersal for National Security and Rational Town Planning." *American City* 63 (September 1948): 5.

"Factory Offices." *Progressive Architecture* 29 (July 1948): 41–47.

Fairfield, John D. "Alienation of Social Control: The Chicago Sociologists and the Origins of Urban Planning." *Planning Perspectives* 7 (1992): 418–34.

Farish, Matthew. *The Contours of America's Cold War.* Minneapolis: University of Minnesota Press, 2010.

Farr, Newton. "Parking Clinic in Kansas City." *Urban Land* 5 (October 1946): 1, 3, 4.

Feinberg, Samuel. *What Makes Shopping Centers Tick.* New York: Fairchild, 1960.

Feiss, Carl. "The Architecture of Redevelopment in USA." *Progressive Architecture* 37 (August 1956): 120–27.

———. Review of *Can Our Cities Survive?,* by José Luis Sert. *Journal of the Society of Architectural Historians* 2 (October 1942): 37–39.

———. "Shopping Centers." *House & Garden,* December 1939, 48–49, 66.

Fernandez, José. *The Specialty Shop (A Guide).* New York: Architectural Book Publishing, 1950.

Ferry, John William. *A History of the Department Store.* New York: Macmillan, 1960.

"A Fifth Avenue Pipe and Tobacco Shop: Eugene Schoen, Architect." *American Architect and the Architectural Review* 122 (July 19, 1922): 58–60.

"50th Anniversary: The American Federation of Arts." *Journal of the American Institute of Architects* 31 (April 1959): 30–31.

Findlay, John M. *Magic Lands: Western Cityscapes and American Culture after 1940.* Berkeley: University of California Press, 1992.

Fisch, Fred W. "Meeting Parking after the War." *American City* 59 (November 1944): 113.

Fisher, Howard T. "Can Main Street Compete?" *American City* 65 (October 1950): 100–101.

————. *The Impact of New Shopping Centers upon Established Business Districts.* Originally presented at the National Citizen's Conference on Planning for City, State and Nation, May 15, 1950. N.p., 1950.

————. "Traffic Planning Opportunities in Shopping Center Design." *Traffic Quarterly* 4 (October 1951): 383–92.

"Fisher Building Garage, Albert Kahn, Inc., Architects." *American Architect* 135 (February 20, 1929): 264–68.

Fishman, Robert. *Bourgeois Utopias: The Rise and Fall of Suburbia.* New York: Basic Books, 1987.

————. "The Regional Plan and the Transformations of the Industrial Metropolis." In *The Landscape of Modernity: Essays on New York City, 1900–1940,* edited by David Ward and Olivier Zunz, 106–25. New York: Russell Sage Foundation, 1992.

————. *Urban Utopias in the Twentieth Century: Ebenezer Howard, Frank Lloyd Wright, Le Corbusier.* New York: Basic Books, 1977.

Fiske, John. *Reading the Popular.* Boston: Unwin Hyman, 1989.

Flanagan, Richard M. "The Housing Act of 1954: The Sea Change in National Urban Policy." *Urban Affairs Review* 33 (November 1997): 265–86.

"Flower Market." *Interiors* 100 (July 1941): 26–27, 46.

Fogelson, Robert. *Downtown: Its Rise and Fall, 1880–1950.* New Haven, Conn.: Yale University Press, 2001.

"Food Market." *Architectural Record* 78 (September 1935): 170.

Forshaw, J. H., and Patrick Abercrombie. *County of London Plan.* London: Macmillan, 1943.

"Fort Worth Plan Excludes Autos." *Progressive Architecture* 37 (May 1956): 81.

Forty, Adrian. *Objects of Desire: Design and Society since 1750.* New York: Pantheon Books, 1986.

"Forty Stores." *Architectural Forum* 88 (May 1948): 93–144.

Fox, Richard Wightman, and T. J. Jackson Lears, eds. *The Culture of Consumption: Critical Essays in American History, 1880–1980.* New York: Pantheon Books, 1983.

"Framingham Picked as New Shopping Site." *American City* 63 (February 1948): 135.

"Frank A. Parsons, Art Educator, Dies." *New York Times,* May 27, 1930, 25.

"Fresno Mall." *Arts & Architecture,* August 1965, 12–14.

Friedberg, Anne. *Window Shopping: Cinema and the Postmodern.* Berkeley: University of California Press, 1993.

Friedel, Robert. "Scarcity and Promise: Materials and American Domestic Culture during World War II." In *World War II and the American Dream: How Wartime Building Changed a Nation,* edited by Donald Albrecht, 42–89. Washington, D.C.: National Building Museum and Massachusetts Institute of Technology, 1995.

Funaro, Bruno, and Geoffrey Baker. "Shopping Centers." Building Types Study No. 152. *Architectural Record* 106 (August 1949): 110–35.

Funigiello, Phillip J. "City Planning in World War II: The Experience of the National Resources Planning Board" (1972). In *Introduction to Planning History in the United States,* edited by Donald A. Krueckeberg, 152–69. New Brunswick, N.J.: Center for Urban Policy Research, 1983.

"Gallen Kamp's Shoe Store, Los Angeles." *Pencil Points* 27 (July 1946): 48–52.

Gallison, Peter. "War against the Center." *Grey Room* 4 (Summer 2001): 6–33.

"Garages Grow Up." *Architectural Forum* 98 (February 1953): 120–41.

Geist, Johann F. *Arcades: The History of a Building Type.* Cambridge: MIT Press, 1983.

"General Houses, Inc., Chicago." *Architectural Record* 75 (January 1934): 18–19.

"General Motors Special Showing" (advertisement). *New York Times,* January 7, 1930, 24.

"General Motors Technical Center." *Architectural Record* 98 (November 1945): 98–103.

"Getting Twenty-Four Hour Service from Store Fronts." *Chain Store Age* (February 1941).

"Ghirardelli Square in Brooklyn: Why Not? Fulton Street Shopping Mall Project." *Progressive Architecture* 49 (November 1968): 52–56.

Giedion, Sigfried. *Architecture, You and Me: The Diary of a Development.* Cambridge, Mass.: Harvard University Press, 1958.

———. *Building in France, Building in Iron, Building in Ferroconcrete.* Translated by J. Duncan Berry. 1928; Santa Monica, Calif.: Getty Center for the History of Art and the Humanities, 1995.

———. "The Heart of the City: A Summing Up." In *The Heart of the City: Towards the Humanisation of Urban Life,* edited by J. Tyrwhitt, J. L. Sert, and E. N. Rogers, 159–63. New York: Pellegrini and Cudahy, 1952.

———. "Historical Background to the Core." In *The Heart of the City: Towards the Humanisation of Urban Life,* edited by J. Tyrwhitt, J. L. Sert, and E. N. Rogers, 17–25. New York: Pellegrini and Cudahy, 1952.

———. "The Humanization of Urban Life." *Architectural Record* 111 (April 1952): 121–29.

———. "In Search of a New Monumentality." *Architectural Review* 104 (September 1948): 117–28.

———. "The Need for a New Monumentality." In *New Architecture and City Planning,* edited by Paul Zucker, 549–68. New York: Philosophical Library, 1944.

———. *Space, Time and Architecture: The Growth of a New Tradition.* Cambridge, Mass.: Harvard University Press, 1941.

———. "The State of Contemporary Architecture II: The Need for Imagination." *Architectural Record* 115 (February 1954): 186–91.

———. *Walter Gropius: Team and Teamwork.* New York: Reinhold, 1954.

Giedion, Sigfried, José Luis Sert, and Fernand Léger. "Nine Points on Monumentality" (1943). In *Architecture Culture, 1943–1968: A Documentary Anthology,* edited by Joan Ockman and Edward Eigen, 29–30. New York: Rizzoli, 1993.

Gillette, Howard, Jr. "The Evolution of Neighborhood Planning from the Progressive Era to the 1949 Housing Act." *Journal of Urban History* 9 (August 1983): 421–44.

———. "The Evolution of the Planned Shopping Center in Suburb and City." *Journal of the American Planning Association* 51 (Autumn 1985): 449–60.

———. "Film as Artifact: *The City* (1939)." *American Studies* 18 (1977): 71–85.

Gina, Francis X. "A Costume Jewelry Shop." *Bulletin of the Beaux-Arts Institute of Design* 17 (January 1941): 3.

"Glamour in Glass." *Men's Wear,* November 8, 1939, 10.

Gold, John R. *The Experience of Modernism: Modern Architects and the Future City, 1928–1953.* London: E & FN Spon, 1997.

Goldhagen, Sarah Williams, and Réjean Legault, eds. *Anxious Modernisms: Experimentation in Postwar Architectural Culture.* Cambridge: MIT Press, 2000.

Goodman, Cynthia. "The Art of Revolutionary Display Techniques." In *Frederick Kiesler,* edited by Lisa Philips, 57–84. New York: Whitney Museum of American Art, 1989.

Goodman, Percival, and Paul Goodman. *Communitas: Means of Livelihood and Ways of Life.* Chicago: University of Chicago Press, 1947.

Goodrich, Ernest P. "The Place of the Garage in City Planning." *Architectural Record* 65 (February 1929): 198.

Grabow, Stephen. "Frank Lloyd Wright and the American City: The Broadacres Debate." *Journal of the American Institute of Planners* 43 (April 1977): 115–24.

"Grand Rapids Parking Plan to Rehabilitate Shopping at the Urban Center." Building Types Study No. 98. *Architectural Record* 97 (February 1945): 86–95.

"Grand Rapids Retail Center Acclaimed as Model." *Women's Wear Daily,* February 15, 1945, 31.

"Grass Grows Green on Main Street." *House & Garden,* July 1943, 31.

"Grass on Main Street." *Saturday Evening Post,* February 13, 1943.

"'Grass on Main Street' Becomes a Reality." *Architectural Forum* 81 (September 1944): 81–93.

Grebler, Leo. "New City Centers in Europe." *Urban Land* 14 (April 1955): 3–7.

———. "Post-war Rebuilding in Western Europe." *Progressive Architecture* 37 (August 1956): 128–35.

"Greenbelt, MD, Ellington and Wadsworth, Architects." *Architectural Forum* 68 (May 1938): 417.

"Greenbelt Towns." *Architectural Record* 80 (September 1936): 215–34.

Greenberg, Clement. "Avant Garde and Kitsch." *Partisan Review* 6 (Fall 1939): 34–49.

Greenberg, Lynda. "Victor Gruen." In *Macmillan Encyclopedia of Architects,* edited by Adolf K. Placzek, 263–64. New York: Free Press, 1982.

Greer, Guy, ed. *The Problem of the Cities and Towns: Report of the Conference on Urbanism, Harvard University, March 5–6, 1942.* Cambridge, Mass.: n.p., 1942.

———. "Syracuse Plans Its Future." In *Planning, 1944: Proceedings of the Annual National Planning Conference.* Chicago: American Society of Planning Officials, 1944.

———. "Syracuse Tackles Its Future." *Fortune,* May 1943, 120–22, 156–60.

———. *Your City Tomorrow.* New York: Macmillan, 1947.

Gris, John M., and James Ford, eds. *Slums, Large-Scale Housing and Decentralization.* Washington, D.C.: President's Conference on Home Building and Home Ownership, 1932.

Gropius, Walter. "Gropius Appraises Today's Architect." *Architectural Forum* 96 (May 1952): 111–12, 166–82.

———. "Principles of Bauhaus Production" (1926). In *Programs and Manifestoes on Twentieth-Century Architecture,* edited by Ulrich Conrads. Cambridge: MIT Press, 1970.

———. *Rebuilding Our Communities.* Chicago: Theobald, 1945.

———. *Scope of Total Architecture.* New York: Harper, 1955.

Gropius, Walter, and Martin Wagner. "A Program for City Reconstruction." *Architectural Forum* 79 (July 1943): 75–86.

Grossman, Andrew D. *Neither Dead nor Red: Civilian Defense and American Political Development during the Early Cold War.* New York: Routledge, 2001.

Gruen, Victor. "Dynamic Planning for Retail Areas." *Harvard Business Review* 22 (November–December 1954): 53–62.

———. *The Heart of Our Cities: The Urban Crisis: Diagnosis and Cure.* New York: Simon & Schuster, 1964.

———. *How To Live with Your Architect.* New York: Store Modernization Institute, 1949.

———. "Planned Shopping Centers." *Dun's Review,* May 1953, 37–38, 113–14, 116–22.

———. "The Planned Shopping Centers in America." *Zodiac* 1 (1957): 159–68.

———. "Retailing and the Automobile." Building Types Study No. 280. *Architectural Record* 127 (March 1960): 191–210.

———. "Sculpture and Architecture: An Architect's View." *Arts Magazine,* April 1, 1955, 11–13.

———. *Shopping Centers of Tomorrow.* Washington, D.C.: American Foundation of the Arts, 1954.

———. "Somewhere in Claustrophobia: A Few Booby Traps along the Glazed Front." In "Forty Stores." *Architectural Forum* 88 (May 1948): 95–96.

———. "What's Wrong with Store Design?" *Women's Wear Daily,* October 18, 1949, 62.

———. "What To Look for in Shopping Centers." *Chain Store Age* 24 (July 1948): 22, 63–66.

Gruen, Victor, and Larry Smith. "Shopping Centers: The New Building Type." *Progressive Architecture* 33 (June 1952): 66–109.

———. *Shopping Towns USA: The Planning of Shopping Centers.* New York: Reinhold, 1960.

Gruen Associates. *A Greater Fort Worth Tomorrow.* Fort Worth, Tex.: Greater Fort Worth Planning Committee, 1956.

Gruenbaum, Victor. "Some Notes on Modern Store Design." *Architect and Engineer* 148 (February 1942): 14–22.

———. "Wohnung eines geistig arbeitenden Ehepaares." *Architektur und Bautechnik* 15 (1933): 137–43.

Gruenbaum, Victor, and Elsie Krummeck. "Face to Face." *Apparel Arts* (June 1940): 52.

Gruzen, Sumner. "Automobile Shopping Centers." *Architectural Record* 76 (July 1934): 43–48.

Gutheim, Frederick. "Pedestrian Millennium Sighted." *Washington Post,* May 30, 1948, B3.

Gutman, Robert. *Architectural Practice: A Critical Review.* New York: Princeton Architectural Press, 1988.

Guzzardi, Walter. "An Architect of Environments." *Fortune,* January 1962, 76–80, 134, 136, 138.

Hagopian, Mahan. "The A. S. Beck Shoe Store." *Architectural Record* 65 (June 1929): 543.

Hale, Peter. "New Haven's Post-war Plan." *1945 Proceedings of the Institute of Traffic Engineers* (1946): 56–61.

Hales, Peter Bacon. *Atomic Spaces: Living on the Manhattan Project.* Urbana: University of Illinois Press, 1997.

Hamlin, Talbot F. "The International Style Lacks the Essence of Great Architecture." *American Architect* 143 (January 1933): 12–16.

———. "Some Restaurants and Recent Shops." *Pencil Points* 20 (August 1939): 485–500.

Hammett, Jerilou, and Kingsley Hammett, eds. *The Suburbanization of New York: Is the World's Greatest City Becoming Just Another Town?* New York: Princeton Architecture Press, 2007.

Hammond, Harold. "Plans for Post-war Traffic Safety." *Proceedings of the Institute of Traffic Engineers* (1944): 106–10.

Hanchett, Thomas W. "Federal Incentives and the Growth of Local Planning, 1941–48." *Journal of the American Planning Association* 60 (Spring 1994): 197–208.

———. "Financing Suburbia: Prudential Insurance and the Post–World War II Transformation of the American City." *Journal of Urban History* 26 (March 2000): 312–28.

———. "U.S. Tax Policy and the Shopping-Center Boom of the 1950s and 1960s." *American Historical Review* 101 (October 1996): 1082–110.

Harbeson, John. "Design in Modern Architecture." *Pencil Points* (January 1930): 227–35.

Hardwick, M. Jeff. *Mall Maker: Victor Gruen, Architect of an American Dream.* Philadelphia: University of Pennsylvania Press, 2004.

Harmon, Robert B. *Victor Gruen: An Architectural Pioneer of Shopping Centers: A Selected Bibliography.* Monticello, Ill.: Vance Bibliographies, 1980.

Harris, Neil. "Spaced Out at the Shopping Center" (1975). In *Cultural Excursions: Marketing Appetites and Cultural Tastes in Modern America,* 278–88. Chicago: University of Chicago Press, 1990.

Harrison, Leonard C. "Rye Aims at City Planning Leadership." *American City* 61 (October 1946): 88–89.

Haskell, Douglas. "Mixed Metaphors at Chicago." *Architectural Review* 74 (August 1933): 47–49.

———. "Review, *Contemporary Art Applied to the Store and Its Display.*" *Creative Art* 6 (May 1930): 109–10.

Hauf, Harold. "City Planning and Civil Defense." *Architectural Record* 108 (December 1950): 99.

Hayden, Dolores. *Building Suburbia: Green Fields and Suburban Growth, 1820–2000.* New York: Vintage Books, 2003.

Hays, K. Michael. "Picturing Collective Consumer Culture: Hannes Meyer's Co-op Vitrine." In *Shopping: A Century of Art and Consumer Culture,* edited by Christoph Grunenberg and Max Hollein, 112–24. Ostfildern-Ruit, Germany: Hatje Cantz, 2002.

"Heart of Gruen's Fresno Plan." *Progressive Architecture* 46 (January 1965): 184–86.

Heimann, Jim, ed. *Shop America: Midcentury Storefront Design, 1938–1950.* Los Angeles: Taschen, 2007.

Held, Roger L. "Endless Innovations: The Theories and Scenic Design of Frederick Kiesler." Ph.D. diss., Bowling Green State University, Ohio, 1977.

Hendrikson, Robert. *The Grand Emporiums.* New York: Stein & Day, 1979.

Henriksen, Margot A. *Dr. Strangelove's America: Society and Culture in the Atomic Age.* Berkeley: University of California Press, 1997.

Herrey, Hermann, Erna Herrey, and Constantine Pertzoff. "An Organic Theory of City Planning." *Architectural Forum* 80 (April 1944): 133–40.

Hersey, John. *Hiroshima.* New York: Alfred A. Knopf, 1946.

Heynen, Hilda. *Architecture and Modernity: A Critique.* Cambridge: MIT Press, 1999.

Hilberseimer, Ludwig. "Cities and Defense" (1945). In Richard Pommer, David Spaeth, and Kevin Harrington, *In the Shadow of Mies: Ludwig Hilberseimer, Architect, Educator, and Urban Planner,* 89–93. Chicago: Art Institute of Chicago, 1988.

———. *The New City: Principles of Planning.* Chicago: Theobald, 1944.

———. *The New Regional Pattern: Industries and Gardens, Workshops and Farms.* Chicago: Theobald, 1949.

"Hill Garage, Los Angeles, Kenneth MacDonald, Jr. & Company, Architects." *American Architect* 133 (April 5, 1928): 480.

Hirsch, Arnold. *Making the Second Ghetto: Race and Housing in Chicago, 1940–1960.* New York: Cambridge University Press, 1983.

Hise, Greg. *Magnetic Los Angeles: Planning the Twentieth-Century Metropolis.* Baltimore: Johns Hopkins University Press, 1997.

Hitchcock, Henry-Russell. "Architectural Education Again." *Architectural Record* 67 (April 1930): 445–46.

———. "The Architecture of Bureaucracy and the Architecture of Genius." *Architectural Review* 101 (January 1947): 3–6.

———. "Modern Architecture, I." *Architectural Record* 63 (April 1928): 337–49.

———. "Modern Architecture, II." *Architectural Record* 63 (May 1928): 452–60.

———. *Modern Architecture: Romanticism and Reintegration.* New York: Payson & Clarke, 1929.

———. "The Place of Painting and Sculpture in Relation to Modern Architecture." *Architects' Year Book* (1947): 12–22.

———. "Review of *Wie Baut America* by Richard J. Neutra." *Architectural Record* 63 (June 1928): 594–95.

Holden, Arthur C., ed. *Planning Man's Physical Environment.* Conference proceedings. Princeton, N.J.: Princeton University, 1947.

———. "Prepare to Meet Your Client." *New Pencil Points* 23 (June 1942): 73–76.

Holleman, Thomas J., and James P. Gallagher. *Smith, Hinchman & Grylls: 125 Years of Architecture and Engineering, 1853–1978.* Detroit: Wayne State University Press, 1978.

Hopper, Parker Morse. "Twentieth Century European Architecture." *Architectural Forum* 50 (February 1929): 209–39.

Hornbeck, James. "Shopping Can Be a Pleasure." Building Types Study No. 250. *Architectural Record* 122 (September 1957): 205–32.

Horowitz, Daniel. *The Morality of Spending: Attitudes toward the Consumer Society in America, 1875–1940.* Baltimore: Johns Hopkins University Press, 1985.

"Hotel, Store and Apartment Properties Figuring in Manhattan Real Estate Activity." *New York Times,* December 3, 1939, 194.

Hough, A. C. "Experience with Off-Street Parking in Pittsburg." *Proceedings of the Institute of Traffic Engineers* (1938): 14–16.

"House for Mr. Charles Mitchell Bliss." *House & Garden,* November 1939, 28–29.

Howe, George. *The Structure and Growth of Residential Neighborhoods in American Cities.* Washington, D.C.: Federal Housing Administration, 1939.

———. "What Is This Modern Architecture Trying to Express?" *American Architect* 137 (May 1930): 22–25, 106, 108.

"How to Build Cities Downtown." *Architectural Forum* 102 (June 1955): 122–31, 164–236.

"How U.S. Cities Can Prepare for Atomic War: MIT Professors Suggest a Bold Plan to Prevent Panic and Limit Destruction." *Life,* December 18, 1950.

Hoyt, Homer. *Market Analysis of Shopping Centers.* Technical Bulletin No. 12. Washington, D.C.: Urban Land Institute, October 1949.

Hubbard, Theodora Kimball, and Henry Vincent Hubbard. *Our Cities To-Day and To-morrow: A Survey of Planning and Zoning in the United States.* Cambridge, Mass.: Harvard University Press, 1929.

Hudnut, Joseph. "The Art in Housing." *Architectural Record* 93 (January 1943): 57–62.

Hunt, John Dixon. "*Ut Pictura Poesis, Ut Pictura Hortus,* and the Picturesque." In *Gardens and the Picturesque: Studies in the History of Landscape Architecture,* 105–38. Cambridge: MIT Press, 1992.

Hurd, Fred. "Holding Customers in the Central District." *American City* 60 (November 1945): 137, 139.

Huyssen, Andreas. "Mass Culture as Woman: Modernism's Other." In *After the Great Divide: Modernism, Mass Culture, Postmodernism,* 44–62. Bloomington: Indiana University Press, 1986.

Ihlder, John. "Coordination of Traffic Facilities." *Annals of the American Academy of Political and Social Science* 133 (September 1927): 1–7.

"In Kansas City, a Framework for the Future." *Architectural Forum* 103 (November 1955): 158–65.

"Innovations in Small Store Design." In "Minor Architecture: Exemplified in Moderate Cost Buildings." *Architectural Forum* 34 (April 1921): 135–38.

"In Oakland There Is No Traffic Problem." *Traffic Engineering* 16 (May 1946): 337.

"Inside Out, Ross-Frankel, Inc." *Interiors* 104 (January 1945): 85.

International City and Regional Planning Conference. *Planning Problems of Town, City and Region: Papers and Discussions at the International City and Regional Planning Conference.* Baltimore: Norman, Remington, 1925.

Isaacs, Reginald. "Are Urban Neighborhoods Possible?" *Journal of Housing* 5 (July 1948): 177–80.

———. "The 'Neighborhood Unit' Is an Instrument for Segregation." *Journal of Housing* 5 (August 1948): 215–19.

Isenberg, Alison. *Downtown America: A History of the Place and the People Who Made It.* Chicago: University of Chicago Press, 2004.

"Is Store Design Vital?" *Architectural Record* 89 (February 1941).

Italian Art and Landscape Foundation. *More Streets for People.* New York: Italian Art and Landscape Foundation, 1972.

"It's a Hit! Be Sure to See It" (advertisement). *New York Times,* November 12, 1938, 6.

Jackson, Kenneth T. *Crabgrass Frontier: The Suburbanization of the United States.* New York: Oxford University Press, 1985.

Jacobs, Jane. "Downtown Is for People." In *The Exploding Metropolis,* edited by the Editors of Fortune. Garden City, N.Y.: Doubleday, 1958.

———. "Two Projects." In *The Pedestrian in the City,* edited by David Lewis. Princeton, N.J.: Van Nostrand, 1965.

"Jacques Coeur House, Bourges." *American Architect* 140 (September 1931): 44.

Jakle, John A., and Keith A. Sculle. *Lots of Parking: Land Use in a Car Culture.* Charlottesville: University of Virginia Press, 2004.

Jameson, Fredric. "Postmodernism, or the Cultural Logic of Late Capitalism." *New Left Review* 151 (July–August 1984): 53–92.

Johns, Michael. *Moment of Grace: The American City in the 1950s.* Berkeley: University of California Press, 2004.

Johnson, David A. *Planning the Great Metropolis: The 1929 Regional Plan of New York and Its Environs.* New York: E & FN Spon, 1996.

Johnson, Donald Leslie. "Origin of the Neighborhood Plan." *Planning Perspectives* 17 (July 2002): 227–45.

Johnson, J. Stewart. *American Modern, 1925–1940: Design for a New Age.* New York: Harry N. Abrams, 2000.

Johnson-Marshall, P. "Rotterdam: How It Is Being Rebuilt." *Architects Journal* (October 27, 1955): 557–70.

"John Wanamaker Men's Store, New York City: Kenneth C. Welch, Architect." *Architectural Record* 80 (August 1936): 117–19.

Jones, Mickey. "109-Store Houston Shopping Center of 1952 to Feature Pedestrian Mall." *Women's Wear Daily,* January 3, 1951.

"Jordan Marsh, Boston, Perry, Shaw and Hepburn, Architects." *National Architect* 3 (August 1947).

"Joseph Magnin Store, Sacramento." *Progressive Architecture* 28 (May 1947): 71–75.

Judt, Matthias. "Reshaping Shopping Environments: The Competition between the City of Boston and Its Suburbs." In *Getting and Spending: European and American Consumer Societies in the Twentieth Century,* edited by Susan Strasser, Charles McGovern, and Matthias Judt, 317–37. New York: Cambridge University Press, 1998.

Justement, Louis. *New Cities for Old: City Building in Terms of Space, Time and Money.* New York: McGraw-Hill, 1946.

Kahn, Ely Jacques. "Essential Details in Store Designing." *Architectural Forum* 40 (June 1924): 245–48.

———. "The Modern European Shop and Store." *Architectural Forum* 50 (June 1929): 795–97, 804.

Kahn, Louis. "Toward a Plan for Midtown Philadelphia." *Perspecta* 2 (1953): 11–27.

"Kalamazoo Keeps Her Customers." *Traffic Engineering* 16 (August 1946): 458.

"Kansas City Flanks Business District with Six Modern Parking Lots." *Traffic Engineering* 16 (April 1946): 274.

Kaufmann, Eugene C. "Neighborhood Units as New Elements in Town Planning." *Journal of the Royal Institute of British Architects* (December 19, 1936): 165–75.

Kawneer Company. *Kawneer Sales-Building Store-Fronts.* Niles, Mich.: Kawneer, 1944.

———. *Machines for Selling.* Niles, Mich.: Kawneer, 1946.

Kayden, Jerold S. *Privately Owned Public Space: The New York City Experience.* New York: John Wiley, 2000.

Keally, Francis. "How Airports Will Affect Zoning Laws." *American Architect* 136 (December 1929): 20–21, 100–102.

———. "A New Effect with Stucco." *House Beautiful,* October 1931, 302–3.

Kelly, Barbara M. *Expanding the American Dream: Building and Rebuilding Levittown.* Albany: State University of New York Press, 1993.

Kelly, Burnham. "The Necessity for Dispersion." In *Proceedings of the Conference "Building in the Atomic Age," Massachusetts Institute of Technology Department of Civil and Sanitary Engineering, June 16–17, 1952*; reprinted in *Journal of the American Institute of Planners* 19 (Winter 1953): 20–25.

Kennedy, G. Donald. "The Parking Problem Can Be Solved." *Rotarian,* April 1946, 44–46.

"Kent Automatic Parking Garage, New York, Jardine, Hill and Murdock." *American Architect and Architecture* 133 (June 20, 1928): 835–37.

Kentgens-Craig, Margret. *The Bauhaus and America: First Contacts, 1919–1936.* Cambridge: MIT Press, 1999.

Ketchum, Morris, Jr. "An Architect Looks at the Shopping Center of the Future." *Empire State Architect* 16 (July–August 1956): 20, 34.

————. *Blazing a Trail.* New York: Vantage Press, 1982.

————. "Civil and Industrial Defense: A Special Summary Report." *Bulletin of the American Institute of Architects* 7 (March–April 1953): 35–37.

————. "Current Trends in Store Design." *Architectural Record* 103 (April 1948): 109–44.

————. "A Decorators Accessory Shop." *Bulletin of the Beaux-Arts Institute of Design* 19 (1943): 7.

————. "A Merchandise Display Window." *Bulletin of the Beaux-Arts Institute of Design* 18 (March 1942): 3.

————. *Morris Ketchum Jr., Architect.* New York: Architectural Catalog, n.d., ca. 1941.

————. "A Mural for a Handicraft Shop." *Bulletin of the Beaux-Arts Institute of Design* 17 (February 1941): 4.

————. "The Open Faced Shop." *Interiors* 101 (July 1942): 44–47.

————. "Services for Sale." *Architectural Record* 90 (July 1941): 83–99.

————. "A Shopping Group and Motion Picture Theater Entrance." *Bulletin of the Beaux-Arts Institute of Design* 20 (February 1944): 28–30.

————. *Shops and Stores.* New York: Reinhold, 1948.

————. "What to Look for in Shopping Centers." *Chain Store Age* 24 (July 1948): 23, 58, 62.

Ketchum, Morris, Jr., and Jedd S. Reisner. "Master Room." In "The New House 194X." *Architectural Forum* 77 (September 1942): 92–95.

Kiek, Robert. "Europe's Fifth Avenue." *Urban Land* 13 (October 1954): 1, 6.

Kiesler, Frederick. *Contemporary Art Applied to the Store and Its Display.* New York: Brentano's, 1930.

————. "Design Correlation: A Column on Exhibits, the Theater and the Cinema." *Architectural Record* (February 1937): 7–15.

————. "Manifesto of Tensionism" (1925). In *Contemporary Art Applied to the Store and Its Display.* New York: Brentano's, 1930.

————. "On Correalism and Biotechnique: A Definition and Test of a New Approach to Building Design." *Architectural Record* 86 (September 1939): 60–75.

————. "Shop Window Displays, Saks and Company, New York City." *Architectural Record* 66 (September 1930): 215–20.

————. "Space House." *Architectural Record* 75 (January 1934): 44–61.

————. "The Space House: Annotations at Random." *Hound & Horn* 7 (January–March 1934): 292–97.

Kimball, Fiske. "Modern Architecture: An Exhibition in the Galleries of the Museum." *Pennsylvania Museum Bulletin* 27 (April 1932): 131–35.

————. "What Is Modern Architecture?" *The Nation,* July 30, 1924, 128–29; reprinted in *Western Architect* 33 (October 1924): 114–16.

Kincaid, H. Evert. "Chicago Plans." *Proceedings of the Institute of Traffic Engineers* (1943): 36–55.

Klaber, Eugene H. "Urban Exodus: A Quandary for Planners." *American City* 63 (March 1948): 104.

Knight, Warren A. "Parking Headache Gone in Montclair." *New York Times,* September 11, 1949, 59.

Knowles, Morris. "City Planning as a Permanent Solution to the Traffic Problem." In International City and Regional Planning Conference, *Planning Problems of Town, City and Region: Papers and Discussions at the International City and Regional Planning Conference,* 48–62. Baltimore: Norman, Remington, 1925.

Koch, Harry. "Parking Facilities for the Detroit Central Business District." *Proceedings of the Institute of Traffic Engineers* (1939): 73–76.

Kocher, A. Lawrence. "The Country House: Are We Developing an American Style?" *Architectural Record* 60 (November 1926): 385–95.

———. "Early Architecture of Pennsylvania." *Architectural Record* 48 (January 1920): 513–30.

———. "Low-Cost Farmhouse." *Architectural Record* 75 (January 1934): 30.

Kocher, A. Lawrence, and Howard Dearstyne. *Colonial Williamsburg, Its Buildings and Gardens.* Williamsburg, Va.: Colonial Williamsburg, 1949.

Kocher, A. Lawrence, and Albert Frey. "Real Estate Subdivisions for Low-Cost Housing." *Architectural Record* 69 (April 1931): 323–27.

Kohn, Margaret. *Brave New Neighborhoods: The Privatization of Public Space.* New York: Routledge, 2004.

Kopytoff, Igor. "The Cultural Biography of Things: Commoditization as Process." In *The Social Life of Things: Commodities in Cultural Perspective,* edited by Arjun Appadurai, 64–93. New York: Cambridge University Press, 1986.

Koran, Arthur, and Felix J. Samuel. "A Master Plan for London: Based on Research Carried Out by the Town Planning Committee of the M.A.R.S. Group." *Architectural Review* 91 (June 1942): 143–50.

Kotler, Philip, and Gary Armstrong. *Principles of Marketing,* 13th ed. Upper Saddle River, N.J.: Prentice Hall, 2010.

Kowinski, William S. *The Malling of America: An Inside Look at the Great Consumer Paradise.* New York: William Morrow, 1985.

Krieger, Alex, and William S. Saunders, eds. *Urban Design.* Minneapolis: University of Minnesota Press, 2009.

Kuznick, Peter J., and James Gilbert, eds. *Rethinking Cold War Culture.* Washington, D.C.: Smithsonian Institution Press, 2001.

Kyson, Charles. "Advertising and . . . Advertising." *American Architect and Architecture* 139 (April 1931): 48–49.

———. "Architecture: The Sick Profession." *Pencil Points* 11 (September 1927): 563–66.

———. "Blades of Grass." *Pencil Points* 11 (August 1927): 487–89.

Laermans, Rudi. "Learning to Consume: Early Department Stores and the Shaping of the Modern Consumer Culture, 1860–1914." *Theory, Culture, and Society* 10 (1993): 79–102.

"Lakewood Park, Los Angeles County." *Architectural Record* (September 1951): 32–36.

Lapidus, Morris. *Architecture: A Profession and a Business.* New York: Reinhold, 1967.

———. "Basic Plans and Profiles of Store Front Construction." *Architectural Forum* 63 (July 1935): 53.

————. "Free Flow Plan in Tight Areas." Building Types Study No. 110. *Architectural Record* 99 (February 1946): 100–105.

————. "Planning Today for the Store Tomorrow." *Chain Store Age* (April 1944): 24–30.

————. "The Retail Store and Its Design Problems." Building Types Study No. 98. *Architectural Record* 97 (February 1945): 96–107.

————. "Store Design: A Merchandising Problem." Building Types Study. *Architectural Record* 89 (February 1941): 113–35.

————. *Too Much Is Never Enough.* New York: Rizzoli, 1996.

Lapp, Ralph E. "Atomic Bomb Explosions: Effects on an American City." *Bulletin of the Atomic Scientists* 4 (February 1948).

————. *Must We Hide?* Cambridge, Mass.: Addison-Wesley, 1949.

————. "The Strategy of Civil Defense." *Bulletin of the Atomic Scientists* 6 (August–September 1950).

Larkin, John. "A Pilot Study of Planned Industrial Dispersion in the Baltimore Area." *Bulletin of the American Institute of Architects* 7 (March–April 1953): 38–43.

Larsen, Kristin. "Cities to Come: Clarence Stein's Postwar Regionalism." *Journal of Planning History* 4 (February 2005): 33–51.

————. "The Radburn Idea as an Emergent Concept: Henry Wright's Regional City." *Planning Perspectives* 23 (July 2008): 381–95.

Larson, Magali Sarfatti. "Emblem and Exception: The Historical Definition of the Architect's Professional Role." In *Professionals and Urban Form,* edited by Judith R. Blau, Mark E. La Gory, and John S. Pipkin, 49–86. Albany: State University of New York Press, 1983.

Lawrence, Sidney. "Declaration of Function: Documents from the Museum of Modern Art's Design Crusade, 1933–1950." *Design Issues* 2 (Spring 1985): 67–77.

Leach, William. *Land of Desire: Merchants, Power, and the Rise of a New American Culture.* New York: Pantheon Books, 1993.

Lear, John. "Hiroshima, USA: Can Anything Be Done about It?" *Collier's,* August 5, 1950, 15.

Lears, T. J. Jackson. "From Salvation to Self-Realization: Advertising and the Therapeutic Roots of the Consumer Culture, 1880–1930." In *The Culture of Consumption: Critical Essays in American History, 1880–1980,* edited by Richard Wightman Fox and T. J. Jackson Lears, 3–38. New York: Pantheon Books, 1983.

————. "A Matter of Taste: Corporate Cultural Hegemony in a Mass-Consumption Society." In *Recasting America: Culture and Politics in the Age of the Cold War,* edited by Lary May, 38–54. Chicago: University of Chicago Press, 1989.

Lebhar, Godfrey M. *Chain Stores in America: 1859–1950.* New York: Chain Store Publishing, 1952.

Le Corbusier. "L'Habitation moderne." *Population* (July–September 1948).

LeCraw, Charles S. "Allentown Saves Its Shopping Area." *Traffic Quarterly* 3 (January 1949): 63.

————. "City-Owned Parking Lot Experience in Miami Beach, Florida." *Traffic Quarterly* 4 (July 1950): 206–13.

————. "Interior Block Planning." *Traffic Quarterly* 1 (October 1947): 351–66.

Lefferts, E. B. "Should Business Provide Off-Street Parking for Patrons?" *Proceedings of the Institute of Traffic Engineers* (1938): 19–23.

Leffler, Melvyn P. "The Conception of National Security and the Beginnings of the Cold War, 1945–48." *American Historical Review* 89 (April 1984): 346–81.

Lesak, Barbara. "Visionary of the European Theater." In *Frederick Kiesler,* edited by Lisa Philips, 37–45. New York: Whitney Museum of American Art, 1989.

Levine, Lawrence. *Highbrow/Lowbrow: The Emergence of Cultural Hierarchy in America.* Cambridge, Mass.: Harvard University Press, 1988.

Lewis, David, ed. *The Pedestrian in the City.* Princeton, N.J.: Van Nostrand, 1965.

Lewis, Harold MacLean. *Highway Traffic,* vol. 3 of *Regional Plan of New York and Its Environs.* New York: Regional Plan of New York and Its Environs, 1927.

———. *Planning the Modern City,* vol. 1. New York: John Wiley, 1949.

Libbey-Owens-Ford Glass Company. *52 Designs to Modernize Main Street with Glass.* Toledo, Ohio: Libbey-Owens-Ford, 1935.

———. *Visual Fronts.* Toledo, Ohio: Libbey-Owens-Ford, 1945.

Lichtenstein, Susanne Ralston. "Editing Architecture: *Architectural Record* and the Growth of Modern Architecture, 1928–1938." Ph.D. diss., Cornell University, 1990.

Light, Jennifer. "The City as National Resource: New Deal Conservation and the Quest for Urban Improvement." *Journal of Urban History* 35 (May 2009): 531–60.

"The Lighting of Merchandise." Building Types Study No. 95. *Architectural Record* 96 (November 1944): 102.

"The Lijnbaan at Rotterdam." *Town Planning Review* 27 (April 1956): 21–26.

Linder, Mark. "Wild Kingdom: Frederick Kiesler's Display of the Avant-Garde." In *Autonomy and Ideology: Positioning an Avant-Garde in America,* edited by R. E. Somol, 122–53. New York: Monacelli Press, 1997.

"Linen Shop." In "Stores." *Architectural Forum* 71 (December 1939): 433.

Livingston, James. "Modern Subjectivity and Consumer Culture." In *Getting and Spending: European and American Consumer Societies in the Twentieth Century,* edited by Susan Strasser, Charles McGovern, and Matthias Judt, 413–29. New York: Cambridge University Press, 1998.

Locke, Dean. "The Use of Parking Facilities in the CBD of Baltimore, May, 1931." *Proceeding of the Institute of Traffic Engineers* (1931): 28–38.

Lönberg-Holm, Knud. "Architecture in the Industrial Age" (1929). *Arts & Architecture,* April 1967, 22–27.

———. "Gasoline Filling and Service Station with Specification Checking List." *Architectural Record* 67 (June 1930): 561–84.

———. "Monuments and Instruments." *Shelter* 2 (May 1932): 4–9.

———. "New Theatre Architecture in Europe." *Architectural Record* 67 (April 1930): 487–91.

———. "Planning the Retail Store." *Architectural Record* 69 (June 1931): 495–514.

———. "Technical Developments, 1931." *Architectural Record* 71 (January 1932): 59–72.

———. "Two Shows: A Comment on the Aesthetic Racket." *Shelter* 2 (April 1932): 16–17.

Lönberg-Holm, Knud, and Theodore Larson. "The Technician on the Cultural Front." *Architectural Record* 80 (December 1936): 472–82.

"A Long Considered Scheme Develops." *Architectural Record* 87 (June 1940): 114–18.

"Long Span Concrete Arches Used in Garage." *American Architect* 117 (1920): 743–47.

Longstreth, Richard. *The American Department Store Transformed, 1920–1960.* New Haven, Conn.: Yale University Press, 2010.

———. *City Center to Regional Mall: Architecture, the Automobile, and Retailing in Los Angeles, 1920–1950.* Cambridge: MIT Press, 1997.

———. "The Diffusion of the Community Shopping Center Concept during the Interwar Decades." *Journal of the Society of Architectural Historians* 56 (September 1997): 268–93.

———. *The Drive-In, the Supermarket, and the Transformation of Commercial Space in Los Angeles, 1914–1941.* Cambridge: MIT Press, 1999.

———. "The Forgotten Arterial Landscape: Photographic Documentation of Commercial Development along Los Angeles Boulevards during the Interwar Years." *Journal of Urban History* 23 (May 1997): 437–59.

———. "J. C. Nichols, the Country Club Plaza and Notions of Modernity." *Harvard Architecture Review* 5 (1986): 121–35.

———. "The Mixed Blessings of Success: The Hecht Company and Department Store Branch Development after World War II." In *Shaping Communities,* edited by Carter L. Hudgins and Elizabeth Collins Cromley, 244–62. Knoxville: University of Tennessee Press, 1997.

———. "The Neighborhood Shopping Center in Washington, D.C., 1930–1941." *Journal of the Society of Architectural Historians* 51 (1992): 5–34.

———. "River Oaks Shopping Center." *Cite* 36 (Winter 1998): 8–13.

———. "Silver Spring: Georgia Avenue, Colesville Road, and the Creation of an Alternative 'Downtown' for Metropolitan Washington." In *Streets: Critical Perspectives on Public Space,* edited by Zeynep Çelik, Diane Favro, and Richard Ingersoll, 247–58. Berkeley: University of California Press, 1994.

Lovejoy, F. W. "What Can Be Done about Traffic Congestion: Off-Street Parking Facilities." *Civil Engineer Magazine,* May 1946, 202–4.

Lowe, Jeanne R. "What's Happening in Fort Worth." *Architectural Forum* 110 (May 1959): 136–39.

Lowenthal, Milton. "The Suburban Branch Department Store." *Architectural Record* 72 (July 1932): 3–12.

"Lundberg." *Architectural and Engineering News* 9 (February 1967): 50.

"The Lush New Suburban Market." *Fortune,* November 1953, 116–31.

Lynes, Russell. "Highbrow, Lowbrow, Middlebrow." *Harper's,* February 1949, 19–29.

Macauley, David. "Walking in the Urban Environment: Pedestrian Practices and Peripatetic Politics." In *Transformations of Urban and Suburban Landscapes: Perspectives from Philosophy, Geography, and Architecture,* edited by Gary Backhaus and John Murungi, 193–226. Lanham, Md.: Lexington Books, 2002.

MacDonald, Austin F. "Parking Facilities Outside the Traffic Zone." *Annals of the American Academy of Political and Social Science* 133 (September 1927): 76–81.

Macdonald, Dwight. "Mass Cult and Midcult" (1960). In *Against the American Grain.* New York, Random House, 1962.

MacGregor, T. D. "The Shopping Center: Logical Adjunct in Group Housing in Suburban Areas." *Engineering News Record* 156 (August 12, 1948): 16–17.

"Machines for Selling." *Progressive Architecture* 28 (May 1947): 84–88.

Mackesey, Thomas, and Gilmore Clarke. "Planned Communities." Building Types Study No. 73. *Architectural Record* 93 (January 1943): 78–82.

"Main Street Malady Plagues Municipalities." *American City* 61 (September 1946): 7.

"Main Street, USA: Where Design and Dollars Interlock." *Architectural Forum* 70 (February 1939): 73–104.

Mallgrave, Harry Francis. *Modern Architectural Theory: A Historical Survey, 1673–1968.* New York: Cambridge University Press, 2005.

"A Mammoth New Shopping Center." *American City* 64 (February 1949): 78–79.

March, Walter F. "The Problem in Designing Modern Shop Fronts." *American Architect* 133 (June 20, 1928): 783–94.

Marchand, Roland. *Advertising the American Dream: Making Way for Modernity, 1920–1940.* Berkeley: University of California Press, 1985.

Marcus, Leonard. *The American Store Window.* New York: Whitney Library of Design, 1978.

"Markets in the Meadows: Bypassing the Downtown Trap." *Architectural Forum* 90 (March 1949): 114–24.

Marling, Karal Ann, ed. *Designing Disney's Theme Parks: The Architecture of Reassurance.* Montreal: Canadian Centre for Architecture, 1997.

Marquis, Donald E. "The Spanish Stores of Morgan, Walls & Clements." *Architectural Forum* 50 (June 1929): 901–16.

Marsh, Burton W. "Parking and Terminal Problems." *Traffic Engineering* 15 (February 1945): 158–63.

"Marshall Field's New Shopping Center." *Architectural Forum* 95 (December 1951): 188–90, 194–97.

Martin, Reinhold. *The Organizational Complex: Architecture, Media, and Corporate Space.* Cambridge: MIT Press, 2003.

———. "The Organizational Complex: Cybernetics, Space, Discourse." *Assemblage* 37 (December 1998): 103–27.

Marx, Leo. *The Machine in the Garden: Technology and the Pastoral Ideal in America.* New York: Oxford University Press, 1964.

Mason, John W. *The Cold War, 1945–91.* London: Routledge, 1996.

Masters, Dexter, and Katharine Way, eds. *One World or None: A Report to the Public on the Full Meaning of the Bomb.* New York: McGraw-Hill, 1946.

May, Elaine Tyler. *Homeward Bound: American Families in the Cold War Era.* New York: Basic Books, 1988.

"May Company Garage." *Architectural Digest* 6, no. 4 (1930): 78.

Mayer, Albert. "The Need for Synchronized Dispersal." *Bulletin of the Atomic Scientists* 8 (February 1952): 49–52.

———. "A New-Town Program." *Journal of the American Institute of Architects* 15 (January 1951): 5–10.

———. "A Technique for Planning Complete Communities, Part 1." *Architectural Forum* 66 (January 1937): 19–36.

———. "A Technique for Planning Complete Communities, Part 2." *Architectural Forum* 66 (February 1937): 126–46.

Mayer, Albert, and Julian Whittlesey. "Horse Sense Planning, 2." *Architectural Forum* 79 (December 1943): 77–82.

McAndrew, John, ed. *Guide to Modern Architecture: Northeast States.* New York: Museum of Modern Art, 1940.

McAndrew, John, and Elizabeth Kassler, eds. *What Is Modern Architecture?* New York: Museum of Modern Art, 1942.

McCallum, Ian. *Architecture USA.* New York: Reinhold, 1959.

McCrosky, Theodore T. "Decentralization and Parking." *Proceedings of the Institute of Traffic Engineers* (1941): 59–63.

McEnaney, Laura. *Civil Defense Begins at Home: Militarization Meets Everyday Life in the Fifties.* Princeton, N.J.: Princeton University Press, 2000.

McGavin, C. T. "Teamwork Can Solve the Downtown Parking Problem." *Urban Land* 9 (July–August 1950): 1, 3–8.

McKeever, J. Ross. *Shopping Centers: Principles and Practices.* Technical Bulletin No. 20. Washington, D.C.: Urban Land Institute, July 1953.

McLean, Joseph. "Project East River: Survival in the Atomic Age." *Bulletin of the Atomic Scientists* 9 (September 1953): 247–52, 288.

McNeil, Donald H. "Pittsburgh's Downtown Parking Problem." *Proceedings of the Institute of Traffic Engineers* (1946): 28–40.

Meikle, Jeffrey L. *Twentieth Century Limited: Industrial Design in America, 1925–1939.* Philadelphia: Temple University Press, 1979.

Mennel, Timothy. "Victor Gruen and the Construction of Cold War Utopias." *Journal of Planning History* 3 (May 2004): 116–50.

"Men's Shops." Planning Techniques No. 10. *Architectural Forum* 68 (June 1938): 497–506.

"Men's Store Remodeled for Modern Merchandising." *Architectural Record* 92 (October 1942): 60–61.

"Merchants Lose Downtown Blues." *New York Times,* February 27, 1955, F7.

Mickle, D. Grant. *Solutions to Local Parking Problems.* Reprinted from *Proceedings of 30th Annual Michigan Highway Conference.* Washington, D.C.: Automotive Safety Foundation, 1944.

———. "Traffic Planning." *Proceedings of the Institute of Traffic Engineers* (1937): 103.

Mikkelsen, Michael A. "Expansion of the *Architectural Record* for 1930." *Architectural Record* 66 (December 1929): 501–2.

———. "Two Problems of Architecture." *Architectural Record* 65 (January 1929): 65–66.

———. "A Word about the New Format." *Architectural Record* 63 (January 1928): 1–2.

Miller, Daniel. "Consumption as the Vanguard of History: A Polemic by Way of Introduction." In *Acknowledging Consumption: A Review of New Studies,* edited by Daniel Miller, 1–52. New York: Routledge, 1995.

Miller, J. Marshall. "Pasadena Tackles Its Parking Problem." *Traffic Engineering* 15 (August 1945): 441–45.

Miller, Michael B. *The Bon Marché: Bourgeois Culture and the Department Store, 1869–1920.* Princeton, N.J.: Princeton University Press, 1981.

"Millions of People Will Be Attracted by Store Fronts." *Architect and Engineer* 162 (July 1945): 30–31.

"Milliron Department Store." *Architect and Engineer* 179 (November 1949): 20–28.

Mills, C. Wright. *White Collar: The American Middle Classes.* New York: Oxford University Press, 1951.

Mitchell, Robert A. "What Can Be Done about Traffic Congestion: Traffic Engineering and Enforcement Methods." *Civil Engineering Magazine* 16 (June 1946): 260–62.

Mock, Elizabeth, ed. *Built in USA: 1932–1944.* New York: Museum of Modern Art, 1944.

"A Model Shopping Village in Texas." *Architectural Record* 70 (September 1931): 197–98.

"Modern Architectural Design for Sacramento." *Architect and Building News* 167 (December 1946): 12–13.

"Modernism and Tradition: On Modernism by Irving Morrow and on Tradition by Enrest E. Weihe." *Journal of the American Institute of Architects* 16 (September 1928): 459–64.

"Modernize Main Street." *Architectural Record* 78 (July 1935): 72.

"Modernize Main Street Competition Awards." *Architectural Record* 79 (October 1935): 205–66.

"Modern Theory Is Used in Beverly Mass to Design the North Shore Shopping Center." *American City* 62 (July 1947): 124–25.

Moholy-Nagy, Sibyl. "If Shopping Centers Must Be: Review of *Shopping Towns USA: The Planning of Shopping Centers,* by Victor Gruen and Larry Smith." *Progressive Architecture* 41 (September 1960): 204–5.

Monson, Donald. "City Planning in Project East River." *Bulletin of the Atomic Scientists* 9 (September 1953): 265–67.

Monteyne, David. *Fallout Shelter: Designing for Civil Defense in the Cold War.* Minneapolis: University of Minnesota Press, 2011.

Montgomery, Roger. "Improving the Design Process in Urban Renewal" (1965). In *Urban Renewal: The Record and the Controversy,* edited by James Q. Wilson, 454–87. Cambridge: MIT Press, 1966.

Moos, Stanislaus von. *Le Corbusier: Elements of a Synthesis.* Cambridge: MIT Press, 1979.

Moot, R. D. "Directional Traffic Engineering: Experience of Schenectady." *City Planning* 4 (July 1928): 214–19.

"More Cars, Superhighways Will Set Post-war Pattern for Commercial Building." *American Builder and Building Age,* June 1943, 40, 97.

Morris, Meaghan. "Things to Do with Shopping Centers." In *Too Soon Too Late: History in Popular Culture,* 64–92. Bloomington: Indiana University Press, 1998.

Morse, Margaret. "An Ontology of Everyday Distraction: The Freeway, the Mall, and Television." In *Logics of Television: Essays in Cultural Criticism,* edited by Patricia Mellenkamp, 193–221. Bloomington: Indiana University Press, 1990.

Mott, Seward H. "The Federal Housing Administration and Subdivision Planning." *Architectural Record* 79 (April 1936): 257–62.

Mott, Seward H., and Max Wehrly. *Shopping Centers: An Analysis.* Technical Bulletin No. 11. Washington, D.C.: Urban Land Institute, July 1949.

Mozingo, Louise A. *Pastoral Capitalism: A History of Suburban Corporate Landscapes.* Cambridge: MIT Press, 2011.

Mumford, Eric. *The CIAM Discourse on Urbanism, 1928–1960.* Cambridge: MIT Press, 2000.

Mumford, Eric, and Hashim Sarkis, eds. *Josep Lluís Sert: The Architect of Urban Design, 1953–1969.* New Haven, Conn.: Yale University Press, 2008.

Mumford, Lewis. "Death of the Monument." In *Circle: International Survey of Constructive Art,* edited by J. L. Martin, Ben Nicholson, and N. Gabo, 263–70. London: Faber & Faber, 1937.

———. "The Highway and the City." *Architectural Record* 123 (April 1958): 179–86.

———. "Machinery and the Modern Style" (1921). In *Roots of Contemporary American Architecture,* edited by Lewis Mumford, 196–200. New York: Reinhold, 1952.

———. "The Modern City." In *Forms and Functions of Twentieth-Century Architecture,* edited by Talbot Hamlin, vol. 4, 775–819. New York: Columbia University Press, 1952.

———. "Modern Design" (1934). In *Sidewalk Critic: Lewis Mumford's Writings on New York,* edited by Robert Wojtowicz, 121–23. New York: Princeton Architectural Press, 1998.

———. "Monumentalism, Symbol and Style." *Architectural Review* 105 (April 1949): 173–80.

———. "The Neighborhood and the Neighborhood Unit." *Town Planning Review* 24 (January 1954): 256–70.

———. "The Sky Line: A Walk through Rotterdam." *New Yorker,* October 12, 1957, 174, 177–84.

———. "The Sky Line: New Faces on the Avenue." *New Yorker,* September 9, 1939, 62–64.

———. "The Sky Line: Preview of the Past." *New Yorker,* October 11, 1952, 66, 69–76.

———. "The Sky Line: The Laundry Takes to Architecture." *New Yorker,* November 26, 1932, 36–37.

———. "The Sky Line: The Modern Restaurant." *New Yorker,* June 23, 1932, 50–52.

———. "The Sky Line: The New York Lunchroom." *New Yorker,* May 19, 1934, 44, 46, 48.

———. "The Sky Line: What Might Have Been." *New Yorker,* March 19, 1932, 71–72.

———. "Two Restaurants and a Theater" (1938). In *Sidewalk Critic: Lewis Mumford's Writings on New York,* edited by Robert Wojtowicz, 219–22. New York: Princeton Architectural Press, 1998.

Mumford, Lewis, et al. "The Planned Community." *Architectural Forum* 58 (April 1933): 253–74.

"Municipal Off-Street Parking Systems in the NY Metropolitan Region." *RPA Bulletin* (August 1950): 5.

"Municipal Programs for Off-Street Parking Facilities." *Urban Land* 8 (October 1949): 1, 3, 4.

"Munsey Park, Business Center." *American Architect* 144 (July 1934): 67–70.

Museum of Modern Art. *Look at Your Neighborhood.* New York: Museum of Modern Art, 1944.

———. *Two Cities: Planning in North and South America.* New York: Museum of Modern Art, 1947.

Myers, Howard. "Was the Architect of Tomorrow Here Yesterday?" *Journal of the American Institute of Architects* 2 (July 1944): 13–17.

National Conservation Bureau, Traffic Division. "Demonstrating to Retail Businessmen the Relative Unimportance of Curb-Parked Vehicles." In *Traffic Survey Manual.* New York: National Conservation Bureau, 1941.

———. "Street and Off-Street Parking Study." In *Traffic Survey Manual,* 95a–f. New York: National Conservation Bureau, 1941.

National Defense Committee. "Architecture and War." *Journal of the American Institute of Architects* 14 (October 1950): 147–48.

———. "Shortages Are Opportunities." *Journal of the American Institute of Architects* 15 (February 1951): 63.

———. "Short-Run, Long-Run." *Journal of the American Institute of Architects* 15 (January 1951): 3.

National Interregional Highway Committee. *Interregional Highways.* Washington, D.C.: National Interregional Highway Committee, 1944.

National Register of Historic Places. *Merchants Square and Resort Historic District.* Washington, D.C.: U.S. Department of the Interior, 2006.

National Resources Committee. *Our Cities: Their Role in the National Economy.* Washington, D.C.: Government Printing Office, 1937.

National Resources Committee, Research Committee on Urbanism. *Supplementary Report of the Urbanism Committee to the National Resources Committee.* Washington, D.C.: Government Printing Office, 1939.

National Retail Dry Goods Association. *Planning the Store of To-morrow.* New York: NRDGA, 1945.

National Security Resources Board, ed. *National Conference on Industrial Dispersion: Proceedings.* Washington, D.C.: National Security Resources Board, 1951.

National Security Resources Board, Civil Defense Office. *Survival under Atomic Attack.* Document 130. Washington, D.C.: National Security Resources Board, 1950.

"Neighborhood Shopping Centers." *Architectural Record* 71 (May 1932): 325–32.

Nelson, George. "Architects of Europe Today." *Pencil Points* 16–17 (1935–36): 1–4.

———. "Foreword." In Emrich Nicholson, *Contemporary Shops in the United States,* 5–9. New York: Architectural Book Publishing, 1945.

———. *Main Street: Now and Postwar.* Revere Pamphlet 13. New York: Revere Copper and Brass, 1943.

———. "Stylistic Trends in Contemporary Architecture." In *New Architecture and City Planning,* edited by Paul Zucker, 569–76. New York: Philosophical Library, 1944.

Nelson, Richard L., and Frederick T. Ashman. *Conservation and Rehabilitation of Major Shopping Districts.* Technical Bulletin No. 22. Washington, D.C.: Urban Land Institute, February 1954.

Neuhardt, Oskar. "Licht im Landhaus." *Moderne Welt: Almanache der Dame* (May 1934): 40.

Neutra, Richard. "Peace Can Gain from War's Forced Changes." *Pencil Points* 23 (November 1942): 28–41.

"New Arrangement for Bringing the Inside Outside." *Architectural Record* 101 (February 1947): 101–4.

"New Beverly Trading Center to Have Space for 3,00 Cars." *Christian Science Monitor,* October 29, 1946, 4.

"New Buildings for 194X." *Architectural Forum* 78 (May 1943): 69–151.

"New City within a City." *National Architect* 6 (May 1950): 8.

"New Elements in House Design." *Architectural Record* 66 (November 1929): 397–414.

"New Fifth Avenue Shop Fronts." *American Architect* 120 (August 17, 1921): 105–7.

Newhouse, Victoria. *Wallace K. Harrison, Architect.* New York: Rizzoli, 1989.

"The New House 194X." *Architectural Forum* 77 (September 1942): 65–152.

"A New Model Shopping Center Developed by Realtor Firm." *National Real Estate Journal* 39 (January 1938): 46–48.

"New Thinking on Shopping Centers." *Architectural Forum* 98 (March 1953): 122–45.

"New Towns." *Architectural Forum* 95 (November 1951): 137–42.

"New Towns for American Defense." *Journal of the American Institute of Architects* 15 (January 1951): 3–50.

"New York's Shopping District and the Shifting of Trade Centers." *American Architect* 110 (December 20, 1916): 386–88.

Nicholson, Emrich. *Contemporary Shops in the United States.* New York: Architectural Book Publishing, 1945.

"Nine Garages for City of Chicago Make a Frontal Attack on Parking Problem." *Architectural Record* 115 (March 1954): 152–58.

"1951 Design Survey." *Progressive Architecture* 32 (January 1951): 45–97.

1948 Store Modernization: Clinics and Forums. New York: Store Modernization Show, Inc., 1948.

Nolting, Orin, and Paul Oppermann. *The Parking Problem in Central Business Districts, with Special Reference to Off-Street Parking.* Chicago: Public Administration Service, 1938.

"No. 1: Shopping Center at River Oaks, Houston." In "Suburban Shopping Centers." *National Real Estate Journal* 39 (December 1938): 29.

North, Arthur T. "A Modern Store Alteration." *Architectural Forum* 50 (June 1929): 957–58.

Northern Westchester Joint Planning Program. "Appendix A: Economic Base of Mount Kisco." In *Northern Westchester: A Series of Planning Reports for Six Municipalities.* Westchester County, N.Y.: Northern Westchester Joint Planning Program, 1951.

"Northgate: Suburban Shopping Center." *Architect and Engineer* 183 (September 1950): 14–19.

"Northland's Sculpture in a Gallery, Models at the Jacques Seligmann Galleries." *Interiors* 114 (May 1955): 10.

Norton, C. McKim. "Report on Project East River." *Journal of the American Planning Association* 19 (June 1953): 87–94.

———. "Report on Project East River, Part II: Development of Standards." *Journal of the American Planning Association* 19 (September 1953): 159–67.

Norton, Peter D. *Fighting Traffic: The Dawn of the Motor Age in the American City.* Cambridge: MIT Press, 2008.

Nystrom, Paul H. *Bibliography of Retailing.* New York: Columbia University Press, 1928.

———. *Chain Stores,* rev. ed. Washington, D.C.: Chamber of Commerce of the United States, Domestic Distribution Department, 1930.

———. *Retail Selling and Store Management.* 1914. Reprint, New York: Appleton, 1925.

Oakes, Guy. *The Imaginary War: Civil Defense and American Cold War Culture.* New York: Oxford University Press, 1994.

Obituary for Frederick Kiesler. *Architectural Design* 36 (April 1966): 162.

Obituary for Frederick Kiesler. *Architectural Record* 139 (February 1966): 36.

Ockman, Joan. "Art, Soul of the Corporation: Patronage, Public Relations, and the Interrelations of Architecture and Art after World War II." *SOM Journal* 5 (2008): 170–86.

———. "Toward a Theory of Normative Architecture." In *Architecture of the Everyday,* edited by Steven Harris and Deborah Burke, 122–52. New York: Princeton Architectural Press, 1997.

"Offices Move to the Suburbs." *Business Week,* March 17, 1951, 79.

Official Guide Book of the New York World's Fair, 1939. New York: Exposition Publications, 1939.

Ogburn, William. "The Politics of Atomic Power." In *The Atomic Age Opens,* edited by Gerald Wendt and Donald Porter Geddes. Cleveland: World Publishing, 1945.

"Olympic Shopping Circle." *Los Angeles Times,* September 22, 1950, 18.

"100 Per Cent Locations." *Architectural Forum* 68 (June 1938): 524–25.

Oral History of Gordon Bunshaft. Interviewed by Betty J. Blum. Chicago Architects Oral History Project, Ernest R. Graham Study Center for Architectural Drawings, Department of Architecture. Chicago: Art Institute of Chicago, 1990.

Oral History of Norman J. Schlossman, rev ed. Interviewed by Betty J. Blum. Chicago Architects Oral History Project, Ernest R. Graham Study Center for Architectural Drawings, Department of Architecture. Chicago: Art Institute of Chicago, 2005.

Oral History of Richard Marsh Bennett. Interviewed by Betty J. Blum. Chicago Architects Oral History Project, Ernest R. Graham Study Center for Architectural Drawings, Department of Architecture. Chicago: Art Institute of Chicago, 1991.

Owings, N. A. "Economics of Department Store Planning." *Architectural Record* 101 (February 1947): 87–91.

Pai, Hyungmin. *The Portfolio and the Diagram: Architecture, Discourse, and Modernity in America.* Cambridge: MIT Press, 2002.

"Parfumerie et magasin a Vienne." *Architecture D'Aujourd'hui* (April 1938): 5–6, 19, 20.

Paris, W. Franklyn. "Modernism." *Pencil Points* (December 1930): 753–55.

Park, Robert E., Ernest W. Burgess, and Roderick D. McKenzie, eds. *The City.* 1925. Reprint, Chicago: Midway Reprint, 1984.

"Park and Shop." *American City* 52 (October 1937): 71–72.

"Parking Deck." *Progressive Architecture* 35 (September 1954): 104–5.

"Parking Deck, Smith, Hinchman & Grylls, Inc., Architects." *Architectural Record* 90 (October 1941): 68–69.

"Parking Facilities Relieve Traffic Congestion." *American City* 57 (January 1942): 79.

"Parking Garage: Series of Unit Buildings." *Architectural Record* 110 (September 1951): 168–71.

"Parking Lots for Mineola." *American City* 61 (September 1946): 145.

"Parking 1,000 Cars." *Architectural Forum* 69 (December 1938): 20.

"Parking Regulations and Reactions in Several Large Cities." *American City* 45 (March 1930): 122–23.

Parnes, Louis. *Bauten des Einzelhandels und ihre Verkehrs und Organisationsprobleme* [Buildings of the retail trade and their circulation and organizational problems]. Zurich: Orell Füssli, 1935.

———. "Intermediate Floors for Greater Efficiency in Storage and Service." Building Types Study No. 122. *Architectural Record* 101 (February 1947): 95–97.

———. *Planning Stores That Pay: Organic Design and Layout for Efficient Merchandising.* New York: F. W. Dodge, 1948.

Parsons, K. C. "Shaping the Regional City: 1950–1990: The Plans of Tracy Augur and Clarence Stein for Dispersing Federal Workers from Washington, D.C." In *Proceedings of the Third National Conference on American Planning History.* Hilliard, Ohio: Society for American City and Regional Planning History, 1990.

Pasmore, Victor. "Connection between Painting, Sculpture and Architecture." *Zodiac* 1 (1957): 63–71.

Passanti, Francesco. "The Skyscrapers of the Ville Contemporaine." *Assemblage* 4 (October 1987): 52–65.

Patricios, Nicholas. "The Neighborhood Concept: A Retrospective of Physical Design and Social Interaction." *Journal of Architectural and Planning Research* 19 (Spring 2002): 70–90.

Pawley, Frederic Arden, comp. "The Retail Store." *Architectural Record* 77 (July 1935): 50–58.

"Pedestrian Malls Tried in Toledo, Kalamazoo." *Architectural Forum* 111 (September 1959): 11.

Pells, Richard H. *The Liberal Mind in a Conservative Age: American Intellectuals in the 1940s and 1950s,* 2nd ed. Middletown, Conn.: Wesleyan University Press, 1989.

Perkins, G. Holmes. "New Towns for America's Peacetime Needs." *Journal of the American Institute of Architects* 15 (January 1951): 1–15.

———. "The Regional City." In *The Future of Cities and Urban Redevelopment,* edited by Coleman Woodbury, 26–43. Chicago: University of Chicago Press, 1953.

Perkins, G. Holmes, and Roger L. Creighton. "The Harvard Studies: The Design of New Towns." *Journal of the American Institute of Architects* 15 (January 1951): 20–35.

Perry, Clarence Arthur. *The Extension of Public Education: A Study in the Wider Use of School Buildings.* U.S. Bureau of Education Bulletin No. 28. Washington, D.C.: Government Printing Office, 1915.

———. "The Neighborhood Unit: A Scheme of Arrangement for the Family-Life Community." In *Neighborhood and Community Planning,* vol. 7 of *Regional Plan of New York and Its Environs,* 22–130. New York: Regional Plan of New York and Its Environs, 1929.

"Philadelphia Plans Again." *Architectural Forum* 87 (December 1947): 66–88.

"Philadelphia Slum Modernization by the Block." *Architectural Forum* 93 (October 1950): 172–75.

Phillips, Stephen. "Toward a Research Practice: Frederick Kiesler's Design-Correlation Laboratory." *Grey Room* 38 (Winter 2010): 90–120.

Phillips, T. Glenn. "The Traffic Problems in Detroit and How They Are Met." *Annals of the American Academy of Political and Social Science* 116 (November 1924): 241–43.

"Pittsburgh in Progress: Towards a Master Plan." *Progressive Architecture* 28 (June 1947): 67–72.

Pittsburgh Plate Glass Company. *There Is a New Trend in Store Design.* Pittsburgh: Pittsburgh Plate Glass Company, 1945.

"Planned Neighborhoods for 194X." *Architectural Forum* 79 (October 1943): 65–142.

"Planned Neighborhoods for 194X." *Architectural Forum* 80 (April 1944): 71–150.

"Planning and Management of Nichols Shopping Centers." *National Real Estate Journal* 40 (February 1939).

"Planning for Economy and Flexibility: Edward D. Stone, J. Stanley Sharp and Cope B. Walbridge." In "The New House 194X." *Architectural Forum* 77 (September 1942): 117–19.

"Planning for Parking in Buffalo." *American City* 55 (June 1940): 67.

"Planning Techniques No. 2: Shoe Stores." *Architectural Forum* 66 (March 1937): 185–96.

"Planning with You." *Architectural Forum* 79 (August 1943): 65–81.

"Planning with You." *Architectural Forum* 80 (May 1944): 69–70.

Platt, S. N. "Sheldon Cheney: Crusader for Modernism." *Archives of American Art Journal* 25 (1985): 11–17.

Plunz, Richard. *A History of Housing in New York City: Dwelling Type and Social Change in the American Metropolis.* 1982. Reprint, New York: Columbia University Press, 1990.

Pommer, Richard. "'More a Necropolis than a Metropolis': Ludwig Hilberseimer's High Rise City and Modern City Planning." In Richard Pommer, David Spaeth, and Kevin Harrington, *In the Shadow of Mies: Ludwig Hilberseimer, Architect, Educator, and Urban Planner,* 16–53. Chicago: Art Institute of Chicago, 1988.

Pommer, Richard, David Spaeth, and Kevin Harrington. *In the Shadow of Mies: Ludwig Hilberseimer, Architect, Educator, and Urban Planner.* Chicago: Art Institute of Chicago, 1988.

Ponte, Alessandra. "Professional Pastoral: The Writing on the Lawn, 1850–1950." In Georges Teyssot, ed., *The American Lawn,* 88–115. New York: Princeton Architectural Press, 1999.

"Postman's Makes the Most of a Narrow Frontage." *Architectural Record* 87 (March 1940): 57–59.

"Post-war Pattern." *Architectural Forum* 74 (May 1941): 309–10.

"Preview of the War We Do Not Want." *Collier's,* October 27, 1951.

Priaulx, Arthur W. "Northgate: Suburban Shopping Center." *Architect and Engineer* 183 (September 1950): 14–19.

"Productive Home Architectural Competition." *Pencil Points* 20 (May 1939): 307–14.

"Professor Kocher Joins the *Architectural Record* Staff." *Architectural Record* 62 (August 1927): 167.

"Profile." *Michigan Society of Architects Bulletin,* March 14, 1939, 101.

Progressive Grocer. *Better Grocery Stores.* New York: Progressive Grocer, n.d.

"Proposed Back Bay Center Development." *Progressive Architecture* 35 (January 1954): 73–85.

"Pros and Cons of Architecture for Civil Defense." *Progressive Architecture* 32 (September 1951): 63–80.

"Providing Parking Spaces in Downtown Business Districts." *American City* 60 (June 1945): 135.

Public Administration Clearing House. "Public Parking Facilities." *Traffic Engineering* 15 (December 1945): 96.

"Radburn: A Suburban Town Planned for the Motor Age." *Architecture* 60 (December 1929): 317–24.

Radway, Janice A. "On the Gender of the Middlebrow Consumer and the Threat of the Culturally Fraudulent Female." *South Atlantic Quarterly* 93 (Fall 1994): 871–94.

"The Ramp Garage." *American Architect and the Architectural Review* 123 (April 25, 1923): 375–82.

Randall, Gregory C. *America's Original GI Town: Park Forest.* Baltimore: Johns Hopkins University Press, 2000.

"Recent Work by Gruenbaum, Krummeck and Auer." *Architectural Forum* 75 (September 1941): 191–200.

"Recessed Shopfronts." *Architectural Forum* 43 (August 1925): 97–112.

Redstone, Louis. *Art in Architecture.* New York: McGraw-Hill, 1968.

———. *New Dimensions in Shopping Centers and Stores.* New York: McGraw-Hill, 1973.

Reed, Peter. "Philadelphia Urban Design." In *Louis I. Kahn: In the Realm of Architecture,* edited by David B. Brownlee and David G. De Long, 304–13. New York: Rizzoli, 1991.

Reeder, Earl. "City Planning and Traffic Surveys." *City Planning* 3 (1927): 194–200.

"Regal Shoes." *Architectural Forum* 65 (October 1936): 316.

Regional Plan Association. "Parking Facilities Found Inadequate in Communities of the Region." *Information Bulletin* 30 (May 18, 1936).

Reid, Kenneth. "The Modernist from Wainscott: Morris Ketchum, Jr." *Pencil Points/Progressive Architecture* 25 (August 1944): 65–66.

———. "New Beginnings." *Pencil Points* 23 (May 1942): 242–43.

———. "To the Readers of *Pencil Points.*" *Pencil Points* 21 (June 1940): 35.

———. "Walter Dorwin Teague." *Pencil Points* 18 (September 1937): 555.

"Remodeling Main Street, Niles Michigan." *Architectural Forum* 81 (October 1944): 100–112.

"Replanning in Rye, N.Y." *Planning and Civic Comment* 12 (July 1946): 19.

"Retailers' Problem: Reviving a Sick Old 'Downtown.'" *Business Week,* January 15, 1955, 42–46.

"Retail Stores Reference Study." *Architectural Record* 83 (February 1938): 101–34.

Richards, Charles R. *Art in Industry.* New York: Macmillan, 1929.

Riesman, David. *The Lonely Crowd: A Study of the Changing American Character.* New Haven, Conn.: Yale University Press, 1950.

———. "The Suburban Sadness." In *The Suburban Community,* edited by William M. Dobriner, 375–401. New York: Putnam, 1958.

Riley, Terence, and Edward Eigen. "Between the Museum and the Marketplace: Selling Good Design." In *The Museum of Modern Art at Mid-century: At Home and Abroad,* 150–75. New York: Museum of Modern Art, 1994.

Robbins, George W., and L. Deming Tilton, eds. *Los Angeles: Preface to a Master Plan.* Los Angles: Pacific Southwest Academy, 1941.

Robertson, Kent A. "The Status of the Pedestrian Mall in American Downtowns." *Urban Affairs Review* 26 (December 1990): 250–73.

Robinson, Charles Mulford. *Modern Civic Art; Or, The City Made Beautiful,* 4th ed. New York: Arno Press, 1970.

Rodgers, Daniel T. *Atlantic Crossings: Social Politics in a Progressive Age.* Cambridge, Mass.: Harvard University Press, 1998.

Rogers, Allan H. "Model Off-Street Parking Provided, Garden City, N.Y." *American City* 53 (September 1938): 105.

———. "Municipal Parking Lots Set Pattern for Business Districts of Future." *Public Management* 20 (September 1938): 278–79.

———. "A New Solution to the Parking Problem." *Public Works* 69 (July 1938): 20–22.

"Roosevelt Field Shopping Center." *Progressive Architecture* 36 (September 1955): 90–97.

Rosa, Joseph. "A. Lawrence Kocher, Albert Frey: The Aluminaire House." *Assemblage* 11 (April 1990): 58–69.

Rose, Kenneth D. *One Nation Underground: The Fallout Shelter in American Culture.* New York: New York University Press, 2001.

Rose, Lisle A. *The Cold War Comes to Main Street: America in 1950.* Lawrence: University Press of Kansas, 1999.

Rose, Mark H. *Interstate: Express Highway Politics, 1939–1989.* Knoxville: University of Tennessee Press, 1990.

Ross, David H. "Magnin's New Store, San Mateo." *Architect and Engineer* 182 (August 1950): 16–20.

Roth, Leland M. *A Concise History of American Architecture.* New York: Harper & Row, 1979.

Rowe, Colin. "Introduction." In Museum of Modern Art, *Five Architects: Eisenman, Graves, Gwathmey, Hejduk, Meier.* New York: Oxford University Press, 1975.

Rowe, Peter. *Making a Middle Landscape.* Cambridge: MIT Press, 1991.

Rubenstein, Harvey M. *Central City Malls.* New York: John Wiley, 1978.

Rubin, Joan Shelley. *The Making of Middlebrow Culture.* Chapel Hill: University of North Carolina Press, 1992.

Rudofsky, Bernard. *Streets for People: A Primer for Americans.* Garden City, N.Y.: Doubleday, 1969.

"Rural Insurance Plant: Connecticut General Life Insurance Company, Bloomfield, Connecticut." *Architectural Forum* 101 (September 1954): 104–7.

Rye, New York. *On Our Way: The Rye Development Program.* New York: City of Rye, 1946.

Saarinen, Aline B. "Art as Architectural Decoration." *Architectural Forum* 100 (June 1954): 133–35.

Saarinen, Eliel. *The City: Its Growth, Its Decay, Its Future.* New York: Reinhold, 1943.

"Sacramento, a Model for Small City Redevelopment." *Architectural Forum* 98 (June 1954): 153–59.

"Sacramento, California: The Joseph Magnin Store." *Architectural Record* 100 (December 1946): 140.

"Sacramento: Joseph Magnin New Store." *Architect and Engineer* 167 (December 1946): 12–13.

Safran, Yehuda, ed. *Frederick Kiesler, 1890–1965.* London: Architectural Association, 1989.

Samson, M. David. "'Unser Newyorker Mitarbeiter': Lewis Mumford, Walter Curt Behrendt, and the Modern Movement in Germany." *Journal of the Society of Architectural Historians* 55 (June 1996): 126–39.

Sanders, S. E., and A. J. Rabuck. *New City Patterns: The Analysis of and a Technique for Urban Reintegration.* New York: Reinhold, 1946.

"San Francisco's Stonestown Shopping Center." *National Architect* 7 (February 1951): 4.

Sasagawa, K. William. "Technique for Neighborhood Planning." *American City* 63 (August 1948): 112–13.

"A Satellite Town for the Detroit Area." *Architectural Forum* 79 (October 1943): 91–97.

Scalzo, Julia. "All a Matter of Taste: The Problem of Victorian and Edwardian Shop Fronts." *Journal of the Society of Architectural Historians* 68 (March 2009): 52–73.

Schwartz, Frederick J. *The Werkbund: Design Theory and Mass Culture before the First World War.* New Haven, Conn.: Yale University Press, 1996.

Scott, Allen J., and Edward W. Soja, eds. *The City: Los Angeles and Urban Theory at the End of the Twentieth Century.* Berkeley: University of California Press, 1996.

Scott, Felicity. "Allegories of Nomadism and Dwelling." In *Anxious Modernisms: Experimentation in Postwar Architectural Culture,* edited by Sarah Williams Goldhagen and Réjean Legault, 215–37. Cambridge: MIT Press, 2000.

Scott, Mel. *American City Planning since 1890.* Berkeley: University of California Press, 1969.

———. *Cities Are for People: The Los Angeles Region Plans for Living.* Designed by Alvin Lustig, with drawings by Bob Holdeman. Los Angeles: Pacific Southwest Academy, 1942.

———. *Metropolitan Los Angeles: One Community.* Designed by Alvin Lustig. Los Angeles: Haynes Foundation, 1949.

Scully, Vincent. *American Architecture and Urbanism.* New York: Praeger, 1969.

"Selling Architecture." *Pencil Points* 5 (August 1924): 33.

Sert, José Luis. *Can Our Cities Survive? An ABC of Urban Problems, Their Analysis, Their Solutions.* Cambridge, Mass.: Harvard University Press, 1942.

———. "Centres of Community Life." In *The Heart of the City: Towards the Humanisation of Urban Life,* edited by J. Tyrwhitt, J. L. Sert, and E. N. Rogers, 3–16. New York: Pellegrini and Cudahy, 1952.

———. "Cidade dos Motores, Brasil." *Pencil Points* 27 (September 1946): 52–73.

———. "The Human Scale in City Planning." In *New Architecture and City Planning,* edited by Paul Zucker, 392–410. New York: Philosophical Library, 1944.

———. "A Short Outline of the Core." In *The Heart of the City: Towards the Humanisation of Urban Life,* edited by J. Tyrwhitt, J. L. Sert, and E. N. Rogers. New York: Pellegrini and Cudahy, 1952.

"Service Men's Centers: Harrison, Fouilhoux & Abramovitz, Architects, Morris Ketchum Jr., Associate." *Architectural Forum* 77 (December 1942): 38–43.

Sexton, R. W. *American Commercial Buildings of Today.* New York: Architectural Book Publishing, 1928.

Shanken, Andrew. "Between Brotherhood and Bureaucracy: Joseph Hudnut, Louis I. Kahn, and the American Society of Planners and Architects." *Planning Perspectives* 20 (April 2005): 147–75.

———. "From the Gospel of Efficiency to Modernism: A History of Sweet's Catalogue, 1906–1947." *Design Issues* 21 (Spring 2005): 28–47.

———. *194X: Architecture, Planning, and Consumer Culture on the American Home Front.* Minneapolis: University of Minnesota Press, 2009.

Sharp, Thomas. *Town Planning.* New York: Penguin, 1940.

Sheldon, Roy, and Egmont Arens. *Consumer Engineering: A New Technique for Prosperity.* New York: Harper & Brothers, 1932.

Shepley, Henry R. "Park Square Garage, Boston, Ralph Doane, Architect." *Federal Architect* 7 (October 1936): 18.

Sheumaker, Helen, and Shirley Teresa Wajda, eds. *Material Culture in America: Understanding Everyday Life.* Santa Barbara, Calif.: ABC-CLIO, 2008.

"Shop and Store Reference Number." *Architectural Forum* 40 (June 1924).

"Shop Fronts." *American Architect* 110 (December 20, 1916): 383–85.

"Shoppers' World." *Architectural Forum* 95 (December 1951): 180–84.

"Shoppers' World at Framingham Applies New Ideas." *Architectural Record* 110 (November 1951): 12–13.

"Shopping Center." *Architectural Forum* 85 (August 1946): 76–79.

"Shopping Center." *Architectural Forum* 86 (June 1947): 84–93.

"The Shopping Center Back Where It Started." *Business Week,* July 17, 1954, 106–8.

"Shopping Center Designed to Attract Shoppers." *American City* 60 (August 1945): 87.

"Shopping Center for a Satellite Town near Olympia Fields, Illinois." *American City* 62 (January 1947).

"Shopping Center Round Up." *Chain Store Age* (July 1950).

"Shopping Centers." *Architectural Forum* 100 (June 1954): 102–19.

"Shopping Centers." Building Types Study No. 203. *Architectural Record* 114 (October 1953): 178–205.

"Shopping Centers: A Neighborhood Necessity." *Urban Land* 3 (October/November 1944): 5–7.

"Shopping Centers: A New Building Type." *Progressive Architecture* 29 (June 1952).

"Shopping Centers for War Workers." *Architectural Record* 92 (July 1942): 40–44.

"Shopping Centers of Tomorrow Exhibition, prepared by V. Gruen." *Arts Digest,* November 15, 1954, 28.

"Shopping Facilities in Wartime." *Architectural Record* 92 (October 1942): 62–78.

"Shopping Near a Defense Center." *Progressive Architecture* 32 (December 1951): 15.

Shurcliff, Sidney N. "Shoppers' World: The Design and Construction of a Retail Shopping Center." *Landscape Architecture* 42 (July 1952): 145–51.

Silver, Christopher. "Neighborhood Planning in Historical Perspective." *Journal of the American Planning Association* 51 (Spring 1985): 161–74.

Silver, Janet G., ed. *Design for Better Living: The Architecture of Richard Marsh Bennett, 1937–1973.* New York: Mercantile, 1985.

Simpson, Hawley S. "Downtown Storage Garages." *Annals of the American Academy of Political and Social Science* 133 (September 1927): 82–90.

Siry, Joseph. *Carson Pirie Scott: Louis Sullivan and the Chicago Department Store.* Chicago: University of Chicago Press, 1988.

"Skillful Enlargement." *House & Garden,* September 1939, 6–7.

Skinner, Alton. "Parking Lots—and 30-Minute Meters to Encourage Their Use." *American City* 55 (November 1940): 51–52.

"Skyscraper Garages Offer Solution to City Parking Problem." *Dun's International Review* 54 (November 1929): 38–40.

"A Small Stores Development." *Bulletin of the Beaux-Arts Institute of Design* 19 (1942–43): 22–28.

Smiley, David. "Making the Modified Modern." *Perspecta* 32 (Spring 2001): 39–54.

———, ed. *Sprawl and Public Space: Redressing the Mall.* New York: Princeton Architectural Press, 2003.

Smith, Terry. *Making the Modern: Industry, Art, and Design in America.* Chicago: University of Chicago Press, 1993.

Smith, Whitney R. "No Cars on Main Street." *Better Homes and Gardens,* January 1945, 20, 21, 67–69.

Smith, Wilbur S. "Business Aids Traffic Problems." *Traffic Quarterly* 8 (January 1954): 23–32.

Smith, Wilbur S., and Charles S. LeCraw. *Parking.* Saugatuck, Conn.: Eno Foundation, December 1946.

Snaith, William T. "How Retailing Principles Affect Design" (1959). In *Stores and Shopping Centers,* edited by James Hornbeck, 2–10. New York: McGraw-Hill, 1962.

———. "Serving the Suburban Customer through Branch Stores." In National Retail Dry Goods Association, *Planning the Store of To-morrow,* 102–7. New York: NRDGA, 1945.

Solnit, Rebecca. *Wanderlust: A History of Walking.* New York: Viking Press, 2000.

Solomonson, Katherine. *The Chicago Tribune Tower Competition: Skyscraper Design and Cultural Change in the 1920s.* New York: Cambridge University Press, 2001.

Somes, Dana. "Recent Shop Fronts in New England." *Architectural Forum* 40 (June 1924): 249–52.

"Something New in Stores: Grand Entrance through the Roof." *Architectural Forum* 90 (June 1949): 104–11.

Sorkin, Michael, ed. *Variations on a Theme Park: The New American City and the End of Public Space.* New York: Hill and Wang, 1992.

"Southdale: It's Always Spring in This Roofed Market Square in the Suburbs." *Interiors* 116 (May 1957): 96–101.

"Southdale Shopping Center." *Architectural Forum* 106 (April 1957).

"Special Design Award: City Planning, Redevelopment Study, Sacramento." *Progressive Architecture* 36 (January 1955): 104–7.

Spigel, Lynn. *Make Room for TV: Television and the Family Ideal in Postwar America.* Chicago: University of Chicago Press, 1992.

"The Splashiest Shopping Center in the U.S." *Life,* December 10, 1956, 61–62, 65–66.

Staeheli, Lynn A., and Don Mitchell. "USA's Destiny? Regulating Space and Creating Community in American Shopping Malls." *Urban Studies* 43 (May 2006): 977–92.

"A Station for a Shopping Center, Henry S. Churchill, Architect." Building Types Study No. 86. *Architectural Record* 95 (February 1944): 76–77.

Stein, Clarence S. "City Patterns . . . Past and Future." *New Pencil Points* 23 (June 1942): 52–53.

————. *Toward New Towns for America.* Cambridge: MIT Press, 1957.

Stein, Clarence S., and Catherine Bauer. "Store Buildings and Neighborhood Shopping Centers." *Architectural Record* 75 (February 1934): 175–87.

Steinbaugh, V. B. "Underground Parking for Detroit." *American City* 61 (February 1946): 112, 115

Stephan, Regina, ed. *Erich Mendelsohn: Architect, 1887–1953.* New York: Monacelli Press, 1999.

Stern, Robert A. M. "The Thirties." *Journal of the Society of Architectural Historians* 24 (March 1965): 6–10.

Stern, Robert A. M., Gregory Gilmartin, and Thomas Mellins. *New York 1930: Architecture and Urbanism between the Two World Wars.* New York: Rizzoli, 1987.

Sternlieb, George, and James W. Hughes, eds. *Shopping Centers, U.S.A.* New Brunswick, N.J.: Rutgers University, Center for Urban Policy Research, 1981.

Stetson, Damon. "From Municipal Lots to Complete Parking Program." *American City* 56 (August 1941): 95, 97.

Stiverson, Cynthia Zignego. *Architecture and the Decorative Arts: A Catalogue of the A. Lawrence Kocher Collection of Books at the Colonial Williamsburg Foundation.* West Cornwall, Conn.: Locust Hill Press, 1989.

Stoever, F. Wallace. "No. 3: 'Park and Shop' Developments, Washington, D.C." In "Suburban Shopping Centers." *National Real Estate Journal* 39 (December 1938): 32–33.

Stone, Edward Durell. *Evolution of an Architect.* New York: Horizon, 1962.

Stonorov, Oscar, and Louis I. Kahn. *Why City Planning Is Your Responsibility.* New York: Revere Copper and Brass, 1943.

————. *You and Your Neighborhood: A Primer for Neighborhood Planning.* New York: Revere Copper and Brass, 1944.

"Store Block." *Architectural Forum* 73 (October 1940): 294–95.

"Store Building for Sears." *Architectural Forum* 72 (February 1940): 70–76.

"Store Buildings." Technical News and Research. *Architectural Record* 65 (June 1929): 583–606.

"Store Designers Don't Suffer from Tradition Fixations—Thank God." *Pencil Points/Progressive Architecture* 25 (August 1944): 40–41.

"Store Fronts of Tomorrow." *New Pencil Points* 23 (October 1942): 33–36.

"Store Fronts of Tomorrow." *New Pencil Points* 24 (February 1943): 29–47.

"Store Modernizations." *Progressive Architecture* 29 (October 1948): 81–88.

"Store-on-Stilts." *Architectural Forum* 92 (February 1950): 102–3.

"Stores." *Architectural Forum* 71 (December 1939): 427–45.

"Stores in Urban and Suburban Shopping Centers." *Architectural Record* 146 (July 1969): 135–50.

"Stores of the Future." *New Pencil Points* 25 (August 1944): 42–62.

Stowell, Kenneth Kingsley. *Modernizing Buildings for Profit.* New York: Prentice Hall, 1935.

Strasser, Susan. *Satisfaction Guaranteed: The Making of the American Mass Market.* Washington, D.C.: Smithsonian Books, 1989.

Striner, Richard. "Art Deco: Polemics and Synthesis." *Winterthur Portfolio* 25 (Spring 1990): 21–34.

"Suburban Retail Districts." *Architectural Forum* 93 (August 1950): 106–22.

"Suburban Shopping Centers." *National Real Estate Journal* 39 (December 1938).

Suga, Yasuko. "Modernism, Commercialism and Display Design in Britain: The Reimann School and Studios of Industrial and Commercial Art." *Journal of Design History* 19 (Summer 2006): 137–54.

Sukert, Lancelot. "The Retail Shop: An Opportunity for Architect and Merchant." *American Architect* 143 (November 1933): 25–34.

"Sunlight Towers." *Architectural Record* 65 (March 1929): 307–10.

"Sunlight Towers, an Apartment House." *American Architect* 135 (May 5, 1929): 563.

"Superblock versus Gridiron." *Architectural Forum* 73 (July 1940): 66–67.

"Super-servicenter for Jersey City Shopping Center." *Architectural Record* 76 (December 1934): 454.

"Swimming Pools: Standards for Design and Construction." *Architectural Record* 65 (January 1929): 68–87.

"Symphony in Stores: Two Inspirations within the Reach of Many." *Store of Greater New York,* August 1939.

Tanner, Ogden. "Closed to Traffic." *Architectural Forum* 110 (February 1959): 88–93.

Taylor, A. D. "Kingsford Heights." *Pencil Points* 23 (October 1942): 58–66.

Taylor, Don. "Hollywood Tackles the Parking Problem." *Architectural Record* 88 (December 1940): 45–48.

Teaford, Jon C. *The Rough Road to Renaissance: Urban Revitalization in America, 1940–1985.* Baltimore: Johns Hopkins University Press, 1990.

"A Technique for Accelerated Planning." *New Pencil Points* 24 (August 1943): 31–50.

Teegan, Otto. "Here Stands the B.A.I.D." *Journal of the American Institute of Architects* 2 (October 1944): 191–96.

Telchin, Charles, and Francis X. Gina. "AR Time Saver Standards: Planning Units for Retail Stores." *Architectural Record* 87 (April 1940): 107–9.

———. "Retail Fronts, Comparative Details." *Pencil Points* 20 (August 1939): 508.

Teller, Edward, J. Marshak, and L. R. Klein. "Dispersal of Cities and Industries." *Bulletin of the Atomic Scientists* 2 (April 15, 1946).

"Ten Miles High." *Architectural Forum* 124 (January–February 1966): 30–31.

Teyssot, Georges. "Public Space and the Phantom Agora." *Via Architectura* 2 (1998).

"Three Small Shops." *Architectural Record* 91 (March 1942): 47–49.

Tobin, Kathleen. "The Reduction of Urban Vulnerability: Revisiting 1950s American Suburbanization as Civil Defense." *Cold War History* 2 (January 2002): 1–32.

Tomlan, Michael. "Architectural Press, U.S." In *Encyclopedia of Architecture: Design, Engineering and Construction,* edited by John Wilkes, vol. 1, 266–94. New York: John Wiley, 1988.

"To Park or Not to Park." *American City* 35 (October 1926): 461–64.

"To Prevent the Utter Destruction of Urban Civilization." *American City* 61 (February 1946): 5.

"To Relieve Traffic Congestion in New York." *American Architect* 119 (March 30, 1921): 395.

"The Town of Willow Run." *Architectural Forum* 78 (March 1943): 37–54.

"Traffic and Parking in Beverly Hills." *Architectural Record* 104 (December 1948): 94–100.

"Traffic Congestion, Parking Facilities and Retail Business." *American City* 35 (June 1926): 664–67.

"Traffic Jams Business Out." *Architectural Forum* 72 (January 1940): 64–65.

"Traveling Exhibition Brings Design to the Public." *Progressive Architecture* 35 (July 1954): 74–77.

"Triangular Site Suggests Circular Mall." *Architectural Record* 106 (August 1949): 129.

"Triple-Threat Store." *Architectural Forum* 96 (May 1952): 124–26.

Troedsson, Carl Birger. "The City-Town: A Rehabilitation Program Based on a City as It Is and as It Could Be." *California Arts & Architecture,* October 1942, 36–37, 50.

———. "Plan for Pedestrians." *Architectural Forum* 76 (March 1942): 10.

Trowbridge, Edwin. "New Shop Fronts, 1." *Brickbuilder* 16 (August 1907): 136–40.

———. "New Shop Fronts, 2." *Brickbuilder* 16 (September 1907): 158–62.

"Trust Rides Shopping Center Boom." *Business Week,* July 1950, 80–84.

Tuttle, Bloodgood. "To Stimulate Renovization." *Pencil Points* 17 (January 1936): 41–43.

"Typical Downtown Transformed." *Architectural Forum* 104 (May 1956): 146–55.

Tyrwhitt, Jaqueline. "Cores within the Urban Constellation." In *The Heart of the City: Towards the Humanisation of Urban Life,* edited by J. Tyrwhitt, J. L. Sert, and E. N. Rogers. New York: Pellegrini and Cudahy, 1952.

———. "The Size and Spacing of Urban Communities." *Journal of the American Institute of Planners* 15 (Summer 1949): 10–17.

Uhlfelder, Eric, ed. *Origins of Modern Architecture: Selected Essays from "Architectural Record."* Mineola, N.Y.: Dover, 1998.

Uhlig, Klaus. *Pedestrian Areas: From Malls to Complete Networks.* New York: Architectural Book Publishing, 1979.

"Under One Roof." *Architectural Record* 68 (December 1930): 452–54.

Upton, Dell. *Architecture in the United States.* New York: Oxford University Press, 1998.

"Urban Design." *Progressive Architecture* 37 (August 1956): 97–127.

Urban Land Institute. *Automobile Parking in Central Business Districts.* Technical Bulletin No. 6. Washington, D.C.: Urban Land Institute, July 1946.

"Urban Traffic Forum." *Architectural Forum* 98 (February 1953): 110–19, 164–84.

U.S. Census Bureau. "Transportation Indicators for Motor Vehicles and Airlines: 1900 to 2001." In *Statistical Abstract of the United States: 2003.* Washington, D.C.: U.S. Census Bureau, 2003.

U.S. Department of Commerce. *Retail Store Design Problems.* Washington, D.C.: U.S. Department of Commerce, 1926.

U.S. Department of Commerce, Area Development Division. *Industrial Dispersion Guidebook for Communities: A Technique for More Secure Location of New Defense-Supporting Plants.* Domestic Commerce Series No. 31. Washington, D.C.: Government Printing Office, 1952.

U.S. Federal Housing Administration. *Planning Neighborhoods for Small Houses.* Technical Bulletin No. 5. Washington, D.C.: U.S. FHA, 1936.

———. *Planning Profitable Neighborhoods.* Technical Bulletin No. 7. Washington, D.C.: U.S. FHA, 1938.

"Victor Gruen, Obituary." *Journal of the American Institute of Architects* 69 (March 1980): 110.

Vogelgesang, Shepard. "Architecture and Trade Marks." *Architectural Forum* 50 (June 1929): 897–900.

Wachs, Martin, and Margaret Crawford, eds. *The Car and the City: The Automobile, the Built Environment, and Daily Urban Life.* Ann Arbor: University of Michigan Press, 1992.

Walker, Ralph. "Alert." *Journal of the American Institute of Architects* 14 (August 1950): 51–52.

———. "Architecture of Today: An American Architect's View." *Creative Art* 5 (July 1929): 460–65.

Wall, Alex. *Victor Gruen: From Urban Shop to New City.* Barcelona: Actar, 2005.

Wall, Henry V. "Unique Community Planning Follows Expansion of Defense Industries." *American City* 57 (January 1942): 55–56.

"Wallach's New York." *Architectural Forum* 65 (October 1936): 318.

Walters, Henry L. "Modern Store Fronts." *Architectural Review* 14 (June 1907): 153–61.

Watkin, William W. "The Advent of the New Manner in America." *Pencil Points* 12 (July 1931).

Weinberg, Robert C. "For Better Places to Park." *American City* 52 (June 1937): 99–101.

———. "The Spirit of a City." *Journal of the American Institute of Planners* 19 (Winter 1953): 45–49.

Weiss, Marc A. "The Origins and Legacy of Urban Renewal." In *Urban and Regional Planning in an Age of Austerity,* edited by Pierre Clavel, John Forester, and William W. Goldsmith, 53–79. New York, Pergamon, 1980.

———. *The Rise of the Community Builders: The American Real Estate Industry and Urban Land Planning.* New York: Columbia University Press, 1987.

Welch, Kenneth C. "The Apparel Store." *Architectural Record* 77 (July 1935): 62–63.

———. "Convenience vs. Shopping Goods." *Women's Wear Daily,* December 26, 1946, 82–83.

———. "The Department Store." *Architectural Record* 81 (January 1937): 3–12.

———. "Department Stores." In *Forms and Functions of Twentieth-Century Architecture,* edited by Talbot Hamlin, vol. 4, 36–83. New York: Columbia University Press, 1952.

———. *The Effect of Retail Distribution on the City Plan.* AIA Great Lakes District Seminar, October 3, 1947. N.p.: February 24, 1948.

———. "The Logic of Layout." *Architectural Forum* 58 (May 1933): 346–52.

———. "Modernizing for Wartime Efficiency." *Apparel Arts* (March 1942).

———. "Modern Shopping Centers." *American Planning and Civic Association Annual* (1949): 126–30.

———. "Neighborhood Shopping Centers and Parking Problems." *Planning and Civic Comment* 12 (October 1946): 17.

———. "New Concepts in Store Lighting." *Architectural Record* 100 (August 1946): 117–20.

———. "Plan Fundamentals for the Men's Shop." *Architectural Record* 80 (August 1936): 154.

———. "Planning a Small Men's Shop." *Architectural Record* 76 (September 1934): 183–87.

———. "Reflection Factors in Store Windows." *Architectural Record* 100 (August 1946): 107–10.

———. "Regional Shopping Centers." Building Types Study No. 172. *Architectural Record* 109 (March 1951): 121–36.

———. "Self-Selection Is Sensible." *Apparel Arts* (October 1943).

———. "Urban Planning." *Michigan Society of Architects Weekly Bulletin* 18 (April 18, 1944): 67, 69, 71, 74.

————. "Where Are Department Stores Going?" *Architectural Record* 96 (November 1944): 91–96.

Welch, Kenneth C., and Bruno Funaro. "Traffic Problems in Shopping Centers." *Architectural Record* 112 (October 1952): 223–28.

Wendt, Gerald, and Donald Porter Geddes, eds. *The Atomic Age Opens.* Cleveland: World Publishing, 1945.

Wendt, Lloyd, and Herman Kogan. *Give the Lady What She Wants! The Story of Marshall Field Company.* Chicago: Rand McNally, 1952.

"What Housing for Willow Run?" *Architectural Record* 92 (September 1942): 51–54.

"What Makes a Mall Plan Practical? Lincoln Road Project, Miami Beach, Fla." *Chain Store Age* (executive ed.) 35 (March 1959): 28–30.

"What Makes a 1940 Store Obsolete?" *Architectural Forum* 90 (July 1950): 62–79.

"When Controls End—More New Stores than Ever." *Business Week,* August 25, 1951.

"Where Sales Depend on Economic Health." *Architectural Record* 89 (March 1941): 65.

Whitfield, Stephen J. *The Culture of the Cold War.* Baltimore: Johns Hopkins University Press, 1991.

"Who Did What for Niles, Michigan." *Architectural Forum* 105 (November 1956): 135–37.

Whyte, William H. *The Organization Man.* New York: Simon & Schuster, 1956.

————. *The Social Life of Small Urban Spaces.* Washington, D.C.: Conservation Foundation, 1980.

"Wide Store Space with Open Front." *Architectural Record* 97 (February 1945): 104–6.

Wigley, Mark. *White Walls, Designer Dresses: The Fashioning of Modern Architecture.* Cambridge: MIT Press, 1996.

Willier, Thomas. "Parking Needs of a Modern City." *Proceedings of the Institute of Traffic Engineers* (1944): 28–37.

Wilson, Richard Guy, Dianne H. Pilgrim, and Dickran Tashjian. *The Machine Age in America, 1918–1941.* New York: Harry N. Abrams, 1986.

Windels, Paul. "How Should Our Cities Grow?" *Journal of the American Institute of Architects* 14 (October 1950): 148–53.

————. "How Should Our Cities Grow?" *Journal of the American Institute of Architects* 14 (November 1950): 223–27.

————. "How Should Our Cities Grow?" *Journal of the American Institute of Architects* 14 (December 1950): 257–61.

Winkler, Allan M. *Life under a Cloud: American Anxiety about the Atom.* New York: Oxford University Press, 1993.

"Winners of Productive Home Competition Are Announced." *Architectural Forum* 70 (May 1939): 14, 16, 18.

"Winners of Productive Home Competition Are Announced." *Architectural Record* 85 (May 1939): 53–58.

"Win $1,000 Prizes for Post Offices." *New York Times,* July 13, 1938, 19.

Wirth, Louis. "Urbanism as a Way of Life" (1938). In *Cities and Society,* edited by Paul K. Hatt and Albert J. Reiss Jr. Glencoe, Ill.: Free Press, 1957.

Wirth, Louis, and Edward Shils. "Urban Living Conditions." In *Urban Planning and Land Policies,* vol. 2 of *Supplementary Report of the Urbanism Committee to the National Resources Committee.* Washington, D.C.: Government Printing Office, 1939.

"Withering Grass." *Architectural Forum* 85 (December 1946): 12, 14.

Wojtowicz, Robert. *Lewis Mumford and American Modernism: Eutopian Theories for Architecture and Urban Planning.* New York: Cambridge University Press, 1998.

———, ed. *Sidewalk Critic: Lewis Mumford's Writings on New York.* New York: Princeton Architectural Press, 1998.

Wolfe, W. S. "Shoppers Parking Deck, Detroit, Smith, Hinchman & Grylls." *Architectural Concrete* 5 (1939): 24–26.

Woltersdorf, Arthur F. "Carnival Architecture." *American Architect* 143 (July 1933): 10–20.

"Women's Specialty Shop . . ." *Architectural Forum* 85 (October 1946): 132–33.

Woodburne, C. W. A. "The Drug Store." *Architectural Record* 77 (July 1935): 64–65.

Woodbury, Coleman, ed. *The Future of Cities and Urban Redevelopment.* Chicago: University of Chicago Press, 1953.

"Wood Panels Designed by George Wittbold for Setting of Exhibition of General Motors Products." *Pencil Points* 14 (May 1933): 242.

Woods, Mary N. *From Craft to Profession: The Practice of Architecture in Nineteenth-Century America.* Berkeley: University of California Press, 1999.

Wright, Frank Lloyd. "The Art and Craft of the Machine." *Brush and Pencil* 8 (May 1901): 77–90.

———. "Broadacre City." *Architectural Record* 77 (April 1935): 243–54.

Wright, Gwendolyn. *USA.* London: Reaktion, 2008.

Wright, Henry. Letter to the editor. *Progressive Architecture* 32 (November 1951): 10, 12.

———. *Rehousing Urban America.* New York: Columbia University Press, 1935.

Wurster, William W. "The Need for Change." In *Building for Modern Man,* edited by Thomas H. Creighton, 174–78. Princeton, N.J.: Princeton University Press, 1949.

"Wynn Furniture Store in LA Is Designed for Motorist Attention and Minimum Cost." *Architectural Forum* 86 (April 1947): 88–89.

"The Year's Work." *Interiors* 102 (September 1942): 32–33.

Yocum, James C. *Municipal Provision of Parking Facilities—State Laws and City Projects.* Research Monograph No. R-44. Columbus: Ohio State University, Bureau of Business Research, 1946.

Zorbaugh, Harvey W. "The Natural Areas of the City." In *The Urban Community,* edited by Ernest W. Burgess, 217–29. Chicago: University of Chicago Press, 1926.

INDEX

Abbott, Hunley, 100, 256n13

Ackerman, Frederick: Munsey Park Business Center, 128–29; Radburn Plaza Building, 128–29, 141

Adams, Frederick J., 160, 165, 166, 259n37

Adorno, Theodor W., 7, 39–40

advertising: by architects, 49, 61, 65, 70; modernism movement and, 43, 56; storefronts as vehicles for, 20, 58; by stores, 5, 26, 77, 255n9, 255–56n10. *See also* goods: selling; merchandising

air-conditioning, 4, 89, 239, 241

Alexander, Robert, 277n42

Altman-Kuhne Candy shop (New York City, Gruen, 1939–40), 54, 61

Aluminaire House (New York, Kocher and Frey, 1931), 32

America House (Ketchum), 65

American Federation of the Arts (AFA), 197, 285n63, 285n68

American Institute of Architects (AIA): and civil defense planning, 178, 180–83, 186, 188; Urban Planning Committee, 123

American Planning Association: *The City*, 7, 224

American style, 31, 32

American Union of Decorative Artists and Craftsmen (AUDAC), 42–43, 48, 261n77

Anaheim, California: parking plan, 112, 113

Appleton, Wisconsin: Gruen's proposal for, 229, 231, 288n47; Valley Fair Shopping Center, 255n2

Arcade, The (Providence, Rhode Island, 1827), 259n39

arcades, 31, 103, 137, 150, 170, 288n47; Eighth Street, New York City, 101, 102; Gruen's designs of, 54, 55, 56, 58, 76; Parisian, 25, 241, 245, 259n39; pedestrian, 101, 125, 161; in shopping centers, 100, 123, 130, 143, 156, 166, 167, 192, 215; in store designs, 25–31, 44, 52, 85, 263n12. *See also* storefronts; vestibules

architects and architecture, modern, 17–49, 52, 65, 257n40; advertising by, 49, 61, 65, 70; art joined with, 197–204; civil defense dispersal planning, 175–92; commerce's tensions with, 9, 48–49; consumption's tensions, 49, 173, 199, 220, 265n44; economic aspects of profession, 210, 211, 213; European, 12, 38–39, 47; industrialization integrated with, 31, 36; merchandising and, 4, 35–36, 199, 207–8, 237; modernists vs. traditionalists debates, 17–19, 22, 24, 32, 54, 100; openness in, 7, 43, 83; pedestrian focus, 54, 226, 253; planning role of, 4, 132, 208–11, 213; postwar, 234–39; in retail design, 9–10, 75; role in normalizing modernism, 10, 12–15, 90–91, 253; shopping centers work, 207–11, 213, 224; specialization in, 6, 14–15, 31; store design work, 6, 17–18, 265n44; urban, 96–97, 123, 232, 234–35. *See also* modernism; modernity

Architects Civic Design Group of Grand Rapids (Michigan), 120

Architectural Forum (journal): format change, 31; "How to Build Cities Downtown" conference, 236–37; "New Buildings for 194X" issue, 148–60, 158; postwar building issue, 154–59; Productive Home competition, 65; special feature on stores, 71; Urban Traffic Forum, 236, 237

Architectural Record (journal): building type issues, 210, 211, 213; cover design change, 31; retail stores issues, 32, 35, 71, 72

art: commerce mixed with, 52–53; countering Cold War anxieties with, 14; modernism in, 39, 40, 42, 43, 47; shopping centers as venue for, 197–204, 205, 224. *See also* culture; Museum of Modern Art

art deco style, 24, 32, 48, 83

Artek furniture showroom (Ketchum and Gina, 1941–42), 65, 68

"Art of This Century" gallery (Kiesler, 1942), 47

Arundell Display School (London), 45, 261n85

A. S. Beck Shoe Store (Brooklyn, Hagopian, 1929), 33

Atget, Eugène: *Avenue des Gobelins,* 243, 244

atomic bomb, 175–92; fears created by, 14, 183–84, 186, 281n2; firebreaks, 178, 181, 182, 184, 186; target zones, 179, 184

atriums, 6, 29, 251–53

AUDAC. *See* American Union of Decorative Artists and Craftsmen

Auer, Michael: Canterbury Shop, 54, 56, 57, 61

Augur, Tracy B., 176, 177

automobiles: city redesigns to accommodate, 123, 145, 163; separating pedestrians and, 143, 165, 232, 234–39, 256n24; store access from, 29–30, 35, 95–97, 100–118, 120, 126–30, 166, 191–92, 284n53. *See also* cities: traffic in; parking

Avalon store (Jacobs, 1924), 54

avant-garde style, 4, 45; European, 38–39, 47; Kiesler's use of, 40, 42

Avedon shop arcade (New York City, Jacobs, 1925), 25, 26, 54

Bach, Richard F., 42, 285n63

Bacon, Edmund: Penn Center, Philadelphia, plans, 235

BAID. *See* Beaux-Arts Institute of Design

Bakema, Jaap, 235, 289n57

Baker, Geoffrey, 286n3; *Shopping Centers,* 208, 209, 210, 213

Banham, Reyner, 40

Barclay-Vesey Building (New York City, Ralph Walker, 1926), 259n37

Bartholomew, Harland: parking plan by, 112, 114, 270n16

Barton's Bonbonniere (New York City, Gruen, 1939–40), 54, 61

Bauer, Catherine, 136, 141, 180, 235

Bauhaus Building (Dessau, Germany), 256n24

Bauhaus style, 19, 32, 35, 42, 45, 48, 56

Bayfair Shopping Center (San Leandro, California, Gruen, 1957), 2–3, 4, 6

Beauregard, Robert A., 13

Beaux-Arts Institute of Design (BAID), 65, 67, 69, 80, 265n51

Becket, Welton: Stonestown Shopping Center, 214–15

Bedell Store (New York City, Urban, 1929), 29

Behrendt, Walter Curt: Buffalo, New York, parking plan, 111–12

Bel Geddes, Norman, 5, 47, 48, 53, 255–56n10, 262n10

Belluschi, Pietro, 153, 209; McLoughlin Heights shopping center, 143, 144, 146,

149, 224; Mondawmin Shopping Center, 241, 290n76; "New Buildings for 194X" submission, 151; in PPG catalog, 83, 84–85

Benjamin, Walter, 241, 243, 245

Bennett, Richard, 152, 265n53; Old Orchard Shopping Center, 217, 219, 287n27; Park Forest Plaza, 147, 219–20, 287n28

Bergen County Shopping Center (New Jersey, Kelly and Gruzen, 1948), 148

Bertoia, Harry, 203; *Golden Trees* sculptures, 240–41

Beverly Hills, California: parking plans, 109, 112, 114

Beverly Shopping Center (Boston, Ketchum, Gina and Sharp, 1947), 167, 168, 169, 170, 171, 224, 287n25; modernist style of, 166–68; open spaces in, 196, 216; parking at, 169, 280n82

Bigger, Frederick, 267n84

Bittermann, Eleanor, 203

Black, Russell Van Nest, 27, 149

Blucher, Walter, 149, 273n62

bomb shelters: in shopping centers, 188, 190, 284n49; in subways, 183, 283n31

Boston, Massachusetts, 136, 137. *See also* Beverly Shopping Center

Bourdieu, Pierre, 257n40

Bowlby, Rachel, 263n19

Boyd, John Taylor, Jr., 25, 27

Boyer, M. Christine, 13

Brambilla, Roberto, 246, 247, 290n11

Brancusi, Constantin, 43

Breines, Simon, 246, 247, 290n6, 291n13

Breuer, Marcel: dispersal study, 180

Bristol Parfumerie (Vienna, Gruen, 1935), 53, 54

Broadacre City (Wright, Frank Lloyd), 176

Broek, J. H. van den, 235, 289n57

Brooks, Van Wyck: usable past concept, 224

Buffalo, New York: parking plan (Behrendt), 111–12

buildings: aluminum construction, 4, 67; civic, 142, 155; commercial, 35, 160–61, 235; fireproof, 187–88; fronts of, 31–32; glass-and-steel construction, 67, 77–78, 264n34; historical, 249; iron-and-steel construction, 20, 22; mixed-use, 160; monumental, 221; New York World's Fair, 48, 53, 64, 264n37, 264n38; office, 10, 99, 100, 151, 178; open areas around, 184, 193; on pedestrian streets, 150, 156; postwar, 154–55; rehabilitation of, 22, 80, 96, 100–103, 132, 152–53; residential and institutional, 90, 130; setback, 103, 128–29; tall, 229. *See also* architects and architecture, modern; garages, parking; shopping centers; stores

Bullocks Wilshire store (Los Angeles, Parkinson, 1929), 109

Bunshaft, Gordon, 264n36

Burdick, Henry H., 190

Burgess, Ernest, 136

Burke, Eugene: *Modern Store Design,* 87, 88, 268n100

Calder, Alexander, 203

Caldwell, Alfred, 176

Calkins, Earnest Elmo, 255–56n10

Canterbury Shop (White Plains, New York, Gruenbaum, Krummeck and Auer, 1940), 54, 56, 57, 61

Carrère and Hastings: storefront elevations by, 24

cars. *See* automobiles

Carson, Pirie, Scott & Co. store (Chicago, Sullivan, 1899), 12

Case Study Houses, 90–91

Century of Progress exhibition (Chicago, 1933), 18

chain stores, 5–6, 60, 71, 73, 75, 258n23. *See also* Grayson's Ready-to-Wear

Channel Heights plan (Neutra, 1942), 137, 139

Chapman Garage (Los Angeles), 271n25

Chareau, Pierre, 43

Cheney, Sheldon: and Martha Candler Cheney, 48

"Chicago Plan," 228–29, 230

Chicago school: on planning territory, 136

Church, Thomas, 166, 213

Churchill, Henry, 146–47

CIAM. *See* Congrés Internationaux d'Architecture Moderne

Cincinnati, Ohio: parking plans, 116, 117

Ciro store (New York City, Gruen and Ketchum, 1939), 54, 56, 63, 264n27

cities: aging, 148, 152; civil defense dispersal planning, 175–92; congested, 26–27, 180, 198–99; decentralization of, 155, 178, 181–82, 184; green areas in, 140, 224, 225; historic, 217; inner cores, 3–4, 15, 150, 152, 155, 160, 226–29, 232–34; modernist design of, 7, 15, 125–27, 135–40, 161, 226–28, 231, 246; pedestrianization of, 140–48, 160, 162; planning, 148–53, 161, 181–82; remaking, 95–97, 100–118, 123, 163, 184, 225; retailing in, 9–10, 24, 160, 189–90; social life in, 135, 137, 152, 178, 189, 233–34, 246; suburbanization of, 248–50; traffic in, 95–107, 134, 148, 152, 226–27, 279n77, 288n47; walking in, 134, 135, 136, 152, 161. *See also* downtowns; Fort Worth Plan; new towns; Rye, New York: redevelopment plan; urban areas; urban renewal

citizenship, 5, 7–9, 224, 250

City, The (film, American Planning Association), 7, 224

civil defense, 177, 181–90, 192

Clarke, Gilmore, 96, 136

class consciousness, 136, 204, 245

Clearview shopping center (Princeton, New Jersey, Ketchum, Gina, and Sharp, 1952), 224, 225

Coates, Welles, 39

Cold War, 14, 186, 203, 204–5, 224. *See also* dispersal planning, Cold War

Colomina, Beatriz, 13

Colonial Williamsburg: Gloucester Street shopping area, 101; restoration of, 31, 166

Comey, Arthur C., 232

commerce: architecture's tensions with, 9, 48–49; citizenship and, 224; curbside model of, 132; mixing with art, 52–53; modernism movement and, 9, 43, 47; pedestrian-focused, 146, 147–48; planning's relationship to, 146, 173; tensions between culture and, 12, 15, 19–20, 22, 25. *See also* goods: selling; merchandising

commodities. *See* goods

communities: compartmentalized, 183, 188; empty shopping centers in, 250, 251; neighborhood development in, 139–40; organic, 133, 224; pedestrian-focused, 146; planned, 133, 143; remaking urban core into, 135, 155, 184, 232–34; satellite, 177; self-sufficient, 180. *See also* neighborhoods; social life; units

community centers, 3–4; shopping centers as, 196, 198–99, 204, 220–21, 224, 233–34, 251

Conant Real Estate Trust, 165–66, 280n84

congestion. *See* cities: congested; cities: traffic in

Congrés Internationaux d'Architecture Moderne (CIAM): *Heart of the City,* 232–34; new monumentality concept, 203–4, 205; planning projects, 3–4, 136, 167, 256n34; Stevenage, Great Britain, plans, 232; Tumaco, Colombia, plans, 232

Connecticut Avenue Park and Shop (Washington, D.C., Lönberg-Holm, 1931), 130, 142

Connecticut General Life Insurance Company: suburban office building, 178

consumer engineering, 5, 48–49; use of term, 255–56n10

consumption, 6, 13, 48, 53, 197, 240, 245; architecture's tensions with, 49, 173, 199, 220, 265n44; culture of, 5–7, 134, 256n16; inner city patterns of, 227–28; mass, 20, 165, 203; modernism movement and, 14, 47, 58, 243–44; postwar, 58, 61, 165, 204–5

Contini, Edgardo, 188

continuity: as modernist technique, 31, 42, 71–72, 80, 89, 166

Coolidge, William, 165

Co-op Vitrine project (Meyer, 1924), 39

Copenhagen, Denmark: streetscape redevelopment in, 249

Corbett, Harvey Wiley, 125, 260–61n72

correalism, 42, 47

Country Club Plaza parking facilities (Kansas City, Delk, 1923), 100–101, 128, 142

Court House Square, 275n87

courtyards, 29–30, 143, 147, 240–41, 245. *See also* open spaces

Crawford, Margaret, 13

Creighton, Thomas H., 83, 182

Cret, Paul, 18

Crosby, Bing, 280n85

Cross Country Center (Yonkers, Douglass, 1950–54), 215, 287n21

crystallization points, 191, 199, 233, 234, 284n51

culture, 155, 200; Cold War, 176, 190, 191; of consumption, 5–7, 134, 256n16; mass, 24, 203; of modernism, 8, 47, 65; in shopping centers, 155, 159; tensions between commerce and, 12, 15, 19–20, 22, 25. *See also* art

curbside paradigm, 132, 163, 192; challenging, 97–100, 107, 109, 123–30; moving beyond, 14, 140–48, 173. *See also* automobiles: store access from; 100 percent locations

Curtis Lighting company, 35

Davison, Robert, 99, 259n47; as *Architectural Record* editor, 31

De Boer, S. R., 142–43

decentralization, 123, 163, 190; of cities, 155, 161, 181–82; Cold War tensions and, 175–78, 183–84, 186, 204

de Certeau, Michel, 7

de Klerk, Michael, 18

Delk, Edward Buehler, 274n80; Country Club Plaza, 100–101, 128, 142

department stores, 36, 106, 256n14, 265n44, 285n55; arts in, 261n81, 285n64; nineteenth-century, 6; parking

garages, 98, 100; in shopping centers, 156, 245

design correlation. *See* correalism

Deskey, Donald, 40

De Stijl movement, 42

Detroit, Michigan: highway loop, 115; parking plans, 112, 114, 120, 226, 273n65

Deutsch, Karl: and Wiener's life belt system plan, 283n38

Deutscher Werkbund, 19, 42

Deutsch Herren Moden (Vienna, Gruen), 54

Disneyland (Anaheim, California, 1954): Main Street model, 215

dispersal planning, Cold War, 175–92, 283n38. *See also* Cold War

display cases, 84; continuous, 78, 166; floating, 75, 76, 125; glass, 54, 263n12

displays, 19, 29, 69; emphasis on, 20, 22; entire store serving as, 38, 44, 65; Kiesler on, 39–40; merging outdoor space with, 75, 125. *See also* arcades; merchandising; storefronts

display windows, 27, 35, 38, 58, 72, 104, 109

distribution, 38, 39, 65, 71, 72, 226

Dixie Square Mall (Harvey, Illinois), 250

Doesburg, Theo van, 256n14, 260n67

Doubleday Doran Bookshop (Chicago, Lapidus, 1936), 75

Douglass, Lathrop: Cross Country Center, 215

downtowns: aging, 8, 10; congestion in, 149; renewal of, 226, 234–39; shopping in, 80, 165. *See also* cities: inner cores

Dreiser, Theodore, 6

Duiker, Jan, 18

Durkheim, Émile, 136

Eames, Charles, 149, 153

Eames, Ray, 153

Eastland Shopping Center (Hudson Company, Gruen, unbuilt), 188, 191, 196, 220, 225, 284n53; discourse of dispersal and, 189, 190–92

East Wing of the National Gallery (Washington, D.C., Pei, 1976), 251, 253 eclecticism, 18, 48, 99

Edwards, Paul, 176

efficiency: modernism characterized by, 38, 51, 72, 84, 87, 227–28

Eighth Street, New York City: arcade concept, 101, 102

Eimer & Amend Apothecary (New York City, Lapidus, 1934), 267n81

Ellington, Douglas: Greenbelt shopping center, 136, 141–42

Eno Foundation: traffic study by, 109, 111

Erikson Electric Company, 35

Esperdy, Gabrielle, 12–13

ethnic groups: urban renewal and, 246. *See also* race: urban renewal and

Europe: architects and architecture in, 37, 38–39, 47

Euwer, Campe (Allentown, Pennsylvania), 95

exteriors. *See* arcades; display windows; interior-exterior spatial overlap; storefronts

Fagin, Henry (Regional Plan Association), 162

Feiss, Carl, 236, 277n34; shopping center proposal, 142, 146

Fernandez, José, 83, 87, 89

FHA. *See* U.S. Federal Housing Administration

Fifth Avenue, New York City: proposed pedestrianization of, 26, 214, 246, 247, 259n37

Film Arts Guild Theater (New York City, Kiesler, 1929), 40, 42

Fisher, Howard, T., 259n47; as *Architectural Record* editor, 259n47; auto-shopping proposal, 126–27; Lincoln Plaza, 127, 147; Marshall Field Skokie Shopping Center competition, 217, 218, 219

Fisher Building garage (Detroit, Kahn, 1928), 99

Fishman, Robert, 13

Flint, Michigan: parking plans, 114

flow: use of term, 260n61

Fogelson, Robert, 13

Fooshee and Cheek: Highland Park Village, 129, 130, 275n87

Ford, George B., 270n16

Ford, Henry, 277n39

Ford Foundation headquarters (New York, 1976, Roche), 251, 252

form following function, 51–52, 77

Fort Worth Plan (Gruen, 1955), 15, 226–28; addressing traffic congestion problems, 229, 231, 288n39, 288n43; use of pedestrian zones, 234, 235, 237

Fouilhoux, André, 64, 69, 72

Foulks, William, 266n63

Fourier, Charles, 245

Frankel, Evan, 267n77

Frankl, Paul: Mosse Linen Shop, 64

Frederick Loesser and Company store (Brooklyn), 266n65

Fredericks, Marshall, 200

Frey, Albert, 30, 130; Aluminaire House, 32; Sunlight Towers, 31–32

friction: aesthetic, 38, 49; use of term, 260n61

Fuller, Buckminster, 18, 36

Fulton Mall (Brooklyn, New York, Urban Design Group and Pomeroy, 1975), 246

Fulton Mall (Fresno, California, Gruen, 1964), 246

Funaro, Bruno: Eighth Street arcades, 102; *Shopping Centers*, 208, 209, 210, 213, 286n3

function: form follows, 51–52, 77; modernism's emphasis on, 13, 49

functional equivalent argument, 291n21. *See also* privately owned public spaces

Furno, Vincent, 279n74

Gabo, Noam, 43, 201

garages, parking, 98–100, 114, 237, 289n64; Fort Worth Plan, 226, 227; styles of, 128, 271n25. *See also* parking

Garden City, New York: parking plans, 109, 110

garden city movement, 232. *See also* green spaces; town greens

garden courts. *See* courtyards

Gehl, Jan, 248

General Houses, Inc., 126

General Motors Technical Center (Eero Saarinen), 166, 213

Giberson, Earl F.: Linda Vista Shopping Center, 143, 144, 146, 224, 225, 276n21, 277n38

Giedion, Sigfried, 133, 204, 245, 284n51; on modern architecture, 7, 18, 32, 43, 256n24; on shopping centers, 10, 233–34

Gina, Francis X., 69; Artek furniture showroom, 65, 68; Clearview shopping center, 224, 225; *Machines for Selling,* 82; Middlesex Center, 168, 169, 172; store designs, 105, 108. *See also* Beverly Shopping Center; Rye, New York: redevelopment plan

glass: invisible line of, 65, 77–78; on storefronts, 20, 22, 25, 43; in store interiors, 166, 271n35. *See also* buildings: glass-and-steel construction; display cases: glass; plate glass

glazing. *See* storefronts: glazed

Goodhue, Ruth, 154

goods: access to, 7, 58, 83, 165, 204, 241; display of, 25, 29, 40, 47, 56, 73, 76; distribution of, 19, 38, 39, 42–43, 226; modernity's embrace of, 243, 245; movement of, 5, 38, 72, 87, 90, 127; pedestrians' relationship to, 43–45; production of, 18, 43, 71; representation of, 20, 22; selling, 17, 24, 32, 40, 52–53. *See also* consumption; merchandising

Goodwin, Phillip, 64

Gordon, Witold, 64

Graham, John: Northgate Shopping Center, 196–97, 214, 216

Grand Rapids Parking Plan (Welch, 1945), 120–23, 162–63

Grand Rapids Planning Commission, 118

Grand Rapids Store Equipment Company (GRSEC): consulting work, 266n65, 266n66; store fixtures diagram, 36; Welch as vice president of, 35, 70–73

Grand River Court (Grand Rapids, Michigan, Welch, 1945), 120–23, 156

Grayson's Ready-to-Wear: San Francisco store, 60; Seattle store, 58, 59, 60, 61, 221

Greek Revival style, 65

Greeley, William Roger, 133

greenbelts, 150; as bomb-related firebreaks, 178, 181, 182, 184, 186

Greenbelt shopping center (Maryland, Wadsworth and Ellington, 1937), 136, 141–42

green spaces, 143; in shopping centers, 166, 167, 192, 255n2. *See also* garden city movement; open spaces; pastoralism; town greens

Greenwich, Connecticut: parking plans, 109

Grimm, Sergei, 278n49

Gropius, Walter, 32, 38–39, 152, 209; dispersal study, 180; drugstore design, 84; in PPG catalog, 83–84, 85; on units, 136, 137

GRSEC. *See* Grand Rapids Store Equipment Company

Gruen (Gruenbaum), Victor, 13, 69, 125, 177, 268n93; Altman-Kuhne Candy shop, 54, 61; Appleton, Wisconsin, proposal, 229, 231, 288n47; *Architectural Forum* proposal, 153–60, 192; art in shopping centers project, 14, 199–204, 286n72; Barton's Bonbonniere, 54, 61; Bayfair Shopping Center, 2–3, 4, 6; Bristol Partumerie, 53, 54; Canterbury Shop, 54, 56, 57, 61; Ciro store, 54, 56, 63, 264n27; on civic functions of shopping centers, 220–21, 224, 250, 251; on civil defense functions of shopping centers, 187–90; cluster plan, 196–97, 216–17, 220; Deutsch Herren Moden, 54; Eastland Shopping Center, 188, 189, 190–92, 196, 220, 225, 284n53; Fulton Mall, 246; Kalamazoo Mall, 109, 246, 248; Los Angeles shopping center proposal, 159–60, 192, 220; on merchandising, 52–61; Midtown Plaza, 245; Milliron's Department Store, 104; "New Buildings for 194X" submission, 151, 153–60; New York World's Fair participation, 224,

262n9; Olympic Shopping Circle, 107, 192, 220–21, 222, 223, 285n55; Paris Decorators shop, 264n27; pedestrianization and, 153–60, 171, 173, 234; in PPG catalog, 83, 84–85; pragmatism of, 54, 198; remaking buildings for parking, 103, 106, 107; self-promotion by, 61, 262n4, 269n107, 284n45; shopping center designs, 1–3, 4, 157, 158, 159–60, 189, 192, 209–11, 220, 226, 241, 246; *Shopping Centers of Tomorrow* exhibit, 197–99; *Shopping Towns USA,* 285n66; and shop windows, 243, 269n109; site section study, 193–94; store designs, 90, 221, 224, 269n109; storefront designs, 54, 56, 58; at Store Modernization Show of 1947, 89; Strasser Studio, 54, 264n27; use of modernist style, 14, 54, 76, 81, 87, 155, 234–36, 269n109; work for Bel Geddes, 262n10; Wynn Furniture Store, 221, 224. *See also* Fort Worth Plan; Lederer de Paris store; Northland Shopping Center; Southdale Shopping Center
Gruzen, Sumner: Bergen County Shopping Center, 148; Jersey City Big Bear Shopping Center, 129, 220–21, 275n84

Hackensack, New Jersey: parking plans, 108
Hagopian, Vahan: A. S. Beck Shoe Store, 32, 33
Hale, Peter: "New Haven's Post-war Plan," 104
Halprin, Lawrence, 219
Hamlin, Talbot, 6, 8, 54, 134
Harbeson, John, 18
Hardwick, M. Jeff, 13
Harkness, John: dispersal study, 180
Harris and Brown, 287n21
Harrison, Wallace, 64
Harrison, Fouilhoux & Abramovitz, 64
Harvard University, Graduate School of Design, 137, 237
Haskell, Douglas, 47, 183, 259n47; as *Architectural Record* editor, 31
Hauf, Harold, 175

Heap, Jane, 40
Hempstead, New York: parking plans, 108, 109
Hersey, John: *Hiroshima,* 177
Highland Park Village (Dallas, Fooshee and Cheek, 1930), 129, 130, 275n87
highways, 226, 237, 250, 256n24; civil defense planning and, 182, 184, 186; Detroit loop plan, 115; parking connected to, 97, 112, 113, 116, 120, 123; shopping center access from, 123, 155, 166. *See also* streets
Hilberseimer, Ludwig, 136, 152, 175
Hitchcock, Henry-Russell, 18, 208, 259n47; as *Architectural Record* editor, 31; *Modern Architecture,* 12; as 1932 MOMA exhibit curator, 47–48; on relationship of art and architecture, 201, 203
Hoffmann, Josef, 260n68
Holabird and Root, 83
Hollywood, California: parking plan, 112
Hook of Holland housing complex (Oud, 1929), 35, 37, 38, 48
horizontalism, 43
Hornbeck, James, 219–20
housing, 100, 126, 140, 186; adjacent to shopping centers, 142, 143, 219, 251; research on, 102, 146, 259n47, 283n34; urban development and, 182, 237, 239, 280n82. *See also* Hook of Holland housing complex; Parkchester housing project
Houston Galleria (HOK), 251
Howard, Ebenezer, 98
Howe, George, 18
Hoyt, Homer, 160, 279n72
Hudnut, Joseph, 146
Hudson Company: art program at Northland, 199–200; shopping center plans, 188, 189, 190, 192–97

Illinois Institute of Technology (Mies van der Rohe), 213
industrial design and designers, 36, 47, 48, 53, 255–56n10, 268n100
industries, 77, 186; Cold War dispersal

plans, 175, 178, 183–84, 186; modernism integrated with, 43, 80, 81. *See also* production

infrastructure, urban, 10, 137, 161, 186

Inness, George: *The Lackawanna Valley,* 2, 3

Institute for Environmental Action, 248

interior-exterior spatial overlap, 89, 251; arcades creating, 75, 245; easy transition, 52, 58; intermediate zone between, 54, 77–78; as modernist technique, 2–3, 4; use of glass, 65, 243; visual connections, 83, 84, 85

International City and Regional Planning Conference (New York City, 1925), 97–98

International Style, 18, 48, 49, 54

"International Theater Exposition" (New York City, 1926), 40

Interregional Highways report (1944), 113

intervention, urban, 95, 97, 132, 237, 239, 289n68. *See also* urban renewal

Isaacs, Reginald, 140, 149

Isenberg, Alison, 13

isochron analysis, 273n58, 280n87

Italian Art and Landscape Foundation, 290n11

Italianate style, 271n25

Ivel Corporation: Gruen's work for, 53

Jacobs, Harry Allen, 259n37; Avalon shop arcade, 25, 26, 54

Jacobs, Jane, 227–28, 237, 248, 288n43

Jakle, John A., 95

Jameson, Fredric, 251

Jennings, Richard, 200

Jersey City Big Bear Shopping Center (Gruzen, 1934), 129, 220–21, 275n84

Johnson, Phillip: *Modern Architecture,* 12; as 1932 MOMA exhibit curator, 47–48

Jordan Marsh store (Boston, Perry, Shaw and Hepburn), 280n88

Joseph, Seymour R.: *New Pencil Points*– Kawneer competition prize, 78, 79

Kahn, Albert, 72; parking garage designs, 98–99

Kahn, Ely Jacques, 19, 25, 35, 69

Kahn, Louis, 149; Philadelphia plan, 149, 237, 238; *You and Your Neighborhood,* 139, 139, 140. *See also* Stonorov and Kahn

Kalamazoo Mall (Michigan, Gruen, 1959), 109, 246, 248

Kansas City, Missouri: parking plan, 112

Kant, Immanuel, 7

Kawneer Company: Ketchum's work for, 265n55, 268n91, 268n93; *Machines for Selling,* 80–81, 82, 83, 89, 166, 268n88; Store Fronts of Tomorrow competition, 77–80

Kawneer Prize, 69

Keally, Francis, 64, 264n34, 264n37

Kebbon, Eric, 64

Kelly, Burnham, 178

Kennedy, G. Donald, 149

Kent Automatic Parking Garage system, 98–99

Kepes, Gyorgy: *The New Landscape,* 282n26

Ketchum, Morris, Jr., 61–70, 77, 264n32, 264n36, 280n89; America House, 65; Artek furniture showroom, 65, 68; Beverly Shopping Center, 196, 216, 224, 287n25; Ciro store, 54, 56, 63, 264n27; Clearview shopping center, 224, 225; dispersal discourse and, 177; Kawneer Company work, 265n55, 268n91, 268n93; *Machines for Selling,* 82, 83, 166; Marshall Field shopping center competition, 216–17; Middlesex Center, 168, 169, 172; Mosse Linen Shop, 64; Myrtle Beach Club riding academy, 65; Niles, Michigan, Main Street redevelopment project, 80, 81, 89, 95; 1939 World's Fair participation, 264n37; Paris Decorators shop, 264n27; parking plans, 103, 107; pedestrian plans, 160–62, 171, 173, 279n77; pragmatism of, 64, 70, 161, 183; Project East River, 14, 182–86, 283n33, 283n36; Reid article on, 69–70, 282n30; Sharp's partnership with, 265n41; Shoppers' World, 169, 215, 216, 224, 225;

shopping center work, 112, 134, 186, 192, 204, 213, 214; *Shops and Stores,* 89–90, 125, 143, 145, 146, 208, 269n105; Steckler Shop, 65, 66, 67, 264n27; store blocks, 105, 149, 156, 160, 161; store designs, 80, 90, 104, 105, 235, 280n82; storefront designs, 56, 65; at Store Modernization Show of 1947, 89; suburban work of, 162–69; use of modernist style, 14, 87, 266n58. *See also* Beverly Shopping Center; Lederer de Paris store; Rye, New York: redevelopment plan

Kiesler, Frederick: "Art of This Century" gallery, 47; "City in Space," 40; *Contemporary Art Applied to the Store and Its Display,* 39–40, 43–45, 46, 47; department store designs, 256n14, 261n81; "Endless Theater," 40; Film Arts Guild Theater, 40, 42; Saks Fifth Avenue window designs, 40, 41, 42, 260–61n72; shop window designs, 243, 245; "Space House," 47; "Space Stage," 40; storefront designs, 44, 45, 46; theatrical design work, 42, 260n67, 260n68, 260n71, 260–61n72; use of modernist style, 13, 47, 48, 56

Kimball, Fiske, 18, 259n47; as *Architectural Record* editor, 31

Kingsford Heights, Indiana: community plan, 146

kitsch, 200, 286n71

Klein, Alexander, 260n61

Klein, Richard, 290n7

Kober, Edgar: *Modern Store Design,* 87, 88, 268n100

Kocher, A. Lawrence, 130, 259n48, 259n49; Aluminaire House, 32; as *Architectural Record* managing editor, 31–32

Korean War, 176, 182, 188

Kraft, Arthur, 200, 203; *Baby Elephant,* 202

Krummeck, Elsie, 262n9; Canterbury Shop, 54, 56, 57, 61; Los Angeles shopping center proposal, 159–60, 192, 220

Lakewood Shopping Center (Los Angeles, Martin, 1954), 195, 196, 215, 216

Lapidus, Morris, 73–77, 267n75, 267n76; in *Contemporary Shops in the United States,* 87; on display cases, 125; Doubleday Doran Bookshop, 75; Eimer & Amend Apothecary, 267n81; Miami plan, 112; *New Pencil Points* "Store Fronts of Tomorrow" competition, 267n85; Postman's retail shop, 75, 76; in PPG catalog, 83, 84–85; Sachs Furniture Store, 75; shopping center designs, 169–71, 172, 281n96; on shop windows, 243; store designs, 125, 221; storefront designs, 65, 73, 74, 75–77, 235; at Store Modernization Show of 1947, 89; on urban shopping core, 130, 132; use of modernist styles, 13, 14

Lapp, Ralph E., 177, 281n8

Larson, Theodore, 259n47; as *Architectural Record* editor, 31

Laszlo, Paul: Los Angeles shopping center design, 219

Lazarsfeld, Paul, 262n6

Le Corbusier, 47, 53; machinic metaphors of, 18, 39, 81; *pilotis* argument, 100; urban design theories, 7, 8, 125, 133; on urban pedestrians, 133; Ville Radieuse, 125, 134

Lederer de Paris store (New York City, Ketchum and Gruen, 1939), 53, 54, 55, 61, 62, 63, 65, 263n12, 264n27

Léger, Fernand, 204

Lescaze, William, 72, 77, 83, 267n83

Lever House (New York City, SOM, 1952), 103, 220

Lewis, Harold MacLean: parking plans, 98, 116

Lexington, Kentucky: Drive-In project (Neutra, 1929), 128–29

Libby-Owens-Ford Company, 72, 267n83; *Visual Fronts* pamphlet, 83, 268n93

life belt system (Norbert Wiener), 186–87, 188–89, 283n38

Lijnbaan urban reconstruction project (Rotterdam, the Netherlands), 234–35, 289n57, 289n61

Lincoln Plaza (Chicago, Fisher, 1951), 127, 147

Lincoln Road shopping district (Miami), 112

Linda Vista Shopping Center (San Diego, Giberson and Whitney Smith, 1943), 143, 144, 146, 224, 225, 276n21, 277n38; *New Pencil Points* "Store Fronts of Tomorrow" competition, 267n85

lobbies, 77–78, 80. *See also* storefronts; vestibules

Loebl, Schlossman and Bennett: Olympia Fields shopping center proposal, 147

Loewy, Raymond, 5, 48, 53, 87, 255–56n10

Lönberg-Holm, Knud: Connecticut Avenue Park and Shop, 130, 142; on merchandising, 38, 39, 56, 65; shopping center designs, 130; on shop windows, 43, 243; store designs by, 35–36, 71, 72; use of modernist style, 13, 47–48, 87; utilitarianism of, 141

Longo, Gianni, 192, 220, 248

Longstreth, Richard, 12, 29, 128, 275n82, 275n90

Los Angeles: Gruen and Krummeck shopping center proposal, 159–60, 192, 220; parking plans, 109, 112

Los Angeles Drive-In Market (Neutra, 1929), 30, 32, 118, 123, 128

Luce, Henry, 149

Lundberg, Elmer A., 86, 268–69n102; *Progressive Architecture* article, 86

Lunden, Samuel E., 267n84

Lux, Gwen, 200; *Bird Flight,* 201

Macdonald, Dwight, 200

MacKaye, Benton: townless highway concept, 182

Mackesey, Thomas, 136

Macy's, Inc.: nighttime delivery system, 98

Main Street(s): aging, 8, 10; *Architectural Record* design competition, 72; curbside model of commerce, 132; double-decked, 169; grassed-over, 143, 163–65; Mount Kisco, New York, redevelopment plan, 162, 279n80; Nelson's proposals for, 148, 149–50, 151, 153; Niles, Michigan, remodeling project, 80, 81, 89, 95; pedestrianized, 148–53, 162, 163–64, 290n7; remaking to accommodate automobiles, 107–18, 123; shopping centers as replacement for, 170–71, 214–16

malls: grassed-over, 142–43, 160–61; pedestrian, 143, 149, 169, 192, 229, 246, 277n42, 289n61; in shopping centers, 225; urban, 162, 279n80; use of term, 7. *See also* pedestrianization; shopping centers

Mangel, Sidney, 267n77

Mangel's chain store, 73

Marshall Field Skokie Shopping Center competition, 216–17, 287n23, 287n26, 287n27; Fisher's submission, 217, 218, 219; Ketchum's submission, 216; SOM's submission, 220, 221

Marshall Field Wholesale Store (Chicago, Richardson, 1887), 12

Marston, Van Pelt and Mayberry: Pasadena Arcade, 29

Martin, Albert C.: Lakewood Shopping Center, 195, 196, 215, 216

Marx, Leo, 2–3, 220, 239

Matisse, Henri, 43

May Company Garage (Los Angeles), 271n25

Mayer, Albert, 142, 180; on planning for parking, 101–3

Mayer and Whittlesey, 277n39

Mayers, Murray & Phillip, 64, 264n37

McAndrew, John, 54, 61, 264n27

McClintock, Miller, 270n16

McCroskey, Theodore T., 137

McKim, Mead & White, 18, 24, 64

McLoughlin Heights shopping center (Vancouver, Belluschi, 1942), 143, 144, 146, 149, 224

Mendelsohn, Erich, 39, 43

Mennel, Timothy, 239

merchandising, 47–49, 51–91; arcades' role in, 31; architectural planning around, 4, 10, 12–15, 24, 52, 207–8, 237, 241; art

integrated into, 203; in cities, 9–10, 125–
26; expanding representations of, 77–91;
Gruen's work, 52–61; Ketchum's work,
61–70; Lapidus's work, 73–77; mass, 5,
60; pedestrianization as outgrowth of,
253; planning for, 116, 128, 132; rationalist approach to, 130, 210; stores
designed for, 19, 25, 32, 35–36, 38–39,
43–45; suburban, 128, 168; Welch's
work, 70–73. *See also* advertising; displays; retailing; storefronts

Merchants Association of Allentown,
Pennsylvania, 95

metropolitan areas, remaking, 180–82, 204.
See also regional districts; urban areas;
urban renewal

Metropolitan Grand Rapids Planning Association (Michigan), 118, 120

Metropolitan Museum of Art (New York
City), 42

Meyer, Hannes, 38; Co-op Vitrine project, 39

Miami: parking plan, 112

Mickle, Grant, 149

Middlesex Center (Framingham, Massachusetts, Ketchum, Gina, and Sharp, 1948),
168, 169, 172

Midtown Plaza (Rochester, New York,
Gruen, 1962), 245

Mies van der Rohe, 43, 47, 77, 153; Illinois
Institute of Technology, 213; "Museum
for a Small City," 149; Tugendhat dining
area semicircle, 267n76

Mikkelsen, Michael A., 31, 259n45, 259n46

Milliron's Department Store (Los Angeles,
Gruen, 1947), 104

Milwaukee, Wisconsin: parking plan, 112

Mineola, New York: parking plans, 116

Miró, Joan, 203

Mock, Rudolf: as curator of MoMA *Look at
Your Neighborhood* exhibit, 139–40

moderne style, 24, 32, 35, 48, 64, 83

modernism: aesthetics of, 38, 40, 49, 65, 80,
83; architecture's role in normalizing, 10,
12–15, 29, 69, 90–91, 253; arts and, 39,
40, 42, 43, 47, 197–204; CIAM-based,

167, 232–34; consumption and, 14, 47,
58, 243–44; culture of, 8, 47, 65; dispersal plans and, 180–82; glass-and-steel, 67,
77–78; Gruen and, 52–61, 155; industries and, 43, 80, 81; language of, 65, 87,
168, 207–41; parking problems addressed
through, 100–107; pedestrian focus, 134,
136, 140–48, 153, 160, 169–73, 203,
234, 245–40, 253; social/psychological
barriers broken down by, 43, 47, 135–36,
137; spatial patterns of, 147–48, 184;
steel-and-glass, 13–14; in store design,
4–5, 9–10, 29, 36, 39–40, 51–52, 72, 87,
89–90; techniques of, 13, 15, 24, 48, 61,
77, 81, 85; tensions in, 24, 49, 135; traditionalists' debates with, 17–19, 22, 24,
32, 100. *See also* cities: modernist design
of; pragmatism, modernist; rationalism,
modernist; shopping centers: modernist
design of; urban areas: modernism movement and; utilitarianism

modernity: in architecture, 4, 24; in garage
designs, 99–100; in store design, 87, 243,
245; suburban, 240

modernization, 3, 81, 86; architecture's
intersection with, 12–15, 48–49, 77;
FHA loan program for, 72, 73; pedestrianization and, 140, 250; in shopping center design, 5, 239–41; in store design, 39,
54, 86, 129–30. *See also* urban renewal

Moltke, Willo von, 146; shopping sketch,
7, 8

Mondawmin Shopping Center (Baltimore,
Belluschi), 241, 290n76

Monopoly game (Milton Bradley), 94

Montclair, New Jersey: parking plans, 108

monumentality, new, 220, 224; CIAM's pursuit of, 203–4, 205

Moran, Malcolm, 200

Morgan, Walls & Clements: Mullen and
Bluett Store, 32, 34; Plaza Market, 30,
32, 128

Moses, Robert, 283n31

Mosse Linen Shop (New York City, Frankl
and Ketchum, 1938), 64

"Motor City" (Brazil, Paul Wiener and Sert), 161, 164

Mount Kisco, New York: redevelopment plan, 162, 279n80

Mullen and Bluett store (Pasadena, Morgan, Walls & Clements), 32, 34

Mumford, Lewis, 140, 182, 224; on modernism, 54, 235; on pedestrianization, 173, 248; on store design, 18, 32

Munsey Park Business Center (Ackerman, 1930), 128–29

Museum of Modern Art (MoMA): Bauhaus exhibit of 1938–39, 48; "Brazil Plans a City" exhibit, 161; *Built in USA* exhibit, 143; *International Exhibition of Modern Architecture* (1932), 18, 38, 47–49, 267n81; *Look at Your Neighborhood* exhibit, 139–40; *Machine Art* exhibit of 1934, 48; new building for, 64

Myers, Howard, 9, 10, 64, 69, 148, 154, 269n105

Myrtle Beach Club riding academy (Ketchum), 65

National Gallery, East Wing (Washington, D.C., Pei, 1976), 251, 253

National Research Corporation (NRC), 165

National Retail Dry Goods Association: "How to Build Cities Downtown" conference, 236–37

National Security Resources Board (NSRB), 178

National Suburban Centers, Inc. (NSC), 165

neighborhoods: Harvard's studies of, 137; inner cities contrasted with, 7–9; planning guide, 139; postatomic bomb planning for, 178, 180, 181; remaking to accommodate automobiles, 100–107; schools and, 138, 181; shopping centers in, 130, 131, 141, 154; walking in, 139. *See also* units: neighborhood

Nelson, George: as *Architectural Forum* editor, 9; city planning by, 116, 148–53, 224, 278n52; Main Street proposals, 148, 149–50, 151, 153; "New Buildings for 194X," 148–54; on pedestrian precincts, 171, 173; and shopping district creation, 14; store designs by, 10, 69, 87

Nelson, Otto, 183

Neues Bauen, 32. *See also* Bauhaus style

Neutra, Richard: Channel Heights plan, 137, 139; Lexington, Kentucky, Drive-In, 128–29; Los Angeles Drive-In Market, 30, 32, 118, 123, 128

New Haven, Connecticut: "Post-war Plan" (Hale, 1945), 104

New Pencil Points "Store Fronts of Tomorrow" competition, 77–80, 267n84, 267n85

new towns, 137, 140, 180, 181, 182

New York City: Eighth Street arcade concept, 101, 102; pedestrianization programs, 15, 245–46, 248, 249; subway bomb shelters, 183, 283n31

New York Life Insurance company, 283n33

New York University School of Retailing, 268n101; Store Modernization Show of 1947, 89

New York World's Fair (1939): buildings at, 48, 53, 64, 264n37, 264n38; Gruen's participation in, 224, 262n9

Nichols, Jesse Clyde, 274n80, 274n81, 275n82; Country Club Plaza, 100–101, 128

Nicholson, Emrich, 87, 268n98

Niles, Michigan: Main Street redevelopment project, 80, 81, 89, 95

Nixon, Richard M.: shopping center campaign stops, 250, 251

no-build zones, 178. *See also* dispersal planning, Cold War

nodes. *See* units

Northgate Shopping Center (Seattle, Graham, 1950), 196–97, 214, 216

Northland Shopping Center (Southfield, Michigan, Gruen, 1954), 1, 3, 193–97, 285n59, 287n24, 289n61; art program at, 14, 199–204, 286n72; cluster plan, 216–17, 220; efficiency of, 226, 231

Norton, C. McKim, 283n34
Nowicki, Matthew, 147
NSC. *See* National Suburban Centers, Inc.
NSRB. *See* National Security Resources Board

Oakes, Guy, 176
Oakland, California: parking lots, 109
objectivity, German *(Sachlich),* 18, 32, 36,
    258n9
Ogburn, William, 176
Old Orchard Shopping Center (Skokie, Illi-
    nois, Bennett, 1954–56), 217, 219,
    287n27
Olympia Fields shopping center proposal
    (Chicago area, Loebl, Schlossman and
    Bennett, 1947), 147
Olympic Shopping Circle (Los Angeles,
    Gruen, 1950), 107, 192, 220–21, 222,
    223, 285n55
100 percent locations, 10, 128, 137; auto-
    mobile's influence on, 166, 192; pedestri-
    anization and, 249–50; rethinking, 97,
    98, 130, 132. *See also* curbside paradigm
open spaces: parking and, 108, 193; in shop-
    ping centers, 143, 167; in store design,
    43, 52, 83; in urban redesign, 96, 237.
    See also courtyards; greenbelts; green
    spaces; parks; pastoralism
Orr, Douglas, 178
Oud, J. J. P., 18, 43; Hook of Holland proj-
    ect, 35, 37, 38, 48
Ourossoff, Nicolai, 248–49

Palm Drive-In (Severance, 1929), 30, 128
Paris Decorators shop (New York City,
    Ketchum and Gruen), 264n27
*Paris Exposition Internationale des Arts Déco-
    ratifs et Industriels Modernes* (1925), 24,
    40, 42
Park, Robert E., 136
park-and-shop concept, 95–97, 132
Park and Shop game (Milton Bradley), 93–
    95, 96, 269n2, 269n6
Park and Shop, Inc. (Allentown, Pennsylva-
    nia), 95

Parkchester housing project (New York City,
    Shreve, Lamb and Harmon, 1939–41),
    72, 280n82
Parker and Unwin, 98
Park Forest Plaza (Park Forest, Illinois,
    Bennett, 1947–52), 147, 217, 219–20,
    287n28
parking: altering buildings to accommodate,
    100–107; cities' need to redesign, 95–97,
    229; diverted around town greens, 145,
    161; downtown, 149, 246; ground-floor
    insets, 100, 103; highway access, 97, 112,
    113, 116, 120, 123, 155; lots for, 99;
    modernist solutions for, 100–107; off-street,
    98, 100, 109, 113, 129, 237; park-and-
    shop concept, 95–97, 132; peripheral,
    123, 156, 164, 232, 241; rear, 32, 34,
    108–9, 112, 141, 146–47, 162; ring
    design, 192–93; rooftop, 103–4, 106,
    123, 274n67, 274n69; setbacks, 103,
    128–29; shopping center, 143, 154, 155,
    159–60, 191–92, 220, 277n42; store
    access from, 14, 120, 129–30; on
    superblocks, 112, 120; underground, 112,
    156. *See also* automobiles: store access
    from; garages, parking; Welch, Kenneth
    C.: parking plans by; *and parking plans
    under specific cities*
Parkinson, John and Donald: Bullocks
    Wilshire store, 109
parks, 137, 139, 147, 159, 186, 249, 255n2.
    See also green spaces; open spaces;
    pastoralism
Park Square Garage (Boston), 99–100
Parnes, Louis, 274n72; department store
    work, 256n14; pedestrian promenade by,
    125, 126
Pasadena, California: parking plans, 109
Pasadena Arcade (Marston, Van Pelt and
    Mayberry, 1929), 29
pastoralism, 2–3, 15, 169, 220, 239–41. *See
    also* green spaces; open spaces; parks
pedestrianism: civic, 7–9; Cold War, 204–5;
    postwar, 234–39; in urban renewal, 134,
    234–35

pedestrianization: consumption related to, 5–7, 43–45; Gruen and, 153–60, 171, 173, 234, 289n61; Ketchum's plans for, 160–62, 171, 173, 279n77; of Main Streets, 148–53, 162, 163–64, 290n7; New York City, 15, 245–46, 248, 249. *See also* modernism: pedestrian focus; shopping centers: pedestrian focus

pedestrian precincts, 148, 204–5, 226–29, 231; urban renewal based on, 228–29, 231, 232–34, 237, 239. *See also* shopping districts

pedestrians: automobiles' separation from, 127, 143, 165, 232, 234–39, 256n24; as citizens, 7–9; planning for, 226–31; shopping centers oriented toward, 199, 214–16; shopping districts oriented to, 126, 134, 263n19; stores' efforts to attract, 9, 14, 29–30, 54, 83, 104, 263n19; unit concept built around, 135, 139–40, 145; use of term, 7. *See also* walking

Peekskill, New York: pedestrianization in, 290n7

Pei, I. M.: National Gallery, East Wing, 251, 253; Roosevelt Field Shopping Center, 10, 11, 169, 234, 288n43

Penn Center, Philadelphia: Bacon's plans for, 235

perimeter plan. *See* "Chicago Plan"

Perkins, G. Holmes: dispersal study, 180

Perkins and Will, 216

Perry, Clarence: and neighborhood unit creation, 7, 14, 135, 137, 180

Perry, Shaw and Hepburn: Jordan Marsh store, 280n88

Philadelphia: urban renewal plans, 149, 237, 238

Phoenix, Arizona: SOM's department store in, 256n14

Picasso, Pablo, 43

Pico Boulevard Sears store (Los Angeles, 1939), 103

picturesque design strategy, 217, 219–20, 224

Pittsburgh: parking plans, 114, 116, 135

Pittsburgh Plate Glass (PPG): *Design of the Month* brochure series, 86; *There Is a New Trend in Store Design*, 79–80, 83–86

Plainfield, New Jersey: parking plans, 109

planners and planning: architects' involvement in, 4, 132, 208–11, 213; cities', 148–53, 161, 181–82; commercial, 146, 173; dispersal planning, 175–92, 283n38; large-scale, 24, 132, 134, 146, 148; postwar, 77, 79, 145; rationalist, 141, 180. *See also* Regional Plan Association; *Regional Plan of New York and Its Environs;* site planning and plans

Plan Viosin (Le Corbusier, 1925), 125

plasticity: design considerations regarding, 40, 69, 80

plate glass: development of, 4, 20, 22; in storefronts, 25, 43, 52, 54, 67, 69, 243

Plaza Market (Morgan, Walls & Clements, 1929), 30, 32, 128

plazas, 125–26, 249; in shopping centers, 155, 220; urban streets becoming, 232–33, 234. *See also* courtyards; malls

Pomeroy, Hugh, 149

Pomeroy, Lee Harris: Fulton Mall (Brooklyn, New York), 246

POPS. *See* privately owned public spaces

Portman, John: atriums designed by, 251

Postman's retail shop (New York City, Lapidus, 1939), 75, 76

PPG. *See* Pittsburgh Plate Glass

pragmatism, modernist: Gruen's, 54, 198; Ketchum's, 61, 64, 70, 183; Lapidus's, 75–76; of merchandising, 19, 35–36, 71, 87; in Niles, Michigan, project, 80; parking problem addressed through, 102–3, 116, 118; pedestrian problem addressed through, 134; Shepley's, 100; Taylorist, 31; urban renewal and, 135, 152, 180; Welch's, 72

precincts. *See* pedestrian precincts; shopping districts

Prince, Harry, 181

Princeton University: "Planning Man's Physical Environment" conference, 133, 143, 275n2 privately owned public spaces (POPS), 253, 291n21

production: mass, 31, 39, 71, 83, 243, 245, 286n71; modernism movement in, 36, 47, 48

programming: design considerations regarding, 39, 51, 69, 72, 80, 104, 145; in shopping centers, 208, 233

Progressive Architecture: shopping center planning feature, 209–10, 211, 212, 213, 216; store modernizations feature, 86

Project East River (atomic bomb survival study, Ketchum), 14, 182–86, 283n33, 283n36

promenades, 29, 125, 147, 152, 221. *See also* sidewalks; walkways

Pruneyard v. Robins (1980), 291n21

Quincy, Massachusetts: parking plans, 108

race: urban renewal and, 136, 204, 246

Radburn Plaza Building (New Jersey, Ackerman, 1929), 128–29, 141

Rapson, Ralph: *New Pencil Points* "Store Fronts of Tomorrow" competition, 267n85

rationalism, modernist, 18, 47–48, 54, 176–77; economic, 91, 140; Gruen's, 58; Ketchum's, 70; Lapidus's, 75–76, 77; merchandising and, 83, 210, 251; in 1920s store design, 31–39, 43, 49; as planning tool, 141, 180; unit concept and, 137, 146; urban questions approached with, 102, 232

Rawls, Huston, 165, 280n86, 280n89

Raymond & May Associates, 290n7

recentralization, 10, 120, 161, 166, 176, 191

regional districts, 123, 181, 204, 246; dispersal planning for, 178, 181, 182, 184, 186; shopping centers in, 155, 190

Regional Plan Association (RPA), 108, 136; report of 1936, 100, 101

Regional Plan of New York and Its Environs (RPNYE), 98, 125, 135, 136, 259n37

Reid, Kenneth, 77, 266n57; article on

Ketchum, 69–70, 282n30; as PPG catalog editor, 79–80

Reimann School (Berlin), 45, 261n85

Reisner, Jedd, 69; *New Pencil Points* "Store Fronts of Tomorrow" competition, 267n85

retailing, 120, 197; architects specializing in, 5, 14–15, 75; cities as traditional sites of, 9–10; modernism and, 54, 90–91, 130; shopping centers' as future of, 187, 189–90; superblocks for, 169–71. *See also* merchandising; shopping centers; shopping districts; stores

Retail Recentralization, Inc. (RRI), 165, 166

Revere Copper and Brass, 139, 149–50, 276n22

ribbon vitrines, 76

Richardson, H. H., 12

Ringstrasse (Vienna, Austria), 221

River Oaks (Houston, 1937), 129, 130

roadways. *See* highways; streets

Robertson, Jacquelin, 246, 248

Roche, Kevin: Ford Foundation headquarters, 251, 252

Rockefeller Center (New York City, 1929), 125, 256n24

Roosevelt Field Shopping Center (Queens, Pei, 1956), 10, 11, 169, 234, 288n43

Root, John W., 72

Ross-Frankel, Inc.: Lapidus's work at, 73, 75

Rotterdam, the Netherlands, 289n57. *See also* Lijnbaan urban reconstruction project

Rousseau, Jean-Jacques, 7

Rowe, Colin, 13

RPA. *See* Regional Plan Association

RPNYE. *See Regional Plan of New York and Its Environs*

Rudofsky, Bernard: *Streets for People,* 248

Rye, New York: Main Street redesign, 165, 169, 232; redevelopment plan (Ketchum, Gina and Sharp, 1946), 160–62, 163, 279n72, 279n74, 279n75

Saarinen, Aline B., 203

Saarinen, Eero: General Motors Technical

Center, 166, 213; in PPG catalog, 83, 268n95; Willow Run town center, 145, 146

Saarinen, Eliel, 98, 152; parking plans by, 120

Saarinen, Lily: *Great Lakes* sculpture, 200, 202

Sachlich. See objectivity, German

Sachs Furniture Store (New York City, Lapidus, 1936), 75

Saks Fifth Avenue store: Kiesler's window displays, 40, 41, 42, 260–61n72

Salvisberg, Otto, 274n72

Sanders, Morris, 83

Santillana, Giorgio de: and Wiener's life belt system plan, 283n38

Schoen, Eugene: store design by, 19–20

Scott, Mel: *Cities Are for People,* 140

Sculle, Keith, 95

Sears, Roebuck store (Los Angeles, 1939), 104

Segoe, Ladislas, 118

selling. *See* advertising; goods: selling; merchandising

Sert, José Luis: *Can Our Cities Survive?,* 125–26; "Motor City," 161, 164; on role of architect, 3–4, 10, 204; on shopping centers as communal places, 233–34; on unit concept, 136

Severance, J. B.: Palm Drive-In, 30, 128

Sexton, Randolph W., 17, 18–19, 22

Shaker Square (1928), 128–29

Shanken, Andrew, 13, 118, 137

Sharp, Stanley, 69, 265n41, 265n54; Clearview shopping center, 224, 225; *Machines for Selling,* 82; Middlesex Center, 168, 169, 172; *New Pencil Points* "Store Fronts of Tomorrow" competition, 267n85; store design, 105, 108. *See also* Beverly Shopping Center; Rye, New York: redevelopment plan

Sharp, Thomas, 219

Sheeler, Charles, 43

Shelter magazine, 36, 38

Shepley, Henry R., 99–100

shop fronts: use of term, 20. *See also* store-fronts

shoppers: seduced, 9; upper-class, 19, 245; women seen as typical, 6–7, 168, 200, 203

Shoppers' World (Framingham, Massachusetts, Ketchum, 1951), 169, 215, 216, 224, 225

shopping centers: advent of, 1–3; applying principles to urban renewal, 228–29, 231; architectural discourse regarding, 207–11, 213, 224; as art venues, 197–204, 205, 224; cities' competition with, 80, 235–36; civic functions of, 166, 191, 196–97, 220–21, 224–26, 250–51; civil defense functions of, 14, 186–90, 192–93, 284n49; as community centers, 155, 198–99, 204, 220–21, 224, 233–34, 251; cultural activities at, 155, 159; design strategies for, 225, 251; drive-through, 123, 126–27, 281n96; economic risk of, 1–2, 168; empty, 250–51; highway access to, 123, 155, 162–63, 166; large-scale, 154–55, 156, 213–26, 239; Main Street as model for, 165, 214–16; as models for remaking urban cores, 233–34; modernist design of, 4–5, 12–15, 125–26, 166–68, 207, 234–35, 239–41, 245; neighborhood, 130, 131, 140, 141, 145, 154; parking at, 109, 112, 155, 159–60, 191–92, 220; parks in, 159, 255n2; pedestrian focus, 134, 140–48, 159–60, 163–64, 169–71, 193–97, 199, 204–5; as public spaces, 251, 253, 291n21; regional, 155, 165–69, 204, 239; retail districts distinguished from, 208–9; social functions of, 10, 190–97, 199–200, 203, 220–21, 224–25, 233–34, 240; strip form, 141, 147; suburban, 5, 165–69; urbanity of, 193, 196–97, 203, 217, 234. *See also* arcades: in shopping centers; Gruen (Gruenbaum), Victor: shopping center designs; *and specific shopping centers*

Shopping Centers of Tomorrow exhibit (Gruen), 197–99

shopping districts: design of, 14, 95–97,
142; downtown, 246; facade plans, 142;
parking in, 109, 114, 128, 135; pedes-
trian-oriented, 125, 134, 170, 173; shopping centers distinguished from, 208–9;
suburban, 127–30. *See also* store blocks
shopping mall: use of term, 255n2. *See also*
malls
Shreve, Lamb and Harmon: Parkchester
housing project, 72, 280n82
Shurcliff, Arthur A., 166; Gloucester Street
shopping area, 101
Shurcliff, Sidney N., 166
sidewalks: elevated, 125–26; in shopping
centers, 192; stores' relationship to, 27,
29, 52, 65, 77–78, 104, 130. *See also*
promenades; walkways
Simmel, Georg, 136
site planning and plans: accommodating
automobiles, 107–18, 130; in architectural and social organization, 135–36,
137; L-shaped, 215, 287n21; pedestrian-
focused, 140–48; shopping center, 208–
11, 213, 217, 224–25, 251; types of,
14–15. *See also* planners and planning
Sitte, Camillo, 219
Skidmore, Owings and Merrill (SOM): in
Contemporary Shops in the United States,
87; Lever House, 103, 220; Marshall
Field Skokie Shopping Center competition, 220, 221; Phoenix department store,
256n14; in PPG catalog, 83, 84–85;
Willow Run planning, 277n39
Skokie Shopping Center (Illinois). *See*
Marshall Field Skokie Shopping Center
competition
slums, urban, 177–78, 181, 182. *See also*
urban renewal
Smith, Larry, 210, 285n66
Smith, Whitney: Linda Vista Shopping
Center, 143, 144, 146, 224, 225, 267n85,
276n21, 277n38
Smith, Wilbur S., 97
Smith, Hinchman & Grylls, 189
Snow, Richard B., 64

social life: art's importance in, 43, 200, 203;
in cities, 135, 137, 152, 178, 189, 233–
34, 246; medieval, 152, 288n25; stores'
role in, 39, 48, 90–91. *See also* communities; shopping centers: social functions of
SOM. *See* Skidmore, Owings and Merrill
Soriano, Raphael: in *Contemporary Shops in
the United States,* 87
Southdale Shopping Center (Edina, Minnesota, Gruen, 1956), 1, 2, 199, 228,
239–41; as symbol of modernism, 5, 15,
245, 251
standardization, 36, 60, 83, 85, 89
Starrett & Van Vleck, 35
St. Dié, France: city plan (Le Corbusier),
125
Steckler Shop (New York City, Ketchum,
1945), 65, 66, 67, 264n27
Stein, Clarence, 136, 141, 147, 152, 176,
182, 277n40
Stevenage, Great Britain: CIAM plans for,
232
Stone, Edward Durell, 64, 69, 87, 264n36,
265n41, 265n54
Stonestown Shopping Center (San Francisco,
Becket, 1952), 214–15
Stonorov, Oscar: Philadelphia plan, 149,
236, 237, 238; *You and Your Neighborhood,* 139
Stonorov and Kahn: neighborhood planning
guide, 139; in PPG catalog, 83, 84–85;
unit concept use, 140; Willow Run planning, 277n39
store blocks, 10, 103–4, 129–30; Ketchum's
design of, 105, 149, 156, 160, 161. *See
also* shopping districts; superblocks
store design, 6, 17–49, 85; articles on, 21;
car access, 29–30; conventional, 19–24;
Lapidus on, 75–77; for merchandising,
32, 35–36, 38–39, 70–73; modernism
debates in, 17–19, 22, 24, 49; modernist,
4–5, 43, 49, 51–52, 72, 79–81, 87, 89–
91; openness in, 52, 83; rationalist, 31–
39; role in acceptance of modernism,
9–10, 12–14; streets' relationship to, 25,

29–30, 77–78; tensionist, 39–47; traditionalist, 17–18, 19; use of plate glass, 20, 22, 25; vestibules, 25–31, 33. *See also* arcades: in store designs; modernism: in store design

storefronts: all-glass, 20, 22, 25, 43; articles on, 21, 23; conventional, 19–24; glazed, 38, 65, 69, 77–78, 80, 85, 269n109; Gruen's, 54, 56, 58; Ketchum's, 56, 65; Kiesler's, 44, 45, 46; Lapidus's design of, 65, 73, 74, 75–77, 235; merchandising role of, 20, 38, 56; modernist, 47, 89; open-faced, 52, 65, 265n46; recessed, 29, 31, 33, 44, 54, 55, 57, 78, 235; use of term, 20. *See also* arcades; display cases; displays; vestibules; windows

Store-on-Stilts proposal (Ketchum, Gina and Sharpe), 107, 108

stores, 32, 71, 125; advertising, 5, 77, 255n9, 255–56n10; cities' relationship, 24, 160; dual entry, 104, 109, 112, 169, 192; modernizations of, 86; pedestrian access to, 14, 27, 29–30, 52, 65, 263n19; service function of, 38, 266n58; setbacks for parking, 128–29; use of glass in, 166, 271n35. *See also* automobiles: store access from; department stores; displays; merchandising; retailing; shopping centers; store blocks; streets: stores' relationship to

Storey, Walter Rendell, 47

Stowell, Kenneth Kingsley, 48, 69, 72, 267n86

Strasser Studio (Gruen, 1939–40), 54, 264n27

Strawbridge and Clothier stores: Ardmore, Pennsylvania, 266n63; Jenkintown, Pennsylvania, 266n65

streets, 145, 221, 274n81; closing for pedestrian use, 161, 215, 227, 229, 232–34, 237, 245–50, 276n22, 277n26, 297n77; commercial, 81; loop, 246; multisectioned, 270n18; pedestrianization of, 235, 249, 289n61; service, 111–12, 114, 116, 235, 277n42; shopping centers' imitation of, 225, 241; stores' relationship to, 25–27,

29–30, 58, 61, 65, 73, 77–78, 84, 86; traffic, 116, 125; transformation of, 246, 250. *See also* highways; Main Street(s); parking

Stübbin, Josef, 98

Suburban Centers Trust (SCT), 165, 168–69

suburbanization, 15, 191; applying principles to urban renewal, 226–27, 228–29, 231; civil defense dispersal planning and, 175–82, 186–88; as impetus for pedestrianization, 248–50; of shopping, 5, 10, 165–69

suburbs: competition for cities, 95, 246; emerging, 12, 127–30; investing in, 165–66; pedestrian focus of, 140–48; sprawling, 191, 198–99. *See also* metropolitan areas, remaking; regional districts; urban areas

subways: bomb shelters in, 183, 283n31

Sukert, Lancelot, 266n66

Sullivan, Louis: Carson, Pirie, Scott & Co. store, 12

Sunlight Towers project (Frey, 1929), 31–32

superblocks: in cities, 136, 137, 140; for commercial districts, 169–71; Ketchum's use of, 161, 229; parking on, 112, 120; pedestrian-focused, 173, 229; shopping centers and, 156, 239; use of term, 135; Welch's use of, 162–63. *See also* store blocks; units: neighborhood

Supplementary Report of the Urbanism Committee to the National Resources Committee, 136–37

survivability (atomic bomb), 14, 176–86, 282n25. *See also* dispersal planning, Cold War; vulnerable urban districts

Swanson, J. Robert: Willow Run town center, 145, 146

Syracuse, New York: city planning in, 149, 278n49

Tanner, Edward, 274n80

taxes. *See* U.S. Internal Revenue Code: 1954 changes to

Teague, Walter Dorwin, 5, 48, 87, 268n88

Telchin, Charles, 268–69n102
Teller, Edward, 175
tensionism, 39–47
territories, 135–40, 156, 177, 180. *See also* pedestrian precincts; shopping districts; units
Texas Electric company, 226–27
Times Square (New York City): pedestrianization of, 15, 245, 248
Tönnies, Ferdinand, 136
town centers, 137, 145, 150, 152, 166, 288n47
town greens, 140, 224, 225. *See also* green spaces: in shopping centers; parks
towns, medieval, 142, 152, 220, 224, 288n35
Trade Winds Shop (Ketchum), 65
traditionalists: modernists' debates with, 17–19, 22, 24, 32, 100
traffic congestion. *See* automobiles; cities: traffic in; parking
Traffic Game, Inc., 95
transit systems, 98, 186, 237. *See also* highways; streets
transparency: as modernist technique, 4, 13, 58, 65, 69, 71–72, 80, 83, 91, 266n58
Troedsson, Carl, 277n26
Trowbridge, Edwin, 22
Truman, Harry S., 182, 188. *See also* U.S. National Production Authority
T-Square magazine. *See Shelter* magazine
Tumaco, Colombia: CIAM plans for, 232
Tyrwhitt, Jaqueline, 140, 182, 282n26

units: cities based on, 229, 231; for civil defense dispersal planning, 176–82, 184, 186; neighborhood, 7, 14, 135–40, 145, 148, 239; overuse of, 277n27; pedestrian-focused, 140–48, 173; satellite, 177–82, 184, 199; settlement, 136, 176–77, 181, 183–84, 186, 188, 199; shopping centers utilizing, 156, 191; urban renewal based on, 161, 204, 234, 239. *See also* pedestrian precincts; regional districts; shopping districts
Upton, Dell, 12

Urban, Joseph: Bedell Store, 29
urban areas, 10, 152; congestion in, 14, 148, 236, 246; dual-use concept in, 187–90; modernism movement and, 43, 123, 239; neighborhoods contrasted with, 7–9; reducing congestion in, 176, 177–78, 180–82, 184, 186–87; reorganization of, 156, 190–91; shopping center concept applied to, 225, 228–29, 231, 233–34; vulnerability of, 183–84, 186, 191. *See also* cities; intervention, urban; metropolitan areas, remaking
Urban Design Group: Fulton Mall (Brooklyn, New York), 246
Urban Land Institute (ULI), 279n72, 287n15; reports on shopping centers, 211, 213, 235
urban renewal: modernist principles applied to, 15, 125, 140, 234–39; parking, 14, 120; pedestrianism and, 134, 152, 229, 231, 232–34, 237, 239; precursors to, 132, 161. *See also* intervention, urban; parking; pedestrianization; slums, urban
"usable past" concept, 224
U.S. Federal Housing Administration (FHA): commercial loan liberalization program, 72, 73
U.S. Internal Revenue Code: 1954 changes to, 2, 239
U.S. National Production Authority, 188, 190, 192
utilitarianism, 18, 35, 38, 141
utopianism and utopianists, 152, 169–70, 171, 245

Valley Fair Shopping Center (Appleton, Wisconsin, George Narovec, 1955), 255n2
Vantongerloo, Georges, 43
variety store plan, 105
Veblen, Thorstein, 39–40
vestibules, 25–31, 33, 54. *See also* arcades; lobbies; storefronts
Ville Radieuse (Le Corbusier, 1929–30), 125, 134

Voorhees, Walker, Foley and Smith, 184
vulnerable urban districts (VUDs), 183–84, 185, 186, 191

Wadsworth, Reginald: Greenbelt shopping center, 136, 141–42
Wagner, Martin, 136, 137, 180
Walbridge, Cope, 265n54
Walker, Frank R., 266n70
Walker, Ralph T., 18, 178, 184; Barclay-Vesey Building, 259n37
walking: in cities, 134, 135, 136, 152, 161; in neighborhoods, 137, 139; shopping and, 136, 255n2. *See also* pedestrianization; pedestrians
walkways, 125–26, 143, 235. *See also* promenades; sidewalks
Wall, Alex, 13
Wank, Roland, 267n84
Warwick, Virginia: town center, 288n47
Washington, D.C.: parking plan, 113
Weinberg, Robert, 100–101, 232–33
Welch, Kenneth C., 70–73, 266n61, 268–69n102, 274n68, 280n89; city planning work, 273n60, 273n65; Grand River Court, 120–23, 156; Mondawmin Shopping Center proposal, 241, 290n76; parking plans by, 118–27, 162–63, 274n67, 274n69; on pedestrian precincts, 171, 173; shopping center designs, 124, 127, 209, 216; store designs, 14, 87, 90, 125, 243, 266n62, 280n87; at Store Modernization Show of 1947, 89; suburban work of, 162–69; as vice president of Grand Rapids Store Equipment Company, 35
Welch-Wilmarth Corporation, 70–71, 266n60

Wheaton, William, 184; dispersal study, 180
Whitten, Robert, 270n16
Whittlesey, Julian: on planning for parking, 101–3
Whyte, William: *The Social Life of Small Urban Places,* 248
Wiener, Norbert: life belt system, 186–87, 188–89, 283n38
Wiener, Paul Lester: "Motor City," 161, 164
Wigley, Mark, 13
Willow Run town center (Michigan, Eero Saarinen and Swanson, 1943), 145, 146, 277n39
Wilmarth Show Case Company, 70
Windels, Paul, 178
windows: display, 54, 58, 72, 87–89, 245; in 1920s store design, 44, 45; shop, 43, 243, 269n109. *See also* plate glass; storefronts
Winter, Foster, 190, 284n47
Wittbold, George: Gruen's work for, 53
women: as typical shoppers, 6–7, 168, 200, 203; in workforce, 263n21
Woodbury, Coleman, 176, 184
World War II, 6, 58, 126, 165, 224
Wright, Frank Lloyd, 24, 176
Wright, Gwendolyn, 12
Wright, Henry, Jr., 9, 10, 136, 148, 282n25
Wright, Russell, 87
Wurster, William, 134, 166
Wynn Furniture Store (Inglewood, California, Gruen, 1947), 221–24

Yale University: and Bureau of Highway Traffic, traffic study by, 109, 111
York and Sawyer, 64, 264n37

Zola, Émile, 6

DAVID SMILEY teaches at the Graduate School of Architecture, Planning, and Preservation at Columbia University.